Marriage Customs
of the World

Marriage Customs of the World

From Henna to Honeymoons

George P. Monger

ABC CLIO

Santa Barbara, California
Denver, Colorado
Oxford, England

Library of Congress Cataloging-in-Publication Data
Monger, George P.
Marriage customs of the world : from henna to honeymoons / George P. Monger.
    p.   cm.
  Includes bibliographical references and index.
  ISBN 1-57607-987-2 (hardback : alk. paper) — ISBN 1-57607-988-0 (e-book)
  1. Marriage customs and rites.   I. Title.

GT2690.M65   2004
392.5—dc22

2004017586

07   06   05   10 9 8 7 6 5 4 3 2

This book is also available on the World Wide Web as an eBook. Visit abc-clio.com for details.

ABC-CLIO, Inc.
130 Cremona Drive, P.O. Box 1911
Santa Barbara, California 93116-1911
This book is printed on acid-free paper.

Manufactured in the United States of America

Contents

Introduction

The propensity of human beings to form partnerships and establish family units is almost universal, and often in establishing these marriage partnerships, some form of ceremony is carried out. Further, there are remarkable similarities of thought, ideas, and symbolism across cultures in these ceremonies. The ceremony is usually a public event so that the community to which the couple belong can witness the union—this public aspect of the ceremony is very important in marriage throughout the world. The differences in ceremony usually relate to, and reflect, cultural and religious views of marriage and the role of the sexes in society.

Throughout Europe, for example, where the Christian church managed to gain control of the marriage ceremony and impose a Christian morality on the institution of marriage, there are great similarities in performance, dress, and philosophy. The church marriage ceremony became so ingrained in European culture that where the state has managed to break church control over marriage, through revolution, for example, and has instituted civil registration as *the* legal act of marriage, a church service is often still observed. In some European cultures the marriage may not be considered by the community to be "proper" without the religious ceremony. Consequently, throughout Europe, the differences in the marriage act are not always apparent and are usually expressed in variations of custom and/or dress.

It is remarkable how some customs seem to be almost universal. The practice of "barring the way"—members of the community of the bride or groom put barriers across the path in front of the wedding party going to or from the wedding to block their way—is a good example. The party is allowed to pass upon payment—usually by the groom or his party. Perhaps the groom is being required to pay into the community or make a contribution to the bride's family and friends as compensation for taking her away. In the Orkney Islands, the local children would demand payment from the groom to be used for a football for the boys—a sort of fine for taking the bride. Such customs are found in England, throughout Europe, in Russia, and in Thailand.

Many apparently inexplicable customs and ceremonies associated with life events have a function that may be practical and/or spiritual. In looking at marriage ceremonies and customs we can discern several distinct, but not mutually exclusive, functions. Marriage customs or ceremonies may function:

- As a public announcement to the community that a new family unit has been established
- To help the couple set up home as an independent economic unit
- As a popular adjunct to the legal requirement
- To bring luck and good fortune to the couple and the new family unit

When written records were scarce and most people were illiterate (and, of course, photography had yet to be invented), it was essential that the community observed and took part in the wedding to mark the occasion in the collective mind and to witness the event. Members of the community in many places would soon make their feelings known if they did not agree with the match. Therefore, custom and ceremony are really a public show and an affirmation of what is essentially a private arrangement. In very few cases and cultures is marriage considered exclusively as a personal arrangement of the couple. In Europe and the United States, seen as free societies with a high degree of personal choice, there is very often an element of community agreement to the wedding (if the community disapproved they had ways of expressing their disapproval). Among landed families there was little free choice—marriages were often arranged to cement alliances or to gain control of property. There was also very little interclass marriage—this can also be seen in many cultures where there is an overt or hidden class system. For example, in some societies a girl is likely to marry a young man whose family is in the same trade or profession as her father.

The second reason for custom and ceremony is to help the couple set up home as an independent unit. In addition to help from parents and close family, such customs as penny weddings, biddings, showers, and the giving of wedding presents, and other means of raising money for the couple—such as the auctioning of gloves or pieces of the bride's garter or pinning money to the clothing of the bride and groom—represent the efforts of the larger community to ensure that the couple have a solid financial beginning. In contemporary Russia, for example, on the second day of the celebrations, the remaining guests, the families, and close friends scatter money around the room, which the bride has to sweep up. Symbolic help is sometimes given to the couple through these customs, so that in Britain and the United States, the custom of walking on gold (silver)—the bride has a coin in her shoe—is a wish that the couple will not want for money.

Third, customs and ceremonies are deeply ingrained in the psyche of cultures and communities such that there are few societies that do not have some form of ceremonial recognition of the marriage, and such ceremonies are often based upon some form of tradition. Where governments have tried to suppress this ceremony or introduce practices from outside cultures they have met with resistance and have had little success. In Russia, after the Revolution in 1915, the governing authorities attempted to reduce the working time lost in the celebration of marriage by making it a quick civil event with no frills. But authorities soon found that people wanted some frills, and so wedding halls were developed that allowed a minimal ceremony. Post-perestroika Russia has gone back to pre-Revolution traditions. In Turkey during the 1920s, the Turkish government introduced a Civil Code for marriage, based on that of Switzerland, which ignored traditional practice and caused offense. The need for ceremony is exemplified by the fact that humanists, atheists, and gays wish for a form of ceremony to recognize and formalize their unions. Same-sex couples in many places are legally prevented from entering into marriage. One of the arguments from legislators opposing same-sex marriage is that in some curious way the wish for the couple to form a marriage alliance undermines the institution of marriage.

Finally, wedding ceremonies are often thought to bring luck and good fortune to the couple. Marriage is, for most cultures, the beginning of a new life. Marriage is said to be one of the "rites of passage," and it was, and is still, considered part of growing up—part of the transition from being a child to becoming an adult. In Ireland, an unmarried man of any age was often still considered to be a child and under the authority of his parents—a married man of any age would be deemed to have achieved adulthood. This is not an unusual view. At pivotal times in life, or of the year, there are thought to be dangers from demons, bad luck, or other malevolent forces, and marriage is one of those pivotal times. The malevolent forces that could wreck the happiness of the day and the couple's future life have to be averted with prayers, blessings, and actions, such as firing guns into the air when the couple process to or from the marriage ceremony. The bride is considered to be especially vulnerable to evil influences and spirits at this time of change. Some brides wear clothes or ornaments believed to offer protection from demons. A Tibetan bride may wear an engraved silver reliquary around her neck to protect her from evil spirits as she leaves the protection of her family gods to be under the protection of her husband's family gods. For similar reasons, the bride in China is not allowed to touch the ground in her journey from her childhood home to that of her new husband.

The bridal couple also need continued protection and good fortune for the whole of their married life. The wish for good fortune is embedded in traditions throughout the world. In Europe and the United States, this wish is expressed in the confetti thrown over the couple, in such practices as putting a silver or gold coin into the bride's shoe, and in the appearance of lucky characters, such as a chimney sweep, at the wedding. In many cultures, children are thought to be the couple's future and fortune; they represent the future and the continuity of the family line—a form of immortality. In biblical Jewish tradition, if a married man died childless, his brother was expected to marry his wife and father children in his name. A Bulgarian Gypsy bride carries a child over the threshold of her new home to ensure her fertility.

The "magic" of the wedding, however, acts in two ways. The good wishes, symbolism, and charms may bring the bride (and groom) good luck and good fortune, but in societies where there has been free choice in marriage partner, and where getting married was seen as an essential part of achieving adulthood,

meeting a suitable partner was often a matter of luck and good fortune. Consequently, items that have been in contact with the bride or have been part of the celebrations were considered to have some magical properties or to bring good fortune through association. Traditions whereby the woman who catches the bride's bouquet is the next to be married can today be found at Korean weddings and at Palestinian-American weddings. A variation is found in Colombia, in South America—each bachelor at the wedding places one of his shoes under the bride's dress and the groom picks one of the shoes. The owner of the shoe is the next to be married. A girl may place a piece of wedding cake under her pillow to dream of her future husband.

Marriage and weddings are often portrayed as female events—there is usually more preparation for the woman than for the man, and the woman's preparations are often more elaborate. In Western society, the bride-to-be and her family have traditionally made most of the arrangements and, by tradition, paid for the celebrations. In many societies the marriage is the culmination of the woman's expectations; her role in life is to become a man's partner in marriage and to have children. This is evident in Muslim and Christian societies. Although the Koran says that there should be equity in marriage, this is not always so in practice. Christian tradition has been governed by the teachings of St. Paul, which declared that the man is "the head of the wife" and that wives should submit themselves to their husbands (Eph. 5.22–33).

But, ironically, in many respects and in many societies, marriage is more advantageous for the man than for the woman. In middle-class European society, a "good" marriage for a woman would support her for life, but she sacrifices freedom as she subjugates herself to her husband. In weddings, as with many traditional turning points in life or seasons, we can observe a form of topsy-turvydom—the bride is the central character, with the groom apparently playing a secondary and reluctant role. In some societies the bride is expected to put on a show of reluctance at leaving home (and this may not be totally fake—in many cases, she is going into completely unknown territory in joining her husband's family household). In Western society the groom is seen to be the reluctant one because he is seen as losing his freedom (in practice the bride is the one who loses more of her freedom and independence). Yet, at the same time, in some societies a man was not considered to have achieved adulthood until he had married. There are many social dichotomies inherent in marriage—in what it means and in the social roles of the participants before, during, and after marriage.

The nineteenth-century reformer Barbara Leigh Smith Bodichon, in her 1854 book *A Brief Summary in Plain Language of the Most Important Laws Concerning Women; Together with a Few Observations Thereon* (quoted in Hellerstein et al. 1981), noted that in the marriage service an Englishwoman heard her husband promise her all his worldly goods. But, in fact, after the marriage all her belongings and her body were, by law, considered her husband's property. Even into the second half of the twentieth century, a married woman could not enter into a contract without her husband's consent (yet she could still be prosecuted for a criminal offense in her own right).

Today, the concept of the companionate marriage is becoming more and more accepted around the world. In societies with the tradition of arranged marriage, parents are now having to come to terms with the fact that their children now often prefer to meet and fall in love with a person of their own choice. This move away from such traditional practice is most noticeable in groups that have had substantial contact with the West. This often causes intrafamily tensions. The companionate marriage is not new in societies where there has been free choice of partner, but in European and American culture among, especially, the landed classes,

marriage was often a business arrangement used to secure alliances, bolster fortunes, and amalgamate families. This often caused infidelity—to which the marriage partner and the society often turned a blind eye unless the indiscretion became too blatant and public. But there was enormous importance placed on producing a son and heir to carry on the family name and inherit the fortune. It is this imperative that decreed that the bride should be a virgin and that the wife should be faithful to her husband. In Muslim and Jewish tradition an elder son and heir was required to carry on the family name and to offer prayers for the father's soul after his death. The purity and fidelity of the bride also ensured that a man did not support another man's child. But in some societies, particularly where there is little emphasis on property and a greater cooperation in land and food production, fidelity is not paramount and virginity is a state of mind rather than a physical thing. Contemporary marriage in Western societies has changed remarkably over the years, partly due to the sexual revolution in the latter part of the twentieth century, so that virginity is not always considered important for the bride (it was rarely as important for the groom to be a virgin).

Beginning in the nineteenth century, weddings in Britain and the United States, especially, have received the attention of a "wedding industry," with etiquette books detailing how things should be done, couples registering with shops so that guests can buy a wedding present from the list at that shop, and magazines of bridal fashions. The industry continues today, with wedding fairs where exhibitors advertise wedding services—photographers, cake bakers, florists, wedding outfit suppliers, limousine suppliers, and toastmasters.

There are now also many sites on the Internet that can put wedding organizers in touch with various services and suppliers. Hindu and Islamic Internet sites give details of available women and men looking for marriage partners. Traditional differences among cultures are often proudly described in articles on the Internet, but there has been a homogenization in many aspects of weddings throughout the world. The Western white wedding dress is now recognized in most parts of the world as a symbol of weddings. At the mass weddings organized by the Unification Church, with thousands of couples being married in a stadium in Seoul, Korea, the brides all wear white wedding dresses. At the mass weddings organized in Iraq by Saddam Hussein, the brides wore white wedding dresses. And in Japan, about half of the weddings are in the Western style. Often the rejection of tradition and traditional dress is influenced by fashion and a wish to rise to a more affluent class. In nineteenth-century Norway, young women rejected the use of the traditional bridal crown. However, it became chic to return to traditional roots, and it is now fashionable to marry in traditional Norwegian costume.

For purposes of reviewing marriage traditions, culture is not confined within "national" boundaries. The wedding practices of Muslims transcend national boundaries. Although there may be localized customs and modes of dress—typical bridal dress in Palestine, for example, differs from region to region—the way of marrying and the overall practice is remarkably the same from North Africa to Afghanistan. All Muslim brides have a "henna night" before the wedding day. Similarly, in European culture there are many customs and traditions across national boundaries, and the intent of the different customs is very much the same. In just about every culture where there is a wedding ceremony and community celebration, the bride and groom, especially the bride, are dressed up and decorated to elevate them above the norm for the day—often they are regarded as royalty for their wedding day. But the details of the celebration are not immune from influences from outside cultures. In Britain toward the end of the twentieth century it became fashionable for the female guests to be given a small net package of sugared almonds—an idea borrowed from Greek weddings.

Marriage and weddings are peculiar and complex constructs that have a plethora of meanings and functions, both legal and social. They demonstrate cultural differences and similarities. Where we find similarities of custom, the meanings of those customs are also often similar. In the United States, which has been a melting pot for cultures, most forms of marriage are to be found. In this encyclopedia, it is hoped that the major customs, traditions, and marriage practices studied will assist in the understanding of contemporary marriage practice. But there are as many slight differences of marriage custom and tradition as there are cultures and communities, and it would be impossible to chronicle all the differences and all the customs. The entries in this book will attempt to demonstrate aspects of the concept of continuity and change in tradition and performance. We can see a continuation of the reason for a tradition, at the same time that the performance is being updated.

But, in the end, however the wedding is carried out, whether with elaborate ritual, through exchange of gifts, or with a simple civic ceremony and signing of a register, the couple are equally married—confetti does not have to be thrown, the bride does not have to wear an elaborate white dress, and, as the Sioux Medicine Man, Lame Deer (1980, 144), has said, "One ceremony is as good as another." They all achieve the same result.

References

Fire, John /Lame Deer, and Richard Erdoes. [1972] 1980. *Lame Deer: Sioux Medicine Man.* London, New York: Quartet Books.

Hellerstein, Erna, Hume Olafson, Leslie Parker, and Karen Offen, eds. 1981. *Victorian Women: A Documentary Account of Women's Lives in Nineteenth Century England, France, and the United States.* Brighton, England: Harvester Press.

Abduction, Marriage by

Marriage by abduction was a theory suggested by some nineteenth-century anthropologists, notably John F. McLennan (1865). Others have considered this to be a rare form of marriage, and some have even doubted that it ever occurred as a widespread and valid marriage form.

According to the Hindu Laws of Manu, of eight forms of marriage recognized, four are considered "blessed," and the other four are condemned as "blamable" unions. One of these is known as *râkshasa,* a union by forcible abduction of a maiden from her home, either by stealth or by breaking into her house and slaying or wounding her kinsmen. There are some cases in Britain that appear to have been genuine cases of abduction. Abduction, especially of heiresses, was a problem in Britain. Legislation was enacted to prevent the practice. A statute of 1487 (at the time of Henry VII) ranked abduction as a felony, and an Elizabethan act of 1596 denied those found guilty of abduction the benefit of clergy. There were some high-profile cases of abduction, such as that of the daughter of Sir Thomas Puckeringe, Jane, who was abducted in 1649 while walking with her maid in Greenwich Park, London, by a group of mounted men led by one Joseph Walsh. She was carried off to Dunkirk and then to a religious house at

Nieuport, Flanders, at that time under Spanish rule. Although steps were immediately taken to secure the release of Jane Puckeringe, it was not until some eight years later that this was achieved. Joseph Walsh and his associates were apprehended, handed over to the British authorities, and indicted for a felony.

Another case that occurred in the early nineteenth century involved an elaborate plot to abduct and marry a sixteen-year-old heiress, Ellen Turner. The plot was hatched by one Edward Gibbon Wakefield and his brother William. A note was sent to the girl at school in Liverpool saying that her mother was ill in London and that she was to accompany the servant who delivered the letter, in the carriage provided by the physician attending her mother. At a carriage stop in Manchester she was persuaded to accompany Edward and William Wakefield to Carlisle to meet her father. They drove through Gretna Green, where Edward was married to Ellen. After the marriage, the couple traveled south at considerable speed to catch a boat to cross the English Channel to Calais. The headmistress at Ellen's school became suspicious and went to Ellen's family home. Realizing that the school had been duped, the school authorities set the law onto William, who was apprehended in Calais and brought back to England. The bride was returned to her parents, and the marriage, which had not been consummated, was annulled by act of Parliament. The Wakefield brothers were imprisoned for three years by the Lancaster Spring Assizes in March 1827 for conspiracy.

There are occasional contemporary accounts of abduction of women for marriage. For instance, in 1995 in China, where there is a shortage of marriageable women due to the government policy of allowing only one child per family and the cultural imperative for that child to be a boy, two hundred women, who had been abducted and sold as wives to farmers, were rescued in one province.

It is doubtful that there can be a true marriage by capture. Forcible abduction and the subsequent unwilling consummation would be rape and the relationship at best more like concubinage. Apart from the Laws of Manu, the major examples to support the concept of marriage by abduction or capture are practices where there is an outward sign of resistance on the part of the bride to going with the groom so that there may be a ritualized battle between the groom and his followers and the bride's attendants. Plutarch (a Graeco-Roman period writer and historian from about A.D. 90) wrote of the Spartans that the bride might have been carried off by force, and there might have been some violence, but the abduction was planned by the couple. Similarly, some form of reluctance and force on behalf of the bride and of the groom, respectively, has often been noted among the ancient Greeks and Romans.

Burckhardt (1831) noted that, among the Bedouins and Wahabys, a young woman returning with the cattle in the evening might be met and abducted by her future spouse and his supporters and carried to her father's tent. She might defend herself with sticks and stones; the more she fought, struggled, and bit her assailants, the more her peers applauded her. A common practice in Gypsy marriage is for the couple to elope, which could be interpreted as deriving from capture or abduction. However, in this, as in most recorded marriage practices where there is an apparent abduction or some form of mock battle or contest between the supporters of the bride and those of the groom, the event is prearranged and the marriage agreed to by the bride and groom. It is probably a means for the bride to show modesty and her reluctance to lose her virginity and to leave her family and friends. In eighteenth-century Connecticut, it was the practice for a group of young men to abduct the bride immediately after the wedding and take her to a country tavern. The bridegroom and his supporters would ride after the abductors and gain the release of his bride by providing them with a meal. This apparently happened in 1783 in Hadley to a Mrs. Job Marsh. Alice Morse Earl, writing on the customs of New England in 1893, noted that even then in parts of Rhode Island the young men would break down the door of the bridal chamber and abduct the bride, forcing the young husband to rescue her. During the wedding reception in modern Russia, the groom's friends abduct the bride and extract a ransom from him for her return.

See also Bed, Marriage; Capture, Marriage by; Concubine; Consummation; France; Gretna Green

References

Burckhardt, John Lewis. 1831. *Notes on the Bedouins and Wahabys.* London: H. Colburn and R. Bentley.

Fonseca, Isabel. 1995. *Bury Me Standing: The Gypsies and Their Journey.* London: Chatto and Windus.

McLennan, John F. 1865. *Primitive Marriage, An Inquiry into the Origin of the Form of Capture in Marriage Ceremonies.* Edinburgh: A and C Black.

Scott, George Ryley. 1953. *Curious Customs and Sex and Marriage.* London: Torchstream.

Aborigines (Australian)

Western writers have written that there seems to have been little, if any, ceremony in the aboriginal method of marrying. Westermarck (1894) wrote: "In Australia, wedding ceremonies are unknown in most tribes, but it is said that in some there are a few unimportant ones." The Kaurna aboriginal group from South Australia provides a model of Australian aboriginal society and mores and demonstrates that Westermarck's remarks above were simplistic. They were based on a misunderstanding of the society and were written from a European viewpoint. Observers viewed the practices of Aborigines from the viewpoint of nineteenth-century white Christian morality. Westermarck (1894, 388) also quoted Fison and Howitt, writing of the South Australian group in 1880, who said that marriages were brought about "most frequently by elopement, less frequently by captures, and least frequently by exchange or by gift."

The organization of Kaurna society involved independent family groups working and traveling a specified territory known as a *pangkarra;* these territories were grouped into larger units called *yerta*—meaning earth, land, or country and derived from words meaning earth and mouth, so that the overriding concept portrayed by the term is one of an area that can sustain the group. Of great importance to the study of marriage customs are the differing moral views of sex and sexual relations. In Kaurna society, marriage was not seen as a barrier to sexual relations, and sexual intercourse with a member of the family group was offered as a part of hospitality. Adultery was not a concept recognized or understood by the Kaurna, and indeed it was common for a woman to have sexual relations with a number of men with the full approval and encouragement of her spouse. To the British settlers, this exemplified the low moral standards of the Aborigines. In 1819 the assistant chaplain in New South Wales wrote in a letter to the secretary of the New Zealand Mission that the natives were "the most degraded of the human race. . . . as they increase in years, they increase in vice" (Woerlee 2003). Other Christian ministers in Australia writing to friends were no less denigrating. Well into the late nineteenth century, the Aborigines were portrayed as being brutal savages. An anonymous writer in the *Chambers Journal* of 22 October 1864 described the ways of the Aborigines:

> In nothing is the brutality of their nature more clearly shown than in their treatment of females. Among them, women are considered as an inferior class, and are used almost as beasts of burden. . . . Courtship, as the precursor to marriage, is unknown among them. When a young warrior is desirous of procuring a wife, he generally obtains one by giving in exchange for her a sister, or some other female relative of his own; but if there should happen to be no eligible damsel disengaged in the tribe to which he belongs, then he hovers round the encampment of some other blacks until he gets an opportunity of seizing one of their *leubras,* whom perhaps he has seen and admired when attending one of the grand corroborries. His mode of paying his address is simple and efficacious. With a blow of his *mulla-mulla* (war club) he stuns the object of his "affections," and drags her insensible body away to some retired spot, whence, as soon as she recovers her senses, he brings her home to his own gunyah in triumph. (Scott 1953, 56)

Wife-stealing (*milla mangkondi*) was prevalent among aboriginal groups, but this did cause great acrimony among community groups. However, all indulged in the practice as it was seen as a method of increasing the gene pool. All tribal groups had a great antipathy toward wife-stealing, and the worst affront that could be dealt to a group was for a young wife to be stolen from an elder. The writer went on to describe the stealing of a wife at night, the man using his spear to ensnare the woman's hair and draw her from her group, and the subsequent ordeal to prevent fighting between the family groups in defense of the young woman and young man.

It was with the onset of puberty that an aboriginal girl became a woman, able to join the group of marriageable women and take part in the family hospitality laws. This usually happened around the age of ten or twelve years, and she was expected to join her promised spouse soon afterward. However, no man married before the age of about twenty-five, after he had passed through his initiation into manhood; indeed, it was more advantageous for a girl to marry an older man who commanded higher food distribution rights. However, younger men were not barred from having sexual relations with the wives of the older men. The belief was that the sex act was a gift of the gods and that people should enjoy it at their discretion.

Ceremonial activity did occur between the families, and accounts in some of the anthropological and popular writings are missing the social subtleties. It was usual and expected that the young woman would marry into a different family group to ensure an increase in the gene pool; it was very rare for the couple to know each other before the wedding. Aboriginal groups usually identified with certain totem groups, and there were rules about which totem groups could intermarry. Arrangements and negotiations did not begin until the parents were sure that the girl would survive to marriageable age. Two groups, one from each of the yerta, would meet together to discuss the arrangements to transfer the woman from her family group to that of her spouse. Polygamy was allowed in aboriginal society, usually polygyny (multiple wives) and sometimes polyandry (multiple husbands), although, as mentioned above, the woman was not expected or required to reserve her sexual favors for only her husband (similarly the man was not expected to be faithful to one woman or to his harem).

The groom's family group camped near the bride's group for about two days and through a series of rituals established that they were gathered for a marriage. During this time the groom's family sent an emissary to the bride's group to negotiate the marriage transaction, discussing the relationships and settlements in great detail. Once agreements had been achieved, each of the negotiators returned to their family group to announce that the marriage could take place. The actual marriage occurred at daybreak following the completion of the negotiations. Usually the bride's brother would hand her to her new husband, although occasionally this was done by her father. She would immediately begin to live and work with her new family group. Her new life was more difficult if she joined a harem—as the older harem members would sometimes give her a hard time—and easier for her if she entered a monogamous marriage.

In some groups, before a young man was able to make a choice of bride, the parents of the eligible girls would stand around him and beat him; he would not retaliate, but would not speak to any of them again, not even to the parents of the one he chose. He indicated his choice by presenting the parents with food, and, if the girl agreed, he led her away from her family group. There were instances of couples falling in love and eloping. The couple would have to ensure that they eloped to an area well away from their family routes. If they were caught he would be injured with a spear through his thigh, and the girl would be hit on the head with a club. Any offspring resulting would be killed. If they kept away for some years, they could eventually rejoin their family group by taking a gift of food to the young man's parents.

The white settler population did not recognize the validity of aboriginal marriage—marriages were to be conducted under English law—and the clergy disapproved of marriage between the natives and the settler population. The Anglican bishop of Adelaide had forbidden such marriages; consequently those mixed marriages that did occur had to take place in a civil ceremony.

See also Capture, Marriage by; Civil Ceremonies; Elopement; Maori Weddings; Polyandry; Polygyny

References

Murphy, Brian M. 1978. *The World of Weddings: An Illustrated Celebration.* London: Paddington.

Scott, George Ryley. 1953. *Curious Customs of Sex and Marriage.* London: Torchstream.

Westermarck, Edward. 1894. *The History of Human Marriage.* 2d ed. London: Macmillan.

Woerlee, Bill. 2003. "Kudnarto." Available at *http://www.kudnarto.tripod.com* (accessed 8 June 2004).

Adultery

Adultery, having sexual relations with a person other than a marriage partner, has been considered a very serious, if not capital, offense, in many societies. Some societies have developed cruel punishments for the offense, ranging from death to humiliation. In some societies, the punishment is harsher for the woman than for her partner. In Britain, legislation was enacted in 1650 that made adultery a capital offense (punishable by hanging). But this law was not usually enforced—during this period there were social movements advocating free love, sexual freedom, and greater equality of the sexes. Adultery was usually tolerated in sixteenth- and seventeenth-century society if it was sufficiently discreet. Society would only take action if there was a complete and public marital breakdown. In this case the local community would ostracize the couple with a public display, such as "rough music" (people gathered outside the home and banged pots and pans and other items to make a terrific din) or "riding the stang" (carrying effigies of the couple involved on a pole around the community accompanied by a "rough band" and a crowd of followers). Many of the aristocracy lived somewhat openly in some form of adultery, and there was not shame in concubinage or in producing a child out of wedlock. The important point was for the eldest son to marry and have a son by his wife to ensure kinship, inheritance, and the continuance of the family line.

In ancient Egypt, villages were insular and quite xenophobic, and adulterous relationships were seen as threatening the family alliances within the village. The Egyptians considered both males and females as responsible for adultery. Egyptian literary texts suggested that the punishment for adultery for both parties was death at the hands of the betrayed party. However, there is little evidence that this punishment was used, and legal texts suggested that the usual punishment for a guilty male was some form of fine and for the woman most likely a divorce. It is unclear (but it is unlikely) whether an aggrieved wife could divorce an adulterous husband.

In Hindu writing, the punishment for adultery depended on the caste of the perpetrators. If the man committed the offense with a woman of a higher caste, he would be put to death—if with a woman of an equal or lower caste his possessions would be confiscated and he would be castrated and carried around on an ass. If he committed the adultery by fraud with a woman of the same or lower caste, he would be stripped of his possessions, branded on the forehead, and banished. If any man from an inferior caste should commit the act with a woman from a superior caste, he would be dismembered, tied to a hot plate, and burned to death. However, those from the highest caste could commit adultery with those from an inferior caste with only a fine as punishment, and a Brahmin, or a priest, would only suffer having his hair cut off.

But there are many cases where, as noted above, the punishment was death. An eighteenth- or nineteenth-century eyewitness account from Java (published by T. Little in *The Beauty, Marriage-Ceremonies, and Intercourse of the Sexes, in all Nations,* in 1824, and quoted by Scott 1953) described the execution for adultery of thirteen of the emperor's women by poisoning. In parts of New Guinea, capital punishment was used only for the crime of adultery. Disfigurement of the adulterer was another common punishment. Among several North American Indian groups, an aggrieved husband would bite or cut off the nose of the guilty woman; among the Creeks and Chittagong Hill tribes, the ears of a woman found guilty of infidelity were cut off. Another North American Indian tribe, the Muskogees, simply forced adulterers to remain celibate for the period of four full moons. According to the ancient laws of Sweden and Denmark, an aggrieved husband was allowed to kill his wife and castrate her lover.

There were less draconian punishments. Westermarck (1894) wrote that in the Up-lands-lag, an old Swedish provincial law, an adulteress had to pay a fine of forty marks. If she was unable to pay, she would lose her hair, nose, and ears. Punishments sometimes, it seems, were intended to make the guilty woman unattractive to her lover or any other person.

Among the Central African Lele people, if a woman dies in childbirth, she is believed to have committed adultery and her purported lover would be liable to pay a blood debt. Among the Bemba people of Zambia, a bridegroom took to his new household salt, meat, firewood, and a bow and arrow to shoot game and to protect his wife against adulterers. Adultery on the part of his wife was considered an infringement of his rights. This suggests one of the reasons for such draconian punishments for adultery. The act was seen as a form of theft on the part of the male partner and a treachery on the part of the woman—and likely to undermine the family relationships within the community and to subvert lines of inheritance and certainty of kinship because of the likelihood of bringing an outsider's child into the family. Consequently, punishments were often harsher for women than for men.

In Britain, although there were laws enacted to punish adultery, there was a certain amount of acceptance, and it was only when the adulterous behavior could not be ignored and "public decency" was offended that the community intervened. It was not always only the couple involved who would be ostracized—public wrath and condemnation was often directed at the cuckolded husband because adultery was seen as reflecting poorly on his reputation and ability to rule his household. Within English society, and particularly within the richer classes, there existed a significant double standard in that a wife was expected to ignore or overlook her husband's infidelities while being ostracized should she commit adultery. However, it is also suggested that the English ambivalence

toward, and tacit acceptance of, adulterous relationships was due to the almost impossibility of obtaining a divorce. If the marriage was unhappy or the couple had lost feelings of attachment to each other, there was no way out, as there is in other societies where the possibility of divorce or the creation of a polygamous household exists. As Macfarlane (1986, 244) wrote: "High prostitution and adultery rates may have been the price the English paid from the sixteenth to the nineteenth century for the rigid marriage code."

See also Rough Music/Rough Band

References
Depla, Annette. 1994. "Women in Ancient Egyptian Wisdom Literature." In *Women in Ancient Societies,* edited by Léonie J. Archer, Susan Fischler, and Maria Wyke. London: Macmillan.
Gillis, John R. 1985. *For Better, For Worse: British Marriages, 1600 to the Present.* Oxford: Oxford University Press.
Macfarlane, Alan. 1986. *Marriage and Love in England, 1300–1840.* Oxford: Basil Blackwell.
Mair, Lucy. 1971. *Marriage.* Harmondsworth, Middlesex: Penguin.
Scott, George Ryley. 1953. *Curious Customs of Sex and Marriage.* London: Torchstream.
Stone, Lawrence. 1990. *The Family, Sex, and Marriage in England, 1500–1800.* Abridged and revised ed. London: Penguin.
Westermarck, Edward. 1894. *The History of Human Marriage.* 2d ed. London: Macmillan.

Afghanistan

In Afghani society, when a couple becomes engaged to be married, there is usually a huge party, and from then until they are married the couple are treated almost like royalty. The engagement is often very long, sometimes lasting a year. The wedding usually occurs at night, with the celebrations continuing well into the next morning and, after a brief respite for sleep, maybe continuing through the next day. On the wedding day, the couple are treated like a king and queen, although the ceremony is very simple. The bride enters the marriage room with an entourage of women and sometimes children and processes to where the groom awaits her, where they sit on two thronelike chairs. The Koran is passed over their heads, and henna is put into their hands for good luck. The children also are given some henna on their palms—this makes them part of the celebration and is said to bring them good luck and happiness. After congratulations, the bride and groom lead a traditional dance and everyone joins in, and then the feasting, the dancing to the music of the *tabla* and *hamounia,* and the general celebrations begin. The guests make a great deal of noise and shoot guns into the air. During the reign of the fundamentalist Muslim Taliban government in Afghanistan, the wedding became more subdued, and all forms of music were banned.

See also Islamic Marriage
Reference
Wiggins-Azimi, Lydia. 1997. "An Afghan
    Wedding: 'From an American Perspective.'"
    Available at *http://www.afghanmagazine.com/
    articles/afghanwedding.html* (accessed 4 January
    2004).

African Weddings
See Egypt; Niger; Nuer Weddings; Yoruban Weddings; Zulu Weddings

Age at Marriage
The age of the couple at marriage varies among cultures according to religious and civil law and local custom. According to Sharia (Islamic) law, for example, a girl should marry soon after puberty—presumably to ensure that she retains her virginity for her husband. Thus, an Iranian girl may be married at the age of nine years. Tibetans generally marry in their mid-twenties. Polish Gypsy girls would generally be married at around twelve or thirteen years of age. Romanian Gypsy girls are still married at about fourteen. These ages seem to have been common across many cultures. Puberty has been seen as the acceptable age at which a girl could marry. However, such a young age has become less and less acceptable over the last century or so.

The Hindu Laws of Manu set out the ideal age difference between a man and a woman for marriage, saying that the man should be three times the age of the girl—a man of twenty-four should marry a girl of eight. However, it also occurred in Hindu writings that a man of thirty should marry a girl of twelve (the age difference here being two-and-a-half times the girl's age) and that it would be sinful for a man to breach this rule. Early Hindu religious writers wrote that a girl should be married by the age of ten or twelve years, and if she was not married by this age, she should be immediately married off, even in the season when marriage was prohibited. However, intercourse before puberty was forbidden.

The age at which a person can be married is obviously related to the legal "age of consent" for sexual intercourse, which in turn relates to the age of puberty, to perceived ages of adulthood (although in many communities adulthood is perceived to be arrived at upon marriage—in Ireland, for instance, an unmarried man of any age would be treated as a child in his family, unless, of course, he had entered the priesthood), and to the ability of couples to set up individual family units. Again there are exceptions. In Britain, a married couple living with the parents of one of the partners until the couple's own home can be set up is not unusual, and among some peoples, such as the Albanian Gypsies, the couple may live in an extended family unit, with the young wife being under the authority of her husband's mother.

However, the age for betrothal or spousal may have had little relationship to the age of puberty and may be much younger than the age of marriage. Betrothal was the contract between two families and was often viewed as tantamount to being married (but without the sexual rights). In Hindu practice, it was quite common for a young girl to be promised in marriage to an older boy or man. In British and European practice, it was not uncommon for young children to be espoused, but with the actual wedding not taking place until the boy was fourteen and the girl twelve—that is, when they had reached puberty. However, these spousals could be undone, since, by definition, they could only be *espousal de futuro* (a promise to marry in the future); one of the basic tenets of wedding agreements is that of consent of both parties, and young children could not be considered to have given their informed consent. Generally, the form of *espousal de futuro* depends on the couple using the words "I will take thee," indicating a promise for the future. Although binding, it was possible to break the contract by mutual agreement or if one of the party did not fulfill the promises or conditions contained in the original promise, such as the failure to wed or perform the marriage ceremony at a particular time or within a suggested time frame. Similarly, if one of the couple was found guilty of heresy, apostasy, or infidelity, the contract could be null and void.

Historically, in Europe, child spousals were not common, and occurrence was usually among the upper and ruling classes. Generally, population studies have shown that a high proportion of people married in their mid-to-late twenties. There were several reasons for this, such as the need to accumulate enough money and goods to be able to set up home (for women this could mean leaving home and going into "service"—becoming a servant—to earn enough money to accumulate goods to take into the marriage).

In Britain during the first half of the eighteenth century, the mean age of first marriage for males was 27.5 years, whereas the mean age for females was 26.2 years. By the end of the century this had dropped to 26.4 years and 24.9 years, respectively (Gillis 1985, 110). In the first part of the nineteenth century, the mean ages had dropped even further to 25.3 years and 23.4 years. Similar age ranges are found in the United States. But this entry from the *Parish Register* of Hilton, Dorsetshire, from 1739, appears to be at odds with general society in sug-

gesting that celibates and those holding back from marriage for financial reasons should be penalized: "Ordered, that all young unmarried persons above seventeen years of age do forthwith go to service, or be proceeded against according to law" (Dyer 1891, 126). Dyer offers no explanation for this statement.

Between the two world wars of the twentieth century, the average age of marriage in Britain had risen to twenty-six years for men and twenty-four years for women; by 1950 these average ages had both fallen by two years, probably due to the greater ability of couples to be financially independent, along with an increase in housing construction in this period and the consequent greater availability of housing.

As noted above, in Britain the youngest age for marriage was twelve for a girl and fourteen for a boy. This hampered British nineteenth-century reformers in attempts to prevent child prostitution by increasing the age of sexual consent; these attempts were further harmed by Lord Coleridge saying that the age must be twelve—that was the age, in common law, at which a girl could marry. The Criminal Law Amendment Act of 1885 raised the age of consent to sixteen, and the penalty for an assault on a girl under thirteen was whipping or penal servitude. However, it was not until 1926 that the youngest age for marriage of both boys and girls was raised to sixteen. There appears to be a disparity between the legal age of sexual consent for girls (sixteen years from 1885) and the lowest legal age at which she could be married (until 1926, it was twelve years of age), given that, in civil and ecclesiastical marriage practice, consummation of the marriage is expected (nonconsummation being grounds for annulment).

Currently in Britain the legal age at which a man and a woman can marry with parental consent is sixteen, and the age at which they can marry without this consent is eighteen, which was lowered from twenty-one on 1

January 1970. Eighteen is also the voting age in Britain.

See also Islamic Marriage; Spousal
References
Dyer, T. F. Thiselton. 1891. *Church-Lore Gleanings.* London: A. D. Innes.
Gillis, John R. 1985. *For Better, For Worse: British Marriages, 1600 to the Present.* Oxford: Oxford University Press.
Laslett, Peter. 1971. *The World We Have Lost.* 2d ed. London: Methuen.
Pearsall, Ronald. 1971. *The Worm in the Bud: The World of Victorian Sexuality.* Harmondsworth, Middlesex: Pelican.
Stone, Lawrence. 1990. *The Family, Sex, and Marriage in England, 1500–1800.* Abridged and revised ed. London: Penguin.

Almonds

At a Greek Orthodox wedding, the bridal couple is showered with sugared almonds; this is not part of the prescribed wedding service but is a folk tradition that has been incorporated into the ceremony. During the part of the service known as the Dance of Isaiah, when the couple and the priest, along with the wedding sponsors, make three circuits around the center of the church, sugared almonds and rice are poured over the couple. Additionally red-colored sugared almonds, known as *mándoles,* are thrown. Often this develops into a battle, with guests throwing the almonds at one another and deliberately trying to hit the groom and the priest. Sometimes the children hide in the upper women's gallery of the church so that they can get a good aim.

Sugared almonds feature prominently in Greek wedding ceremonies today but are a relatively recent phenomenon. Earlier, just almonds were used, which, along with other fruits, were poured over the heads of the couple to suggest a "watering" of the couple to make the new life together sprout and bring forth new life in the form of children. The almond tree is the first tree to bloom in Greece in the spring and can therefore be seen as a sign of spring and renewed life.

Greek Orthodox Christians, however, refer to the biblical story of Aaron's rod being thrown onto the ground and bearing almond blossoms (Num. 17.8). The connection of the almond with renewal and fertility seems clear. And the whiteness and sweetness of the sugared almond is said to represent purity, virginity, and the sweetness of marriage. Indeed, the practice among the Jews in eighteenth-century Poland—where the wedding started on the Sabbath with the bridegroom reading from the Law—was for the women in the gallery to shower him with almonds and raisins as a symbol, or wish, for the fruitfulness of the marriage as he went up to carry out this task. The children would scramble to collect the nuts and fruit.

In Greece, sugared almonds are thrown over the couple as they leave the church—in the same way that confetti is thrown—but without the aggression associated with the almond-throwing in the church. Sugared almonds are distributed to the guests as they leave the church—sometimes they take a large handful from a basket or they may be given some wrapped in a tulle bag tied with a ribbon. These may be a mixture of white, pink, and sometimes red sugared almonds (*mándoles*) and may include a small ceramic ornament (*boboniéra*). This is similar to a French practice and is sometimes a part of British weddings.

Occasionally, in some villages in North Cephalonia, when the bridal couple arrive at the groom's house, the bride is met at the door by her mother-in-law with a plate of *kouphéta,* a mixture of rice and almonds. The bride takes a handful of the mixture and throws it three times to the back and front for good luck and fertility before being embraced by her mother-in-law and entering the house.

Almonds are an important part of the period before the wedding. Sugared almonds may be given to the relatives and close friends who attend an engagement supper. North American Greeks often include *boboniéra* in the engagement party with a table set aside with a tray with sugared almonds and the wedding rings and an icon. Sometimes a priest will bless the tray of rings and almonds—the rings will be worn on the left hand as an engagement ring, to be transferred to the right hand at the wedding. In Greece, almonds are served at receptions at the bride-to-be's house in the days before the wedding, and in some parts of Greece married women go around the village bidding people to attend the wedding, carrying a basket containing sugared almonds, pomegranates, a bottle of ouzo, and a mixture of walnuts and almonds.

Sugared almonds are sometimes used for divinations. Unmarried girls place three sugared almonds from their *boboniéres* under their pillow so that they will dream of their future husband. Thought to be especially useful for divination are sugared almonds that have been on the tray carrying the wedding crowns—because they have been blessed by the priest. But any sugared almonds that have been in the church or have been in contact with the groom or thrown by the groom outside the church are believed to be effective. It is important for this divination that the sugared almonds have been at the wedding—sugared almonds that had been used at a funeral or baptism, where they are also featured, would not be effective.

Among the Berber people in Morocco, on the morning after the wedding night, the bride's supporter and witness throws a handful of almonds to the children, who scramble for the nuts, which are considered to be impregnated with the bride's good fortune.

See also Cake, Wedding; Confetti; Divinations; Greek Weddings; Rice

References

Edwards, Thornton B. 1996. "The Sugar Almond in Modern Greek Rites of Passage." *Folklore* 107: 49–56.

Hazel, Jeff. 1991. "Wedding Customs—Sugared Almonds." *FLS News* 13 (July): 9.

Murphy, Brian M. 1978. *The World of Weddings: An Illustrated Celebration.* London: Paddington.

Rouvelas, Marilyn. 1993. *A Guide to Greek Traditions and Customs in America.* Bethesda, MD: Nea Attaki.

Anniversaries

Wedding books tell us that, according to tradition, wedding anniversaries are to be celebrated as the following: First—Paper; Second—Cotton; Third—Leather; Fourth—Silk; Fifth—Wood; Sixth—Iron; Seventh—Bronze; Eighth—Electric; Ninth—Ceramic; Tenth—Tin; Eleventh—Steel; Twelfth—Linen; Thirteenth—Lace; Fourteenth—Ivory; Fifteenth—Crystal; Twentieth—China; Twenty-fifth—Silver; Thirtieth—Pearl; Thirty-fifth—Coral; Fortieth—Ruby; Forty-fifth—Sapphire; Fiftieth—Gold; Fifty-fifth—Jade; Sixtieth—Diamond. Variations include the first as cotton and the second as paper; the seventh as wool and the eighth as bronze; and the fifty-fifth as emerald; and the addition of a seventy-fifth wedding anniversary repeating as diamond.

However, there seem to be few accounts of celebrations of wedding anniversaries, and even some etiquette books advise that, apart from the silver, gold, and diamond years, the celebration of anniversaries ought to be a private event. And there does seem to be a commercial motive in this list. (How traditional is an electrical anniversary?) The indefatigable Victorian chronicler of marriage customs and traditions, John Cordy Jeaffreson (1872), makes no mention of wedding anniversary celebrations or presents.

However, as with weddings, tradition has developed for the celebration of the silver, gold, and diamond wedding anniversaries. For instance, for a silver wedding anniversary, the presents should be of silver or tied with a silver ribbon. The celebration is recommended to be a private family affair, with the addition of the original best man and chief bridesmaid. A cake may form a centerpiece, cut as at the original wedding, with a few speeches made. The gold and diamond wedding anniversaries are recommended to be celebrated in a similar manner, but with the latter being a much lower-key occasion "because of the age of the couple" and with both events usually arranged by the eldest son, with the assistance of his brothers and sisters (Heaton 1986, 145).

See also Cake, Wedding
References
Heaton, Vernon. 1986. *Wedding Etiquette Properly Explained.* Rev. ed. Kingswood, Surrey: Elliot Right Way
Jeaffreson, John Cordy. 1872. *Brides and Bridals.* 2 vols. London: Hurst and Blackett.

Anvil, Firing of

Anvils, used by blacksmiths for beating and shaping hot metal, are commonly only thought of, in the context of weddings, in association with marriages over the anvil at Gretna Green. However, in England there was a widespread custom of "firing the anvil." This dangerous custom involved filling a hole in the anvil with gunpowder and firing it with a red-hot iron as a form of salute to the bridal couple. This custom continued in some places well into the twentieth century—in 1936 the anvil was fired at a wedding at Greatham, County Durham. Unfortunately, this practice did result in injuries and even death. There is an account from Bradfield, Essex, England, concerning the blacksmith, a Mr. John Scrivener, who, in the 1850s, used a sledgehammer to force the plug of gunpowder into the hole. The blow from the hammer ignited the gunpowder and the handle of the hammer was blown through his body, killing him instantly.

See also Cars; Gretna Green; Rough Music/ Rough Band
Reference
King, Frank A. 1957. "Essex Wedding Customs and Superstitions." *Essex Countryside* 5, no. 19: 96–97.

Arabic Weddings

The Arab world comprises countries in the area known as the Middle East to the southwest of Asia—Iraq, Iran, Kuwait, Saudi Ara-

bia, the United Arab Emirates, the former Palestine, Lebanon, Yemen, Oman, Jordan, and Syria—and also countries of North Africa such as Egypt, Libya, and Algeria. (Although Israel is part of the Arabian peninsula, it is not an Arab country.) In all these countries, the predominant religion is Islam, and thus they have similar marriage rites and customs. All theoretically practice polygyny. Weddings are usually arranged (although in some countries the rules on this are relaxing due to Western influences)—the parents or guardians of a young man will seek out a suitable marriage partner for him and undertake all the negotiations.

Traditionally an Arab girl will be veiled when she reaches puberty, around the age of twelve or thirteen. In some cases, she will be veiled at the age of ten or eleven and then looked after by the older women to ensure that she does not lose her purity. She remains veiled and chaperoned until her wedding day. The taking of the veil is a sign of her moving into womanhood, and efforts are made to ensure that she is married as soon as possible after she is veiled. Again, outside influences have relaxed some of the traditional strictures regarding the veil, but contact between the sexes is still discouraged.

In many Arab countries it was usual for first cousins to marry (they would have been brought up in close contact and would know about each other)—despite the Islamic tradition that counsels to "marry amongst strangers, thus you will not have feeble posterity" and the ancient Arab injunction to "marry the distant, marry not the near," meaning the near in relationship. Westermarck (1894, 351) also quotes an Arabian hero poem: "He is a hero, not borne by the cousin, he is not weakly: for the seed of relations brings forth feeble fruit." A young man who has fallen in love may tell his mother, who then makes inquiries about the woman and her family. If his family members are satisfied, they will approach the girl's family with an offer of marriage. The young woman has to agree to the marriage before the parents set a date and go to the mosque to mark the beginning of the engagement period. This is a time for preparation for the couple to set up a home. However, it is not necessary for the young man to fall in love before suggesting to his parents that he is ready to marry. Once he has informed his parents that he is ready for a wife, his parents make every effort to find one for him. The Imam at the mosque explains the Islamic moral code, which the couple is expected to follow. The couple's responsibilities are also clearly defined: The husband and wife are equal partners in the marriage, so that the husband is expected to provide for and protect the family but does not have the right to rule the family. The woman is required to care for the children and run the household; all decisions should be by mutual agreement between the couple.

The bride-to-be begins to collect items that she takes into the marriage, which include gold, clothes, household items, and wool to produce mattresses. In Algeria this is called her *shoura*, which, in the event of her husband divorcing her, remains her property that she will take with her. As such it is part of her dowry. The size of her dowry, which the groom-to-be pays, is negotiated between the families; some of the dowry is used to purchase her *shoura*. The size of dowries and the increasing costs of weddings have forced many young Kuwaiti men to either marry foreign women or remain single, a state of affairs that is being addressed by an Islamic religious charity that offers young men incentives to marry Kuwaiti women. Usually a portion of the dowry (one-third to one-half) is retained to be given to the wife in the event of her husband's death or her being divorced by him. The young man meanwhile buys presents for his bride and her mother as a sign of respect and love.

The marriage settlement, dowry, and all other financial arrangements are arranged by the families of the couple. Such arrangements have been criticized by foreign observers, who suggest that the money changing hands is a form of purchase. However, some of the money paid by the groom's family may be used to purchase household items for the bride to bring with her. The dowry payment may also be a form of bond to marry—if the groom pulls out of the arrangement he loses at least part of his money. Typically an Arab wedding involves either the bride being taken to her new husband's house or the groom collecting his bride; this procession is accompanied by music and singing and a great deal of noise, including the firing of guns into the air. Decorating the bride's hands and feet with henna is a fairly universal practice across the Arab world; this is considered very sensuous, and the application of the henna decorations is a ceremony in itself.

Feasting, singing, and dancing over several days is also an element of the Arab wedding. Such celebrations may be segregated by sexes, as in Yemen. And, as with marriage the world over, the consummation of the marriage is most important, with evidence of the bride's virginity at marriage often required. Often the bride was not expected to talk to her new husband at all on the first night. With some groups in the past the marriage was not considered properly sealed until the wife was proven to be pregnant; thus, among the Bedouin of Mount Sinai, the wife was not allowed to enter her husband's tent until she was advanced in pregnancy.

The territorial disputes between the Israeli and Palestinian governments that have been a feature of the politics of the Middle Eastern region through the latter half of the twentieth century and the early twenty-first century have caused problems for Palestinian couples marrying. Military roadblocks and road closures have sometimes prevented a bridegroom from getting to the home of his bride to collect her, as is the Palestinian custom.

See also Arranged Marriage; Consanguinity; Consummation; Dowry; Egypt; Henna; Islamic Marriage; Kuwait; Yemen

References

Braddock, Joseph. 1961. *The Bridal Bed.* New York: John Day.

Fraser, John Foster. 1911. *The Land of Veiled Women*. London: Cassell.

Murphy, Brian M. 1978. *The World of Weddings: An Illustrated Celebration*. London: Paddington.

Westermarck, Edward. 1894. *The History of Human Marriage*. 2d ed. London: Macmillan.

Wood, Edward J. 1869. *The Wedding Day in All Ages and Countries*. 2 vols. London: R. Bentley.

Arranged Marriage

Not all cultures have a tradition of courtship as it is known in contemporary North American and European countries, and indeed it was sometimes very difficult for young people to meet. In many cultures, marriages are arranged by the parents, sometimes with the couple having little or no say. Such arranged marriages are often found within societies with a high degree of hierarchy and awareness of social rank. Today, arranged marriages have become a very contentious issue among the children from the second and third generations of the Hindu communities in Britain, who have been brought up in the European courtship and marriage tradition. Newspaper articles from 12 October 1976 in the *Times* (London) reported concerns about young Asian women running away from home rather than being forced into arranged marriages. The practice was defended by a mother, whose daughter had left home for that reason, who argued that the parents are more experienced and that young people do not know enough about the world. She further argued that parents investigate backgrounds and families to ensure that the man can provide for the woman and keep her happy. By running away, her daughter was considered to have brought disgrace to her family.

A survey in 1994 of Sikhs and Hindi, between sixteen and twenty-five years of age and born in Britain, suggested that 60 percent rejected the idea of an arranged marriage (*Manchester Guardian*, 25 June 1994). Forty percent accepted the concept of an arranged marriage but would retain the final say as to whether the marriage would go ahead. But traditionally the couple would not meet until the day of the wedding and would have little or no right to veto the match. Indeed, today it is not unusual for Hindu couples in India to be involved in the arrangements.

Arranged marriages occur in two major forms, both involving the parents of the couple arranging the alliance between the two families, often by using the services of a matchmaker. As noted above, in some cultures the couple have a right of veto. Thus among many African and nomadic tribes the young are allowed some choice. Today, even in societies such as that of the Tuareg people in Niger where at one time marriages were arranged between the parents—and it was not unknown for a prepubescent girl, who had been promised in marriage as a child, to be taken to the encampment of her betrothed and force-fed milk to give her a fully nubile appearance, and then the marriage consummated—the young people are actively involved in choosing a marriage partner. However, the families of Peulh Bororos tribes of Niger still choose the marriage partner for their young children.

In other cultures, notably the Hindu, an alliance through marriage is sometimes arranged between the parents even before the birth of the child, and their children have little or no say in the matter even as young adults. The traditional Chinese practice was for the parents to undertake the bride-seeking process with girls from rich families sought by rich families and the poor also marrying among themselves. The Chinese have a saying, "Bamboo door is to bamboo door as wooden door is to wooden door." Again, practices are changing to allow free, or freer, choice, although matchmakers or other go-betweens are still employed. The matchmaker often simply acts as an intermediary who explains the virtues of a young man or woman to the parents seeking a spouse for their child and makes the dowry and other financial arrangements between the two families.

Historically, among the highest ranks of European aristocracy (despite that one of the central tenets of Christian marriage is and was consent of both parties), arranged marriages—to forge family alliances—were well known; the children might argue against the parental choice but would often bow to the authority of their parents. This was not widespread, although the practice was retained for a much longer period among the higher aristocracy as a way to ensure that estates and fortunes were kept within a circle and to develop alliances for political and financial security. Among the landed classes in twelfth-century France, a daughter was viewed as an adjunct of the estate who could be "disposed of" as her father deemed to his best advantage—even to giving her in marriage to a retainer for some service rendered—a tradition still evident in some fairy stories where a young protagonist may demand the hand of a daughter in marriage in return for some deed.

See also Courtship; Matchmaking
References

Baldizzone, Tiziana, and Gianni Baldizzone. 2001. *Wedding Ceremonies: Ethnic Symbols, Costume, and Rituals.* Paris: Flammarion.

Gillis, John R. 1985. *For Better, For Worse: British Marriages, 1600 to the Present.* Oxford: Oxford University Press.

Macfarlane, Alan. 1986. *Marriage and Love in England, 1300–1840.* Oxford: Basil Blackwell.

Mair, Lucy. 1971. *Marriage.* Harmondsworth, Middlesex: Penguin.

Murphy, Brian M. 1978. *The World of Weddings: An Illustrated Celebration.* London: Paddington.

Westermarck, Edward. 1894. *The History of Human Marriage.* 2d ed. London: Macmillan.

Aztec

See Mexico

Ball Games

One would think that ball games would have little to do with the celebration of a wedding, but there exist traditions in which the bridegroom, usually, was expected to contribute either a football, or the money for a ball, to the local youths or community. Brand (1777) wrote, under the title "Foot-Ball Money":

In the North of England, among colliers and others, it is customary for a party to watch the bridegroom's coming out of the church after the ceremony, in order to demand money for a foot-ball; a claim that admits of no refusal. . . . Coles's Dictionary adverts to another kind of ball money given by a new bride to her old play-fellows. . . . In Normandy the bride throws a ball over the church, which both bachelors and married men scramble for.

Guthrie (1885) described a custom at that time in Scotland:

Formerly it was customary when marriages took place in the church of Pettie for the children of the parish school to barricade the door, and refuse admittance to the party till the bridegroom should either make a present of fourpence to buy a new football, or earn exemption from the custom by kicking the ball over the church. If the would-be benedict could not achieve the exploit of

kicking the ball, and would not pay the pence, the cleverest fellow might take off the bride's shoes. Thus degraded, the bridegroom was allowed to enter the church.

The cathedral session books of Kirkwall, Orkney, in northern Scotland, for 1684, stated that those who married must donate or give money for a football for the scholars of the grammar school. Another Orkney tradition stipulated that if the bride and groom were from different parishes, the best man had to donate a ball, or pay for a ball (ba'siller), for the children of one of the parishes, usually the bride's. If the best man refused to make the donation, the wedding party would be hounded by the boys and, as they emerged from the church, be confronted by the boys demanding their ba'. This practice continued in the Orkneys well into the twentieth century—there is reference to a bridegroom donating a ball to the local schoolboys at Deerness in 1931. It is not only in the north of England and the Orkneys that ball playing and donating traditions were found. In parts of France, a football game, known as *la Soule,* was played at weddings.

The traditions in England and the Orkneys, however, are part of a whole raft of customs by which the wedding party or the couple have to make some form of payment, usually to children, on the wedding day and may be derived from traditions of "paying a footing," that is, making some form of payment or donation to a community when joining that group (or sometimes in the case of a wedding, removing a person from the group).

See also Barring the Way; Ba'siller; Bosseller; Creeling

References

Brand, John. [1777] 1900. *Observations on the Popular Antiquities of Great Britain*. Revised and enlarged by Sir Henry Ellis in 1841 and 1848. 3 vols. London: G. Bill and Sons.

Guthrie, E. J. 1885. *Old Scottish Customs*. London: Hamilton, Adams.

Robertson, John. 1967. *Uppies and Doonies: The Story of the Kirkwall Ba'game*. Aberdeen: Aberdeen University Press.

Bangladesh

The majority (around 85 percent) of the population in Bangladesh is Muslim, approximately 10 percent is Hindu, and the remainder are Christian, Buddhist, or of other faiths. Although the beliefs and cultures of these groups differ, leading to differences in the religious aspects of the wedding ceremony, there are some cultural overlaps in actual wedding practices. In Bangladeshi culture, it is considered a duty and a destiny to marry, and it is rare for a person of marriageable age to be unmarried. Cohabitation is not socially acceptable, and any couple choosing this option would be severely ostracized. One reason for this may be that a wedding is not considered so much a "personal" commitment between the bride and groom as a bond between two families. Consequently, many of the ceremonies *(onushthan)* that are performed over a period of time have as a primary objective for the two families to introduce themselves and get to know and welcome each other. As often the case in Muslim tradition, a marriage is usually arranged, through relatives or friends or, especially in rural areas, through a professional matchmaker (known as a *ghatak*). Today, particularly among the middle classes, nonarranged marriages are acceptable.

The first formal event is the engagement ceremony that follows the marriage agreement between the two families *(paka-katha)*. This may be a large event, and in the case of wealthier people may be two separate functions—one for the bride and one for the groom. The couple themselves do not normally attend each other's engagement ceremonies. The bride-to-be's function is held at her parental home with the groom-to-be represented by members of his immediate and extended family as well as some of his friends. The engagement ring is usually put on the bride-to-be's finger (fourth finger of the right hand) by either her future husband's mother or grandmother. This is followed by a feast. A similar event is held for the man at his family home, where the bride is represented by members of her family and friends. After this formal engagement, the couple are allowed to meet and socialize, generally with a chaperone.

There now begins a time of great preparation for the wedding. This may take place a few weeks or up to within two years of the agreement. During this time the two families will organize the clothes and food, arrange for the religious clerics, issue invitations, arrange venues, decide on music, photographers, and video makers, buy presents for the close family members, and arrange accommodation and travel for out-of-town guests. Some couples also arrange a short holiday after the wedding, but this is uncommon. The wedding itself occurs over four days, with a different "element" occurring on each day. These four parts are the bride's *gai-haldi,* the bridegroom's *gai-haldi,* the wedding itself (the *be-a*), and the *walima*.

The bride's *gai-haldi* takes place at the bride's parental home and involves the bride's close female relatives and friends applying a turmeric *(haldi)* paste to the bride and massaging her from head to foot with oil. The bridegroom's female relatives arrive at the bride's home in procession bearing trays with sweets, outfits for the bride, including bridal saris, shoes or sandals, jewelry, and make-up, and gifts for her family. As a recognition of the traditional role of turmeric in this event, the women usually wear shades of yellow and the young members of each family coordinate patterns or textures on their saris so that each side is easily identifiable.

The event is relatively informal. Family members and friends of the bride and groom get to know each other in a social gathering with music and a meal—and during the evening the families have a series of musical debates in which they sing the praises of their own family and tease the others with their shortcomings (a form of dueling found in the marriage performance in many cultures). The younger members of the family may finish the evening with a water fight (rong-khela) using colored water. Traditionally, the bride wears a yellow sari with a red border and has her head covered, but she only attends the gai-haldi for part of the time. Her important participation is in the bracelet-tying ceremony (rakhi bandhan)—a red and silver cotton bracelet (rakhi) is tied to her right wrist by the mother or grandmother of the groom as a token of eternal bonding. The grandmother then offers the bride a small portion of a sweet dish (laddoo), which is set in front of the bride. Other members of the groom's family then each in turn offer her a small portion of the same dish. Once they have all made their offering, the bride's family follows suit. This order not only shows respect to the groom's family but is also said to be the beginning of her being taken into the groom's family; from now on she is expected to think and behave as a member of the bridegroom's family.

The bridegroom's gai-haldi is very similar to that of the bride, but without the rituals of the turmeric paste and oil massage.

The wedding itself, the be-a, is hosted by the bride's family. A procession of the bridegroom, his immediate family, his relatives, and his friends, which could number as many as two hundred people, the barat, arrives at the door of the wedding venue, where the procession is blocked from entering by the younger brothers, sisters, friends, and relatives of the bride, who demand a payment of entrance money (gate dhora). Although the amount of the gate dhora has previously been arranged, there is a raucous bout of bargaining before the money is paid and the barat is allowed entrance. The money is divided equally among those who barred the way of the wedding party.

After this ritual, the bridegroom's family and the barat are welcomed with sugar, garlands of flowers, showers of flower petals, and the placing of gold or silver bindi (dots) on the foreheads of the female members of the party. The bride remains in a secluded part of the house with her female relatives and friends until later in the ceremony. Meanwhile the bridegroom takes his place on a decorated platform for the religious part of the ceremony (the AKD or nikah). The Mullah, or cleric, with two witnesses, first goes to the bride to ask her consent for the marriage. After she has given her consent and signed the marriage document, the Mullah and witnesses return to the groom for his consent and signature on the document. The document is then signed by the Mullah and the witnesses. The document forms the marriage agreement and includes the den-moha-rana—the settlement the bride will receive in event of a divorce. The signing of the document seals the marriage both legally and in the eyes of society. The Mullah concludes this part of the ceremony with a sermon extolling the virtues and goodness of marriage. The bridegroom's family celebrates the sealing of the marriage and the alliance of the families by handing out dates and nuts to the company. It is becoming popular for the signing of the wedding agreement to take place earlier in the day rather than at the wedding celebrations.

The bride arrives at the celebrations sometime after the handing out of the dates and nuts wearing a red banarasee sari embroidered with golden thread; she also wears a long sheer scarf (a dupatta) that she uses as a veil during the wedding. The groom wears a long white *sherwani* coat and a *pagri* turban. The couple are seated together to receive their guests and well-wishers until they are called to dinner. There may be several hundred guests for the dinner; arrangements are made for the couple to either be served dinner where they are seated or they may go to a specially laid table. However, it is customary for a close female friend to accompany the bride for the rest of the evening. At the end of the evening a traditional *rusmat* takes place (in some cases this occurs when the bride arrives to sit next to the bridegroom). The bride and bridegroom get to see each other's face in a mirror, perhaps for the first time in the case of a traditionally arranged marriage, and they share food from the same plate and drink from the same glass as a gesture symbolizing the uniting of the couple in marriage.

During the *rusmat* the mother of the bridegroom puts a ring on the fourth finger of the bride's left hand while the bride's mother puts a ring on the bridegroom's finger. The fathers then present the couple with personal gifts and the parents bestow their blessings on the couple. The *rusmat* places a seal of approval and a blessing on the marriage from the two sets of parents. Sometime during the evening, the younger relatives and friends of the bride try to steal *(juto churi)* the bridegroom's shoes. A group of young people from the bridegroom's family attempts to prevent them from getting the shoes. The shoes are returned once the bridegroom has made a payment to the group. Although the payment amount is prearranged, an argument usually takes place concerning the value of the shoes. It is not unusual for the *barat* to take a spare pair of shoes for the bridegroom as a bargaining lever. The end of the dinner and the conclusion of the *rusmat* is a signal for the *barat* to depart, but this time the bride goes with them as she is now part of the bridegroom's family; she is accompanied by an unmarried female relative or friend to help her unpack and settle into her new home.

The final event, the *walima,* takes place a few days later. This is a reception hosted by the bridegroom's family. The bride's family arrives in procession and is greeted by the couple and the bridegroom's family with sugar, garlands, the scattering of flower petals, and the placing of gold or silver *bindi* on the foreheads of the females in the party. A sumptuous meal is served, after which the newlyweds return to the bride's parental home, which is decorated with flowers and colored lights, with the visiting party, to visit and spend a few days with the bride's family.

See also Barring the Way; Henna; Islamic
  Marriage; Shoes
Reference
Personal information from Mrs. Rumana Zuberi,
  Ipswich, Suffolk, November 2002.

Banns

In Great Britain, an approaching wedding has to be officially announced, so that any person with valid objections, or any person who knows of any impediments to the wedding, is able to make these objections known. The announcement is traditionally read out in church on three successive Sundays and is referred to as the reading of the banns. It has been suggested that the word "banns" is derived from the German verb *binden,* which in the imperfect becomes "band"—to bind or join together.

The Church of England's *Book of Common Prayer* prescribes the wording of the announcement: "I publish the Banns of Marriage between *M* of _____ and *N* of _____. If any of you know cause, or just impediment, why these two persons should not be joined together in holy Matrimony, ye are to declare it. This is the first [second, or third] time of asking." If the couple live in different parishes, the banns have to be read in the churches of both parishes; the curate of the church where the wedding is to take place is not allowed to perform the ceremony without a certificate of the banns being thrice announced from the curate of the other parish. In 1974 the Church of England suggested updating the wording of the banns to: "I publish the banns of marriage between *N* of _____ and *N* of _____. If any of you know any reason in law why these persons may not marry each other you are to declare it. This is the first [second] [third] time of asking."

In 1200, Archbishop John Peckham decreed that the banns of marriage should be published in church three times prior to the marriage, and the fourth Lateran Council, in 1215, ordered the publication of banns by canonical law, as well as the public performance of the marriage rite. During the Commonwealth period in England, 1649 to 1660, Parliament decreed that marriage was a civil act and should be performed before a registrar, whose duty included announcing the names of the couple either in church after the service on three successive Sundays or in the marketplace on three successive market days, according to the wishes of the couple.

It was not until 1754, with Lord Hardwick's Marriage Act, that it became by law an offense to be married anywhere other than in a church or public chapel without the prior calling of the banns or without a license. The Act was passed as an attempt to prevent elopements, clandestine marriages (Fleet Weddings), and weddings where a family (usually of the bride) wished to prevent marriage with a partner considered to be a gold digger or otherwise unsuitable. However, this led to the popularity of Gretna Green for elopements, which was the first town over the English border with Scotland, where this law did not apply. In the traditional English folk song, "Come Write Me Down," from the singing of the Copper family (Copper 1971, 271) from Rottingdean, Sussex, England, the penultimate verse begins: "To church they went the very next day and were married by asking as I've heard say." "Asking" or "to be asked" in church was one of several local terms for the reading of the banns. Indeed, it is a term used in the *Book of Common Prayer*. The following note from the *Book of Common*

Prayer giving instructions regarding the case of the couple living in different parishes uses the term "asked" for the announcement of the banns: "And if the persons that are to be married dwell in divers [more than one] Parishes, the Banns must be asked in both Parishes."

The couple in the song were, therefore, married with due announcement to their community and with permission, as opposed to eloping to Gretna Green or obtaining a special license. Other local terms for the reading of the banns included to be "cried" in church, "calling home," to be "thrown over the rannal-bawk," and "spurring." (The rannal-bawk was an iron beam in a kitchen chimney from which kettles were hung.) In parts of the north of England it was customary to ring the church bells after the third reading of the banns; the bell was referred to as the "spurring bell" and was rung to bring a blessing to the couple. After the third reading, the congregation would shout, "God speed 'em well." However, this was frowned upon by some members of the clergy. A vicar in a parish in Yorkshire suppressed the customary good wishes altogether because it "excited unseasonable mirth among the younger portion of the congregation."

Regional superstitions concerning the banns developed. One from Lincolnshire was that if the bell was tolled for the death of a married woman on the same day that the banns were read for the third and last time it would presage that the new bride would not live even one year of her married life. A Perthshire superstition considered that it was unlucky to have the banns read during the end of one quarter of the year and for the couple to marry at the beginning of the next. In some places in Britain it was thought that if an engaged couple heard their banns announced, their first child would be born an idiot or all their children would be born deaf and dumb. However, as it is usual for a couple to hear their banns read, it would seem that few have experienced the consequences of this superstition. Similarly, a superstition from the Leeds area, Yorkshire, stated that it was unlucky for a woman to attend church when her banns were being called—her future children would run the risk of being deaf and dumb.

At one time, if the couple called off the wedding after the third reading of the banns, the clergy could fine them for the offense; calling off the marriage at this stage was interpreted as a scorning of the church. The reading of the banns was seen as the first part of the marriage ceremony, and, if no objections or impediments were raised after the third reading, that constituted an implied communal agreement to the marriage. Therefore, to call off the wedding after the marriage performance had begun would be tantamount to a divorce and would be a slight to the community; the couple could be further punished by the local community who might make "rough music" against them.

In 2001 the Church of England Synod considered dropping the calling of the banns in church because of a decrease in church attendance and to encourage church weddings for attendees at church; however, after three years no action has been taken on this suggestion.

See also Fleet Weddings; Gretna Green;
    Irregular Marriage; Lord Hardwick's Marriage
    Act; Rough Music/Rough Band

References

Book of Common Prayer, The. Oxford: Oxford
    University Press.
Copper, Bob. 1971. *A Song for Every Season.*
    London: William Heinemann.
General Synod. 1975. *Alternative Services Series 3:
    The Wedding Service. A Report by the Liturgical
    Commission of the General Synod of the Church of
    England.* London: SPCK.
James, E. O. 1933. *Christian Myth and Ritual.*
    London: J. Murray.
Monsarrat, Ann. 1973. *And the Bride Wore . . . : The
    Story of the White Wedding.* London: Gentry.
Wright, Elizabeth Mary. 1913. *Rustic Speech and
    Folklore.* Oxford: Oxford University Press.

Barring the Way

This is one of a group of customs found in Britain whereby members of the community, usually children, prevent the newlywed couple from leaving the church until they have paid a toll. This is achieved by tying the gates of the churchyard or by holding some form of barrier, such as a rope, across their path. Sometimes the barrier may be more elaborate. For example, the British national newspaper, the *Daily Sketch* (London), in March 1953, described how in Eyemouth, on the English-Scottish border, the way was barred using fishing creels (baskets) and a rope. The rope was cut by the bride after the bridegroom gave money to the group who erected the barrier. It was important, locally, who paid the toll—usually the bridegroom. And as marriages usually take place in the bride's parish, it can be seen as a way for the bridegroom to pay his way into the community and also to signal to the community that the couple were indeed married, useful for populations that at the time would have largely been illiterate and at a time when there were no cameras to capture the wedding and provide proof of the marriage.

Huddleston (1973) gave an account of barring the way at a wedding at Kildwick Church in Yorkshire, England, where the barring of the gates was carried out by the choirboys. When the organist's daughter married, her father, who had not previously had an opportunity to see the custom, mistakenly paid the toll, which, to at least one choirboy, was proof that the organist-father was the groom—despite the fact that the boy had seen the wedding ceremony.

The custom is found in other parts of Europe, such as in Germany, where in peasant marriages the road was barricaded by young men of the village against the couple traveling to the church. The groom had to pay a toll before they could continue. In modern Germany, when the couple leave the church after the service (which is the day after the civil/legal ceremony) the way may be barred by local children who let the couple pass on payment of sweets and money. Sometimes, in Dungannon, County Tyrone, Ireland, the local youths bar the way for the bride into the church. At weddings in Wales, it was traditional for the groom's party to go to the bride's house to collect the bride and her entourage for a procession to the church. It was the custom for the bride's family and supporters to put obstacles in the way of the groom's party. Straw ropes were stretched across the road with perhaps a quintain game set up that the party would have to play. The quintain (in Welsh, *cwinten* or *gwyntyn*) was an upright pole with a free-swinging arm, a flat board target at one end, and a sandbag counterweight at the other. The rider would have to strike the board and get out of the way before the sandbag came around to strike him. In some parts of Wales, this, along with the straw rope barriers, was so associated with weddings that the barring of the way and the straw ropes were referred to as the *gwyntyn*. There is no suggestion that the groom and his followers had to pay any toll along the way, but at the bride's door the party would have to take part in a ritualized question and answer. Similarly, in Thailand, the groom's procession to the marriage is barred, first by a gold chain held by the friends and relatives of the bride and then by a sturdier barrier held by the bride's parents. At each barrier he has to pay a price to be allowed to pass.

In Vietnam on the day chosen for the groom's family to approach the bride's family to consent to the marriage (arranged by a go-between), a sum of money is paid to the communal fund of the girl's village by the groom's family. On the day of the wedding the groom's family and party process to the bride's home but are not allowed in until they have paid an "entrance fee" (usually brought in a red envelope).

In the Orkney Islands it was a tradition for a bridegroom to contribute a football for the scholars, and football was often played after a wedding. There are other references in Scotland to the donation of the money, or an actual ball, for a mass football game. Additionally, there are accounts of the local children demanding the money for the ball outside the church. This may be the origin of ba'siller—

money scattered to the local children at a wedding in Scotland.

See also Ba'siller; Petting Stone; Thailand

References

Huddleston, Mary. 1973. "A Yorkshire Miscellany." *English Dance and Song* 35, no. 1: 24.

Murphy, Brian M. 1978. *The World of Weddings: An Illustrated Celebration.* London: Paddington.

Radford, E., and M. A. Radford. 1961. *Encyclopaedia of Superstitions.* Edited and revised by Christina Hole. London: Hutchinson.

Robertson, John. 1967. *Uppies and Doonies: The Story of the Kirkwall Ba'game.* Aberdeen: Aberdeen University Press.

Ba'siller

Ba'siller, a Scottish dialect word that translates as "ball silver," is sometimes heard as a demand by children attending a wedding in parts of Scotland or the Scottish Isles. Brand (1777) reports that it was customary in the north of England to demand money for a football from the bridegroom as he emerged from the church. The tradition of donating a football, or the money for a ball, was found in a number of places in Scotland, and the present-day custom of parading a woman, decorated with paper rosettes, through the streets by her workmates on the eve of her wedding is sometimes referred to as "bosseller," which may be a corruption of "ba'siller."

There were local customs in which the bride and groom were prevented from entering the church by the local children until the groom had presented them with money or had kicked a football over the church. If the groom failed to comply, the bride's shoes would be taken and the couple would then be allowed into the church. Similarly in Kirkwall, Orkney, Scotland, it was expected that those who married in the cathedral would donate, or pay for, a football for the local grammar school students. The practice persisted into the first half of the twentieth century, when there is a record from 1931 of a bridegroom donating a ball to the children in Deerness.

See also Ball Games; Barring the Way; Bosseller
References
Brand, John. [1777] 1900. *Observations on the Popular Antiquities of Great Britain.* Revised and enlarged by Sir Henry Ellis in 1841 and 1848. 3 vols. London: G. Bill and Sons.
Robertson, John. 1967. *Uppies and Doonies: The Story of the Kirkwall Ba'game.* Aberdeen: Aberdeen University Press.

Bathing

Ritual bathing—cleansing in preparation for a new beginning—is a rite that has been observed in ancient times and among modern peoples. Crawley (1902) suggested that bathing was a form of purification, "the inner meaning of which is to neutralise the mutual dangers of contact." He cited the Malay tradition of purification by water as an integral part of the customs of birth, adolescence, marriage, sickness, and death and other critical times in life. In all these rituals this was referred to as *tepong tawar,* meaning "the neutralizing rice-flour water."

In South Celebes, the bridegroom bathes in holy water before the marriage and the bride is also fumigated to ensure purity. In parts of Russia, there is a tradition of communal bathhouses where, in a ritual overseen by the local village wizard, or magician, a bride is ritually bathed. During the bathing ritual the bride is flailed with birch twigs and the sweat rubbed off her with a fish that is cooked by her future mother-in-law and eaten by her husband-to-be. The Finnish practice suggests that the ritual bath was a way of cleaning away the old life in preparation for the new life. On the day of the wedding, the bride with her friends goes to the sauna for the ritual bath; when she returns home her hair is unbraided and cut short; she is then presented with a linen cap known as a *tzepy* that she wears from then on, marking her transformation to the married state—a married woman never shows her hair in public.

In Egypt, traditionally, part of the bride's preparation is a visit to the bathhouse. She processes through the streets, covered completely with a red cashmere shawl and wearing a small cap or even a crown, under a silk canopy open only at the front, and accompanied by musicians and her friends. After the bride and her party have visited the bathhouse, they return to the bride's house, again in procession, where she and her companions continue to celebrate with the "henna night." In some societies, henna is considered very sensual. It is used as a beautifying agent and to decorate the hands and feet of brides, often with intricate patterns. The Afghanis consider that henna will bring good luck and happiness. In the context of ritual bathing and purification, Bulgarian Gypsies use henna to ritually "clean" the bride during a week of celebrations. It is said to symbolize the bloodstained sheets of the virgin bride after consummation of the marriage. The longer the henna stays on the longer her husband will love her.

The Turkish tradition was for the bride to be bathed the day before the wedding by two or three women. She was escorted to the baths by her nearest relatives carrying burning torches. Among the ancient Greeks, a procession of the bride and groom to the bathhouse, led by flute players and torchbearers, was an integral part of the wedding ceremonial. A young male child carried a special jar for the bathing of the couple. Among some Jewish peoples, a bride-to-be would be washed in a bath of cold water the day before her wedding, accompanied by a group of women who would make a great commotion during the bathing to draw attention to the fact that the young woman was to be a bride. Sometimes the ritual bathing is only applied to the feet and may have a meaning beyond any purification. In some Hindu ceremonies, for example, the bridegroom's feet may be washed by the bride's father; after he has done this he orders his daughter, the bride, to put her feet into the same water and then tells her that he no longer has anything to do with her and she is now in the "power" of her husband (Braddock 1961, 117).

In some areas where the Zoroastrian wedding ceremony is used, the feet of the bride and groom may be ritually washed. If the couple wear Western-style shoes, the tips of the shoes are washed. In the Sundanese wedding, in Indonesia, after the groom has broken an egg with his right foot, the bride washes this foot and then throws the jug that contained the water away to break it.

According to James (1933), in the Middle Ages a bride would, after washing her feet, sprinkle the waters to the corners of the bedchamber in the belief that a blessing would arise from this action. In Prussia, the bride's feet would be washed, and the washing water sprinkled over the guests, the bridal bed, other parts of the house, and the cattle. According to a letter from a "Gentleman in Northern Scotland," from 1754, in some parts of the north of Scotland on the evening before the wedding, the bridesmaids attended the bride and washed her feet (Heseltine 1951, 172). James (1933) also wrote that in Persia when the bridegroom entered the nuptial chamber, a container of water and a basin would be brought. The right leg of the bride would be placed against the left leg of the groom and both would be washed. He does not say if the water was disposed of in any particular manner.

See also Egypt; Feet; Henna; Hindu Weddings; India; Zoroastrian Weddings

References
Braddock, Joseph. 1961. *The Bridal Bed.* New York: John Day.
Crawley, Ernest. [1902] 1932. *The Mystic Rose: A Study of Primitive Marriage and of Primitive Thought in Its Bearing on Marriage.* 4th ed. Revised and enlarged by Theodore Besterman. London: C. A. Watts.
Gaya, Louis de. 1685. *Matrimonial Ceremonies Displayed.* English translation, 1704. London: Privately printed.
Heseltine, G. C., ed. 1951. *A Bouquet for a Bride.* London: Hollis and Carter.
James, E. O. 1933. *Christian Myth and Ritual.* London: J. Murray.
Murphy, Brian M. 1978. *The World of Weddings: An Illustrated Celebration.* London: Paddington.

Bed, Marriage

In all cultures, consummation of the marriage is the final part of the ritual and constitutes a sealing of the contract. The bridal bed, therefore, has been a focus of rowdy celebration, and a newly married couple would often have been given little privacy. In pre-seventeenth-century England, the church often provided a "wedding house" with a room for the postwedding celebrations and perhaps, as at the house at Braughing in Hertfordshire, England, a bedchamber with a bridal bed. The bedding of the couple would take place with a great deal of ceremony, beginning with the priest blessing the bed. At a royal wedding in the time of Henry VII of England (1485–1509), the bishop and the chaplains would bless the bed. After this the couple were passed a cup of sweetened and spiced wine, again blessed by the priest, known as the "benediction posset." Before this was brought in, the couple would have prepared themselves for bed, and the divination custom of throwing the stocking would have been performed. Two of the groomsmen sit on one side of the bed, with their backs to the center, and two of the bridesmaids sit on the other. Each groomsman had one of the groom's stockings and, likewise, each bridesmaid had one of the bride's stockings. Each in turn threw the stocking over the shoulder, the groomsmen hoping to hit the bride on the head and the bridesmaids hoping to hit the groom. A hit would indicate that the thrower would soon be married. After the benediction posset was drunk, the curtains around the bed were drawn and the company dispersed.

Charles the First of England escaped this ceremony by the simple expedient of barring the door of his state bedroom, to the annoyance of his courtiers; but, as Jeaffreson noted, "The royal example did not abolish the practices, which were maintained among the gentle as well as the simple for more than another century" (1872, 1: 250). In 1665, Samuel Pepys, the well-known London diarist, reported entering the bridal chamber

The blessing of the marriage bed, by Bernard Picart, c. 1724. (CORBIS)

to kiss the bride in bed. Indeed, the bedding practices were fully observed at the wedding of Mary (daughter of James I of England and granddaughter of Charles I) and William Prince of Orange, when it is said that the king, Charles II (Mary's uncle), drew the curtains around their bed after they had emptied the posset bowl.

In some places the bed is one of the first items of a new household to be prepared. Gregor (1881) noted that a girl would begin collecting items for setting up her home from a young age, starting with the feathers for her mattress and pillows. Among fishing communities of northeast Scotland, the household items that a bride was expected to take to her new home included a featherbed, four pairs of white blankets, two bolsters, four pillows, and sheets. The bride's contribution to the new household was known as her *providan* or *plinisan* and was delivered to her new home in

a procession with some ceremony. Two carts were used. In the first was the chest of drawers, with the bed with the blankets, bolster, and pillows on top. The second cart carried the *kist* (chest), tubs, and other hardware.

In the Rosehearty district of northeast Scotland, marriages commonly took place on a Thursday, and the bride's *plinisan* was taken to the new home on Wednesday, when the bed was made up. The groom and his two best men slept the night on it. The bridal bed was made up by the bride's sister—if she had no sister, by her nearest female relative. Sometimes a sixpence was nailed to the back of the bed, perhaps to ensure that the couple would not want for anything during life together, in much the same way a bride in other parts of the country would put a silver sixpence, threepenny bit, or a gold coin into her shoe on the wedding so that she would be "walking on gold" (or silver).

In Gardenstone in the northeast of Scotland, the bridal bed was made up by a woman who was currently breast-feeding, in the belief that if any other woman did so there would be no family. At the *beddan* the unmarried guests filled the room and the bride went to bed first. The bridegroom took off his stocking and threw it among the crowd. The one who caught it would be the next to marry.

There are some superstitions associated with the bridal bed. Some consider it bad luck for the couple to sleep in their new home or permanent home on the wedding night. If the harvest moon shines on the bed, that ensures a long and happy life for the couple. If the husband goes to bed before his new wife, he will live longer than her; but the first to go to sleep on the wedding night will be the first to die. The couple should sleep with their heads to the north to ensure continued happiness; but it is very bad luck for the bride to put her bare feet on the floor on the wedding night. It was unlucky if a flea was found in the marriage bed, arising from the belief that it was placed there by a jealous ex-lover of the bride or the groom. This would cause a quarrel, with each accusing the other of being unfaithful before the marriage. If a pound of Limburger cheese was spread between two towels and placed under the pillow of the bridal bed for the couple's first night together, they would have good fortune and a large family. This seems to be a form of "bed joke" to be played on couples on their wedding nights in much the same way as a "rough band" played outside the couple's bedroom window on the wedding night (which often occurred in Cornwall, England) or placing bushes in the wedding bed or short-sheeting the bed or causing some other disturbance to the couple. Even today, couples in Britain will often endeavor to keep the location of their first night of marriage secret to ensure that their friends do not find a way of disturbing them.

See also Divinations; Posset; Stockings, Throwing of

References
Emrich, Duncan, ed. 1970. *The Folklore of Weddings and Marriage.* New York: American Heritage Press.
Gillis, John R. 1985. *For Better, For Worse: British Marriages, 1600 to the Present.* Oxford: Oxford University Press.
Gregor, Rev. Walter. 1881. *Notes on Folklore of the North East of Scotland.* London: Folklore Society.
Jeaffreson, John Cordy. 1872. *Brides and Bridals.* 2 vols. London: Hurst and Blackett.
Porter, Enid. 1969. *Cambridgeshire Customs and Folklore.* London: Routledge and Kegan Paul.

Bells

In Great Britain, the ringing of the bells, blending with the celebratory organ recessional music as the couple leaves the church after the ceremony, gives a characteristic soundscape to an English church wedding. Bells have been part of the church since the earliest days of Christianity, to summon people to worship, to call a curfew (the curfew bell, still rung in some places), and to mark a celebration or the death of one of a community (the passing bell). In the north of Britain, a tradition developed of ringing the bells after the third reading of the banns of marriage, known as the "spurring bell" ("spurring" was a term used for the calling of the banns).

Many bells were destroyed during the Reformation in the sixteenth century and by the followers of Oliver Cromwell during the British Commonwealth period in the mid-seventeenth century. In the rebuilding after this period and with the Restoration of the monarchy, new methods of hanging church bells were developed, and so began the peculiarly English tradition of change ringing and methods, the sound heard today at church weddings (if the couple have hired bell ringers). Change ringing is a technique whereby the group of bell ringers are able to change the order of the sounding of the bells by varying the pull on the bell ropes; with six bells, for example, there are 720 possible orders of ringing—with seven,

5,040. A "method" is a specified sequence of changes ordered like a musical score. After the Restoration, bell ringing became usual at church feasts, and there was a demand for ringing at family occasions such as birth, baptism, marriage, and death.

During the seventeenth and eighteenth centuries, bell ringing may also have accompanied the procession to the church. It was an honor for the bridal party to be escorted to the church by a throng of people, who, in the north and midlands of England and in Wales, especially enjoyed a "horse wedding," where the participants were mounted on horseback and the crowd would ring bells and fire guns into the air.

Noise is expected in the proclamation and celebration of marriage in most cultures. In many Islamic countries, such as Afghanistan, the celebrants shoot guns into the air. In Portugal, Ireland, and other European countries, the members of the wedding party honk car horns as they drive to the wedding celebrations. In Great Britain, church bells are expected. At one time in Upton St. Leonard, Gloucestershire, England, people would beat pots and pans, to make a rough music, if the bells were not rung.

See also Banns; Cars; Rough Music/Rough Band
References
Camp, John. 1988. *In Praise of Bells: The Folklore and Traditions of British Bells.* London: Robert Hale.

Gillis, John R. 1985. *For Better, For Worse: British Marriages, 1600 to the Present.* Oxford: Oxford University Press.

Besom Weddings

In some parts of Great Britain, to be said to be "living over the brush" means to be living together outside of an official marriage. If the couple then were officially married they would be said to have "wed over the broomstick." In some areas a hasty or irregular marriage may be said to be a "marriage over the broomstick." These expressions refer to a practice found in some parts of Great Britain of "besom weddings," a form of trial marriage that was looked upon by the community as a legal and proper marriage, with all the rights, privileges, and obligations of an official wedding, but which could be undone within a certain time limit (usually within a year).

In Wales, the besom wedding involved the couple jumping over a birch besom—a kind of broom or brush made using twigs or sturdy bushy plants such as broom, the sort of broomstick that witches are popularly depicted as riding. The besom was laid across the doorway of either the bride's or the groom's home (or the couple's prospective home). The man and the woman would each have to jump over the broom without touching it or the doorjamb, in the presence of witnesses, after which the bride might be given a wedding ring. The marriage could be undone within a year by the unhappy partner jumping backward over the broom, again across the doorway, again without touching the broom or the doorjamb, and again in the presence of witnesses. If there was a child from the relationship when the marriage was annulled, the father would be the one to take care of it. After the annulment, both parties would be free to marry again, and the woman would be considered either a widow or a virgin. The usual reason for the annulment would have been incompatibility or a failure of childbearing. Some accounts of besom weddings suggest that both the man and the woman had to hold a broom behind and then jump backward over the broom without letting go. It has been said that British Gypsies held a similar marriage ceremony in which the couple jumped over a broom besom and were then pronounced man and wife by an officiating elder.

Why should a broom be central to such a ceremony? A broom has special associations with the home and the fireside, and by extension the family and family life, and may be credited with special powers (consider witches' flying broomsticks). In parts of Ireland, it was traditional to throw a besom after a departing matchmaker or anyone else going on an important mission, to bring them luck.

See also Broom, Marriage over the; Common-
Law Marriage; Divorce; Handfasting; Shoes;
Temporary Marriage

References

Bloom, J. Harvey. [1929] 1977. *Folk-Lore, Old
Customs, and Superstitions in Shakespeare Land.*
London: Mitchell, Hughes, and Clarke;
Norwood, PA: Norwood Editions.

Evans, E. E. 1957. *Irish Folkways.* London:
Routledge and Kegan Paul.

Gwynn, Gwenith. 1928. "Besom Weddings in the
Ceiriog Valley." *Folklore* 39: 149–166.

Menefee, Samuel Pyeatt. 1981. *Wives for Sale.*
Oxford: Basil Blackwell.

Best Man

The best man, or groomsman, usually a close
friend or relative of the bridegroom, has several duties. In Britain, he accompanies the
groom at his prenuptial celebration (stag
night) with the intention of ensuring that the
groom stays out of trouble; on the wedding
day he ensures that everything runs smoothly
and, usually, is the one to take the wedding
ring or rings to the church and at the correct
time give them over to the groom; at the reception he is expected to take care of the
bridesmaids and ensure that all the arrangements (for example the entertainment) run
smoothly. He (usually—but in the late twentieth century a female "best man" was not unknown) makes a speech and proposes a toast
to the bridesmaids. He is there to support the
bridegroom on the wedding day, and in some
respects, he acts as the groom's representative. This has led some writers to ascribe to
him the function of being the bridegroom's
closest companion in helping him fight the
bride's protectors in "marriage by capture."
However, this suggests some sort of univer-
sality of the practice of marriage by capture.
Such a deduction comes from such practices
as the bride being escorted to church by two
bride's-men; later, during the nineteenth
century, these became page boys. In most
wedding ceremonies around the world the
groom is accompanied by supporters and
helpers who may be siblings, peers, and close
unmarried friends.

The term "best man" does not seem to
have come into common usage until late in
the nineteenth century. Jeaffreson (1872)
used the term "groomsman" and described
his duties as being very similar to those of the
present-day best man. He was expected to be
a close friend of the groom and unmarried.
Charles Dickens asked his publisher, John
Macrone, to be his best man at his wedding
but had to withdraw the invitation on the insistence of his bride-to-be because Macrone
was married. In the twenty-first century,
couples in Britain and the United States are
not usually concerned about the marital status of the best man.

A correspondent to Robert Chambers's
The Book of Days (1863), a Suffolk, England,
clergyman, described the accompanying attendants at a laborer's wedding as being only
three: "the official father, the bridesmaid and
the groomsman, the latter two being, if possible, an engaged couple, who purpose to be
the next pair to come up to the altar on a
similar errand upon their own account."

In many cultures, the wedding couple will
have supporters and helpers for the wedding
day who may act as intermediaries during the
events around and during the wedding and,
in some cases, may help to pay for it. Indeed,
in Britain, the best man is usually the one
who pays for any services that need to be paid
for on the day (albeit with money supplied by
the groom or his family). The groomsman, or
best man, is, in many respects, much like the
shoshbin, the groom's close friend and supporter, traditional in Jewish marriages. The
word appears in Aramaic in the sense of being
a close friend, and he is a close companion to
the groom and gives him assistance and support. This brings financial obligations. He is
expected to give expensive gifts to the
groom, and he may, with other friends of the
groom, give gifts to help defray the costs of
the wedding. In this case, all who send gifts
are referred to as *shoshbins.* The groom is
then expected to return these gifts or give
help at the wedding of his *shoshbin.* (This
bears some similarity to the Welsh practice

of bidding.) The bride is also expected to provide her own *shoshbin*.

See also Bidding; Bridesmaid
References

Chambers, Robert. 1863–1864. *The Book of Days.* Vol. 1. Edinburgh: W. and R. Chambers; Philadelphia: J. B. Lippincott.

Jeaffreson, John Cordy. 1872. *Brides and Bridals.* 2 vols. London: Hurst and Blackett.

Segal, Eliezer. 1999. *Why Didn't I Learn This in Hebrew School?* Northvale, NJ: Jason Aronson.

Betrothal

The first stage of a marriage often was the betrothal, or espousal, arranged by the parents, by a matchmaker, or by free choice. In most Western societies, this process is now referred to as an engagement. Over the years, the status of engagement/betrothal has altered markedly, which is reflected in these names used for this promise to marry. The earlier terms, handfasting, betrothal, and espousal, all have some element of finality and contract. By the nineteenth century, when the term "engagement" came to be used for this promise to marry, betrothals were not being blessed by the church, and the betrothal vows had long been subsumed into the church service for the solemnization of marriage. Consequently, the betrothal was considered less legally binding and came to be called an engagement. This did not prevent women from being able to bring cases of breach of promise against men who reneged on their marriage promise—Dickens portrayed this in the *Pickwick Papers,* although this was in fact a misunderstanding. Mr. Pickwick's landlady, Mrs. Bardwell, thought he had proposed to her, and she was persuaded by her lawyers to bring a case of breach of promise against Mr. Pickwick. (This episode was actually written as a criticism of lawyers.) But elements of the early betrothal, notably the exchange of rings and the public view of the two people as a single unit akin to a married couple, have survived the centuries.

The betrothal was, and is, considered as binding as the wedding itself, and in some societies it is the most important step, often carried out with some ceremony. In the Coptic Church, in Egypt, when a couple become engaged, they go to the church and sign a contract just inside the church (compare this to the European practice of espousal and marriage in the church porch, the covered walkway to the church main entrance doors). The contract is witnessed, prayers are recited, the couple are given the rings to wear, and both are anointed with a holy oil cross on their foreheads, chins, and wrists. This ceremony may be conducted at home if the families are poor. This ceremony is followed by a celebration party with the couple seated on thrones. This is very similar to the wedding itself. Egyptian Muslims, too, have an engagement ceremony that is similar to the wedding, and jewelry is usually given to the bride as a betrothal present. Similarly, Indian Muslims have a ceremony to mark the betrothal where the couple exchange presents of clothing, food, toiletries, and sweets. The bridegroom-to-be places a sweetmeat into the mouth of his future bride, because, as the betrothal is a happy event, the bride's mouth should be sweet.

A Hindu betrothal ceremony, called a *misri,* or sugar, ceremony confirms the promise of the wedding agreed to between the two families. After asking for the blessing of Lord Ganesha, seven married women mark a pot of crystallized sugar *(misri)* with the symbol of Ganesh. The couple, with their parents, perform a *puja* to ask for the blessing of the gods; the two then exchange garlands of flowers to symbolically welcome each other into their lives. Gold rings are also presented. The groom-to-be wears his ring on the fourth finger of the right hand and the bride-to-be wears hers on the fourth finger of her left hand. As in Western cultures, there was a belief that a vein ran from that finger directly to the heart. After the exchange of rings, the young woman is given presents, including a basket of fruit and clothing, to show that she has been accepted into the groom's family, and her parents are fed with the *misri* to finalize the promise of the marriage and the engagement.

Sikh families have a similar betrothal ceremony, held at either the man's family home or at the house of worship (*gurdwara*). The families exchange presents and promises of the marriage, and the two exchange rings.

Jewish weddings combine two ceremonies into one event—the *kiddushin,* the betrothal ceremony, and the *nissuin,* the marriage ceremony. The bride and groom sip from a cup of wine, the rabbi recites the betrothal blessings on the couple, and the groom says, in Hebrew, "You are now consecrated to me with this ring according to the Law of Moses and Israel." He then puts the ring on the index finger of her right hand. It is at this point that the *ketubah,* the marriage contract, is read out—usually in Aramaic with an English translation.

The binding nature of betrothal or espousal has led to changes in the marriage laws, notably Lord Hardwick's Marriage Act, which was enacted in 1753 and came into force in 1754, to prevent abuses of the rights and status implied by betrothal. Before this time, betrothal did not need to be public—a private betrothal was just as binding if hands were shaken on the arrangement and especially if a kiss and gifts, usually a ring, were exchanged. This led to abuses, with unscrupulous men becoming betrothed to young heiresses for monetary gain.

As the betrothal was a promise to marry it was usually carried out with some ceremony in public, often in the church porch, with the clergyman acting as witness. However, private betrothals were still allowed, which accounted for the need for reform in 1754. The public betrothal would have included the recitation of vows, some of which were subsumed into the Anglican Church wedding service, and were often sealed with a kiss and the exchange of gifts—often a ring. It was at the betrothal ceremony that the size of the dowry promised for the wife was announced. However, the betrothal or espousal vows could be either expressed in the present or

the future tense; a betrothal expressed in the future tense could be undone. Sealing the betrothal with a kiss, sometimes termed a "wet bargain," meant that if the marriage did not proceed, the man would have to return all gifts given to him; the woman only had to return half the gifts. If no kiss was exchanged, the couple both had to return all gifts.

The joining of hands through or over some natural phenomenon, such as a holed stone, and vowing to marry was also a recognized form of betrothal. The Scottish poet Robert Burns was betrothed to Mary Campbell. They sealed the contract by washing their hands in the current of the nearest stream in moonlight and clasping hands over the stream.

The giving and exchanging of gifts when a marriage is negotiated occurs in many cultures and is an essential element of betrothal. The usual gift as a token of the betrothal is either a ring or a silver coin. A gimmal ring is a jointed ring, divided between the couple on the betrothal and put back together on the wedding day. Similarly, a coin could be cut, with each taking half, and sometimes worn around the neck. These coins with drilled holes were considered to be lucky, and some people wore such love tokens to protect against evil spirits and bad luck because of the oaths and prayers that had been spoken over the coin. Well into the twentieth century a Japanese betrothal would be sealed with a gift from the man to the woman, not necessarily a ring.

In *Twelfth Night* (written around 1600), act 5, scene 1, by William Shakespeare, after Olivia refers to Cesario as "husband," she calls upon the priest to confirm the contract:

Father, I charge thee, by thy reverence,
Here to unfold—though lately we intended
To keep in darkness what occasion now
Reveals before 'tis ripe,—what thou dost
    know
Hath newly passed between this youth and
    me
Priest: A contract of eternal bond of love

Confirm'd by mutual joinder of your hands,
Attested by the holy close of lips,
Strengthened by interchangement of your
    rings;
And all the ceremony of this compact
Seal'd in my function, my testimony.

This encompasses all the elements of a formal betrothal—the joining of hands, the sealing with a kiss, the giving of rings, and the presence of witnesses.

Because betrothal was as binding as the wedding itself, there were concerns among the clergy and church authorities (and other authorities) that couples would live as a married couple, which the authorities would view as evil and scandalous. Sixteenth-century writers and reformers wrote about the dangers of long betrothals and the temptations to which young couples may be exposed. The Swiss religious reformer Heinrich Bullinger in 1541 spelled out the dangers of a long engagement: "After the hand-fastynge and makynge of the contracte, the church-goying and weddyng shuld not be differed to longe, lest the wickedde sow hys ungracious sede in the meane season." Indeed in betrothal oaths, the wording may include the vow to conclude the wedding within forty days.

> **See also** Egypt; Engagement; Handfasting;
> Jewish Weddings; Lord Hardwick's Marriage
> Act; Rings, Wedding and Betrothal; Spousal

References
Bullinger, Heinrich. 1541. *The Christian State of
Matrimony.* Translated in 1575 by Miles
Coverdale. London.
Jeaffreson, John Cordy. 1872. *Brides and Bridals.* 2
vols. London: Hurst and Blackett.
Monsarratt, Ann. 1973. *And the Bride Wore . . . :
The Story of the White Wedding.* London: Gentry.
Scott, George Ryley. 1953. *Curious Customs of Sex
and Marriage.* London: Torchstream.

Bidding

Bidding, a custom in Wales (and in some parts of Cumberland, England) that took place on the eve of the wedding and on the wedding day, was a social event in which gifts

August 25, 1798.

Having lately entered the Matrimonial State, we are encouraged by our Friends to make a Bidding on the Occasion, on Thursday the 13th Day of September next, at the Dwelling-House of Daniel Thomas, (the young Woman's Father) called Ifcoed-Mill, *in the Parish of St. Ishmael, at which Place we humbly folicit the Favor of your good Company; and whatever Donation you may then be difposed to beftow on us, will be gratefully received, and cheerfully repaid, whenever demanded on the like Occafion, by*

Your moft obliged humble Servants,

Ebenezer Jones,
Mary Jones.

☞ The young Man's Grandmother, and young Woman's Father and Mother, defire that all Gifts of the above Nature, due to them, may be returned to the young Couple on the faid Day, and will be thankful for all Favors conferred on them.—The young Man's Uncle (David Thomas of Ifcoed Ucha') and young Woman's Sifters, will alfo be thankful for any Favors conferred on the young Couple.

Bidding letter, Wales, 1798. (Courtesy of the Museum of Welsh Life)

and money were given to the couple to help them establish themselves as a married couple. There were usually two separate biddings, one for the bride and another for the groom. One of the important features of the bidding was that every gift and donation was recorded because the receiving couple was obliged to give a gift or donation of equal value at the bidding of the donor. Consequently, a married couple with a bidding debt to repay would be obliged to attend this future event. Sometimes couples who were owed a debt would pass them on to relatives or friends to help them begin their married life. There are even examples of bidding debts being passed on in wills.

The first biddings seem to have been occasions mainly for women. At a bidding in Breconshire in 1836, the women outnumbered the men by six to one at the bridegroom's event and by thirteen to one at the bride's. The couple's friends and community would be invited by a "bidder," who would travel the district distributing either a printed invitation or delivering a light-hearted verbal invitation. The event was a great social occasion, especially for the unmarried people in the area who were important to the financial success of the event. Food and drink would also be sold, the profits of which augmented the gifts. There might have been other amusements, as suggested by an advertisement for a bidding published in *The Cumberland Pacquet* of 1803 that announced: "For whose amusement there will be various RACES, for prizes of different kinds; and among others a saddle, and Bridle: and a Silver-tipt Hunting Horn, for Hounds to run for—There will also be leaping, Wrestling, etc. etc. . . . Commodious ROOMS are likewise engaged for DANCING PARTIES, in the Evening."

See also Penny Weddings; Presents; Shower; *Stafell*
Reference
Owen, Trefor M. 1961. "A Breconshire Marriage Custom." *Folklore* 72: 372–384.

Bigamy

Bigamy has come to mean the state of being married to two partners at the same time, generally with both partners unaware of the existence of the other. By definition, bigamy can only occur in societies that follow monogamy as a marriage system, a minority worldwide. However, what today is referred to as bigamy should properly be termed polygamy (further divided into polygyny, to have two or more wives, and polyandry, to have multiple husbands).

English lawyers distinguished between polygamy, meaning to marry more than one spouse at a time, and bigamy, trigamy, etc., meaning to marry more than once, with the previous spouse having died. Jeaffreson (1872, 2: 327) noted that the use of the word bigamy to denote polygamy was modern: "Bigamy is an old word, but its present use, to designate polygamy, is modern. In mediaeval England a male bigamist was a person who, after his first wife's death, made a second

marriage. The widower, who thus acted in defiance of the Church's disapprobation of second marriage, was regarded as a dangerous libertine." It was polygamy that was made a felony in 1603 in Britain, making it an offense to marry a second husband or wife, with the former husband or wife still living.

It has been stated by Goody (1976) that polygamy is more common than monogamy in human marriage systems, and indeed, it is mainly within the Christian marriage culture that there is an insistence on monogamy, (however, although many cultures have allowed polygamy, not everyone in the culture entered polygamous marriages and sometimes it was only the wealthy who were able to do so). Many prominent Christians, such as John Milton and Sir Isaac Newton, and some Christian sects, such as the Munster Anabaptists and the Mormon church, have maintained that polygamy was/is not inconsistent with Christian teaching. Within the Mormon church, founded on the Book of Mormon, polygyny was considered an essential part of the religious system. Although the Mormon church renounced plural marriage in 1835 and again in 1890, and legislation was passed against bigamy in 1862 and 1882 in all territories of the United States, plural marriage is still practiced by some Mormons. However, although the established Christian church teaches monogamy in marriage, during the eighteenth century the Lutheran church was prepared to countenance the bigamous or polygynous marriage of Philip of Hesse and of Frederick William II of Prussia (1744–1797). After the Thirty Years' War between Catholics and Protestants in Germany (1618–1648), a resolution was passed in Nuremberg that every man should marry two women.

Before 1538, when births, marriages, and deaths were directed to be recorded in parish registers, it was difficult to be sure if either of a couple had been married or was still married. Even after this instruction it was difficult to keep records, and it was not until Lord Hardwick's Marriage Act in 1754, in

England, that there was any real legislation that could prevent bigamous and irregular marriages. This act required a public registration of a marriage as an essential part of the process. This was intended to prevent secret pre-contracts and secret marriages and marriages by verbal contracts blessed by itinerant priests in alehouses and such notorious areas as the Fleet Prison in London. This act did not apply in Scotland and was responsible for the large development of the marriage industry in Gretna Green, being the first community over the English-Scottish border.

The Matrimonial Causes Act of 1857 first established a mechanism for secular divorce procedures; but it was not until the twentieth century that a lawful divorce was relatively easy to procure for the majority of the population in Great Britain. At the time of Lord Hardwick's Marriage Act in 1754, one speaker in Parliament said that the crime of polygamy was "now so frequent." However, a good many cases of polygamous marriage (or bigamous marriage as we now term it) were either because the couple had undergone a form of divorce popularly accepted as legal, such as a "wife-sale," or parted by mutual consent or by some other ritual such as jumping backward over a broomstick, or one of the couple had been away for so long that he (usually) was thought to be dead and the apparent widow free to remarry (although that marriage would, strictly speaking, be bigamous). There are several recorded cases where a woman has mistakenly undertaken a bigamous marriage. One such case, quoted by Tegg (1877), recounted how the trio involved overcame their problems by the wife being sold by her first husband to the second husband:

> We often hear of people neglecting to be married, but seldom of one woman being given twice in marriage to the same man. Such a circumstance, however, occurred in Yorkshire. We are told. On the 1st October 1827, Samuel Lumb, sen., of Sowerby, 83 years of age, was married at Halifax, to Mrs. Rachael Heap, to whom he had been previously married about 25 years before. Her first husband had entered the army, and was, at the time of her first marriage, with Mr. Lumb, supposed to be dead. In a few years, however, he returned, and demanded his wife, whom he found living with Mr. Lumb, and by whom she had three children. But, after some negotiation, Heap agreed to sell her, and Mr. Lumb bought her, and she was actually delivered to him in a halter, at Halifax Cross. At her last marriage she was given away at the alter by Mr. Lumb's grandson. Her first husband died the April before.

Jeaffreson (1872, 2: 325–326) presented another account of a mistaken bigamous marriage in which the woman's husband had been away on business for so long that she believed him to be dead and had remarried after a period of mourning:

> When Raphe Goodchilde, "of the Parish of Barking, in Thames Street," after a long absence from home on his lawful business returned in the first year of James the First's reign to his proper abode, he found that his darling wife, Bessie, believing him to have died in foreign parts, had worn mourning for him, laid it aside, and became the wife of some Philip Ray. Instead of slinking off to the nearest public-house, and telling the landlady how badly he had been treated, Raphe Goodchilde crossed his threshold, had an explanation with Bessie, and, finding that he was still the "captain of her dreams," politely requested Philip to move off. Like a sensible woman, Bessie begged her proper master's pardon, and Raphe forgave her for her preciptancy towards Philip.

The couple later went to church to renew their vows to each other. It is also interesting to note that this incident occurred in the same year (1603) that James I's Parliament passed the act making bigamy a capital offense—but this was only for willful bigamists. There were exceptions for people who committed bigamy by accident, as in the case of Raphe and Bessie.

See also Divorce; Gretna Green; Irregular
Marriage; Mormon Church; Polyandry;
Polygyny; Wife-Selling

References
Gillis, John R. 1985. *For Better, For Worse: British
Marriages, 1600 to the Present.* Oxford: Oxford
University Press.
Goody, Jack. 1976. *Production and Reproduction: A
Comparative Study of the Domestic Domain.*
Cambridge: Cambridge University Press.
Jeaffreson, John Cordy. 1872. *Brides and Bridals.* 2
vols. London: Hurst and Blackett.
Macfarlane, Alan. 1986. *Marriage and Love in
England, 1300–1840.* Oxford: Basil
Blackwell.
Stone, Lawrence. 1990. *The Family, Sex, and
Marriage in England, 1500–1800.* Abridged and
revised ed. London: Penguin.
Tegg, William. 1877. *The Knot Tied: Marriage
Customs of All Nations.* London: William
Tegg.

Bonds, Marriage

Marriage bonds are peculiar to Great Britain
and have proven useful to genealogists trac-
ing family histories. Marriage bonds are little
known sources of information and sometimes are the only indication of a marriage,
although, by themselves, marriage bonds are
not evidence of the marriage actually having
taken place. Such legal bonds were only available to the affluent, who would often obtain
a special license from the bishop to allow
them to be married without previous publication of banns for reasons of speed and privacy. Those seeking a special license also had
to sign a "wedding or marriage bond," which
was a promise to indemnify the bishop, with
a payment of usually around £200, in the
event of there being proved later to be some
impediment to the marriage not declared
when the license was issued. The indemnified
sum was prohibitive for most of the population. Marriage bonds were often preprinted,
with the details handwritten.

See also Banns

Reference
"Marriage Bonds." Available at *http://www.york.
ac.uk/inst/bihr/marbnds.htm* (accessed 3 June
2004).

Bosseller

This all-female event is found in industrial
areas of Scotland. It was once usually the
case that a woman would leave work when
she married, and this tradition began as a
form of celebration and farewell to the
bride-to-be. The woman's jacket or coat and
hat are decorated with paper flowers and
streamers. After work her workmates make
her wear the decorated jacket and hat and
she is paraded through the town. A chamber
pot, similarly decorated and often containing salt, a piece of coal, and silver, is also carried in the procession, and several times
during the procession the bride-to-be has to
jump over the chamber pot three times, followed by the bridesmaids jumping over
once, and then each of the guests in turn.
There are variations. The costume could include signs and slogans, or she may have bal-
loons, tin cans, and bottles tied to her;
sometimes the bride-to-be is wheeled in a
wheelbarrow; a bell may be rung or a noise
made by the procession to draw attention to
the event; and the contents of the chamber
pot may include a baby doll. The name of the
custom may be related to other practices associated with weddings. Bosseller may be
derived from *ba'siller,* scrambling *(scrammel)*—a practice where the married couple
scatter money for the local children to
scramble for—and creeling. The "ribbon
girl" is a similar custom found in England,
but it is usually not as elaborate.

See also Ba'siller; Creeling; Premarriage
Customs; Ribbon Girl

References
Monger, George. 1996. "Pre-Marriage
Ceremonies: A Study of Custom and
Function." *Lore and Language* 14: 143–155.
———. 1971. "A Note on Wedding Customs in
Industry Today." *Folklore* 82, no. 4: 314–316.

Bottom Drawer

The Bottom Drawer is the term used in the
United Kingdom for items, usually of linen
or small household items, that a girl collects
for her eventual marriage. The items were

bought or collected and put away, usually in the bottom drawer of her chest of drawers. The Bottom Drawer is also referred to as the hope chest or dower chest. This reflects the tradition found in many countries whereby the woman is expected to supply some of the furniture, linen, and cooking equipment in the setting up of the home. An important part of a woman's skills in many European countries was needlework, and a girl would stitch household linen—sheets, tablecloths, quilts, and perhaps such items as a christening robe. Even a winding sheet, for wrapping a corpse, and the best bed linen for laying out a corpse would form part of the bottom drawer collection. Sometimes, brides in rural Cambridgeshire, England, would embroider a cross on the smock worn by the groom at the wedding, which would then be wrapped and stored in the bottom of the chest of drawers to be used at his funeral. A young woman would augment the items she made with purchased ones. For those who could afford it, some large stores (such as Harrods in London) advertised complete packages of household linens for setting up the home— the package supplied depended on the size of house to be stocked. In some cases the man was expected to provide the larger items of furniture and the equipment with which to support the household. As it was not always easy for a girl to collect everything a household might require to function, there were other, additional traditions where the community helped in the setting up of the home.

Gregor (1881) noted that in fishing communities a woman started at a very young age to collect items for her Bottom Drawer, or, as they called it, her *providan*. She would begin by collecting feathers for her bed and her pillows, and her admirers, or her fiancé, would contribute by shooting wildfowl. She bought a *kist* (chest) from her first earnings and kept adding to her stock of household items until her *providan* was complete.

See also Home, Setting Up; *Stafell*
References
Ballard, Linda May. 1998. *Forgetting Frolic: Marriage Traditions in Ireland*. Belfast and London: Institute of Irish Studies, Queens University, Belfast, and Folklore Society, London.
Gregor, Rev. Walter. 1881. *Notes on Folklore of the North East of Scotland*. London: Folklore Society.

Bouquet

Most brides in a Western wedding carry a bouquet. The flowers may have special meaning for the bride or may have been chosen for their meaning in "the language of flowers." Orange blossoms are supposed to represent innocence, purity, lasting love, and fertility. The tree is an evergreen and therefore symbolizes lasting love. It bears fruit and blossoms at the same time, thus representing the innocence and purity of love and fertility. The bride's bouquet did not appear in its modern form until well into the nineteenth century. Flowers usually appeared as wreathes worn by the bride on her head, or as favors worn by the guests, or as branches of rosemary carried by the guests, or perhaps as petals strewn before the bride and groom coming from the church. The gradual introduction of bridesmaids carrying posies or flower baskets probably led to the bride carrying a posy or bouquet; in country districts this would have been of wildflowers. The type of flowers and style of the bouquet seems to be dictated by fashion and availability. Today, when most flower types can be obtained at any time, the bouquet is usually prepared by a florist, who tries to match the overall design of the wedding, including the bride's dress, the floral decoration in the church, and the bridesmaids' outfits (the color scheme of their bouquets blends with their dresses). The style of the bouquet is dictated by fashion and sometimes emulation of fashionable people or celebrities. At the end of the 1990s, a vogue developed in Britain for brides to carry Thai lemongrass in, or as, the bouquet. This is not a very striking flower, resembling ears of corn which were said to have been carried by Roman brides.

Although it is now a general practice for the bride and her family to make most of the arrangements for the wedding, including the ordering of the flowers, an instructional book for young women getting married, written by "Two Ladies of England" (1932, 83), stated that the bridegroom should provide the flowers to be carried by the bride and the bridesmaids. The bride's bouquet should be sent to her house some hours before the wedding, along with the bridesmaids' bouquets if they were staying with the bride. Otherwise, the bouquets should be sent to their respective houses or to the church. The writers went on to state: "One thing is essential, and that is that the bridesmaids shall know *where* they may expect to find their bouquets, otherwise there will be much unnecessary agitation, and perhaps a misunderstanding which will result in a minor calamity."

It is considered traditional for the bride to throw her bouquet to the guests (especially the unmarried ones) as she leaves the reception for her honeymoon. The guests, usually the female ones, scramble for the bouquet; the one who catches it will be the next to marry. Sometimes the bride will throw the bouquet to a particular person. This custom was not mentioned by nineteenth-century writer John Cordy Jeaffreson in his exhaustive (at the time) work *Brides and Bridals* (1872), which, for example, mentioned the scattering of rice as an innovation. Indeed, he did not include any mention of bouquets. So this practice must be a late-nineteenth-century innovation and can be seen as a continuation of the old tradition of flinging the bride's stocking, which still occurred in some places. As with the bouquet-throwing custom, the person who caught the stocking would be the next to be married. Although the custom of throwing the bouquet is well known in Great Britain, and occasionally observed, it is a staple of weddings in the United States. Occasionally a bride will either give the bouquet to a particular person or will keep a memento such as the ribbon round the bouquet. Some brides also retain some of the flowers, which are pressed and included in a scrapbook or book of memories.

See also Flowers; Stockings, Throwing of
References
Monsarrat, Ann. 1973. *And the Bride Wore . . . : The Story of the White Wedding.* London: Gentry.
"Two Ladies of England." 1932. *The Bride's Book or Young Housewife's Compendium.* London: Gerald Howe.

Breakfast, Wedding

A wedding is usually followed by a celebratory meal or bridal banquet, now often known as the reception. But during the nineteenth century this meal came to be misnamed, according to Jeaffreson (1872), as the wedding breakfast. This celebratory meal is still often referred to as the wedding breakfast in the United Kingdom, regardless of what time of day the wedding is held. This term, as hinted at by Jeaffreson, came into popular use during the latter part of the nineteenth century and came about through a mixture of canonical law, which restricted the hours during which a marriage could be solemnized, and fashion. According to canonical law, until the early part of the twentieth century a marriage could only be solemnized between the hours of eight and twelve in the morning unless a special license was obtained. Marriages had to take place during daylight hours to ensure that everything was aboveboard, but it was not until 1934 in Great Britain that weddings were allowed in the afternoons, and then up to 6 p.m.

As Jeaffreson (1872, 1: 298) noted, this was especially irksome to the Victorian genteel classes: "The canonical hours for marriage do not accord with the domestic and social arrangements of modern England. The Victorian gentlewoman, who seldom rises from her bed before half-past eight, or breakfasts earlier than half-past nine, must be up long before her usual rising hour" (1872, 1: 298). This was not a particular worry for the less well off in Victorian Britain. The weddings of poor or other classes took place early or during some small break in the working day so that not too much in earnings would be lost. Sir George Head, writing in 1840 in

A Home Tour through the Manufacturing Districts and Other Parts of England, Scotland, and Ireland (quoted by Scott 1953, 224), described attending a mass wedding in Manchester on a Monday morning. He had been advised to be at the church by eight in the morning (as were the couples), despite the fact that the marriages were not taking place until two hours later—he noted that eight o'clock was the time for marriages by special license.

Among the Victorian genteel classes it became customary to have a "breakfast" after the ceremony, which was often referred to, by the fashionable, as the "déjeuner" (despite the French for breakfast being "le petit déjeuner," "déjeuner" meaning "lunch"). As Jeaffreson noted, the term "wedding breakfast" came to be used by the fashionable classes in Britain during the nineteenth century and referred to anything from a simple buffet to a complete meal. As with many aspects of the traditional white wedding, the aspiring middle classes and lower classes absorbed this term in attempting to appear fashionable and from the etiquette books that act as instructional manuals. The "Two Ladies of England" (1932) made a distinction between an afternoon tea reception, which was fairly informal, where no toasts to the bride and groom were formally proposed and drunk (guests would toast or lift their glasses to the bride and groom privately if they happened to catch their eye), and a wedding breakfast that was a much more formal affair and about which the authors commented that "there are both toasts and—alas!—speeches." The "Two Ladies" also provided a sample menu for a winter wedding breakfast:

> Consommé de Volaille
> Côtelettes d'Agneau aux petits pois
> Escalopes de Saumon en Mayonnaise
> Mayonnaise de Homard
> Foie gras en caisses
> Salade Russe
> Asperges en Branches
> Poulets rôtis aux Cresson
> Mirotins de Langue

> Galantine de Pigeon
> Jambonde Yorke
> Sandwiches variés
> Gelée à la Macédoine
> Gelée au Maraschino
> Gâteau Napolitaine
> Meringues Glacées á la Crème
> Chartreuse de fruit
> Crème à l'Italienne
> Crème de Café
> Pâtisserie variée
> Glaces

For many in the twenty-first century and from parts of the world other than Britain, the term breakfast for this elaborate meal may seem strange. It should be understood that for the upper and genteel class of Victorian England breakfast menus were quite extensive. Beeton (1880, 999) provided an even more elaborate menu and layout for a wedding (or christening breakfast) for seventy or eighty people:

> It will not be necessary to give here a long bill of fare of cold joints, &c., which may be placed on the side-board, and do duty at the breakfast-table. Suffice it to say, that any cold meat the larder may furnish should be nicely garnished, and be placed on the buffet. Collared and potted meats or fish, cold game or poultry, veal-and-ham pies, game and rumpsteak pies, are all suitable dishes for the breakfast-table—as also cold ham, tongue, &c., &c.
>
> The following list of hot dishes may perhaps assist our readers in knowing what to provide for the comfortable meal called breakfast. Broiled fish, such as mackerel, whiting, herrings, dried haddocks, &c.: mutton chops and rump-steaks, broiled sheep's kidneys, kidneys à la maître d'hôtel, sausages, plain rashers of bacon, bacon and poached eggs, ham and poached eggs, omelets, plain boiled eggs, œufs-au-plat, mumbled eggs, poached eggs on toast, muffins, toast, marmalade, butter, &c., &c.

Although the term wedding breakfast is still used, the wedding reception has become more and more formal so that the afternoon-tea type event is very rare.

See also Bride-Ale; Mass Weddings; Penny Weddings

References

Beeton, Mrs. Isabella. 1880. *The Book of Household Management.* London: Ward Lock and Co.

Jeaffreson, John Cordy. 1872. *Brides and Bridals.* 2 vols. London: Hurst and Blackett.

Monsarrat, Ann. 1973. *And the Bride Wore . . . : The Story of the White Wedding.* London: Gentry.

Scott, George Ryley. 1953. *Curious Customs of Sex and Marriage.* London: Torchstream.

"Two Ladies of England." 1932. *The Bride's Book or Young Housewife's Compendium.* London: Gerald Howe.

Bride-Ale

Bride-ale is really another term for a penny wedding or a bridewain and falls within the traditions of the Welsh bidding custom and other customs in which the community helps the couple set up their home and earn a living. Before the Reformation in sixteenth-century Europe, the friends of the couple would hold "an ale" in the church nave to raise money for the couple. After the Reformation, churches would have a "wedding house" nearby in which the couple could hold their wedding feast and have a "bride-ale." It would appear that churches also kept on hand some of the items for holding a bride-ale; a 1547 inventory from the parish church at Wilsdon, Middlesex, England, included "two masers that were appoynted to remayne in the church for to drynk in at bride-ales" (Monsarrat 1973, 32). The bride-ale was very similar in organization and purpose to other ales held in the parish: A clerk-ale was organized to raise funds for the parish clerk's budget, a church-ale for funds for the church, and a bid-ale was organized by the friends of a bankrupt person to help him start again.

The food and drink was prepared by the bride's family, or sent in by friends and well-wishers, and the event was open to all who paid a fixed amount for the privilege. To raise even more money, sports and other events were held. The village elite disapproved of these events, claiming that they led to bad and dissolute behavior, and probably saw this as undermining charitable work and by extension the dependence of the poor or proletariat on the landowners, therefore undermining their control of the population. But official disapproval and attempts to discourage these events largely failed. They were moved to the alehouse, to a private house, or even to the village green. Signs were set out, usually a stake or a bush—known as a "bride-stake" or a "bride-bush"—either near the house or hung outside or displayed in the window.

The authorities continued to attempt to restrain the excesses of the bride-ale. For example, the authorities of "Hales-Owen" Borough (now known as Halesowen, near Birmingham, England) in around 1573 issued a decree that limited the amount of malt that could be brewed for a single wedding, and hence the amount of ale available, and restricted the number of guests at the bride-ale to "eight messes of persons" (thirty-two people):

> Custom of bride-ale. Item, a payne is made that no person or persons that shall brewe any weddyn-ale to sell, shall not brewe above twelve strike of malt at the most, and that the said persons so married shall not keep nor have above eight messes of persons at his dinner within the burrowe; and before his brydall daye he shall keepe no unlawful games in huys house, nor out of hys house, on pain of 20 shillings. (Jeaffreson 1872, 1: 225)

These events persisted in a number of forms for many centuries and have survived in the word "bridal." The fact is that any public event, weddings included, observed by any social community usually involves some form of feasting, and in poor or isolated communities the need to cooperate and assist each other was obvious and paramount.

See also Bidding; Bridewain; Home, Setting Up; Penny Weddings

References

Gillis, John R. 1985. *For Better, For Worse: British Marriages, 1600 to the Present.* Oxford: Oxford University Press.

Jeaffreson, John Cordy. 1872. *Brides and Bridals.* 2 vols. London: Hurst and Blackett.

Monsarrat, Ann. 1973. *And the Bride Wore . . . : The Story of the White Wedding.* London: Gentry.

Bride-Cake

Bride-cake is an anachronistic term for wedding cake and is rarely used today. But historically the terms may have been interchangeable, as suggested by the seventeenth-century poet Robert Herrick (1591–1674) in his poem "The Bride-Cake," published in 1648 in his work *Hesperides:*

> This day, my Julia, thou must make,
> For mistresse bride, the wedding cake;
> Knead but the dow, and it will be
> To paste of almonds turn'd by thee;
> Or kisse it thou, but once or twice,
> And for the bride-cake ther'l be spice.

The Universal Cookery and Food Exhibition in London in 1888 suggested that there was a difference by providing a class for the large, expensive confections described as "wedding cakes" and another class for "two-guinea bride-cakes." However, in Beeton (1880) a recipe is given for a bride or christening cake, but in giving a bill of fare and table layout for a "ball supper" that could also be used for a wedding or christening breakfast she refers to the central cake—which revealed the type of event the table was prepared for—as a wedding cake. In her cheaper edition *Every-day Cookery and Housekeeping Book,* the term bride-cake does not appear, and her recipe is renamed as a "wedding cake." This would indicate that sometime in the late nineteenth century the term wedding cake replaced bride-cake.

It has been suggested that the English wedding cake was based on the plum cake. In a poem "Jack and Joan," by Thomas Campion (1575–1620), there is the line, "And trim with plums a bridal cake." There are also sug-gestions that the bride-cake was an almond paste–covered spice cake, but one far removed from the contemporary tiered wedding cakes. Herrick's poem "The Bride-Cake" mentions almond paste and spice for the bride-cake, but this could equally be referring to the preparation of spiced buns. In Elizabethan times, small buns made of sugar, eggs, milk, and spices were served. Some were thrown over the heads of the bridal couple as they left the church. The rest were stacked on a table for the bride and groom to kiss each other over.

Jeaffreson (1872, 1: 204) quotes the diarist, John Evelyn (1620–1706), remembering as a boy seeing a bride and groom kiss over the mound of bride-cakes: "When I was a little boy (before the Civil War), I have seen, according to the custom then, the bride and bridegroom kiss over the bride-cakes at the table. It was at the latter end of the dinner; and the cakes were laid upon one another, like the picture of the hew-bread in the old Bibles." The cake referred to by Herrick and other writers was very different from the contemporary wedding cake, which is sometimes referred to as a bride-cake in parts of Scotland.

See also Cake, Wedding
References

Charsley, Simon. 1992. *Wedding Cakes and Cultural History.* London: Routledge.

Jeaffreson, John Cordy. 1872. *Brides and Bridals.* 2 vols. London: Hurst and Blackett.

Bridegroom

The word "bridegroom," or "groom," is used to describe the male partner in the wedding. In many respects the word expresses the man's supporting role in the wedding in Western society, where the wedding day is often seen as the woman's big day. The secondary role of the male in the wedding ceremony contrasts with the dominant role that he is generally expected to play in the household. The old *Book of Common Prayer* of the Church of England included a sermon for after the solemnization of marriage that entreated husbands to love their wives as they love their own bodies. It also said that the duty of the wife, according to St. Paul, is to submit to her husband.

The word bridegroom is derived from the Old English *brўd-guma* and the Old Norse word *brúthgumi*. In both instances the words *brўd* and *brúth* refer to the bride (the root meaning is either "one owned or purchased" or, according to the *Oxford English Dictionary,* is derived from cooking or something similar). *Gumi* (Old Norse), *guma* (Old English), and *gomo* (Old High German) are all words for "man." Although it is possible to see here the relationship between the Old English *brўd-guma* and the modern word bridegroom, this becomes even more clear when considering the Middle English words *brúþguma* or *brўþgome,* where *gome* again means "man." However, this later became *grome* because an intrusive *r* came from the Old English *grom,* or Old Norse *gromr,* meaning "groom boy." The *Oxford English Dictionary* notes that the Middle English *grom* means "male child" and suggests that the origin is unknown.

An alternative, and erroneous, derivation for the word bridegroom is that among various peoples the man would wait at the table on his bride; the word "groom" signified one who served; thus he was so called because he served the bride. However, this idea may have arisen from a misunderstanding. It is sometimes said that in the distant past, in England, one of the groomsmen's duties was to arrange and seat the guests for the banquet. However, if the guests were few the groom would take on this delicate task. A seventeenth-century writer, John Stephens (1615), provided a sketch of "A Plaine Country Bridegroome" (quoted in Jeaffreson 1872, 1: 205). We are given an impression of a fussing country bridegroom who "never was maister of a feast before." The concept of him serving at the feast could easily arise from him being attentive to his guests at the marriage feast. The bridegroom does indeed appear to take a secondary role in the proceedings. In most societies the woman takes the biggest step—moving out of her parental home to that of her husband's family (or his home). In some societies, the woman cuts all ties with her own family and, except for a brief return visit, may not see her family again.

In Great Britain and America it is considered unlucky for the groom to see the bride on the wedding day before she arrives at the altar. Similarly, it is unlucky for him to see her wedding dress before the wedding day. It is bad luck for the bridegroom to drop his hat, drop the wedding ring, or to put the ring only partially on the bride's finger. He should further ensure that the clergyman is paid with an odd sum of money and he should not turn back for anything forgotten after the wedding journey is begun. In parts of Britain it was not only the clergy that the bridegroom had to pay off. Members of the local community also expected him to distribute largesse. These money distribution traditions served to help the man to "pay a footing" or to make some compensation to the community for taking the bride. A Scottish custom well into the twentieth century was for the bridegroom to toss a handful of coins to the crowd as he left the house for the church. An Orkney tradition was for the bridegroom to donate a football to the local schoolboys when he married (sometimes the best man was obliged to pay for the ball). Especially when the bride and groom came from different parishes, the ball, or money for the ball, was donated to the children of the bride's parish. In the northern counties of England, the bridegroom, with his bride, would sometimes throw coins to the children, who scrambled to collect them, outside the house where the wedding reception was being held. (A common prank was to heat the coins first.)

In these customs, and the "barring the way" traditions, there could be an element of the bridegroom making a statement to the community that he was indeed the bridegroom. At a barring the way event at a wedding in Kild-wick Church in Yorkshire, reported by Huddleston (1973), the barring of the gates was carried out by the choirboys, which suggests that it was important that the bridegroom should perform his expected part of the custom so that he could be properly identified (and accepted) by the community. When the organist's daughter married, her father, who had not previously had an opportunity of seeing the custom, mistakenly paid the toll, which, to at least one choirboy, was proof that the organist-father was the groom—despite the fact that the boy had seen the wedding ceremony.

According to wedding etiquette books, the bridegroom's role in a contemporary Western wedding is mainly to turn up and pay for things such as the wedding fees, the bride's and bridesmaids' flowers, flowers for the two mothers, his and the best man's boutonnieres, and the engagement and wedding rings. Additionally, he is expected to make a speech of thanks at the wedding reception. Traditionally he wears his best clothes. In rural districts of Cambridgeshire, England, he may wear a new or best smock that his wife would embroider with a cross after the wedding and pack away, ready to be used to dress him for his funeral. Today, if the wedding is to be very formal, the bridegroom and his attendants wear morning suits, with tailed coats and gray top hats. At less formal weddings he and his best man wear lounge suits—in the United States, tuxedos. As with many aspects of weddings today, the bridegroom's costume is a matter of fashion and contemporary convention.

See also Barring the Way

References

An Anglo-Saxon Dictionary Based on the Manuscript of Joseph Bosworth. [1898] 1964. Edited and enlarged by T. Northcote Toller. Oxford: Oxford University Press.

Huddleston, Mary. 1973. "A Yorkshire Miscellany." *English Dance and Song* 35, no. 1: 24.

Jeaffreson, John Cordy. 1872. *Brides and Bridals.* 2 vols. London: Hurst and Blackett.

Bride-Price

Bride-price, or bride-wealth, was a form of payment that a bridegroom or his relatives gave to the bride's family either before or at the wedding. The bride-price was paid in money, goods, or cattle or in labor and was often seen as compensation to the kin group for the loss of the young woman to another group. To the outsider, the payment of a bride-price or bride-wealth might appear to be a form of purchase. Jeaffreson (1872) concluded from Anglo-Saxon laws of Ethelbert, which placed a monetary value on a woman's virtue, that a suitor more or less bought his spouse from her father. However, Jeaffreson has misinterpreted laws that provided for retribution for rape, seduction, or sexual assault as part of a payment for marriage. He called this only a step forward from "marriage by capture." In fact, the major payment that an Anglo-Saxon bridegroom made was not to the bride's parents but to the bride herself in the form of *morgengifu* (the "morning gift"), which was her property and could be a substantial sum of money or land. This provided a form of insurance for the woman in the event of her husband's death or in case of divorce.

Generally, the interpretation of bride-price as a straight purchase transaction overlooks the subtleties within a society. In Indonesian society, divorce can be obtained, and if the fault lies with the man, he loses the bride-price paid to the family. If the fault is on the woman's part, the bride-price is repaid. Thus this practice provides disincentives to divorce but does not prevent divorce entirely. Among some South African communities, divorce is common and appears to have some correlation with bride-wealth; but there are other, more complex societal factors associated with the frequency of divorce, of which the size of the bride-wealth is only one possible factor.

Weddings in many parts of the world involve some form of financial settlement arranged between the two families or even a fee paid in labor. In the Old Testament of the

Bible we read that Jacob (Gen. 29.27) had to work for Laban for seven years in order to marry his daughter Rachel. Among the tribes of the Nuba Hills in the Sudan, it was customary for a betrothed young man to provide gifts for the young girl's family and provide some services. The betrothal was usually concluded before the girl was sexually mature, and the gifts included two to four goats as a single payment, plus annual payments, for five or six years, of two or three baskets of grain or sesame seeds. The services took the form of two days agricultural work annually between the time of the betrothal and the time that the bride moved into the young man's home. In addition, he and his friends were obliged to build a house for the father-in-law.

Among the Swazi people of South Africa, the bride-wealth tends to increase the bride's family prosperity, and all of her brothers will have a share in that prosperity. At the same time, the brothers had an obligation to assist her if she was in need. Among the Bantu, bride-wealth was provided by the men of the matrilineal line of the bridegroom, and this appears to have given them certain residual rights over the bride. If the husband died, she might be inherited, after an additional payment, by the husband's brother; if the husband proved to be impotent his brother might produce children with the wife.

Bride-price, or bride-wealth, therefore is not a straight purchase. It can be a form of guarantee for the woman or her family against divorce and can be seen as an "earnest" payment to prove an ability to support and work for the wife. The payment, and receipt, of the bride-price also imposed certain obligations upon the groom and his family.

See also Divorce; Dowry; Purchase, Marriage by
References
Fell, Christine. 1984. *Women in Anglo Saxon England and the Impact of 1066.* London: Colonnade Books, British Museum Publications.
Macfarlane, Alan. 1986. *Marriage and Love in England, 1300–1840.* Oxford: Basil Blackwell.
Mair, Lucy. 1971. *Marriage.* Harmondsworth, Middlesex: Penguin.
Radcliffe-Brown, A. R., and Cyril Daryll Forde, eds. 1950. *African Systems of Kinship and Marriage.* London: Oxford University Press.

Bridesmaid

Brides are accompanied by female friends and relatives, bridesmaids, at their weddings. The role of the bridesmaid today is one of support and, in the case of very young bridesmaids, decoration. The costume of the bridesmaids is chosen by the bride to complement her outfit. Many brides have several bridesmaids and perhaps a page boy as part of the wedding procession in the church. However, a correspondent to Robert Chamber's *Book of Days* (1863–1864), a clergyman from Suffolk, England, suggested that in the nineteenth century for many brides (and grooms) the accompanying attendants at a wedding were few. He noted that at a laborer's wedding the attendants were only three: "The official father, the bridesmaid and the groomsman, the latter two being, if possible, an engaged couple, who purpose to be the next pair to come up to the altar on a similar errand upon their own account." In the nineteenth century there was an expectation that brides of the well-to-do would be accompanied by a group of bridesmaids—the lack of them was cause for comment. Tegg (1877) quoted an entry from the *Court Circular* of 18 September 1876: "A somewhat peculiar circumstance in connection with the event was that there were *no bridesmaids.*"

The wedding etiquette books suggest that only the chief bridesmaid or maid of honor has any particular duty in the wedding but that the number of bridesmaids that a bride may have depends on whether the bride wants the wedding to be "simple or magnificent." According to the "Two Ladies of England" (1932), for a simple wedding "two bridesmaids are sufficient," but for a more splendid ceremony, four, six, or even eight bridesmaids may accompany the bride. They should be selected from the bride's (and groom's) immediate family and close relatives. It was further suggested that the bridesmaids should, if possible, be of the same height—and that one should "have pretty bridesmaids if you can." There is usually a chief bridesmaid or maid of honor whose duties are to assist the bride, help her prepare for the wedding, hold the bride's bouquet, and move her veil from her face during the ceremony, and to marshal the other bridesmaids and pages if there are any, ensuring that they are dressed correctly and are in place well before the bride arrives at the church. She may also help in choosing the bridesmaids' dresses, which by convention are paid for by the bridesmaids' parents. The maid of honor may, if she is of the correct age, along with the best man, sign as a witness to the marriage. The profusion of bridesmaids at British and American weddings seems to have developed during the nineteenth century among the upper classes.

Jeaffreson (1872) suggested that there is some remnant of "marriage by capture" in the presence of the bridesmaids and groomsmen (the existence of "marriage by capture" as a marriage form is debatable), citing practices of the groom being taken from his male attendant to be led to the church by the bridesmaids and likewise the bride being escorted by male attendants (albeit page boys). According to the mid-nineteenth-century poem by Edward Chicken, "The Colliers Wedding":

To leave the house now all incline
And haste to church, the clock struck nine;
Two lusty lads, well dressed and strong,
Stept out to lead the bride along:
And two young maids of equal size
As soon the bridegroom's hands surprise.

Some, however, date the tradition of bridesmaids to Anglo-Saxon times when, according to Brand (1777), the bride was led to church by a matron known as the "bride's woman," followed by a group of young women called bridesmaids. It has also been said that the bridesmaids were originally from the groom's family, and in times of "marriage by capture" their function was to guard the bride to ensure she did not escape. Jeaffreson (1872) suggests that when marriages took place at the church porch—in England it was not until the sixteenth century that marriages were allowed to take place inside a church—the chief bridesmaid took charge of the dow-purse (a purse containing a sum of money agreed to as the dowry given by the groom to the bride) presented to the bride by the groom at this time, in much the same way that today the chief bridesmaid holds the bride's bouquet. Brides usually wore gloves in the nineteenth century, and when the priest asked, "Who giveth this woman to be married to this man?" the chief bridesmaid or maid of honor would help her to remove her gloves and hold them for the rest of the ceremony; these the chief bridesmaid claimed afterward as a form of badge of office. Brides in the United States sometimes snipped off the ring finger of the left-hand glove so that the ring could be placed on the finger without the removal of the whole glove.

There appear to have been few superstitions and traditional duties for nineteenth-century bridesmaids. The role was to support the bride, helping her to dress for the ceremony and, after the celebrations, helping her prepare for bed. Jeaffreson (1872) provided a detailed (and in places perhaps fanciful) account of the duties of the bridesmaids at some unspecified, probably medieval but at least pre-nineteenth century, time in our history: As the bride entered the bridal chamber, she would be made to drink and eat by her bridesmaids a concoction of plum buns swimming in spiced ale. This was supposed to restore the energies of a "delicate young lady." They would then assist her in removing her bridal gown and chaplet (wreath of flowers), being careful to remove and discard all pins that she had worn during the day. If a bridesmaid retained even one of the pins she would not be married before the next Whitsuntide. Similarly, if the bride accidentally (or purposely) retained one of the pins, nothing would go right for her.

After various bedchamber rituals, such as the throwing of the stocking and the drinking of the benediction posset, the bridesmaids would clear all the guests from the bedchamber. In the morning they would prepare a morning cup of sack-posset and ensure that the celebrations continued. Jeaffreson (1872, 1: 195) went on to note that although the bridesmaids' duties were onerous, they potentially reaped an ample reward for their trouble: "Affording her an admirable field for the display of feminine cleverness and tact, her office gave her opportunities for exhibiting endowments sure to bring her masculine admiration, and very likely to procure her a husband. The length to which our ancestors protracted their bridal festivities was also favourable to her chances of winning an eligible spouse at the wedding, where she officiated as a gentle serving-maid." The expectation that being a bridesmaid would lead to a reasonably quick marriage is encompassed in the belief, "three times a bridesmaid, never a bride"—if association with a bride and the high profile of the day did not attract a husband after two opportunities, then perhaps there was little hope.

Crawley (1932) suggested a greater role for the bridesmaids than just support for the bride—as bride doubles to protect the bride from malevolent influences such as the evil eye or ill luck. The presence of others dressed like the bride could confuse an ill-wisher. He wrote that an Egyptian bride is "attended by several girls who cluster round her under the same canopy." He also stated that a Zulu bride would be surrounded by a "throng of maidens." When an Abyssinian princess married she was accompanied by her sister dressed the same.

An account of a wedding in the Lorraine district of France in 1854, described by an anonymous Englishwoman in *The English-woman's Domestic Magazine* (quoted by Gutch 1880–1881, 268), supported this idea. But in Lorraine it was the bridegroom whom the young women were intending to confuse. After the bridegroom's party had entered the bride-to-be's house, the bridegroom, Germain, had to pick out his bride, who was seated with three other young women of the same stature covered with sheets and with the peaks of their caps adjusted to the same height. The other women in the room and the bride's companions made sure that she did not give her husband-to-be any clue to her identity. If he chose the correct woman, he "would be entitled to lead off the ball with her, and be her partner without change; but if he failed he must remain contented with dancing with the other maidens through the night."

See also Bed, Marriage; Best Man; Capture, Marriage by; Church Porch, Weddings in; France; Indonesia; Posset; Stockings, Throwing of

References
Brand, John. [1770] 1900. *Observations on the Popular Antiquities of Great Britain*. Revised and enlarged by Sir Henry Ellis in 1841 and 1848. 3 vols. London: G. Bill and Sons.
Chambers, Robert. 1863–1864. *The Book of Days*. Vol. 1. Edinburgh: W. and R. Chambers; Philadelphia: J. B. Lippincott.
Crawley, Ernest. [1902] 1932. *The Mystic Rose: A Study of Primitive Marriage and of Primitive Thought in Its Bearing on Marriage*. 4th ed. Revised and enlarged by Theodore Besterman. London: C. A. Watts.
Gutch, Mrs. 1880–1881. "A Rural Wedding in Lorraine." *Folk Lore Record* 3: 258–274.
Heaton, Vernon. 1986. *Wedding Etiquette Properly Explained*. Rev. ed. Kingswood, Surrey: Elliot Right Way.
Jeaffreson, John Cordy. 1872. *Brides and Bridals*. 2 vols. London: Hurst and Blackett.
Tegg, William. 1877. *The Knot Tied: Marriage Customs of All Nations*. London: William Tegg.
"Two Ladies of England." 1932. *The Bride's Book or Young Housewife's Compendium*. London: Gerald Howe.

Bridewain

Bridewain literally translates as "bride wagon" ("wain" means "wagon"). But in Cumberland in the north of England, it refers to the public celebration after the wedding, when a collection is made for the bride and groom and racing and wrestling form part of the entertainment. The Cumberland bridewain was described in Hone (1841, 794):

> A short time after a match is entered into, the parties give notice of it; in consequence of which the whole neighbourhood, for several miles round, assemble at the bridegroom's house, and join in various pastimes of the county. This meeting resembles the wakes or revels celebrated in other places; and a plate or bowl is fixed in a convenient place, where each of the company contributes in proportion to his inclination and ability, and according to the degree of respect the parties are held in; by which laudable custom a worthy couple have frequently been benefited with a supply of money, from fifty to a hundred pounds.

Hone (1841, 795) reprints an advertisement for a bridewain that seeks to promote the event with exciting prizes and gives the qualities of some of the prizes:

BRIDEWAIN
There let Hymen oft appear,
In saffron robe and taper clear,
And pomp and feast and revelry,
With mask and antic pageantry;
Such sights as youthful poets dream,
On summer eves by haunted stream.

George Hayto, who married Anne, the daughter of Joseph and Dinah Colin, of Crosby mill, purposes having a Bridewain at his house at Crosby, near Maryport, on Thursday, the 7th day of May next, [1789], where he will be happy to see his friends and well-wishers; for whose amusement there will be a variety of races, wrestling-matches, &c. &c. The prizes will be—a saddle, two bridles, a pair of *gands d'amour,* gloves, which, whoever wins, is sure to be married within the twelvemonths; a girdle (*ceinture de Venus*) possessing qualities not to be described; and many other articles, sports, and pastimes, too numerous to mention, but which can never prove tedious in the exhibition.

From fashion's laws and customs free,
We welcome sweet variety;
By turns we laugh and dance, and sing;
Time's for ever on the wing;
And nymphs and swains on Cumbria's plain,
Present the golden age again.

As the name implies, the bridewain was originally the ceremonial transporting of the bride's goods to her new home on a decorated wagon, a very public occasion and an important part of setting up the new home. The procession was an opportunity for people to make contributions to the new household. In Yorkshire during the eighteenth century, the bride would ride on an ox-drawn wagon, sitting in a matronly pose with her spinning wheel and stopping to receive gifts along the way.

See also Bidding; Bottom Drawer; Home, Setting Up; Penny Weddings; Racing; *Stafell*
References
Gillis, John R. 1985. *For Better, For Worse: British Marriages, 1600 to the Present.* Oxford: Oxford University Press.
Hone, William. 1841. *The Table Book.* London: Thomas Tegg.

Broom, Marriage over the

In England, the expression "to be married over a broomstick," "married over the broom," or "married over the brush" is to be what was also known as "living in sin," that is, living together without benefit of a church or registry office ceremony. The expression is derived from a form of trial marriage well known into the nineteenth century and probably into the early twentieth century and practiced in a number of places in the British Isles, whereby a couple was able to live together as husband and wife for a year and a day after having both jumped over a broomstick laid across the doorway and without touching the doorjamb. If, after the year and a day, the couple found that they were not compatible, the union could be undone by jumping backward over the broom. In both cases the ritual was to be performed before witnesses. If the couple decided to discontinue the union, it would be as if they had never lived together, and any children of the union would be cared for by the father. The usual reasons for annulment were incompatibility or infertility. It was expected that after the trial marriage the couple would formalize the union in church, but it is not clear that couples rushed to do this—the public ceremony of jumping the broom would in many minds have been enough. In Warwickshire, England, Bloom noted that a hasty marriage was referred to as a "marriage over the broomstick" (1929), and McKelvie (1963) reported that in the Bradford, England, area a couple cohabiting without benefit of a church or civil marriage ceremony was said to be "living over t' brush."

Marriage over the broom is also often associated with Gypsy marriage. Wood in his autobiographical book (1973) described the weddings of Romany Gypsies in Britain and noted that he knew of two forms of ceremony, one of which was jumping the broomstick.

In contrast, in parts of the United States, notably in West Virginia, there was a belief that an unmarried person who stepped over a broom would remain unmarried and that to be touched by the broom brought bad luck (Gainer 1975, 124–125). In the Ozarks a girl who steps over a broom would be a bad housewife (Randolph 1947, 74).

> **See also** Besom Weddings; Gypsy Weddings; Temporary Marriage
> **References**
> Bloom, J. Harvey. [1929] 1977. *Folk Lore, Old Customs, and Superstitions in Shakespeare Land.* London: Mitchell, Hughes, and Clarke. Norwood, PA: Norwood Editions.
> Gainer, P. W. 1975. *Witches, Ghosts, and Signs: Folklore of the Southern Appalachians.* Grantsville, WV: Seneca Books.
> Menefee, Samuel Pyeatt. 1981. *Wives for Sale.* Oxford: Basil Blackwell.

McKelvie, Donald. 1963. "Aspects of Oral Tradition and Beliefs in an Industrial Region." *Folk Life* 1: 77–94.
Randolph, Vance. [1947] 1964. *Ozark Magic and Folkore.* New York: Dover Books.
Wood, Manfri Frederick. 1973. *In the Life of a Romany Gypsy.* London: Routledge and Kegan Paul.

Buddhism
See India; Thailand; Tibet

Bundling
Bundling was a form of, apparently, chaste courtship whereby the couple was allowed to spend the night together, usually wearing at least underclothes, and usually at the woman's home with the acquiescence of her parents. In parts of the United States, this practice was known as "tarrying," in Holland as *queesten,* and in the Orkney Isles, Great Britain, as "courting in bed." The practice seems to have been common in countries of northern Europe and among the North American Indians into the late nineteenth century. The practice seems to have been confined to communities in which young people were allowed to make their own choice of marriage partner and where privacy and warmth for getting to know a prospective partner were difficult to achieve. Many of the descriptions of bundling are from travelers' accounts, so it is not always possible to determine the situations of bundling. For example, the nineteenth-century traveler and explorer Charles Masson wrote in 1842 of his observation in Afghanistan of a form of bundling known as "mamzet bezé": "The lover presents himself at the house of his betrothed with a suitable gift, and in return is allowed to pass the night with her, on the understanding that innocent endearments are not to be exceeded." This account suggests that the courtship was well-advanced. There may be similarities with a practice in Finland, in which it was customary for a couple to sleep

together, partially clothed, for the week or so before their wedding.

A similar practice is traditionally found among the Zulu tribes in South Africa. Once a young man declared his love and has been accepted, the couple can spend nights together, as long as the girl remained a virgin and has the permission of the senior girls in her kraal, her native village (who offer her sexual instructions) (Murphy 1978, 135). The woman was periodically examined to ensure that she remained a virgin. If she lost her virginity, the suitor, or his family, had to pay a fine and the wedding ceremony would take place. There are accounts of North American Indians practicing forms of bundling that indicated the acceptance of a suitor. A young man would enter the woman's hut, light a stick from the fire, and go to the woman's bed; if she blew the flame out that indicated that she liked him, and he would lie down beside her; pulling the covers over her face indicated that she rejected him, and he would leave immediately. Some of these reports were written by eighteenth- and nineteenth-century non-Indians, and it is difficult to be sure of the interpretations— especially as they may not identify the tribal group. The above account quoted by Scott (1953) is from a 1779 book by William Alexander, *The History of Women from the Earliest Antiquity to the Present Time*.

For the Plains Indians, for whom privacy for courting was almost impossible in a tepee or within the village compound—it was too dangerous to leave the compound and meet on the prairie—a practice of "courting in a blanket" developed that gave couples virtual privacy. The woman would stand outside the tepee with a blanket, which she would wrap around herself and her suitor. Ensuring that their heads were covered, they could get to know each other. Thus covered, they were considered invisible to the rest of the community and were ignored. A woman could meet several suitors in this way in one evening, become acquainted with them, and make her choice.

It is thought that bundling, or tarrying, was brought to the United States by European settlers, where it was a well-known and popular practice in England, Wales, Ireland, Holland, Scandinavia, and Switzerland. There exist many travelers' accounts of the practice. An eighteenth-century traveler, Richard Twiss, in his book *A Tour in Ireland in 1775*, noted that bundling was prevalent and quotes an account of the practice in Holland from a book called *The Travels of Van Egmont and Heyman*:

> In the island of Texel, in North Holland, the women are very fond of courtship, which among the youth of the peasantry is carried on in a manner like *Questing*. This is an ancient custom of evening visits and courtships among the young people in the islands of Vlie and Wieringen, but especially in the Texel. It is indeed of an antiquity the date of which cannot be traced. The spark comes into the house at night, either by the door, which is left upon the latch, or half open; by one of the windows; or through the stable; and makes his way to the bedchamber of his sweetheart, who is already in bed. After a compliment or two, he begs leave that he may pull off his upper garment, and come upon the bed to her. This being of course granted, he lifts up the quilt or rug, lays himself under it, and then *quests* or chats with her till he thinks it time to depart, which is invariably done by the same entrance he came in at.

Sumner (1906) stated that, in the seventeenth century, windows in Holland were constructed to allow easy access for bundling. Although bundling is said to have been innocent—the wearing of undergarments or the woman wearing a shift that is secured onto her "prevented" any untoward activity—some commentators noted that in areas where bundling was well known it was not unusual for children to be born just a few months after the wedding. Again, if pregnancy resulted, the couple would be expected to marry. Indeed, in some communities, such as in Cornish mining communities, where, in the early nineteenth century, work revolved around the "family pit" employing the children and mother, pregnancy before marriage was an advantage to prove the fertility of the woman to ensure a family to work the mine—the possibility of the infertility of the man was not considered. Although bundling was well-known in parts of Europe, it seems to have been practiced more by the lower classes, judging from the comments of writers who encountered and mentioned the practice. Burnaby (1775) described the practice thus:

> A very extraordinary method of courtship is sometimes practiced among the lower people in Massachusetts Bay, called *Tarrying.* When a man is enamoured of a young woman and wishes to marry her, he proposes the affair to her parents, without whose consent no marriage in this colony can take place. If they have no objection, they allow him to *tarry* with her one night, in order to make his court to her. At the usual time, the old couple retire to bed, leaving the young ones to settle matters as they can; who, after having sat up as long as they think proper, get into bed together also, without pulling off their under-garments, in order to prevent scandal. If the parties agree, it is all very well; the banns are published, and they are married without delay; if not they part, and possibly never see each other again; unless, which is an accident that seldom happens, the forsaken fair one proves pregnant, and then the man is obliged to marry her, under pain of excommunication.

Burnaby hinted at the innocence of the practice, and steps were taken to prevent intercourse and reduce temptation, such as a low board fixed along the bed dividing it in two, or placing a bolster down the middle. Some mothers tied their daughter's ankles together or made them wear tight clothes. However, U.S. legal opinion did not subscribe to the innocence of the practice. In a case heard at the New York Supreme Court in 1869, in which the parents of a young woman were suing a man for the seduction of their daughter, the court ruled: "that although bundling was admitted to be the custom in some parts of the State, it being proven that the parents of the girl, for whose seduction the suit was brought, countenanced her practising it, they had no right to complain, or ask satisfaction for the consequences, which, the Court say, naturally followed!" (*Seger v. Slingerland, in* Stiles 1869).

Travelers' tales from the United States suggest that bundling among the immigrant settler population was not just a courtship ritual. There are published tales in which the male visitor was expected to share a bed with the daughter of the house as an act of hospitality. Captain Thomas Anburey arrived in Williamstown, Massachusetts, and was given such hospitality:

> There being only two beds in the house, I enquired which I was to sleep in, when the old woman replied, "Mr. Ensign," (here I should observe to you, that the New England people are very inquisitive as to the rank you have in the army). "Mr. Ensign," says she, "our Jonathan and I will sleep in this, and our Jemima and you shall sleep in that." I was much astonished at such a proposal, and offered to sit up all night, when Jonathan immediately replied, "Oh, la! Mr. Ensign, you wont be the first man our Jemima has bundled with, will he, Jemima?" When little Jemima, who, by the bye, was a very pretty, black-eyed girl, of about sixteen or seventeen, archly replied, "No, father, not by many, but it will be the first Britainer." . . . In this dilemma, what could I do? (1789, 37–40)

See also Handfasting

References
Anburey, Thomas. 1781. "Travels through the Interior Parts of America." In *A Series of Letters.* Vol. 2. London: W. Lane.
Ballard, Linda May. 1998. *Forgetting Frolic: Marriage Traditions in Ireland.* Belfast and London: Institute of Irish Studies, Queens University, Belfast, and Folklore Society, London.
Burnaby, Rev. Andrew. 1775. *Travels in North America.* London: T. Payne.

Erdoes, Richard. 1972. *The Sun Dance People: The Plains Indians, Their Past and Present.* New York: Alfred A. Knopf.

Masson, Charles. 1842. *Journeys in Baloochistan, Afghanistan, the Punjab.* London: J. Maddon.

Murphy, Brian M. 1978. *The World of Weddings: An Illustrated Celebration.* London: Paddington.

Scott, George Ryley. 1953. *Curious Customs of Sex and Marriage.* London: Torchstream.

Stiles, Henry Reed. 1869. *Bundling, Its Origins, Progress, and Decline in America.* Albany, NY: Joel Munsell.

Sumner, William Graham. [1906] 1940. *Folkways.* New York: Mentor Books.

Turner, E. S. 1954. *A History of Courting.* London: Michael Joseph.

Twiss, Richard. [1775]. *A Tour in Ireland in 1775.* London: Printed for the Author.

Cake, Wedding

The wedding cake, symbolic of weddings and in many countries viewed as an English development, is largely a product of the nineteenth-century baking and confectionery industry. Cakes or wheaten bread have long been used in weddings and as part of traditional customs and ceremonies that followed the church or civil ceremony. Although the terms "wedding cake" and "bride-cake" may seem to be interchangeable, there appears to have been a difference identified at the Universal Cookery and Food Exhibition in London in 1888, where there was a class for the large, expensive confections described as "wedding cakes" and another class for "two-guinea bride-cakes." Sometime during the late nineteenth century, the term wedding cake replaced bride-cake. Beeton's *Book of Household Management* (1880) gives a recipe for a "Bride" or "Christening Cake," but in giving a "Bill of Fare for a Ball Supper," which could also be used for a wedding or christening breakfast, she refers to the central cake—which showed the type of celebration the food was for—as a wedding cake; and in the cheaper edition, *Every-day Cookery and Housekeeping Book,* the term bride-cake does not appear, and the recipe is renamed as "Wedding Cake." The bridal cake is mentioned by the seventeenth-century poet Robert Herrick (1591–1674) in his poem "The Bride-Cake":

> This day, my Julia, thou must make,
> For mistresse bride, the wedding cake;
> Knead but the dow, and it will be
> To paste of almonds turn'd by thee;
> Or kisse it thou, but once or twice,
> And for the bride-cake ther'l be spice.

This suggests that the bride-cake was an almond paste–covered spice cake, one quite different from contemporary tiered wedding cakes and usually the product of the confectioner's art. The English wedding cake has often been seen as being based on the plum cake, which may be suggested in Herrick's poem. Indeed the poem "Jack and Joan," by Thomas Campion (1575–1620), contains the line, "And trim with plums a bridal cake." However, Herrick's poem could be interpreted as referring to the preparation of spiced buns. Indeed, in Elizabethan times, small buns made of sugar, eggs, milk, and spices were used, with some of the buns thrown over the heads of the bridal couple as they left church. The rest were stacked on a table for the bride and groom to kiss each other over. The diarist John Evelyn (1620–1706) remembered as a boy seeing a bride and groom kiss over the mound of bride-cakes: "When I was a

Ethel Sillby and Kenneth Harrod cutting their wedding cake in 1928 in England with an axe. Both bride and groom were members of the Woodcraft Chivalry, and this was reflected in their wedding celebrations. (Photo by Edward G. Malindine / Topical Press Agency / Getty Images)

little boy (before the Civil War), I have seen, according to the custom then, the bride and bridegroom kiss over the bride-cakes at the table. It was at the latter end of the dinner; and the cakes were laid upon one another, like the picture of the hew-bread in the old Bibles" (Jeaffreson 1872, 1: 204).

Jeaffreson suggested that it was after the Restoration of the English monarchy in 1660, with Charles II, that wedding cake, as we know it, started to be developed by the French chefs that the king brought from France. This consisted of encasing the buns in a shell composed of hardened white sugar and decorated with toys and figures. The crust could be easily broken to allow the buns to be scattered over the bride's head. This was probably conjecture on Jeaffreson's part, but the traditional bridal "cake" in France and Belgium is the *croquembouche,* which consists of a cone structure,

wide at the base, composed of round choux pastries filled with confectioner's cream and dipped in hot toffee. When cooled, it can be decorated with ribbons, almond figures, and sugared almonds, and at weddings today may be decorated with bride and groom figurines on the top. Jeaffreson wrote that, later, two cakes were prepared, one as an ornament for the bridal table and the other to be broken over the bride's head.

The United States absorbed a number of traditions through the influx of immigrants from Europe, so that by the 1890s two cakes were used at weddings. Pound cake, a cake composed of equal parts of the main ingredients—for example, Mrs. Beeton's recipe for pound cake included 1 pound of butter, 1¼ pounds of flour, 1 pound of loaf sugar, and 1 pound of currants—sometimes with a soft icing or a frosting, was associated with the bride and tended to be called the "bride cake," and a heavier plum cake, often known in the United States as "black" cake, sometimes with a hard icing, was associated with the groom. In the twentieth century, a lighter white cake has been more favored. If more than one cake was required, it was common to stack the cakes in declining size order. The dark bridegroom cake was, according to one recipe book written in 1897, cut by the bridegroom and given to the bridesmaids, with a glass of wine, before going to the church. In Virginia, if both cakes were prepared, they were stacked, with the groom's cake on top. But it was the lighter bride's cake that was cut at the reception, with the bride and groom giving each other a piece to eat—a common bit of whimsy is still for the couple to cut the bride's cake, and, in giving the groom a piece to eat, the bride will push it into his face. The groom's cake was saved for later and regarded as a second cake and of less importance to the event. As time went on, the tradition to provide a second cake disappeared, leaving the white cake as the bride's cake and therefore the wedding cake.

In many parts of Europe, the wedding cake is a light sponge cake, flavored and decorated in different styles. Dutch cakes, for example, are normally iced and decorated with white or pink roses in marzipan. Wedding cakes in other parts of the world are usually copies of European and American styles brought to these societies through popular culture. Multitiered cakes did not develop until the latter part of the nineteenth century, when at first the layers were simply laid one upon the other. Decorative pillars were produced to separate the layers; two, three, and four tiers became fashionable (sometimes one or more of the layers would be a false cake). Occasionally, confectioners and chefs undertake the challenge to make as large and as tall a cake as possible. In a local newspaper—from the London Borough of Havering, England—the *Romford Recorder* of 24 August 1973, there was a report of a ten-foot-high, twenty-seven-tier cake (which nearly collapsed twice

before the couple arrived at the reception to cut the cake). Apparently twenty-seven-tier cakes were a tradition in the bridegroom's family.

Although the nature of the bridal or wedding cake has changed over the years, there are customs and traditions associated with the cake that demonstrate a continuity of tradition. It is said that in ancient Rome a bride held three ears of corn in her left hand and the priest broke and divided a wheaten cake between the bride and groom. In medieval times in Britain, large thin grain biscuits were broken over the heads of the bride and groom. The fragments were collected and distributed to the witnesses. This suggests a link between throwing grain over the couple and the breaking of a wedding cake over the bride's head, with, perhaps, continuity into the twentieth century, when it is still customary to throw a piece of wedding cake, on a plate, over the bridal car or carriage after the wedding. The custom of breaking a bride cake over the bride's head seemed to have survived in the northern counties of Great Britain. In the East Riding of Yorkshire, as the bride and groom left the house, the groom was given a plate with wedding cake, which he threw over the bride's head. The more pieces the plate broke into, the more luck they would have. It was inauspicious if the plate did not break; in this case a quick-witted guest would usually stamp on the plate to preserve the couple's luck.

In Goole, Yorkshire, it was the practice for the bride and groom to cut the cake before the wedding. Someone left behind to look after the house cut up the remainder of the cake. On the return of the bride and groom, a piece of cake, again on a plate, was thrown over the wedding carriage. Again, if the plate broke, they would have good luck, and if it did not break, someone would stamp on it. If there was an icing flower on the cake, this would be given to a single girl to ensure that she would be married. On the Scottish/English border, shortbread was thrown over the couple when they reached their new home, usually before they departed for their honeymoon, on the evening of the wedding day. There also existed customs whereby the bride's mother-in-law would break a cake or a loaf of bread over the head of the bride as she entered her new home. This was said to establish a friendly relationship between the two women. It could, however, also be interpreted as a recognition by the mother-in-law of the girl's equal status as a married woman. In Shetland, the bride cake, sometimes known as "dreaming bread" (if a young girl put a sliver of the cake under her pillow at night, she would dream of her future husband—in some traditions only if the cake was first passed three or nine times through a wedding ring), would be broken into pieces and thrown over the bride's head. And in Ireland there were traditions for the bride's mother to break a cake over the bride's head to give her luck and fertility. At the marriage of the highwayman, William Nevison, known as Swiftnicks (who actually performed the famous ride to York attributed to Dick Turpin in the nineteenth-century novel of the same name by Harrison Ainsworth), there occurred what could either be a genuine good-luck wish or a parody of cake-breaking when one of the onlookers broke a cow pat over the head of the bride.

Over about 150 years, new traditions have become associated with the cutting of the cake. Today it is usual for the bride and groom to cut the first slice of the wedding cake at the wedding reception. However, in some areas, as mentioned above, the cake is cut at home, either before or during the marriage service. Whenever the cake is cut there is a general belief that the first slice should be cut by the bride; otherwise, the marriage will be childless. However, in Dutch tradition, the groom cuts the first slice for his bride, who then slices the cake for the rest of her family. An earlier Jamaican tradition was for a bachelor and an unmarried girl to cut the first slice, both holding the knife. It was thought that by performing this task the couple enhanced their own prospects for getting married in the near future (although not necessarily to each other).

It is now usual for both the bride and groom to hold the knife while making the first cut, and it is said that the one whose hand is uppermost on the knife handle will have the upper hand in the partnership. The bride should not have any part in making her own wedding cake (as she should not be involved with the production of her dress). The wedding cake was thought by some people to be endowed with the ability to ensure that the husband remain faithful to his wife as long as she kept a portion of the cake. The top tier of a wedding cake was often kept to be used as a christening cake for the first child.

See also Bride-Cake; Divinations

References
Beeton, Mrs. Isabella. 1880. *The Book of Household Management.* London: Ward Lock and Co.
Charsley, Simon. 1992. *Wedding Cakes and Cultural History.* London: Routledge.
———. 1988. "The Wedding Cake: History and Meaning." *Folklore* 99, no. 2: 232–241.
Jeaffreson, John Cordy. 1872. *Brides and Bridals.* 2 vols. London: Hurst and Blackett.

Cana, Wedding at

In the preamble to the marriage service in the Church of England's *Book of Common Prayer,* which lays out the order of service for weddings, reference is made to Jesus and his mother attending a wedding at Cana, where he performed his first miracle of turning water into wine (John 2.1–11). The *Book of Common Prayer* preamble states: "Which holy estate Christ adorned and beautified with his presence, and first miracle that he wrought, in Cana of Galilee." In 1974, the Church of England Synod proposed a revision to the marriage service that retained this validation of marriage by Christ: "Our Lord who became a man and who made men was pleased to be present at the wedding in order to confirm the sanctity of the full authority of marriage." The early Christian church, from the writings of Paul, considered celibacy as the ideal, but, realizing that this would lead to the eventual disappearance of the Christian movement, early church elders had to accept marriage as a better condition than couples living together without the benefit of the blessing of the church. James (1933) noted that the early church allowed existing marriage customs or practices to continue as long as they were made subservient to a Christian interpretation of the institution of marriage. The account of Christ's attendance and miracle at the wedding at Cana helped to justify their compromise.

See also Christian Weddings
References
Book of Common Prayer, The. Oxford: Oxford
    University Press.
General Synod of the Church of England. 1975.
    *The Wedding Service: A Report by the Liturgical
    Commission of the General Synod of the Church of
    England.* London: SPCK.
James, E. O. 1933. *Christian Myth and Ritual.*
    London: J. Murray.

Canopy, Bridal

The bridal canopy is associated with Jewish wedding practice, but it has been even more widely used. In Britain, Brand (1777) wrote that the Anglo-Saxons performed the marriage benediction under a "veil," a piece of square cloth held at each corner over the groom and bride to "conceal her virgin blushes." This was known as a "care cloth," and it is evident that such a canopy was still being used well into the fourteenth century, as evidenced by the "wardrobe accounts" of Edward II referring to the purchase of a piece of "Lucca cloth" for use as a veil to "spread over the heads of Richard . . . and Isabela . . . at their nuptial mass" in 1321. The problem with Brand's interpretation of the use of the care cloth is that it was only used during the blessing in the church and after the ceremony proper, which would have taken place outside the church at the door. The cloth, held by officers of the church, would not have been held over the head of either of any couple who had been previously married (and widowed).

Bridal canopies appear to have performed different functions in different societies. In Britain the canopy is said to have been used to hide the blushes of the bride; however, although the Edward II account refers to the canopy as a veil, it cannot be said to be the precursor of the veil, as veils did not come to be generally worn by British brides until the eighteenth or nineteenth centuries. In other societies the canopy has a protective function. A Chinese practice was to hold a sacred umbrella over the bride's head to prevent evil influences from harming that sensitive part of the body (she would also be conveyed to the groom's house in an enclosed sedan chair).

The Bedouin of Ethiopia concealed the bride beneath a canopy. Lane (1836, 170) described the procession escorting an Egyptian bride to the baths on the eve of her wedding beneath a silk canopy: "Then follows the bride, walking under a canopy of silk, of some gay colour, as pink, rose-colour, or yellow: or of two colours composing wide stripes, often rose-colour and yellow. It is carried by four men, by means of a pole at each corner, and is open only in front; and at the top of each of the four poles is attached an embroidered handkerchief." A decorated canopy called a *poruwa* is used in Sri Lanka, in which the couple sit or stand for the wedding ceremony. The canopy is considered such an important part of this culture that even Christians go through a ceremony beneath the canopy after being married in church. Hindu and Jain weddings in India usually take place beneath a canopy called a *mandap,* a wooden canopy erected on four pillars, representing the four parents. Each of the pillars is brightly decorated and blessed before the wedding ceremony. In western Finland most people are followers of the Orthodox Church, rather than the Lutheran, and the Orthodox wedding took place beneath a canopy supported by the bridesmaids and groomsmen, a practice that died out in the twentieth century. The ancient Greeks too used a bridal canopy.

But the canopy is most familiar as part of the Jewish tradition. Traditionally the canopy, the *huppah* or *chuppa,* was erected in the courtyard of the bridegroom's house or in the courtyard of the synagogue. It was said that the canopy should be placed beneath the heavens to symbolize that offspring would be as plentiful as the stars in the heavens. Kibbutz weddings often take place in the open, using a canopy made from the Israeli flag. The canopy was often decorated with flowers and green leaves and sometimes cloths and tapestries. The canopy is sometimes seen as a survival of the bridal bower where the couple went to consummate the marriage after the ceremonies. Some rabbinical authorities say that the *huppah* was the groom's house or a room or any other building than the bride's parental home, where, by entering, she declares her independence from her parents and accepts the protection of her husband. However, the seclusion portion of the wedding is now known as *yichud,* or seclusion or privacy, and the canopy is interpreted as representing the (new) home, the basis for Jewish life, open on four sides to represent hospitality. During the nineteenth century, there was controversy as to whether the *huppah* should be erected within the synagogue, with the suggestion that to do so was to make Jewish practice imitate Gentile custom. However, it should be noted that in Christian tradition, the betrothal and wedding took place outside the church, at the church door, with the wedding being blessed in church. Gradually the church took over the officiating at weddings inside the church. But the marriage "service" takes place beneath the canopy—even in the synagogue—which may suggest that the canopy has a function similar to that of other cultures.

Rabbi Isaac ben Abba Mari, writing in the twelfth century, mentioned a custom, of which he disapproved, of holding a cloth or a *talit* over the heads of the couple during the marriage blessing, which sounds analogous to the fourteenth-century practice in England mentioned above. In Sweden, the bridesmaids hold a canopy over the bride made of shawls to protect her from the evil eye. The earliest references to the four-posted canopy among Jewish communities did not occur until the sixteenth century and it appears to have been accepted with reluctance.

When the couple stands beneath the *huppah,* the balance of power within the marriage can be determined by where they place their feet during the ceremony. If the man puts his right foot on the woman's left foot during the blessing, he will have authority over her in the marriage; however, if she manages to put her left foot on his right then she will have the power in the household. There is a story of a bride who lost this competition, so her father recommended that before the consummation of the marriage she ask her husband to bring her a glass of water. Drinking this would shift the focus of the household power. This is reminiscent of the water from St. Keyne's well in Cornwall, England, which will bestow the power in the marriage to whomever of the couple drinks from its waters first.

See also Church Porch, Weddings in; *Huppah (Chuppa);* Jewish Weddings

References

Cunnington, Phillis, and Catherine Lucas. 1972. *Costume for Birth, Marriage, and Death.* London: Adam and Charles Black.

Deane, Tony, and Tony Shaw. 1975. *The Folklore of Cornwall.* London: B. T. Batsford.

Lane, Edward W. [1836] 1914. *The Manners and Customs of the Modern Egyptians.* Everyman Edition. London: J. M. Dent.

Murphy, Brian M. 1978. *The World of Weddings: An Illustrated Celebration.* London: Paddington.

Ranasinghe, Alex. 1970. "The Betrothal and Marriage Customs of the Hebrews during the Time of Christ." *Folklore* 81, no. 1: 48–62.

Segal, Eliezer. 1999. *Why Didn't I Learn This in Hebrew School?* Northvale, NJ: Jason Aronson.

Capture (Kidnap), of Bride

During wedding celebrations in contemporary Russia, the friends of the couple may kidnap or capture the bride and hold her for ransom, which the bridegroom has to pay. It is up to him to notice that his new wife is missing and to negotiate the price for her return. This may happen several times during the celebrations. Traditionally, in the Santander district of Spain, unmarried men would capture the bride on the eve of the wedding and the groom would have to pay for her release. This seems to be similar to the widespread "barring the way" and other customs—in Orkney a bridegroom had to donate a ball, or the money for a ball, to the boys of the bride's parish. This is a form of "paying a footing" into the community or paying a form of fine to the community for taking one of their members away.

See also Ball Games; Barring the Way; Russian Weddings; Spain

Capture, Marriage by

There are many wedding customs and practices in different parts of the world that include some form of ritual or mock battle or the apparent abduction of the bride by the groom's family and friends. These practices gave rise to the nineteenth-century theory of "marriage by capture" (McLennan [1865]). Others have considered this to be a rare form of marriage. In the Hindu Laws of Manu, eight forms of marriage are recognized. Four are considered blessed and the other four are condemned as "blamable" unions. One of these is known as *râkshasa,* which is a "union" by forcible abduction of a maiden from her home after her house is entered and her kinsmen slain or wounded, or by stealth.

Capture was also said to have been the means by which the founders of Rome obtained their wives and was the beginning of the Roman marriage rites. "The Rape of the Sabine Women" was recounted by the Roman historian Livy (c. 59 B.C. to A.D. 17), in his history of Rome (Book 1), and by the Graeco-Roman writer Plutarch (around A.D 46–119) in his *Parallel Lives.* The story goes that the neighboring nations would not let their daughters marry Romans. To acquire wives, Romulus, the founder of Rome, let it

be known that an altar to a god called Consus had been found hidden underground. To celebrate, he appointed a day for sacrifice, public games, and shows, to which all were invited. Romulus sat at the front among his noblemen, wearing purple robes. As a signal, Romulus stood up and threw his robe over his body. The Romans drew their swords, rushed among the crowd, and carried away many of the young Sabine women. The number of women taken that day is variously given as 30, 527, and 683. Romulus is said to have justified his actions by saying that no married women were taken (except one by mistake), to show that the Romans did not commit the rape in a wanton fashion but instead to form marriage alliances. He said to the women that this would not have happened if their fathers had been willing to marry them to the Romans, and he reassured them that they would have the status of wives, with all the material rewards and citizenship, and that they should now give their hearts to the men who had taken their bodies. The event provoked a war between the Romans and the Sabines, who accused the Romans of violating the laws of hospitality. The women eventually came between the two armies to prevent bloodshed, not wishing the men of their birth families or their new husbands to be maimed or killed in a conflict over them. In ancient Rome, a bride would run to her mother and then would have to be carried away by force by the bridegroom and his friends.

McLennan (1865, 136–137) made no distinction between elopement and mock abduction, but he did acknowledge that his contemporary accounts did not provide evidence that marriage by capture was extant in the nineteenth century. The accounts instead referred to a time when tribes that practiced exogamy (that is marriage outside the tribe) obtained their wives by capture:

If it could be shown that exogamous tribes existed, and that the usual relations of savage tribes to each other were those of hostility, we should have found a social condition in which it was inevitable that the wives should systematically be procured by capture. It also appeared that if the existence of exogamous tribes either actually capturing their wives, or observing the symbol of capture in their marriage ceremonies, should be established in a reasonable number of cases, it would be a legitimate inference that exogamy had prevailed wherever we find a system of capture, or form of capture, existing. . . . We may conclude that wherever capture, or the form of capture, prevails, or has prevailed, there prevails, or has prevailed, exogamy. Conversely, we may say that, wherever exogamy can be found, we may confidently expect to find, after due investigation, at least the trace of a system of capture.

An anonymous correspondent to the *Chambers Journal* of 22 October 1864 (quoted by Scott 1953, 55, and used by Jeaf-freson 1872, 1: 14) described how the Ab-origines of Australia obtained a wife. The writer begins by noting that women were considered much inferior to men and had to carry their belongings from one camp to the next as beasts of burden. Courtship was ap-parently unknown to them, so that if a young warrior wished a wife, he exchanged a sister or other female relative for the woman. However, if there was no woman among his tribe who interested him, he might take one from some other encamp-ment by stunning her with his war club and dragging her insensible body to some se-cluded spot. When she recovered, he took her back to his tribe's encampment in some triumph. Sometimes two young men would work together, spending time to spy on the movements of the women who interested them. When they had made their decision, they would creep naked toward the camp-fire around which the women slept, carry-ing only their "jag-spears." When they got close enough, the man would wind his spear in the woman's hair to entangle it in the barb point; she would be roused from her sleep with a jerk from the spear in her hair,

to find another spear point at her throat. She could then be led away because she was aware that if she made any attempt to escape she might be killed. Once she had been se-cured in a place away from the camp, the young men would return for another young woman. If alarm was given, the prospective abductors would escape to try again another day. The account continues by telling us that a distinguished warrior who had carried off a wife might volunteer to undergo "the trial of spears" to prevent the two tribes having to go to war over the incident. The two tribes would meet, and ten of the young men from the woman's tribe would be given three reed spears and a throwing stick each; the young warrior, armed only with a bark shield (about eighteen inches by six inches), would stand about forty yards away from the men, who, on a signal, would throw the spears at him in rapid succession, which the young warrior had to parry with the shield. Having passed this test (as was usual, be-cause of tribal skill in using the shield) and consequently atoning for the abduction, the two tribes would conclude the event by feasting together.

However, Westermarck (1894, 389) stated that where marriage by capture is said to take place between hostile tribes in Aus-tralia, "we are aware of no tribe—exogamous or endogamous—living in a state of absolute isolation." He went on: "On the contrary, every tribe entertains constant relations, for the most part amicable, with one, two or more tribes; and marriages between their members are the rule. Moreover, the cus-tom, prevalent among many savage tribes, of a husband taking up his abode in his wife's family seems to have arisen very early in man's history. . . . there are in different parts of the world twelve or thirteen well-marked exogamous peoples among whom this habit occurs."

In many wedding practices there is an ap-parent conflict between the bride's party and the bridegroom's party and a show of reluc-tance on the part of the bride to be taken in marriage. This is understandable in the case of arranged marriages where the couple has little say in the choice of partner. However, shows of reluctance are commonly seen in situations where the two have either given consent or made a free choice. In the nineteenth century in Greenland, we are told, after the parents of both of the couple had given their consent to the marriage, the bride was collected, on the day agreed, by two or more women, and she was expected to show reluctance to go with them, so that they appeared to have to use force. When she was eventually taken to the bridegroom's house, she sat in a corner with her hair disheveled and covering her face. She was slowly persuaded to drop the assumed coyness and the wedding was concluded. In the Welsh wedding, the procession of the bridegroom's party had a number of obstacles put in the way, and those in the party had to "battle" to gain access to the bride's house. Even once both parties had begun the procession to the church, the bride and her party forced the groom's party to chase her and catch her. In other events, such as one described in Lorraine, France (Gutch, 1880–1881), the members of the groom's party had to persuade the bride's party/protectors to let them in by answering riddles and through wordplay and guile.

According to African custom, the bridegroom's party and the bride's party may meet halfway between the households or villages of the couple, where there may be a mock battle, gift giving, or apparent payment and abduction. The missionary T. Roscoe, writing of the Ganda people (a branch of the Bantu tribes settled in Uganda) in 1911, described how the two parties met at a halfway point, where the friends of the bridegroom would scatter cowry shells (the local currency) for the bride's party to pick up; while they were thus distracted, the groom's friends would abduct the bride. As they ran off with her, they would drop a trail of cowry shells. However, the bride would refuse to enter the groom's compound, to sit down

with him, to eat, or to go to bed—each time being won over by gifts of cowry shells. The marriages among peoples of Nyanza Province in Kenya involved a mock fight between the girls on the bridegroom's side and those on the bride's side.

It was suggested by McLennan (1865) that the custom of lifting a bride over the threshold of her new home was related to the practice of marriage by capture, making a link with the rape of the Sabine virgins, who did not go voluntarily, and signifying that she loses her virginity unwillingly. It is difficult to say if the practice of taking women as brides by force was ever widespread, but certainly there does exist what is seen as a ritual reluctance on the part of the woman to leave her family group and join her husband's. Even when there is agreement and willingness, she has to give an appearance of resistance—this may be through modesty or because, although she may want to marry, for her, the future is unknown. Generally, at marriage, the woman makes the greatest change. In some cases, as in China, she cuts off all previous family ties.

The observations from anthropologists used by McLennan to develop his theory of marriage by capture may not be vestiges of an older tradition but a continuation of established practice. Similarly we cannot tell how much of the Aborigine capture episode described by the anonymous writer in *Chambers Journal* was actually prearranged and whether he or she, as an outsider, knew the whole story. Curiously, forms of marriage by capture have been recorded in the twentieth century. In 1995, newspaper reports said that in a Lunar New Year crackdown in China, two hundred women who had been abducted to be sold as brides to farmers were rescued from only one province in China (*Manchester Guardian,* 19 January 1995). Additionally, in some areas of India, to get out of paying a dowry, a girl's family might kidnap a likely young man and forcibly marry him to their daughter.

See also Abduction, Marriage by; Hindu
   Weddings; Wales

References

Gutch, Mrs. 1880–1881. "A Rural Wedding in Lorraine." *Folk Lore Record* 3: 258–274.

Jeaffreson, John Cordy. 1872. *Brides and Bridals.* 2 vols. London: Hurst and Blackett.

Mair, Lucy. 1971. *Marriage.* Harmondsworth, Middlesex: Penguin.

McLennan, John F. 1865. *Primitive Marriage, An Inquiry into the Origin of the Form of Capture in Marriage Ceremonies.* Edinburgh: A and C Black.

Roscoe, T. 1911. *The Baganda: An Account of Their Native Customs and Beliefs.* London: Macmillan.

Scott, George Ryley. 1953. *Curious Customs of Sex and Marriage.* London: Torchstream.

Westermarck, Edward. 1894. *The History of Human Marriage.* 2d ed. London: Macmillan.

Cards, Wedding

Jeaffreson (1872) reported that during the nineteenth century in English fashionable circles the bride (and groom) would distribute wedding cards to their friends and acquaintances, giving details of the bride's change of name, her new address, and days when she would be at home to receive the good wishes of friends who might visit her. She would usually serve wine and wedding cake to her visitors. The form, wording, and purpose of the wedding card changed with fashion over the nineteenth century, beginning as an invitation to a "banquet" of sweetmeats with an announcement of the marriage and of her future address. The feast of sweetmeats was dropped, along with the implied invitation to call ceremoniously on the bride. For a time, fashion dictated that the card should just state her new address and give a date when she would be at home after her honeymoon trip. Fashion further evolved to direct that the cards should not give the address; then to a single undated card sent in a plain envelope; then to the contrivance of the ordinary calling cards of the bride and the groom joined with a silver thread. By the 1870s fashion declared these cards to be out of fashion and not tolerated in polite society, and it became a matter of debate whether a bride should send cards or be married "without cards."

See also Honeymoon

Reference

Jeaffreson, John Cordy. 1872. *Brides and Bridals.* 2 vols. London: Hurst and Blackett.

Cars

From the latter part of the twentieth century to the present, cars have become the most common transport to and from a wedding in European and other countries. In Great Britain, many hire a Rolls Royce or a limousine and chauffeur to take the bride and her father to the church or registry office and to transport the newlywed couple to the reception after the ceremony. Wedding cars, in most countries, have some form of decoration, usually a v-shape of ribbons on the car hood and rosettes on door handles. In Russia, along with the usual ribbons on the front, a doll is tied to the radiator grill of the car to symbolize future children. At a Portuguese wedding, all the cars have a wedding favor, a ribbon bow, attached to the antenna (similarly in France, ribbon wedding bows can often be seen tied to car antennas). After the wedding, the drivers sound their horns to draw attention to the wedding party. This is common in many European countries and in many other parts of the world but in the British Isles is only found in Ireland. The practice seems to be related to other traditions intended to celebrate and draw attention to the wedding party, such as "firing the anvil" and the "rough band." Similarly, bridal processions in Egypt are usually led by a group of drummers (and sometimes other musicians) to draw attention to the wedding.

Today most couples will depart for the honeymoon by car, and this car often becomes the target of decoration by the couple's friends. Often slogans, jokes, and pictures (usually risqué puns or double entendres) are plastered all over the car using washable paints or foam, often the sign "just married" is attached to the rear, and very often tin cans, old boots, or other junk is tied to the back bumper so that the couple attract

Friends of newly married couple Ben Parr and Olive Owen decorate their car with a "Just Married" sign and tin cans before they drive off on their honeymoon. (Hulton-Deutsch Collection/CORBIS)

attention to themselves as they drive away. Although most of these practices would appear to be twentieth century, cars only having become common in the latter half of the twentieth century, most of the traditions surrounding the car in the present-day wedding can be seen as evolving from earlier wedding customs and rituals that contribute to ensuring that the wedding is a public event.

See also Anvil, Firing of; Confetti; Favors; Honeymoon; Posset; Rough Music/Rough Band; Russian Weddings; Shoes; Stockings, Throwing of

References
Kaiser, Robert, and Hannah J. Kaiser. 1980. *Russia from the Inside.* London: Hutchinson.
Lane, Edward W. [1836] 1994. *The Manners and Customs of the Modern Egyptians.* Everyman Edition. London: J. M. Dent.
Murphy, Brian M. 1978. *The World of Weddings: An Illustrated Celebration.* London: Paddington.
Thompson, Joyce, and Phyllis Bridges. 1971. "West Texas Wedding Cars." *Western Folklore* 30, no. 2: 123–126.

Cats

In the context of weddings, the cat, specifically the black cat, is considered lucky, one of a number of chance natural indicators of good fortune. In 1971 a correspondent from Cornwall, England, to the *Farmers Weekly* magazine reported that it was lucky to see a black cat on the way to the church to be married (Opie and Tatem 1989, 60), although in other parts of the country, and in other situations, a black cat may be considered unlucky. Such beliefs persist to the present day. In terms of finding a partner, it is said that "wherever the cat of the house is black, its lasses of lovers will never lack." The bride who hears a black cat sneeze on her wedding day will be happy throughout her married life. Similarly if she catches sight of a cat on her way to church, or upon leaving after the ceremony, she may expect to enjoy prosperity as well as happiness. To signify wishes for the bride's happiness, a bride may be given a symbolic black cat charm to carry.

See also Courtship; Tokens
References
Anonymous. 1971. *Essex Countryside* 19, no. 172:
    57.
Opie, Iona, and Moira Tatem, eds. 1989. *A
    Dictionary of Superstitions.* Oxford: Oxford
    University Press.

Ceremony

A wedding involves ceremony. The couple is usually dressed in very special clothing, decorated to make them stand out from their friends and relatives, and they are usually feted almost as royalty for the event. Ceremony provides a communal event out of the ordinary to help people remember the wedding—to fix the event in the memory. Such ceremony may be relatively simple—such as the bride being paraded through the streets to her new husband's house, accompanied by friends and musicians, and with some form of "handing-over" event, or the public exchange of promises and vows. The most important thing is that it be public. There are a few societies where the marriage ceremony is not a very public event. In the matriarchal Galician society, the marriage was performed at night and in secret, with only the priest and essential witnesses knowing the date and time and location. It was a form of sport for the local youths to find out the details of the wedding and await the couple as they emerged from the church, to make a great deal of noise with horns and bells and by rubbing scallop shells together until money was thrown to them to go and drink to the health of the couple (Rey-Henningsen 1994, 103). In Western countries—the United States, Canada, Israel and other Jewish communities, Europe, and areas where there is, or has been, a considerable European influence—the ceremony may have a substantial and overt religious content. However, religion has had a strong involvement in the wedding ceremony only since the twelfth century.

It was not until the reign of Edward VI (1547–1553) in England, and later in Europe, that weddings were allowed to take place within the church. Before that time, the important part of the marriage ceremony took place at the church door or in the church porch (Charles I of England, 1600–1649, married Henrietta Maria, daughter of Henry IV of France, by proxy at the door of Notre Dame cathedral), with perhaps a nuptial mass inside the church afterward. Between the seventh and the twelfth centuries, the church began to establish its authority in questions of matrimony. Although efforts were made in the twelfth century for marriage to be included in the seven sacraments of the church, it did not have the status of a sacrament until 1439, which enabled it to be included in the *Book of Common Prayer.* It was only in 1563, after the Reformation, that the Catholic Church required a priest to be present for the marriage ceremony. James (1933) noted that Christianity was dealing with an established institution and had to incorporate established custom and law that had been observed by many generations into its own sacraments in order for the Christian marriage rites to be accepted.

In the Middle Ages, there were two distinct ceremonies. The first part, the *sponsalia,* the secular aspect of the marriage, was itself in two parts: the *sponsalia,* in which the couple consented to contract the marriage, and the *subarrhatio,* which involved the delivering of the ring by the bridegroom to the bride and the promise of the dowry before witnesses. The second part was the priestly blessing of the marriage (the *matrimonium*), providing the sacramental and spiritual element. This consisted of three major elements: the Mass, during which the couple received communion and made offerings; the benediction, during which a veil or cloth was held over the heads of the couple; and the coronation of the couple upon leaving the church.

The priestly involvement came to assume more and more importance over the centuries, giving a spiritual blessing to the legal contract so that the ceremony before the church door would take place in the presence of the priest who blessed the union. The medieval ritual therefore placed the principal act of the marriage, the consent and settlement between the two parties, at the entrance or porch of the church—a very public place. Aspects of these medieval practices are still very evident in contemporary marriage rites. For example, in France, a civil service precedes, and is independent of, any ecclesiastical rite, as the *sponsalia* was independent of the *matrimonium;* indeed, in many European countries, the church service is an optional extra; in the Orthodox church in Finland, the canopy is still used; and bridal crowns are still used in many cultures, such as in Greece, Norway, and Eastern European countries. However, despite the struggles to install the marriage ceremony as one of the church sacraments—the Christian wedding service is still based on, and follows closely, the medieval ritual—consummation made the marriage, and nonconsummation could lead to the annulment of the union.

The marriage ceremony in most parts of the world is a public handing over of one person to the family or care of another group, and it may also involve the very public showing of the symbols of giving and acceptance, which cement alliances and provide guarantees and insurances agreed to between the two families. The religious element is often an add-on and not necessarily required by the state or community. About the only state where a wedding is required to be solemnized in a religious ceremony is Israel. Since 1953, the people of Israel have had to undergo a religious ceremony for marriage, the legislation mandating that whatever the religion of the couple, they must be married by the clergy of that denomination. Consequently, many Israeli couples fly to Cyprus—which has been called the matrimonial equivalent of Las Vegas for the Israeli people—or do not formally marry before setting up home together. The intention of the legislation was to ensure the continuity of the Jewish faith. But the legislation also applies to couples of other faiths, and in this the government was reinforcing the connection between the state and religion.

See also Consummation; Israel; Jewish Weddings; Spousal
References
Chu, Henry. 2003. "Religion Causes a Wedding Daze." *Los Angeles Times,* 4 June.
Goody, Jack. 1983. *The Development of the Family and Marriage in Europe.* Cambridge: Cambridge University Press.
James, E. O. 1933. *Christian Myth and Ritual.* London: J. Murray.
Rey-Henningsen, Marisa. 1994. *The World of the Ploughwoman: Folklore and Reality in Matriarchal Northwest Spain.* Helsinki: Academia Scientiarum Fennica.

Chamber Pot

Chamber pots appear in wedding celebrations mainly as receptacles for drink, as in the French custom *la soupe* (or *la saucée*), whereby the wedding guests prepare a mixture of drink, cake, and other leftovers from the wedding feast in a chamber pot from which the couple is expected to drink. In the Scottish prewedding custom known as "creeling the bride" or "bosseller," a woman is decorated on her last day at work before her wedding and paraded through the streets. A decorated chamber pot, sometimes filled with salt, coal, and a piece of silver, is included in the procession, which the bride-to-be and her entourage jump over at intervals. In Scottish tradition, salt was considered an aphrodisiac (an old Scottish saying was "fond o' salt, fond o' the lasses"). A tradition in the West of Scotland, noted by James Napier in 1879, called for the bride's presents and outfit to be taken to her future home on the evening before the marriage, led by the bridesmaid, who carried "a certain domestic utensil" filled with salt, the first item to be taken into her new home. Some of the salt was sprinkled over the floor as a protection against the evil eye. Rorie (1934) reported that a chamber pot filled with salt was a common present among the people of the northeast of Scotland. Miniature chamber pots with a gilt inscription "for me and my girl" or with an eye on the foot were sold in Aberdeen markets and were often kept on the mantle shelf of the bedroom as an emblem of the marriage.

See also Bosseller; Creeling

References

Monger, George. 1971. "A Note on Wedding Customs in Industry Today." *Folklore* 82, no. 4: 314–316.

Napier, James. 1879. *Folklore or Superstitious Beliefs in the West of Scotland within This Century.* Paisley: Alex Graham.

Rorie, David. 1934. "Chamber Pots Filled with Salt as Marriage Gift." *Folklore* 45: 162–163.

Van Gennep, Arnold. 1932. *Folklore du Dauphiné.* Vol. 1. Paris: Librairie orientale et américaine.

Child Marriage

The marriage of children occurs mainly among native societies. In developed societies, the age for marriage is based on the age of consent for sexual activity. In Islamic countries, girls are usually veiled when they reach puberty, and efforts are made to ensure that they marry soon after the onset of puberty. It happens in some Muslim countries that a girl of eleven or twelve is married to an older man and becomes a mother in the early teenage years. In Britain and in other European countries, child marriage has been recorded among royalty and gentry. Often in these cases, children are promised in marriage, or betrothed, at a very young age. And there are records of children, at the ages of eight or ten, going through a wedding ceremony and lying in bed together, but not consummating the marriage. These marriages were often performed to protect family property rights and, occasionally, the young people's property.

The seventeenth-century London diarist Samuel Pepys describes a juvenile wedding that took place on 20 September 1695. A boy and a girl from the Bluecoat School in London were each left a large amount of money by two wealthy men. The magistrates thought it best to marry these two to one another, to protect them from being swindled out of their fortunes by suitors and un-scrupulous marriage partners. They were married at the Guildhall Chapel by the dean of St. Paul's, with the bride "given away" by the Lord Mayor. Anthropologists have found many societies in which children were married or promised in marriage at a very early age. This occurred mainly in societies where the parents chose or arranged the marriage partner for their children. Two Chinese women, pregnant at the same time, may promise their unborn children in marriage to each other, providing, of course, that the children were of the opposite sex.

European aristocratic and landed society, well into the nineteenth century, treated their children as a means to stabilize the family fortunes, make alliances, and work toward greater aggrandizement, with marriages arranged by the parents. The children, although adult, may have had little say in the choice of marriage partner. In some cultures it was thought wrong for children at puberty to not be promised in marriage. Hindu tradition promoted child marriage. Women were considered naturally libidinous—if a girl was not married by puberty she would soon find a lover, no matter how closely her parents "protected" her, and once she had lost her virginity she would be unmarriageable (and consequently a disgrace and an economic liability). Furthermore, it was thought that in an ideal marriage the bride should be one-third the age of the groom—a man of twenty-four should marry a girl of eight. But it was also decreed in Hindu writings that a man of thirty should marry a girl of twelve and that it would be sinful for a man to break this rule. Early Hindu religious writers (in the Laws of Manu) wrote that a girl should be married by the age of ten years (although some stretch the point to twelve years), and if she was not married by then, she should be immediately married, even in the prohibited marriage season. Intercourse before puberty was forbidden. It was deemed especially important for Hindi to have male children as soon as possible to provide sacrifices so that the souls of the ancestors could stay in

Lalloo Singh, six, and his seven-year-old bride, Basanti, with her face covered by a veil, during ceremonies at their arranged marriage in the desert state of Rajasthan. Far from uncommon, child marriages such as this one at Bayana, one hundred miles south of New Delhi, take place all over rural India despite more than fifty years of laws prohibiting such unions. (Bettmann/CORBIS)

heaven. It was not uncommon for a man with a wife and child to bring up a young girl to become his second wife when she reached the desired age. If a girl was betrothed as a child and her prospective husband died before she reached the age at which she could marry him, she was treated as a widow and given the low status of a widow and not allowed to "re-marry." (A widower, however, was expected to find a new wife as soon as possible.)

In 1846, the Indian Penal Code made it a criminal offense for a marriage to be consummated before the girl had reached the age of ten; in 1891 this age was raised to twelve. However, the Joshi Report of 1929 (the Report of the Age of Consent Committee) found that few people knew of the 1891 legislation. Child marriage was not just between an adult male and a young female. Isabel Burton (wife of the explorer Sir Richard Burton) described seeing a wedding of two children in Bombay in 1876:

> The little bride and bridegroom were aged nine and ten. There was a profusion of rose-water, bouquets, nuts wrapped in leaves, and cocoa-nuts. The children, covered with jewellery, sit in two chairs opposite each other, and an embroidered sheet is put between them; prayers are recited; she hangs a necklace of strung white blossom round his neck, and he throws a necklace of black beads . . . round hers. The marriage lasts for days. . . . next day she is brought back to her parents, and stays with them until she is ready for practical marriage. (Burton 1889)

Child marriage, or properly, child betrothal, was widely practiced among many different African tribes. The Yoruba tribes of Nigeria would betroth girls at a young age and they would be treated almost as wives. In some African communities, the husband-to-be lived with the girl's parents, and worked for them, until she was old enough for marriage. Anthropologists have found many cases and societies in which children were betrothed at birth or soon after. Travelers among the Eskimo tribes recorded examples of young men requesting marriage to a newborn girl. If he was accepted by her father, the promise would be binding and she would be delivered to him for marriage at the proper age.

See also Age at Marriage; Betrothal; Hindu
   Weddings; India; Yoruban Weddings
References
Braddock, Joseph. 1961. *The Bridal Bed.* New
   York: John Day.
Burton, Isabel. 1889. *Arabia, Egypt, India: A
   Narrative of Travel.* London: W. Mullan and Son.
Eichler, Lillian. 1924. *The Customs of Mankind.*
   London: William Heinemann.
Scott, George Ryley. 1953. *Curious Customs of Sex
   and Marriage.* London: Torchstream.
Sumner, William Graham. [1906] 1940. *Folkways.*
   New York: Mentor Books.
Trevelyan, G. M. 1948. *English Social History: A
   Survey of Six Centuries, Chaucer to Queen Victoria.*
   London: Reprint Society.
Westermarck, Edward. 1894. *The History of
   Human Marriage.* 2d ed. London: Macmillan.

Chimney Sweep

In the British Isles and in Germany it is considered lucky for a chimney sweep, dressed in his "blacks," that is, his working clothes, and with a blackened face, to appear at a wedding. Local newspapers often photograph the bride receiving a kiss from the sweep (the photograph showing a stark contrast between the clean whiteness of the bride and her dress against the black of the sweep). In an article in the *Daily Telegraph* of 26 August 1983, a chimney sweep, Cyril Buckland, claimed that it was more profitable to attend weddings (for which he charged £5 for a five-minute appearance) than to do his job (£4 for twenty minutes of work). With the advent of central heating and the use of vacuums to clean chimneys, the visit of the chimney sweep to wed-

dings, properly dressed in blacks, is a rarity. But miniature chimney sweeps are among the good luck charms today present at weddings.

Perhaps it was thought that if the bride embraced such a dirty character she would have a horror of dirt and would consequently be a clean and tidy housewife. Or the practice may have had to do with dark strangers bringing luck. The chimney sweep also has connections with the hearth and the home. The chimney sweep custom is reminiscent of the Irish strawboy tradition, where a group of men completely covered in straw costumes would visit the wedding celebrations to bring luck to the couple, sometimes, however, the luck-bringers would wear women's clothing and blacken their faces, another traditional form of disguise for luck bringers. In general, it was believed that the sighting and greeting of a chimney sweep brought good luck, and the *Dictionary of Superstitions* (Opie and Tatum 1989) gives several anecdotes that attest to the luck-bringing properties of the chimney sweep. The earliest reference is dated 1885. A writer of a letter to the *People* newspaper, London (a Sunday newspaper), dated 11 September 1960, revealed that her friends had told her to blow three kisses after a chimney sweep and "you'll get a pleasant surprise."

See also Strawboys; Tokens
References
Coote-Lake, E. F. 1960. "Variation on the Theme
   of Sweep's Luck." *Folklore* 71: 260.
Gailey, Alan. 1968. "Straw Costume in Irish Folk
   Customs." *Folk Life* 6: 83–93.
Opie, Iona, and Moira Tatem, eds. 1989. *A
   Dictionary of Superstitions.* Oxford: Oxford
   University Press.
Porter, Enid. 1969. *Cambridgeshire Customs and
   Folkore.* London: Routledge and Kegan Paul.

China

There is a Chinese saying, "A daughter married is like water poured out the door," that refers to the fact that when a girl marries, she leaves her family to become part of her husband's family and, apart from a brief period immediately after the wedding, is completely cut off from her birth family. Twentieth-century population laws in China restrict couples to one child. This, along with the cultural imperative for Chinese men to have a son and heir, has encouraged neglect and abandonment of female babies and children, which, in turn, has led to a shortage of women for marriage. In 1990, government figures suggested that men outnumbered women by ten to one. It is thought that this may serve to empower Chinese women. The situation obviously does give women a greater choice in marriage partner. But this has also led to such atrocities as women being abducted from the city and taken to rural farmers desperate for wives. In 1995, newspapers reported that in a Lunar New Year crackdown in China, two hundred women who had been abducted and were to be sold as brides to farmers were rescued from just one province of China (*Manchester Guardian,* 19 January 1995).

Descriptions of Chinese weddings are complicated by the vast size of the country, differences among provinces, and marriage laws that have followed or been influenced by Western cultures and political ideology. In 1931, the Kuomintang Civil Code attempted to impose equality of women and the right of free choice in marriage. In 1950, the Communist Family Law provided freedom of divorce and equal status for women and defined the rights and duties of children. However, these laws and changes have only slowly had an effect on attitudes toward marriage and the role of women in Chinese society. Outside influences have also impinged upon Chinese society so that marriages have to be registered with a registrar and there may be a religious ceremony of marriage in a church (if the families are Christian) or in a temple.

Traditionally, however, marriages are still arranged between two families. The man's parents search for a prospective bride of the same social and financial status. It was not unusual for parents to arrange, and promise, their children in marriage when they were very young, or even before they were born. In some cases, a young girl may be "bought" by a richer family to be the servant to the rich boy, becoming either his wife or his concubine. Two women pregnant at the same time would sometimes promise their children in marriage (if both were boys or both girls the children would be brought up as brothers or as sisters). It was customary for parents to betroth their children at the age of around ten or twelve, with the marriage being finalized when the girl was about fifteen and the man around twenty.

In urban areas today, men and women often make their own choices, but there are restraints that can delay a wedding, or even lead to the cancellation of the arrangements, such as the cost and availability of housing and sometimes the cost of the wedding itself if the parents insist on too large a guest list. Traditionally, when a young man's parents identified a prospective bride, a spokeswoman was hired to act as a go-between to approach the young woman's family with the offer of marriage. It was the job of this spokeswoman to persuade the prospective bride's family to accept the marriage offer; upon acceptance, the families began to make the marriage plans. The first step, after an agreement was made, was for the young man's parents to send a formal letter to the young woman's family to confirm the agreement, together with a request for the young woman's "eight letters." In the Chinese calendar, twenty-two letters are used to represent dates; two letters from these twenty-two are used to represent each of the time, day, month, and year of the birth date. The eight letters of both the bride-to-be and the groom-to-be were then sent to a fortune-telling master to determine whether or not the two sets of numbers presented a match. If they did not match up, contact between the families would cease and the young man's family would begin again the search for a prospective bride. If the birth dates matched up, the groom's family commissioned the spokeswoman to send gifts to the woman's family, along with a "gift letter," a list giving the quantity and description of the gifts. To further confirm the marriage agreement, the formal gifts to the bride's family were sent by the groom's family on a propitious day. The gifts included money, cakes, other food, and sacrifices for worshipping ancestors. The fortune-telling master was further employed to suggest a good day for the wedding, determined from the couple's birth dates, as well as those of their families. After the day had been chosen, a man considered to have had good fortune throughout his life would be hired to move the bridal bed into the correct place; a woman, also of good fortune (measured by having a healthy, living husband and sons), would make the bed and leave fruit and foods denoting good fortune on the bed. The bed was then left until the day of the wedding. A few days before the wedding, the bride sent gifts to the bridegroom, including jewelry, kitchen utensils, linen, and clothes.

The night before the wedding, both of the couple showered or bathed, changed to new underwear, and burned incense as they had their hair combed. This combing was carried out by a "good fortune" woman or man and was symbolic of the adulthood of the couple. The hair was combed four times: The first symbolized "from beginning to end," the second, harmony until old age, the third, many sons and grandsons, and the fourth, wealth and a long-lasting marriage. If one of the couple had been married before, this event was skipped. Today, many couples choose to omit this from the marriage preparations.

On the wedding day, the houses of both the bride and groom were decorated with red—the Chinese wedding color. The bride put on a red wedding gown and jewelry given to her by her parents and then was ready for the sedan chair sent by the groom to collect her. This was decorated in red and carried by four servants. The procession to the groom's house was accompanied by musicians; gifts were also brought for the bride's family. The groom's spokesman entered the bride's

house and carried her on his back to the sedan chair—her feet were not allowed to touch the ground until she arrived at the groom's house. The bride's relatives threw rice into the air to distract any chickens that were around to keep them from pecking the bride, and also to distract bad spirits, and a red umbrella was put up to shield her from evil spirits and also to be a symbol of producing many descendants for the groom's family. At this stage, her relatives bade her farewell as she was now leaving home for good. In some places she was carried in a locked sedan chair, accompanied by male relatives and others carrying lanterns decorated with the ancestral names of the bride and groom cut from red paper. The sedan chair was followed by a bearer carrying a large red umbrella, torch bearers, and musicians. The procession was met halfway to the groom's house by his representatives and relatives. The bride was handed over to them to accompany her the rest of the way.

When the bride arrived at the groom's home, the couple worshipped the ancestors and the heaven and earth and then served tea to the groom's family; the relatives gave the couple red packets (of money) or bridal jewelry in return. This was followed by a banquet, as large as the couple could afford, which in some villages could last up to seven days. Three days after the marriage, the bride was expected to return home to her parents, taking presents and a roasted pig for her family. In some regions she would be accompanied by her new husband. This would be the last time she would see her birth family and she would sometimes stay for a couple of days. Tradition demanded that the bride's family return some of the gifts to the groom's family as a courtesy, and in some regions they returned the head and tail of the roasted pig to symbolize a good beginning and end of the wedding.

The modern Chinese wedding has changed in details over the years, although the form of the wedding has remained the same. As noted above, the Chinese population today contains more men than marriageable women. The women, therefore, have a greater choice of marriage partner, and there is more possibility for the couple to make their own choices rather than having the partner chosen by their parents and a go-between. A wedding in Hong Kong today might follow Chinese traditions, with adaptations to take account of the circumstances of the city and the contemporary world and influence from the Western world. For example, there may be a bridal shower before the wedding and the groom may have a bachelor party.

The checking of compatibility between the bride and groom will only be carried out if the families are particularly superstitious; if the fortune-teller suggests that the two are compatible, the families will exchange family trees. However, the Chinese calendar will still be consulted to find a propitious day for sending the wedding gifts by the groom's family to the bride's. Today, often the gifts are some gift-wrapped food—dried seafood and fruit baskets—and this represents both the initial gifts and the formal gifts that were once sent on separate occasions. Instead of a monetary gift the groom will pay all or a portion of the cost of the wedding, but this can lead to problems and delay in the marriage if the two families cannot agree on the number of guests and tables each can have at the banquet.

Because of problems of housing in China today, it is not always possible for the couple to have a new bed and a new home. Today, the bed linen is changed to traditional red as a symbol of the making of the new bridal bed. The tradition of the bridal gift to the groom is usually not followed by modern couples, but the bride may help in paying for the banquet, and this is sometimes seen as being the bride's gift to the groom. The bride is still collected from her house by the groom and the groomsmen, but today, if possible, they will go in decorated cars, with the bridesmaids trying to prevent them from collecting the bride by making them answer questions and perform tasks to prove the

groom's love and ability to look after the woman. The groom is aided in these tests by his groomsmen. After he has passed all the tests and has given the bridesmaids some red packets, the groom and his party are allowed into the house to greet and collect the bride. At this point, the couple serves tea to the bride's family, beginning with her parents and followed by her other relatives. The relatives give the couple a present in return, usually red packets or jewelry. Sometimes families follow tradition in throwing rice or using a red umbrella as the bride leaves home, and sometimes her parents and relatives will go with the couple to the marriage registrar or church for the wedding ceremony. Before going to the registrar, the couple first go to the groom's family home, where they serve tea to the groom's family, again with the parents served first, followed by his other relatives, each giving the bride a present of red packets or jewelry. All then go to the government marriage registrar for the signing of the marriage license.

The wedding feast follows, probably considered the most important part of the celebrations. This is more of a parental event than any other part of the wedding. Although the groom, or the couple, usually pays for the feast, each set of parents seeks to impress relatives and command respect for the size and lavishness of the feast. This is sometimes a source of tension between the families. The groom's family does not want the bride's family to outnumber them, and at the same time the bride's parents will want to put on a good show for their own relatives. Once the guest list has been agreed to, there follows the problem of choosing the menu, which will include about twelve courses, including appetizer, roast pig, shark fin soup, fried rice or noodles, dessert, and fresh fruit. Each of the guests at the feast presents a monetary gift, but these barely cover the costs of the food. Before the food is served, the guests may play mahjong, the Chinese national game, and have their photographs taken with the bride and groom. The best man and maid of honor will toast the bride and groom. When the food is ready to be served, it is announced by the waiters playing a form of xylophone. As the soup is served, the bridal couple go from table to table toasting the guests; during the meal the couple's friends, groomsmen, and bridesmaids play tricks on the couple, trying to get the groom to publicly show his love for his bride. Some of the games are very outrageous.

During her wedding day the bride will change her clothes four or five times, and after the meal she changes again. When the guests leave, the couple, along with their parents and other relatives, form a line at the door to thank the departing guests for coming. The bridal party then go home; if the couple are staying in a hotel for the night, some of their more persistent friends will track them down and play more tricks on them. The custom of the bride returning to her parental home with gifts after three days is still sometimes observed. In some regions this is simplified to the bride returning home on the same day as the wedding (depending on the distances involved), but she may also leave the house and immediately return and then go to the groom's house and count that as the "returning home."

Contemporary population laws that have limited families to one child have not only led to a great imbalance of the sexes but have promoted divorce, so that a woman who has a female child is likely to be divorced so that her husband can remarry and try for a male child. There is an imperative within Chinese society to ensure that there are offspring to carry on the name and to worship ancestors. A girl will leave her family on marriage and become part of her husband's family and consequently have to pay respects to his ancestors.

See also Canopy, Bridal; Divorce; Evil Eye, Protection from; Indonesia; Rice; Shower; Stag Night
References
Gillan, Audrey. 2002. "Lost Babies, Found Babies." *Manchester Guardian: Weekend,* 10 December, 18–30.
Murphy, Brian M. 1978. *The World of Weddings: An Illustrated Celebration.* London: Paddington.
Scott, George Ryley. 1953. *Curious Customs of Sex and Marriage.* London: Torchstream.

Christian Weddings

The contemporary view of marriage within Christianity is very different from that of the founders of Christianity. Today, marriage is considered the foundation of the family, which is often considered the essential building block of the Christian community. But Jesus told his disciples to leave their families to follow him, and Paul, in his writings, decries the way of the flesh (Revised Standard Version):

> For God has done what the law, weakened by the flesh, could not do: sending his own Son in the likeness of sinful flesh and for sin, he condemned sin in the flesh, in order that the just requirement of the law might be fulfilled in us, who walk not according to the flesh but according to the Spirit. For those who live according to the flesh set their minds on the things of the flesh, but those who live according to the Spirit set their minds on the things of the Spirit. To set the mind on the flesh is death, but to set the mind on the Spirit is life and peace. For the mind that is set on the flesh is hostile to God; it does not submit to God's law, indeed it cannot; and those who are in the flesh cannot please God.
> But you are not in the flesh, you are in the Spirit, if in fact the Spirit of God dwells in you. . . . for if you live according to the flesh you will die, but if by the Spirit you put to death the deeds of the body you will live. (Rom. 8.3–13)

Paul had much to say about the followers of Christ and marriage. In 1 Corinthians, he gives a long answer to the question of marriage:

> But because of the temptation to immorality, each man should have his own wife and each woman her own husband. The husband should give to his wife her conjugal rights, and likewise the wife to her husband. For the

wife does not rule over her own body, but the husband does; likewise the husband does not rule over his own body, but the wife does. . . . I wish that all were as I myself am. But each has his own special gift from God, one of one kind and one of another.

To the unmarried and the widows I say that it is well for them to remain single as I do. But if they cannot exercise self-control, they should marry. For it is better to marry than to be aflame with passion. (1 Cor. 7.2–10)

In other versions, for example, in the 1611 translation of the Bible, the last sentence is given as "for it is better to marry than burn," which is often quoted to support the concept of Christian marriage.

Later in this same passage, Paul wrote, regarding virgins, that it is better to not marry. But if a virgin does so, she has not sinned, although he cautions against marriage:

The unmarried man is anxious about the affairs of the Lord, how to please the Lord; but the married man is anxious about worldly affairs, how to please his wife, and his interests are divided. And the unmarried woman or girl is anxious about the affairs of the Lord, how to be holy in body and spirit; but the married woman is anxious about worldly affairs, how to please her husband. (1 Cor. 7.32–34)

This taught that the ideal path to salvation and purity was through celibacy and virginity; but St. Augustine came to the conclusion that marriage, with its carnal implications, was not actually sinful. And the early church had great debates about Mary and whether her hymen had actually been broken since it was important to Christianity that she be in a state of purity. However, the founding fathers of the Christian church, taking the writings of Paul as their cue, considered that followers of Christ's teaching should, therefore, eschew families and marriage, and opt for a celibate life. But his writings also dealt with marriage and the woman's place in the marriage:

Wives, be subject to your husbands, as to the Lord. For the husband is the head of the wife as Christ is the head of the church, his body, and is himself its Savior. As the church is subject to Christ, so let wives also be subject in everything to their husbands. Husbands, love your wives, as Christ loved the church and gave himself up for her. . . . Even so husbands should love their wives as their own bodies. He who loves his wife loves himself. . . . "For this reason a man shall leave his father and mother and be joined to his wife, and the two shall become one flesh." This mystery is a profound one, and I am saying that it refers to Christ and the church; however, let each one of you love his wife as himself, and let the wife see that she respects her husband. (Eph. 5.22–33)

Paul's writings have governed the church's views of marriage and married relations even to the present day and are still evident in the Christian marriage service. But it is obvious that Paul considered marriage to be second best as a lifestyle choice. This made the church's position regarding marriage difficult to reconcile in later years. However, Paul's phrase "it is better to marry than burn" gave enough justification for marriage, even though St. Augustine struggled personally to justify marriage intellectually. The contemporary Church of England marriage service still uses Christ's attendance at the marriage at Cana as evidence that marriage is a state endorsed by God. Over the years, the church has developed various orthodoxies and sought to exert control over marriage and other issues of kinship. Not surprisingly various groups have developed in Europe that were considered to be heretical in their views—such as the heresies propagated between 1020 and 1030 by the Cathars in southern France and northern Italy, who denied that salvation could be obtained through marriage or sexual generation (citing the teachings of Paul and linked with the denial of Mary being anything other than a virgin). The clerks of Orleans and the laity of Arras also rejected the rules of marriage imposed by the Christian authorities, including rules of consanguinity, kinship relationships, and rules that imposed marriage prohibitions; these "heretics" were consequently condemned as promoting debauchery and incest.

As Goody argued (1983), Christian philosophy regarding marriage, apart from avoiding what would be viewed as fornication as defined by Paul, was governed to some extent by the control it could have over society, inheritance, and governance. By the thirteenth century, the church had managed to establish and control the principles of marriage law for monogamous, indissoluble relationships, had outlawed incest, had denied property rights to bastards, and had prescribed punishment for adultery and fornication. However, the wedding did not become a sacrament of the church until the fifteenth century; and only after the Reformation, in 1563, did the Roman Catholic church insist upon the presence of a priest for a binding and valid marriage. During the sixteenth century, weddings came to be permitted to take place within the church. Before this, weddings would take place at the church porch, perhaps followed by a communion and blessing service in the church.

During the sixteenth and seventeenth centuries, the power of the church in society increased so that the clergy and many of the population considered that a church wedding was a crucial ceremony for a valid marriage, although in civil law a promise or exchange of vows before witnesses was considered as equally valid. And, although consummation of the marriage was, and still is, considered a key part of the act of marrying, this became enshrined in law in 1540 in a statute from Henry VIII so that he could legalize his marriage to Catherine Howard (the first cousin of his second wife—prohibited under the church rules of consanguinity), which stated that, after consummation, a marriage could not be annulled by reason of precontract or affinity, apart from those laid out in "the Law of God." The philosophy of Christian authorities and church leaders has changed since the times of Christ and his disciples from the view that marriage was the second-best option for the Christian, to pragmatic acceptance, to the realization that by imposing their ideals and rules, the church authorities were able to keep some control over society. Today marriage is seen as the cornerstone of civilized society.

See also Consanguinity

References
Cameron, Averil. 1994. "Early Christianity and the Discourse of Female Desire." In *Women in Ancient Societies,* edited by Léonie J. Archer, Susan Fischler, and Maria Wyke. London: Macmillan.
Goody, Jack. 1983. *The Development of the Family and Marriage in Europe.* Cambridge: Cambridge University Press.
Stone, Lawrence. 1990. *The Family, Sex, and Marriage in England, 1500–1800.* Abridged and revised ed. London: Penguin.

Church Porch, Weddings in

There is a saying, "Happy the bride that the sun shines on, woe to the bride that the rain rains on." The age of this saying is unknown, but Robert Herrick, in his *Hesperides* (1648), wrote: "Your praise, and bless you, sprinkling you with wheat; / While that other do divine, / Blest is the bride on whom the sun doth shine." The phrase may have come from the practice in which couples were married in the church porch, thus outside the church, only entering the church for a blessing from the clergy. This practice is alluded to in "The Wife of Bath's Tale" in Chaucer's *Canterbury Tales:* "She was a worthy woman all her live, / Husbands at the church-dore she had five." The practice of marrying in the church porch extended across all sectors of society. Henry III of England (1216–1272) married Eleanor of Provence on 14 February 1236 in the porch of Canterbury Cathedral. It was not until the reign of Edward VI (1547–1553) in England, and later in Europe (Charles I of England, 1600–1649, married Henrietta Maria, daughter of Henry IV of France, by proxy at the door of Notre Dame Cathedral), that weddings were allowed to take place within the church. In the early church, celibacy was considered the ideal, but recognizing that this would lead to the demise of the Christian community, the church fathers (such as Paul) reluctantly allowed marriage. Marriage did not have the status of a sacrament until 1439, when it came to be included in the *Book of Common Prayer*. It was only in 1563, after the Reformation, that the Catholic Church required a priest to be present for a marriage to be valid and binding.

The *Sarum Missal* (the book of words for services produced by the Sarum/Salisbury Cathedral) directed the procedure for ceremony in the church porch: The priest stood before the church door and published the banns thrice. The woman was given by her father, or by friends, with her hand uncovered (if she was a widow the hand would be covered). The man says: "I [name], take thee [name], to my wedded wife, to have and to hold from this day forward, for better for worse, for richer for poorer, in sickness and in health, till death us depart, if holy Church will it ordain, and thereto I plight thee my troth." The woman made a similar vow but with a slight change in wording, "to be boner and buxom in bed and at board till death us depart." The man then gave the priest the ring, which was blessed and sprinkled with holy water and returned to him to put on three fingers and the thumb, repeating at each digit, "In the name of the Father, Son and Holy ghost. Amen." After some prayers, the party then went into the church to the altar steps where the priest recited more prayers.

However, marriage was seen as a secular arrangement, with financial and other settlements being negotiated between the families, so that on betrothal and final marriage, for example, a promise of the dowry, and the confirmation of the dowry, in public, was an essential part of the wedding. This usually took place in the church porch, which in many communities was a very public place and the local meeting center, a place where public announcements and transactions took place. Transactions that occurred in the porch were many and varied and included payment of rents and of bequests. For example, the will of a seventeenth-century yeoman, William Falckward, of Winston, Suffolk, read: "I bequeath to my sonne, Sill Reve, with Elizabeth, his wife, one shilling to be paid to him or his wife, at the church porch of Winston by my executrix. Proved, 18 Oct. 1684." Edward VI's proclamations, allowing weddings in church, began the period when the established church began to take control of marriage.

See also Christian Weddings; Dowry

References
Dyer, T. F. Thiselton. 1891. *Church-Lore Gleanings.* London: A. D. Innes.
Jeaffreson, John Cordy. 1872. *Brides and Bridals.* 2 vols. London: Hurst and Blackett.
Monsarrat, Ann. 1973. *And the Bride Wore . . . : The Story of the White Wedding.* London: Gentry.
Pound, N. J. G. 1994. *The Culture of the English People: Iron Age to the Industrial Revolution.* Cambridge: Cambridge University Press.

Civil Ceremonies

Strictly speaking, a wedding is a civil contract between the two people getting married, or in some societies, between the two families involved. It is not therefore necessary to be married in a church for the marriage to be recognized as legal, although some churches may have a problem with recognizing and accepting a wedding conducted by a qualified and empowered registrar. It was not until the reign of Edward VI in England, and later in Europe, that weddings were allowed to take place within the church. Before this time a wedding would take place in a public place, usually at the church porch, maybe followed by a blessing in the church. The priest, as an official of the prevailing authority, perhaps oversaw and witnessed the exchange of vows. Moving the wedding into the church combined the exchange of vows with the blessing of the marriage and a communion service, and the marriage became a sacrament of the church. Martin Luther (1483–1546, an Augustinian friar and leader of the Reformation in Germany) believed that marriage should be a civil event and not regulated by the church. But this view was not accepted by the legislators of the Protestant church, and in 1563 the Council of Trent declared marriage an essentially religious ceremony.

In 1653, the English Parliament (a Puritan government after the English Civil War) declared that all marriages should be civil and were not valid unless performed before a justice of the peace. All couples wishing to validate their marriages had first to go to the proper parochial registrar, who took the couple's names and address, and if they were under twenty-one, the names of their parents, guardians, or overseers. The registrar was required to publish the banns of marriage either in the church or chapel in the parishes of each on three "Lord's Days," in succession, after the morning service, or at the marketplace on three successive market days between the hours of eleven in the morning and two in the afternoon. The registrar could then issue a certificate, which the couple would take to a justice of the peace, who would complete the marriage by having the couple join hands and repeat the vows.

After the Restoration of the monarchy, the authorities allowed church marriages again. However, because there were many examples of clandestine and fraudulent marriages, Lord Hardwick's Marriage Act was enacted in 1753, taking effect after 25 March 1754. The act required that marriage should be solemnized with the publication of banns or with a license, and that a wedding should be solemnized in the parochial church or chapel where the "banns of matrimony had been usually published." Any clergyman who solemnized a marriage without banns or license or in any other place than a church or public chapel where the banns should be published would, on conviction, "be deemed and adjudged to be guilty of felony, and should be transported to some of His Majesty's plantations in America for the

space of fourteen years." This act did not apply in Scotland and was directly responsible for the rise of the wedding trade at Gretna Green. The act, however, discriminated against Catholics and nonconformists other than Quakers and Jews:

> Provided likewise that nothing in this Act
> shall extend to the part of Great Britain
> called Scotland, nor to any marriages among
> the people called Quakers, or among the
> persons professing the Jewish religion, where
> both the parties to any such marriage shall be
> of the people called Quakers, or persons
> professing the Jewish religion respectively,
> nor to any marriage solemnized beyond the
> seas. (Jeaffreson 1872, 2: 189)

This meant that Catholics and other nonconformists had to solemnize their marriages in a Protestant church for the marriage to be legal, making marriage more of a religious event than a civil arrangement as before. This remained the case until the new Marriage Act of 1836, which introduced civil registrars and removed the requirement for Catholics to be married at an Anglican ceremony. Legally, weddings continued to be regarded as civil contracts, but, as Jeaffreson wrote (1872, 1: 45), the authorities were happy to allow and encourage couples to view the event as a high ceremonial occasion:

> There are those amongst us who, in
> harmony with catholic teaching, declare
> marriage to be a sacrament whilst others
> maintain that it is a mere civil contract.
> The law of the land, without undervaluing
> the ecclesiastical sanctions of wedlock,
> takes the latter, whilst the sentiment of the
> majority of religious persons is in the
> direction of the former view. In dealing
> with the rights of married persons, in so far
> as wedlock affects them, the law regards
> marriage as a civil agreement; but it
> concurs with popular feeling in
> encouraging our brides to think that
> marriage should be beautified and hallowed
> with religious observance. Prevailing
> opinion may be said to hold that, though

matrimony may be *lawful,* it can scarcely be called *holy* unless it has received the sanction of spiritual authority.

The role of the church from 1754 on became very important, so that, despite the relaxation of the marriage laws less than a hundred years later, by the end of the nineteenth century, registry office or civic weddings were mainly used by runaway couples or by pregnant brides because they were seen as affording privacy. This view, of the civic ceremony being private, continued well into the twentieth century, despite the fact that the law said that the doors of the wedding venue must be kept open or unlocked. Marriage as a civil ceremony was first introduced in France after the French Revolution in 1791; gradually more and more countries declared marriage to be a civil arrangement. After the Russian revolution (1917), authorities in Russia tried to suppress the old values and beliefs, and, with some similarities to the Commonwealth Period in Great Britain (for example, in the 1920s the use of the wedding ring was discontinued), weddings were performed at a civic registration ceremony. (After the death of Stalin, dissent began to emerge, and brides would wear white wedding dresses as a form of dissident activity.) In Germany, a wedding must be conducted at a registry office by an appointed official, who should not be a priest. Consequently, couples often have two weddings—the civic ceremony, followed by a church ceremony on the following day. In Sweden, a marriage is first and foremost a civil event, so that a couple wishing to marry have to apply to the parish authorities, who will issue a certificate showing that there is nothing to prevent the marriage (the *hindersprövning*), after which they may opt for a Church of Sweden wedding or may apply to the district court where a registrar will follow a form of service, with vows exchanged and a marriage license issued.

See also Ceremony; Church Porch, Weddings in; Commonwealth Period; Gretna Green

References

Gillis, John R. 1985. *For Better, For Worse: British Marriages, 1600 to the Present.* Oxford: Oxford University Press.

Herrick, Robert. 1961. *Selected Poems.* Edited by John Hayward. Harmondsworth, Middlesex: Penguin.

Jeaffreson, John Cordy. 1872. *Brides and Bridals.* 2 vols. London: Hurst and Blackett.

Macfarlane, Alan. 1986. *Marriage and Love in England, 1300–1840.* Oxford: Basil Blackwell.

Monsarrat, Ann. 1973. *And the Bride Wore . . . : The Story of the White Wedding.* London: Gentry.

Murphy, Brian M. 1978. *The World of Weddings: An Illustrated Celebration.* London: Paddington.

Westermarck, Edward. 1894. *The History of Human Marriage.* 2d ed. London: Macmillan.

Colors

White is traditionally worn by the groom at a Buddhist wedding, and the Japanese wear white at commencement ceremonies (ceremonies to mark a beginning). As a marriage marks the beginning of a new family unit, the beginning of a new life for the couple, so a Japanese bride in traditional costume will wear white beneath a robe of red and gold—the colors of festivals and rejoicing. The wedding color for the Russian Orthodox church is white. This took on an added significance after the death of Stalin in 1953 when brides would wear a white dress as a form of dissent. White—new, clean—is associated with renewal and a new start, a commencement. It is often taken as symbolic of purity. In Western societies, from about the middle of the eighteenth century, white became the symbol of virginity. White as a wedding color was well established in the eighteenth century, when white favors were worn at weddings and white gloves were given to guests. Colors in weddings have been ascribed symbolic significance, which has been put into verse and often quoted:

Married in white, you have chosen all right;
Married in gray, you will go far away;
Married in black, you will wish yourself back;
Married in red, you'd better be dead;

Married in green ashamed to be seen;
Married in blue, you'll always be true;
Married in pearl, you'll live in a whirl;
Married in yellow, ashamed of the fellow;
Married in brown, you'll live out of town;
Married in pink, your spirits will sink.
(Polson 1926, 13)

Another shorter version of this rhyme from Oxfordshire is very similar:

Married in black, you'll wish yourself back;
Married in Green, not fit to be seen;
Married in Brown, you'll never live in a
     town.

It is, however, possible that these rhymes and color symbolisms are more a product of the etiquette books and fancy than of any strong folk traditions. A wedding etiquette book (Woodman 1949), after quoting a rhyme similar to the one from Polson, goes on to say:

The following colour interpretations are calculated to be more correct, and for several centuries they have been accepted as faithful portents—more or less—of the future.
     White is a symbol of purity and of high virtues. Green typifies youth, hope and happiness. Red is a sign of vigour, courage and great passion. . . . Violet denotes dignity, pride and a condition of high ideals.

The line "Married in Brown, you'll never live in a town" suggested a late-eighteenth- or nineteenth-century origin for this color symbolism. In many nineteenth-century English novels, town manners were considered superior to country manners, and country people were considered coarse and unsophisticated. Moving from the country to the town was seen as a step up the social and economic ladder.

Of the other colors mentioned, black and red are colors of mourning. Black would presage the early death of one of the couple. There are strong traditions that try to ensure the separation between marriage and death and prevent a wedding party from meeting a funeral party. But condemned prisoners to be hanged at Tyburn Hill, London, during the eighteenth century, often treated their hanging as a form of wedding, with observers sometimes noting that the prisoner was dressed in white or in the manner of a bridegroom.

Some believe that red is the color of fire and consequently the color of the devil. However, Bengali wedding colors are red and yellow. During the American Revolution, brides in the United States wore red outfits as a sign of revolution (in some etiquette books, red is a sign of vigor, courage, and passion). But there is also a tradition that says that red is an unlucky color for love, and it was considered unlucky to write a love letter in red ink. Red flowers and red hair were considered unlucky. Red cars are supposed to be lucky, and red thread was often used as an amulet against the evil eye or bad luck.

Green is often considered an unlucky color. Traditionally associated with fairies, it was considered unlucky to wear green, at least in Scotland and some other parts of the United Kingdom. Henderson (1866) wrote: "Green, ever an ominous colour in the lowlands of Scotland, must on no account be worn there at a wedding. . . . In fact nothing green must make its appearance that day; Kale and all other green vegetables are excluded from the wedding dinner." As the chosen color of the fairies, mortals wearing green would be unlucky, or even destroyed, for the insult of wearing the fairies' color. Bloom (1929) interpreted green as being the color of promiscuity (and fairy women were often considered promiscuous). In the midlands of England, green was also considered symbolic of being forsaken: "Green and white / Forsaken quite." In some areas, there was a tradition for an unmarried older sister to dance in a pig's trough, sometimes wearing green stockings or a green garter, at the wedding of her younger sister. However this taboo came into being and however widely observed the taboo was, the superstitious belief that green is an unlucky color is well known today. Cunnington and Lucas (1972) quoted a mid-fifteenth-century description of a bridal couple who managed to combine two unlucky colors: "Sir William was clad in a garment of green checkery and Joan (his bride) one of a red colour."

The color blue was considered unlucky in some areas of England (such as in Yorkshire and the Isle of Wight), despite the injunction that a bride should wear "something old, something new; something borrowed, something blue." In the Polson rhyme, the wearer will be "true." It is possible that since the color was associated with the Virgin Mary it carried associations with desired properties of virtue and constancy. It may also have had connotations of popery, and thus would have been prohibited.

See also Dancing in a Hog (Pig) Trough; Dress, Wedding

References

Bloom, J. Harvey. [1929] 1977. *Folk Lore, Old Customs, and Superstitions in Shakespeare Land.* London: Mitchell, Hughes, and Clarke. Norwood, PA: Norwood Editions.

Cunnington, Phillis, and Catherine Lucas. 1972. *Costume for Birth, Marriage, and Death.* London: Adam and Charles Black.

Henderson, William. 1866. *Notes on the Folklore of the Northern Counties of England and the Borders.* London: Longmans, Green.

Monger, George. 1991. "Colour in Marriage." In *Colour and Appearance in Folkore,* edited by John Hutchings and Juliette Wood. London: Folklore Society.

Polson, Alexander. 1926. *Our Highland Folklore Heritage.* Dingwall, Inverness: G. Souter (*Northern Chronicle* office).

Woodman, Mary. 1949. *Wedding Etiquette.* London: W. Foulsham.

Common-Law Marriage

A common-law partnership, in Great Britain, involves a couple cohabiting as a married couple without a recognized civil or religious ceremony. During the twentieth century, such a couple would sometimes be described as "living in sin." Lord Hardwick's Marriage Act of 1754 aimed to prevent clandestine and irregular marriages, some of which would

have been considered common-law marriages, and made these unions more difficult. Perhaps due to the great difficulty involved in legally ending a marriage through divorce and in being remarried in church, the concept continued by popular custom among the poorer classes. It was only really in the nineteenth and twentieth centuries that the practice attracted wide disapproval.

There are many types of irregular, trial, or temporary marriages, especially among itinerant populations, such as canal and railway workers, fruit and vegetable sellers (costermongers), and others in the poor laboring classes. Even into the twentieth century, there were churches in London and Manchester where mass weddings were held so that unions could be "regularized," according to the mores of the state and the upper and middle classes, and to offer a low-priced marriage service for the poor who might not have been able to afford a "proper" wedding. Mayhew (1861–1862) wrote:

Only one-tenth—at the outside one-tenth—of the couples living together and carrying on the costermongering trade, are married. In Clerkenwell parish, however, where the number of married couples is about a fifth of the whole, this difference is easily accounted for, as in Advent and Easter the incumbent of that parish marries poor couples without a fee. Of the rights of "legitimate" or "illegitimate" children the costermongers understand nothing, and account it a mere waste of money and time to go through the ceremony of wedlock when a pair can live together, and be quite well regarded by their fellows without it. (Quennell 1951, 53)

Common-law marriages were not registered in official documents, but their existence can sometimes be deduced if there is a mismatch between marriage and death records and baptism records, as Leslie Bradley found in his researches into the parish records of Eyam, Derbyshire, in the decades 1641 to 1660, where the incumbent of the church appears to have been prepared to baptize the children resulting from such common-law unions (Drake 1982, 112). However, contrary to common belief, English law does not recognize or acknowledge the status of a common-law wife or husband, and a cohabiting partner has no rights in law if the partnership ends. In 2004 there is still a common belief that a couple living together for at least seven years would thereafter have the legal status of "husband and wife." (Some believe that the time period is shorter.) If one of the couple dies, the other is not recognized as "next of kin" by law, regardless of how long the couple had been together, and if the couple separate, there is no automatic property division nor any rights for maintenance payments.

The situation is more complicated in the United States where the concept of common-law marriage is more accepted. Eleven states recognize and accept the validity of a common-law marriage. And the U.S. Constitution requires all states to recognize as valid a common-law marriage that is accepted as a valid marriage in other states. The situation of acceptance varies from state to state, but generally the couple must live together, they must present themselves as a married couple (such as using the same last name and filing a joint tax return), they must have been together for a significant period of time, and must have an intention to be married. If the partner can prove that the partnership is a common-law marriage, there are inheritance, property, and next-of-kin rights. On the other hand, if the partnership breaks down, the couple have to go through divorce procedures, possibly involving complex separation arrangements and court proceedings.

See also Besom Weddings; Broom, Marriage over the; Handfasting; Mass Weddings; Wife-Swapping

References

Drake, Michael, ed. 1982. *Population Studies from Parish Registers.* Matlock Derbyshire: Local Population Studies.

Gillis, John R. 1985. *For Better, For Worse: British Marriages, 1600 to the Present.* Oxford: Oxford University Press.

Leiter, Richard A., ed. 2003. *National Survey of State Laws.* 4th ed. Detroit: Thomson Gale.

Mayhew, Henry. 1861–1862. *London Labour and the London Poor.* London: Griffin, Bohn, and Company.

Quennell, Peter, ed. 1951. *Mayhew's London: Being Selections from "London Labour and London Poor."* London: Spring Books.

Commonwealth Period

The Puritan parliamentarians who ruled Britain after the English Civil War (1642–1649) and during the English Commonwealth Period (1649–1660) are often portrayed as humorless and colorless, banning maypoles and traditional pastimes and generally being killjoys. It is commonly said that they banned marriage in churches using the *Book of Common Prayer* and the wedding ring. To some extent this is true, but there is also a lot of misunderstanding behind this perception. To understand why they discouraged church weddings and the associated paraphernalia, it is necessary to understand some of the background to the parliamentarian view of marriage and the church.

The philosophy of government of the parliamentarians was a mixture of nonconformist views, ideas of the equality of people, and twentieth-century ideals such as the sharing of labor and partnership in marriage. In the parliamentarian view, adultery was not a sin (and a 1650 act against adultery was not enforced) and marriage should be for love and not for money or for sealing alliances or deals between families. The established church, by the 1640s, had taken control of marriage and acted as a moral enforcer. It was not until the sixteenth century that marriages were allowed to take place inside the church. Before that time, the betrothal vows and later the wedding vows (which basically confirmed the betrothal vows) were taken in public in the church porch led by the priest as a witness to the vows. It was after the vows that the couple would enter the church for a mass or blessing. The church made money from fines imposed upon people for marrying without a license, and, as the average cost of the license was around 10 shillings (representing about twelve days of wages for the average seventeenth-century agricultural laborer), licenses were a form of status symbol for the middle and upper classes and may have led the poor to despise church marriage.

The nonconformists saw the established church as taking advantage of its authority and disagreed with some of the church views on, for example, the role and status of women, especially within marriage, where women were accorded a subservient status to men. Nonconformists wanted to restore marriage to its original status of being a civil contract between two people. They were also opposed to the outward symbols and manifestations of this subservient role. The banning of the use of the wedding ring reflected their disapproval of a "heathenish" symbol. They saw the ring as a shackle, a view imperfectly expressed in Samuel Butler's poem "Hudibras" (1663):

> Others were for abolishing
> That tool of matrimony, a Ring,
> With which th' unsanctified Bridegroom
> Is married only to a thumb
> (As wise as ringing of a pig
> That used to break up ground and dig)
> The bride has nothing but her will,
> That nulls the after marriage still.

In 1653, Parliament declared that all marriages should be civil and would not be valid unless performed before a justice of the peace. All couples had to first go to the proper parochial registrar who took the couple's names and address and, if they were under twenty-one, the names of their parents, guardians, or overseers. The registrar was required to publish the banns of marriage either in the church or chapel in the parish of each of the intended on three "Lord's Days," in succession after the morning service, or at the marketplace on three successive market days between the hours of eleven in the morning and two in the afternoon. The registrar could then issue a certificate that they would take to a justice of the peace, who would complete the marriage, the couple joining hands and repeating the vows: "I [name], do here in the presence of God, the searcher of all hearts, take thee, [name], for my wedded wife; and do also, in the presence of witnesses, promise to be to thee a loving and faithful husband." The bride responds: "I, [name], do here in the presence of God, the searcher of all hearts, take thee, [name], for my wedded husband; and do also, in the presence of God, and before these witnesses, promise to be to thee a loving, faithful and obedient wife."

The Parliament did not try to prevent couples from also having a church wedding, either after or before the civil wedding, and instructions for the solemnization of marriages were contained in the *Directory of Public Worship.* The minister led a prayer, made a declaration about the role of marriage, and then asked the couple to join hands and repeat the vows (no rings were exchanged). The *Directory of Public Worship* instructs:

> After solemn charging of the persons to be married, before the great God, who searcheth all hearts, and to whom they must give strict account at the last day, that if either of them know any cause, by precontract or otherwise, why they may not lawfully proceed to marriage, that they now discover it; the minister (if no impediment be acknowledged) shall cause, first, the man to take the woman by the right hand, saying the words: "I, *M,* doe take thee *N.,* to be my married wife, and doe in the presence of God, and before this congregation, promise and covenant to be a loving and faithful husband unto thee, untill God separate us by death." Then the woman shall take the man by the right hand, and say these words: "I, *N.,* doe take thee, *M.,* to be my married husband, and I doe, in the presence of God, and before this congregation, promise and covenant to be a loving, faithful and obedient wife unto thee, untill God shall separate us by death." Then without any further

ceremony, the minister shall, in the face of the congregation, pronounce them to be husband and wife, according to God's ordinance; and so conclude the action with prayer to this effect. (Jeaffreson 1872, 2: 70n)

The marriage act of the first Parliament of this period (the Barebones Assembly) was ratified by the next assembly (the Protectors Parliament) in 1656, with the law slightly softened by the exclusion of the clause from the wording of the previous act, "that no other marriage whatsoever within the Commonwealth of England shall be held or accounted a legal marriage." Many couples at this time preferred to be married twice, once by the magistrate and once by the minister, to ensure that they were legally and properly married. There were also cases where rings were exchanged and the service from the *Book of Common Prayer* was used—just to be sure. One famous case was that of Stephen Marshall, Presbyterian minister of Finchingfield, Essex, who performed the marriage service of one of his daughters using the *Book of Common Prayer* and a ring, because he did not want her returned to him for want of a legal marriage. This may have also been the motive behind an entry in the parish records of St. Mary's Church, North Stifford, Essex, England: "1658: 'Octobr ye 28 were married Grace Heath and Thomas Ffish, strangers both, by Mr. John Stone, Ministr of Greyse, ye banns not published.'" The couple involved may have wanted to ensure that their marriage was proper in the eyes of God but may have gone to another parish so as not to draw the attention of the authorities where they lived.

Upon the Restoration of the monarchy in 1660, parliamentary marriage was abolished and justices of the peace were relieved of their matrimonial duties, thus returning marriage ceremonial to the pre-Commonwealth form; however, although marriages during this period were perfectly valid, to make a political point and to consolidate their authority, the returning authorities quickly passed legislation to declare the validity "of all marriages by justices of the peace since 1st May 1642, or marriages performed according to the direction or true intent of any Act or Ordinance, or reputed Act or Ordinance, of one or both Houses of Parliament, or of any Convention sitting at Westminster, under the name, style or title of a Parliament."

See also Betrothal; Christian Weddings; Spousal
References
Hill, Christopher. 1985. *The World Turned Upside Down: Radical Ideas during the English Revolution.* Harmondsworth, Middlesex: Penguin.
Jeaffreson, John Cordy. 1872. *Brides and Bridals.* 2 vols. London: Hurst and Blackett.

Concubine

A concubine is a woman who cohabits with a man and is not his legal wife; in polygynous societies, a concubine may be a woman who is part of a man's household and a sexual partner, but not a legal wife. King Solomon in the Bible was said to have had "seven hundred wives, princesses, and three hundred concubines" (1 Kings 11.3). The *Oxford English Dictionary* suggests that a concubine may be a secondary wife; however this is a Eurocentric view, since a secondary wife in polygynous societies may be properly married to the man, according to the customs of that society. However, secondary wives were often of a lower class than the husband and were of a lower standing in the household than the first wife, who had authority over them.

Most commonly, a concubine is considered to be a regular consort of a man, but in early days there was little difference between a wife and a concubine; among the ancient Hebrews, a concubine who lived in a man's house continuously for three years would become his wife. Among the ancient Romans, concubines were the companions of the priests. In China, a man was almost expected to have a concubine as part of the household. By law, a Chinese man was not allowed to take a second wife during the lifetime of the first wife, so there was a form of legalized concubinage practiced. Again, the wife had power and authority over the concubines—

they had to request her permission to sit with her, and she could refer to her marriage partner with the term that corresponded to the word "husband," but the concubines referred to him as "master."

In the account of his travels, Marco Polo wrote of the king of the Tartars, a man named Kublai, who ruled during the latter part of the thirteenth century, that "he has four ladies, who always rank as his wives. . . . He maintains also a number of concubines." Westermarck (1894, 445) wrote that "among the Ainos, Mongols, and Tangutans, one man can take only one lawful wife, though as many concubines as he pleases." Concubinage, in an official and sanctioned sense, is often associated with Middle Eastern and Far Eastern cultures—indeed it appears to have been common in cultures where the practice was/is for arranged marriages or for marrying very young—but in England and other parts of Europe, it was common and an accepted part of life up to the eleventh century. Lady Montague, visiting Vienna in 1739, noted that it was the established custom for a lady to have two husbands, one whose name she bore and another to "perform the duties." However, although the concept of concubinage was frowned upon in European culture, adultery was an accepted norm (unless it became too obvious or appeared to be offending the mores of the community).

See also Adultery; Open Marriage; Polygyny
References
Macfarlane, Alan. 1986. *Marriage and Love in England, 1300–1840.* Oxford: Basil Blackwell.
Scott, George Ryley. 1953. *Curious Customs of Sex and Marriage.* London: Torchstream.
Stone, Lawrence. 1990. *The Family, Sex, and Marriage in England, 1500–1800.* Abridged and revised ed. London: Penguin.
Westermarck, Edward. 1894. *The History of Human Marriage.* 2d ed. London: Macmillan.

Confetti

Confetti has been intimately associated with weddings, but paper confetti is a relative newcomer. Confetti was scattered at weddings in France in the late nineteenth century. By the 1890s, it was gaining popularity in England and replacing rice, which itself had been introduced only a few years earlier, replacing wheat. By the beginning of the twentieth century, the use of paper confetti was firmly established in England (although it remains unpopular with those who have the job of cleaning up after the wedding). Originally, confetti consisted of small bonbons (sweets) or paper or plaster imitations thrown during carnivals in Italy. Over the years, confetti evolved to be paper discs scattered over the couple and then the lucky charm or rose petal–shaped colored paper that is used today.

In 1909, a patent application was lodged with the Patent Office in London for a device for holding and scattering "Luck or Love-charms, Tokens or the like." The patent application began: "The object of this invention is to provide a combination of luck or love charms or tokens, amulets, and such like, particularly in combination with a cornucopia or horn-of-plenty with Cupid embellishments, mainly for use at weddings, or other functions or events." This product, if it was ever produced, must not have proved popular, since there are no known examples surviving.

The custom of scattering confetti over the couple is usually considered to have developed from customs of scattering wheat or rice over the couple—with the obvious symbolism of good luck and fertility. Additionally, there were also traditions, among the landed classes, for rose petals and flowers to be scattered in the path of the bride and groom as they left the church. It would appear that the scattering of confetti in England brought together these two separate practices.

See also Almonds; Flowers; India; Rice; Tokens
References
Monserrat, Ann. 1973. *And the Bride Wore . . . : The Story of the White Wedding.* London: Gentry.
Patent Office. 1909. Application 6339. London.

Consanguinity

Most societies that do not practice strict rules of exogamy have rules of consanguinity that prevent couples from the same bloodline from marrying, ensuring that couples do not commit incest. In many cases, these rules were originally designed by religious authorities but have been subsumed, by virtue of being established by a moral authority, within general morality and law. Rules of consanguinity in the Protestant and Catholic churches are based upon the rules laid down in the Bible in Leviticus (18.6–18):

> The nakedness of thy father, or the nakedness of thy mother, shalt thou not uncover: she is thy mother; thou shalt not uncover her nakedness. The nakedness of thy father's wife shalt thou not uncover: it is thy father's nakedness. The nakedness of thy sister, the daughter of thy father, or daughter of thy mother, whether she be born at home, or abroad, even their nakedness thou shalt not uncover. The nakedness of thy son's daughter, or of thy daughter's daughter, even their nakedness thou shalt not uncover: for theirs is thine own nakedness. The nakedness of thy father's wife's daughter, begotten of thy father, she is thy sister, thou shalt not uncover her nakedness. Thou shalt not uncover the nakedness of thy father's sister: she is thy father's near kinswoman. Thou shalt not uncover the nakedness of thy mother's sister: for she is thy mother's near kinswoman. Thou shalt not uncover the nakedness of thy father's brother, thou shalt not approach to his wife: she is thine aunt. Thou shalt not uncover the nakedness of thy daughter in law: she is thy son's wife; thou shalt not uncover her nakedness. Thou shalt not uncover the nakedness of thy brother's wife: it is thy brother's nakedness. Thou shalt not uncover the nakedness of a woman and her daughter, neither shalt thou take her son's daughter, or her daughter's daughter, to uncover her nakedness; for they are her near kinswomen: it is wickedness. Neither shalt thou take a wife to her sister, to vex her, to uncover her nakedness, beside the other in her life time.

The "Table of Kindred and Affinity" in the *Book of Common Prayer* listed thirty "relations" that a man or woman were forbidden to marry. This list was first published in 1560 when the church authorities were becoming increasingly concerned that incestuous unions were taking place. This list of forbidden degrees of marriage became enshrined in English law in 1835. The Puritans of New England, however, considered the English to be lax regarding prohibited degrees of marriage, and in 1680, with the leadership of Increase Mather, a law against incestuous marriages was passed that forbade marriage to the wife's sister or niece. This act remained in force until 1785. The southern states of the United States followed the rules of the Church of England, and thus first-cousin marriage was acceptable.

In 1907 it became lawful in Britain for a man to marry his deceased wife's sister, although the *Book of Common Prayer* in the 1950s continued to include "wife's sister," as above, in the list of relatives a man is forbidden to marry. However, this had long been a controversial prohibition, since, according to a passage in the Old Testament of the Bible, in Deuteronomy (25. 4–10), a man was duty-bound to marry his brother's widow if the brother died without fathering any children. It was the man's duty to father a child with the woman to carry on the brother's name. If he were to reject her he would be publicly shamed:

> Then shall his brother's wife come unto him in the presence of the elders, and loose his shoe from off his foot, and spit in his face, and shall answer and say, So shall it be done unto that man that will not build up his brother's house. And his name shall be called in Israel, The house of him that hath his shoe loosed.

Today, in Jewish tradition, a man is under less of an obligation and can forego this right and obligation. However, some men have taken advantage of this and forfeited their right on receipt of a cash payment from the widow. In the Muslim tradition, similar rules of consanguinity apply. The Koran (4.23) states:

> You are forbidden to take in marriage your mothers, your daughters, your sisters, your paternal and maternal aunts, the daughters of your brothers and sisters, your foster-mothers, your foster sisters, the mothers of your wives, your step-daughters who are in your charge, born of the wives with whom you have lain (it is no offence for you to marry your step-daughters if you have not consummated your marriage with their mothers), and the wives of your own begotten sons. Henceforth you are forbidden to take in marriage two sisters at one and the same time. Allah is forgiving and merciful.

In the Institutes of Vishnu (Vishnu is one of the two major gods in Hinduism and is the protector and preserver of the world and the restorer of the moral order), "sexual connection with one's mother, or daughter, or daughter-in-law, are crimes in the highest degree" (Westermarck 1894, 310).

Christianity built upon the biblical prohibitions and the Saxon prohibitions that forbade marriage between first cousins. In the eleventh century, marriage between second cousins was forbidden, and, later, third cousins were forbidden to marry. The Fourth Lateran Council in 1215 set the prohibitions quite wide—to the fourth degree by canonical computation so that a man could not marry his, or his wife's, fourth cousin, or any nearer relative. However, the church leaders widened further the prohibitions to include spiritual consanguinity, so that they prohibited marriage between a woman and her godfather or a man and his godmother (a form of spiritual incest). A man and a woman who had stood as godparents to the same child were forbidden to marry because they had contracted a spiritual marriage, a contract deemed incompatible with bodily marriage. A person was forbidden to marry his or her child's godparent because of the spiritual intermarriage between the spiritual parent and natural parent. A man and woman having common godparents were also forbidden to marry, because they were deemed to be spiritual siblings and marriage would be considered an incestuous union. Some ecclesiasticals extended areas of consanguinity to those who touched a child at baptism or even accidentally brushed against the robe of a newly baptized infant. However, it was possible to obtain dispensation to marry a person deemed to be in the prohibited line by paying a fee to the church.

In 1540 the lines of prohibited kinship were narrowed so that marriage was allowed with all but close family, which included aunts, uncles, nephews, and nieces. First-cousin marriage became legal, but was often subject to disapproval. Prohibition, however, extended to the spouse's family, because on marriage a couple was deemed to become of "one blood." Consequently, a man could not marry his wife's aunt, should the opportunity arise, even though they were not blood relatives. These prohibitions continued after a spouse's death. For example, a man could not marry his deceased wife's sister. As noted above, this last prohibition was lifted in 1907.

The Council of Trent (1545–1563)—which convened as a reaction to the Reformation, a sixteenth-century European movement that tried to reform the Catholic church and which led to a break with the Pope by the Protestant churches—revised the baptismal consanguinity laws, limiting relationships said to be occasioned by a baptism, so that persons should not be numbered among the baptismal kin who may have only touched the baptized infant.

The ancient Egyptians sometimes have had the reputation of allowing incestuous marriages, but this idea seems to have arisen from the special case of the royal family. For reasons of legitimacy, a pharaoh might marry his half-sister or, in some cases, one of his own daughters. However, in the early years of Egyptology, this reputation developed because the literal interpretation of the words for lovers and married people are "sister" and "brother." It is clear, however, that incest was not commonly practiced and that rules of consanguinity were probably followed.

In African cultures, marriage outside the lineage is often the rule, although there are some groups that practice arranged marriages, usually within the clan (a form of endogamy), because the parents are aware of the family, history, and the temperament of the chosen spouse. Lineage and kinship can be a complicated matter, and perceptions and arrangements of kinship can differ from society to society so that there are not always clear-cut lines of consanguinity. Rules of allowable alliances may follow lines of clan or class. The common theme is that human society seeks to avoid sibling marriage and incestuous relationships, of which there is a general abhorrence. But there is a more prosaic reason for forbidding sibling and close kin relationships—the high probability of exacerbating genetic abnormalities or medical conditions.

See also Endogamy/Exogamy

References

Crawley, Ernest. [1902] 1932. *The Mystic Rose: A Study of Primitive Marriage and of Primitive Thought in Its Bearing on Marriage.* 4th ed. Revised and enlarged by Theodore Besterman. London: C. A. Watts.

Goody, Jack. 1983. *The Development of the Family and Marriage in Europe.* Cambridge: Cambridge University Press.

Jeaffreson, John Cordy. 1872. *Brides and Bridals.* 2 vols. London: Hurst and Blackett.

Macfarlane, Alan. 1986. *Marriage and Love in England, 1300–1840.* Oxford: Basil Blackwell.

Manniche, Lise. 1987. *Sexual Life in Ancient Egypt.* London: KPI.

Westermarck, Edward. 1894. *The History of Human Marriage.* 2d ed. London: Macmillan.

Consummation

The consummation of the marriage and the beginning of sexual relations between the bride and bridegroom is taken as the final act of the wedding performance, if such a term can be used, and is a pivotal enough event for the Christian church and the law to cite non-consummation as a reason for annulment of a marriage. Indeed, by the early Middle Ages in England, it was considered that formal consummation actually made the marriage. In Britain, there were, especially for the well-to-do, five steps to a marriage—the legal contract; the spousal; a public proclamation of the intent to wed through the publishing of the banns (although many of the well-to-do by-passed this by obtaining a special license); the public ceremony in the church; and the consummation of the marriage. In civil law, the spousal before witnesses was considered a crucial part of the marriage contract. If the spousal was *de futuro,* an agreement to marry in the future, and was not followed by consummation, this engagement could be easily broken. If the spousal was followed by consummation, the agreement was legally binding for life.

It also was important in some traditional societies to show that the bride was a virgin, thus ensuring that the first child, hoped to be male and therefore inheriting the family line and property, was the child of the groom and thus the rightful heir. These traditions appear to be stronger among peoples and communities with a strong sense of inheritance, such as patrilineal societies; where there is a sense of "honor" in relationships; and where sexual intercourse, whether consensual or through rape, could be viewed as an act of violence or violation against the men of the family or community. Consequently, some groups demanded a public display of the bride's virginity. Among the Kalderash Gypsies in Spain, this was overseen by four matrons, who would display a bloodied handkerchief. Among Bulgarian Gypsies, young couples elope, often to avoid an arranged marriage or even reduce the marriage settlement. The couple go away for a night and have sexual intercourse; they then take the bloodied sheet back to the man's parent's house, where the sheet is inspected and tested as proof of the young woman's virginity. After this event the families go through the formalities of a public wedding.

A Kuwaiti tradition calls for the women of the household to sit in a room adjoining the bridal chamber to listen for any sounds that may come through the wall, to indicate that the marriage has been consummated and that the bride was a virgin.

Wyndham (1936) describes the marriage rites of the Wolof peoples of coastal Senegal. On the wedding night, the bride was escorted to the bridal chamber by her grandmothers and other older female relatives and prepared for bed. The bridegroom was summoned and the old women left. They would then listen for a scream from the bride, whereupon they would rush into the room, and the bridegroom would leave. The girl was expected to have fainted, and the women would revive her and remake the bed, replacing and taking away the sheet. The sheet was exhibited to the guests the next morning. If it showed signs of the loss of virginity there would be rejoicing and the bride would be showered with gifts.

Similarly, in Yoruban marriage, there were rewards for the family if their daughter is found to be a virgin on marriage. A mother expects a gift of cowrie shells from her new son-in-law after the consummation of the wedding. If her daughter is found to be not a virgin, the cowries would be inferior. A Nyakysus girl, from Tanzania, would preferably be married soon after her first menstruation, with a bull given to her family if she proves to be a virgin on inspection at the marriage, or if the husband attests that he has taken her virginity. Balfour (1951) recounted how the guests waited outside the bridal house for confirmation of the bride's virginity. Once the bride's honor had been confirmed there were celebrations, and three bursts of gunfire announced to the world that all was well. The display of evidence, and the retaining of that evidence, of the bride's virginity goes back to biblical times. In Deuteronomy (22.13–17) the laws are written that:

If any man take a wife, and go in unto her, and hate her,

And give occasions of speech against her, and bring up an evil name upon her, and say, I took this woman, and when I came to her found her not a maid:

Then shall the father of the damsel, and her mother, take and bring forth the tokens of the damsel's virginity unto the elders of the city in the gate:

And the damsel's father shall say unto the elders, I gave my daughter unto this man to wife and he hateth her;

And, lo, he hath given occasion of speech against her, saying, I found not thy daughter a maid; and yet these are the tokens of my daughter's virginity. And they shall spread the cloth before the elders of the city.

However, virginity is not always expected or required in a marriage in some societies. At the consummation ceremony, after the bridewealth negotiations between the families are completed, the Nuer bridegroom asks the bride's mother's permission to take the bride. The consummation takes place at the man's village, after a feigned reluctance on the part of the bride to go with him. However, Evans-Pritchard (1951) noted that she would rarely be a virgin—that, for the Nuer people, "maidenhead is a social, not physical state."

To ease the breaking of the hymen, it was the custom for a Persian bride to throw a hen's egg against a wall to break it, while facing Mecca. This was meant to ensure that her hymen was broken easily and also to promote fertility. There exist practices whereby the hymen was broken before sexual intercourse by someone other than the new husband. A Samoan practice was for the bride's hymen to be publicly ruptured by the chief. She would be escorted to a white carpet on the ground in the center of a square by two elderly women who acted as bridal companions; she would sit cross-legged on the carpet and the chief would sit cross-legged facing her. While the women held her by the waist, he would break her hymen with the forefingers of the right hand.

Similarly, anthropologists have described practices of central Australian Aborigines where the bride's hymen was artificially perforated. The assisting men, in a stated order, then have intercourse with the woman. We find records of similar practices where a group of men have sexual access to the bride for the period of the wedding ceremonial. Crawley (1902) wrote that among the Wataveta people from Kenya the bridegroom has to catch his bride, and he is assisted by four friends, who have intercourse with her during the five days of festivities.

A French anthropologist, Dr. Tautain (1895), described a marriage on the Marquesas Islands in the South Pacific, where, at a sign from the bridegroom, all the men formed a queue. Singing and dancing and in a strict order of hierarchy, the eldest and low born first, each had intercourse with the new bride, the last being her new husband.

These rites have been taken as examples of the promiscuity of primitive peoples. Others have compared them to so-called *jus primæ noctis* or *droit de seigneur,* whereby, it is said, the bride would spend her first married night not with her husband but with her feudal lord. Although the existence of such a rite has been disputed, there is some suggestion that *droit de seigneur* was exercised by Scottish royalty. Crawley (1902) suggested that this practice was "simply a barbarous sort of assertion of despotic authority of the patriarchal sort, appearing for instance in feudal and similar stages of society." However, this practice was mentioned as an ancient custom in fourteenth century England by supporters of the king spreading propaganda against the feudal lords to raise public support for the king against the lords (Jones and Ereira 2004, 15).

There appear to be a number of taboos among tribal societies relating to menstrual blood, and sexual intercourse also seems to have been viewed with some caution among some tribes. It was thought to weaken the man, perhaps causing effeminacy because of contact with a woman, and to have dangers for both the man and the woman. Group sex, under ritual conditions, was sometimes interpreted as removing or lessening the dangers of first sexual intercourse for the husband, and perhaps for the wife.

In some societies, consummation of the marriage was deferred for a period after the marriage ceremony, sometimes for up to four weeks. Various theories have been put forward for this practice. The demons might expect a form of *droit de seigneur* with the new wife. The couple should remain pure as they enter the "sacred world" of marriage. Perhaps there are elements of all the theories, including a wish to demonstrate that the marriage was not brought about by lust but by a desire to establish a stable family unit. The couple was usually not expected to display such restraint without help. An old woman or a child would sleep between the two or there would be some other form of chaperone.

See also Gypsy Weddings; Honeymoon; Kuwait; Nuer Weddings; Spousal; Yoruban Weddings

References

Balfour, Patrick. 1951. *The Orphaned Realm, Travels in Cyprus.* London: P. Marshall.

Braddock, Joseph. 1961. *The Bridal Bed.* New York: John Day.

Clébert, John-Paul. 1963. *The Gypsies.* Translated by Charles Duff. London: Vista Books.

Crawley, Ernest. [1902] 1932. *The Mystic Rose: A Study of Primitive Marriage and of Primitive Thought in Its Bearing on Marriage.* 4th ed. Revised and enlarged by Theodore Besterman. London: C. A. Watts.

Evans-Pritchard, E. E. 1951. *Kinship and Marriage among the Nuer.* Oxford: Oxford University Press.

Fonseca, Isabel. 1995. *Bury Me Standing: The Gypsies and Their Journey.* London: Chatto and Windus.

Jones, Terry, and Alan Ereira. 2004. *Medieval Lives.* London: BBC Books.

Mair, Lucy. 1971. *Marriage.* Harmondsworth, Middlesex: Penguin.

Stone, Lawrence. 1990. *The Family, Sex, and Marriage in England, 1500–1800.* Abridged and revised ed. London: Penguin.

Tautain, L. F. 1895. *Etude sur le mariage des polynesiens des Iles Marquises.* Vol. 6. Paris: Anthropologie.

Wyndham, Richard. 1936. *The Gentle Savage: A Sudanese Journey in the Province of Bahr-el-Ghazal.* New York: W. Morrow.

Contracts

The wedding contract is often just a verbal agreement to marry, but nevertheless it is a legal and binding contract—until the end of the twentieth century, a man would be wary of breaking an engagement for fear of being sued for "breach of contract." Written contracts are now often drawn up for Hollywood and celebrity weddings. These contracts, or prenuptial agreements, which appear to be a new idea, serve the purpose of protecting one of the partnership by limiting the financial and property settlement in the event of divorce. Some modern contracts are drawn up to ensure that the bride has some means of support in the event of her husband divorcing her (the function of contracts in the past). Such written contracts have a long history.

Contracts are found in many literate societies, including Muslim and Jewish. In these groups the negotiating and signing of the contract is an important part of the marriage

Ketubah *(detail of upper half) from Istanbul, 1853. This Jewish marriage contract was written for the bride Kadan ben Nissim Avraham Alcolambri and the groom Shabtai Chayyim ben Yosef Chayyim. Ink, watercolor, and powdered gold on paper. (Erich Lessing / Art Resource, New York)*

ceremony. Historically, a contract was especially important in the marriages of wealthy landowners in Britain, and contracts tended to outline any property exchanges and financial arrangements for the woman should she become widowed or be divorced by her husband. Before the middle of the eighteenth century, marriage for the landed classes usually required five distinct steps, with the first step being the negotiation of financial arrangements between the two sets of parents, which was signed as a written legal contract. This was followed by the espousal, which was also a form of contract, since it included an exchange of verbal promises, before witnesses.

In the Jewish wedding ceremony, the reading and the signing of the *ketubah* (or *ketubbah*), the marriage contract, is an important part of the ceremony. The groom has to read and accept the terms of the *ketubah,* which gives details of the duties and responsibilities of the Jewish husband—notably to provide food, clothing, and conjugal rights. However, it also details the settlement that the husband will give his wife in the event of him divorcing her (a previously married woman would receive half the amount that would be paid to a virgin). The *ketubah* may additionally list the dowry that the bride brings with her. He is responsible to her and her heirs for the maintenance of this dowry, and he may match the value of the dowry with a personal payment to his new wife. The *ketubah* is read out to the bride, usually in Aramaic, and then witnessed. Today, many of these *ketubahs* conform to a standard text and are often read out in a cursory manner, partly because the settlement in the event of the man divorcing the woman is at the heart of the contract and is a little sensitive to be read out beneath the wedding canopy. There are extant *ketubah* texts from as early as the fifth century B.C., which show how Jewish tradition has changed. These texts, from Elephantine, an island in the River Nile where Jewish mercenaries in the pay of the Persian emperor lived, have clauses detailing

the penalties incurred by the person within the marriage who initiates a divorce—that is, either the husband or the wife could initiate the divorce. In later Jewish law it was considered impossible for the woman to divorce her husband.

Written marriage contracts are found in other communities. For example, the Coptic Christians in Egypt sign a contract just inside the church before the engagement ceremony.

See also Dowry; Islamic Marriage; Jewish Weddings

References

Murphy, Brian M. 1978. *The World of Weddings: An Illustrated Celebration.* London: Paddington.

Segal, Eliezer. 1999. *Why Didn't I Learn This in Hebrew School?* Northvale, NJ: Jason Aronson.

Stone, Lawrence. 1990. *The Family, Sex, and Marriage in England, 1500–1800.* Abridged and revised ed. London: Penguin.

Courtship

Courtship is the period when two people get to know each other and decide whether they are compatible for marriage. The concept of romantic love and traditions of courtship based upon mutual attraction—rather than pairings in the interests of the families—are mainly Western ones, although there are examples of courtship and marriage through choice and attraction in some non-Western societies. Courtship is practiced in societies where there is free choice in marriage and mechanisms for young people to meet those of the opposite sex. Anthropologists have found little evidence of courtship rites and customs among non-Western societies. But there are degrees of freedom even within societies that have arranged marriage. In most Muslim countries, for example, although the marriage is arranged between the two families, both the man and the woman have the option to reject the person chosen for them, even though there is no courtship period, in the sense of the couple spending extensive time together and getting to know each other.

In societies where there is more freedom of association between the sexes, marriages may be arranged between families, for reasons of inheritance, property rights, and wealth, and there may be a period of courtship where the couple can get to know each other before the wedding. Where a matchmaker is employed, that person can either be contracted to find a suitable partner—usually by the parents of a young man wishing to marry—or to act as a go-between for a couple who have made their own choice. In some North American Indian tribes, for example, a grandmother acted as a go-between for a couple, though not as a matchmaker, and the couple would pay her with a horse.

Courtship involves many rituals and practices—even in contemporary Britain and the United States. Sometimes these rituals are generational and not overt. It is, for example, considered usual for the man to make the first approach to a woman, which would be to make a "date" to attend some usually public event together, such as a film or a concert. If the couple have enjoyed each other's company, further "dates" might follow and the two may become more intimate, doing more and more things together and exchanging presents until they are recognized by their friends and relatives as a "couple."

The first step in any courtship is, of course, meeting a likely partner, which, even in free and open societies, can sometimes be difficult. People come to know of areas or streets of a town where young people congregate and meet up with someone of the opposite sex and perhaps ask them out on a date. This was especially so in areas with a great deal of workplace segregation, that is, in industries in which, apart from secretaries and office staff, most of the workforce was male—mining or heavy industry—or areas with workforces that were predominantly female—cotton mills, textile factories, and light industry. Between about 1890 and 1939, Oldham Street in Manchester, England, on Saturday and Sunday nights was the venue for the "monkey-rank," where single young men and women would congregate and promenade up and down until they "clicked" with someone. Similarly, in Preston, Lancashire, England, different areas of the town were known for different classes of people. At Chorley, in Lancashire, the venue for this weekly promenade was known as "the drag" and had a "tuppence-ha'penny side," where the factory workers promenaded, and the "tanner side" for the office girls and clerks. Similar forms of segregation could be found in London and elsewhere.

In many places, Saturday and Sunday were the days for courting. In East Lancashire, Friday night was most definitely not the time for courting. If a couple were caught meeting on a Friday evening, the neighbors and friends were alerted by someone beating a frying pan, and the couple would be given a hard time. A children's rhyme from Cornwall designates Saturday night as the night for courting:

> Saturday night is courting night,
> I wish the time was come,
> For my house is swept and sanded,
> So all my work is done.
> (Deane and Shaw 1975, 52)

A well-known traditional rhyme suggests when courtship is allowed: "When the gorse is not in bloom, then kissing's not in season." Gorse is always in bloom. Meeting and getting to know people of the opposite sex can be a problem for members of isolated and nomadic tribes. Consequently, there are a variety of "events" for this, such as fairs and matchmaking. The Guizhou Miaos, for example, from the highland area of western Guizou in the Liupanshui region of China, have an annual love festival known as the *Tiaohuapo* or "dance on the flowery meadow." About forty thousand people attend this festival, some as spectators. But for unmarried young men and women, it is the chance to meet others and to flirt and "seduce"— through music, song, dance, smiles, and furtive glances—members of the opposite sex with a view to finding a marriage partner.

Similarly, matchmaking is a feature of the annual fair held in the town of Lisdoonvarna in Northern Ireland, which takes place in September. Here it is still possible to contract a matchmaker for help in finding a marriage partner; but it is well known and accepted that the social events and dances are very much for allowing couples to meet to establish courtships and eventual marriages. At Crowan, in West Cornwall, England, "taking-day" was an annual event at which young people chose their partner to take to the praze-an-beeble fair (held on or around 16 July). Young people attended church on that Sunday before the fair, and after the service went to nearby Clowance Park, where they would choose this partner. It was said that "many a happy wedding has resulted from the opportunity afforded for selection on 'taking-day' in Clowance Park" (Courtney 1890, 48). There is some similarity between this and the old Russian "woman show" held on Whit Monday, a day for arranging marriages, usually through a matchmaker.

North American Indian males were bashful and had trouble expressing their feelings for a woman, and meeting suitable marriage partners was very difficult. Flutes were only used in courtship and could convey a range of feelings and messages. The "big twisted flute" of the Sioux Indians was supposed to allow a man to entice the woman of his choice. This was a flageolet made from cedar wood and decorated with a figure of a horse (which was considered the most ardent of all animals) by a shaman, who would also compose and instruct the young man in the music to be played on the flute. The flute was only effective when it played the magical music that was conveyed to the shaman in a dream. If played correctly, the young woman of his choice would find the music irresistible and would go with the young man. But there were a number of ways that a young man could meet and express an interest in a girl; he would know that at certain times of day she would collect water, and he could by

chance be on the same path, or she would be returning from collecting vegetables at a certain time with her female companions, so that he and his companions would meet them and have a play battle to try and get the vegetables from the girls; a girl would signal her liking for a young man by making it easy for him to "strike coup," that is, capture the vegetables. A Plains Indian woman looked for a man who would be a good hunter and a brave warrior. Men sought young women who were modest, virtuous, and skilled in beadwork and tanning. However, both would also look for someone attractive—both men and women devoted a great deal of time to appearance. "Courting in a blanket" was a way of providing privacy—a girl would stand in front of the family tepee with a blanket, which she would wrap around herself and her suitor, completely covering them both, and they were free to get to know each other. A girl could see several prospective husbands in an evening in this way.

In parts of Britain, the United States, and the rest of Europe, where a combination of long working hours and cold environments made difficulties for couples to have some privacy, a courtship practice known as "bundling" or "tarrying" was observed. The couple was allowed to spend the night together, usually wearing at least underclothes and usually at the woman's home, with the blessing of the parents. Also known as "courting in bed," this practice is still observed by Amish couples, where a young couple is allowed to share the woman's bed. This would have been anathema to the Puritans of New England, who were very strict regarding meetings between members of the opposite sex and proposals for marriage. In 1672, a certain Jonathan Coventry was indicted at Plymouth for making overtures of marriage without asking for formal consent, and earlier in 1660, Arthur Hubbard was prosecuted by a girl's father and fined £5 for trying to gain the girl's affections. In the Connecticut Valley, it is said that during the eighteenth century, courting couples had to communicate through a "courting stick," a hollow tube about six to eight feet long, about an inch in diameter, and fitted with mouthpieces and ear-pieces. The couple would have to sit at either side of the fireplace, with the rest of the family present, and talk and whisper their "sweet-nothings" through this tube.

An account written in about 1640, of how a courtship was agreed upon in the East Riding of Yorkshire, England, suggested a high degree of formality. First, either the man or his father would write to the girl's father to inquire if the man would be welcome at the house. If the girl's father made some excuse, the man would take that as a refusal. If the answer was favorable, the man would visit twice to see if the girl agreed to the courtship. If she liked him, he would visit for the third time, and this time he would take some token, such as a piece of gold or a ring up to the value of about ten shillings, or some other gift of twice that value. The next time he visited, he would take her a pair of gloves, and the next time a small gift of less value. The courtship would last approximately six months. Obviously such a couple would both be from fairly affluent families. Guthrie (1885) described an "ancient highland" courtship custom:

> The ancient courtship of the Highlanders had these curious customs attending it. After having privately obtained the consent of the fair one, the enamoured swain demanded her of her father. The lover and his friends assembled on a hill allotted for that purpose in every parish, and one of the latter was despatched to obtain permission to wait upon the daughter. If he proved successful, he was again sent to invite the father and his friends to ascend the hill and partake the contents of a whisky cask, which was never by any chance forgotten. The lover then advanced, took his father-in-law by the hand, and plighted his troth, whereupon the maiden was handed over to him.

In Sussex, England, a young man going courting sometimes took a "honeysuckle stick" to indicate his intentions and to bring him luck. A honeysuckle stick was a piece of hazel that had been disfigured with a deep twisting groove and ridges of bark caused by honeysuckle growing up the stick. The clinging honeysuckle was said to symbolize a woman's clinging love and faithfulness and therefore brought luck to the suitor in his courtship. During courtship, a young man may give his sweetheart tokens of his affection; sometimes these would be made by him to show his handicraft skills, such as the Welsh love spoons, lace bobbins in lace-making areas, and knitting sheaths in the Yorkshire Dales in England. In Finland, domestic items such as distaffs for spinning were given as a token of love and as a demonstration of a man's practical abilities; in Germany, a carved and decorated washboard or a mangle board may be given. Other gifts could include combs, necklaces, and even gingerbread molds (in Czechoslovakia).

See also Betrothal; Bundling; Engagement; Love
    Spoons; Matchmaking; Tokens

References

Baldizzone, Tiziana, and Gianni Baldizzone. 2001. *Wedding Ceremonies: Ethnic Symbols, Costume, and Rituals.* Paris: Flammarion.

Courtney, M. A. 1890. *Cornish Feasts and Folklore.* Penzance: Beare and Son.

Deane, Tony, and Tony Shaw. 1975. *The Folklore of Cornwall.* London: B. T. Batsford.

Earle, Alice Morse. 1893. *Customs and Fashions in Old New England.* London: David Nutt.

Gillis, John R. 1985. *For Better, For Worse: British Marriages, 1600 to the Present.* Oxford: Oxford University Press.

Guthrie, E. J. 1885. *Old Scottish Customs.* London: Hamilton, Adams.

Macfarlane, Alan. 1986. *Marriage and Love in England, 1300–1840.* Oxford: Basil Blackwell.

Creeling

Creeling was a Scottish custom that, according to Chambers (1863), died out at the beginning of the nineteenth century. The day after the wedding, the couple and their friends met early, and a creel (a form of basket) was filled with stones and fixed to the young husband's back. He had to run around the town with the creel on his back, followed by a group of the men to make sure that he did not drop the burden. If, or when, his wife went after him and gave him a kiss, he could stop. A description of the custom from Ayreshire suggested that the couple and their friends made an event of the custom. The second day after the wedding, the couple and their friends met, and a creel was filled with stones. The young men took turns carrying it and allowing themselves to be caught by the women, who received a kiss when they succeeded. At last the creel fell to the new husband, who was obliged to carry it for a long time before his new wife took pity on him and caught him—this was proof of her satisfaction with her husband. The creeling continued for a while before the whole group retired to dine.

See also Ball Games; Racing
References
Chambers, Robert. 1863–1864. *The Book of Days.*
     Vol. 1. Edinburgh: W. and R. Chambers.
     Philadelphia: J. B. Lippincott.
Tegg, William. 1877. *The Knot Tied: Marriage
     Customs of All Nations.* London: William Tegg.

Crowns

Wedding crowns are familiar in Norwegian and Greek weddings and are worn by brides in German, Danish, and Polish weddings. Crowns and crownlike headdresses have been, and are today, widely used in Christian and non-Christian marriages. It is possible that the floral chaplet, or circlet, worn by many brides in Great Britain and the United States is derived from the tradition of crowning the bride. In many descriptions of weddings, it is often observed that the bride and groom, as the center of attention, are treated as queens and kings on their day. At weddings in the Coptic church in Egypt, the man and the woman are both dressed with a red sash, gold cloak, and gold-colored crowns—like a king and queen. (The couple remove the cloaks and crowns after the prayers and before they leave the church.)

In a Greek wedding, the couple is crowned with two crowns (or garlands of flowers) joined with white ribbon. The crowns are swapped from head to head three times, and then the couple each take three spoonfuls of wine. This is seen as one of the defining moments of the marriage—"to be crowned" means to be married—and many older people refer to couples who have been married in a registry office as "uncrowned," that is, not properly married. The crowns are kept in a "crown case" or *stephanothíki,* which has an icon inside and is placed over the couple's bed. (The wedding crown is eventually buried with the deceased.)

In Norway, the bride often wears a bridal crown made from beaten silver, although in the nineteenth century it was considered fashionable to reject the crown in favor of a wreath of flowers tied with a long ribbon that reached down to the bride's waist. Some of these crowns became family heirlooms, although in some districts it was common to have communal crowns that would be lent to brides. In her book *Through Norway in June,* a Mrs. Stone, a nineteenth-century English traveler in Norway, described seeing a wedding of four couples at the same time and specifically commented on the bridal crowns and described them:

> They are of beaten silver, but their appearance is entirely spoiled by being brassed over in parts in imitation of gold. This doubtless enhances their value to Norwegians, as silver is with them too plentiful to be held in much esteem. They are from four to eight inches high. One was entirely covered with brass; the other three looked older and showed in parts the silver. Two of them had silver pendants dangling about them, and three had either real or imitation stones inserted.
> (quoted in Lovett 1885, 191)

The crown was also a feature of weddings in Finland until about 1920. On the day of the wedding, after a ritual bath, the bride's hair would be cut and she would be presented with a linen cap called a *tzepy*. After being dressed, the bridal crown would be placed on her head. This she had to wear throughout the wedding celebrations, which could last three days. Brides in Sweden would also sometimes wear bridal crowns, and some churches had a wedding coronet that was loaned to the bride for the day.

The Christian scholar E. O. James tells us that the crowning of the bride and groom was a feature of the marriage rites of the early church. But efforts were later made to abolish this practice because of its heathen associations, especially where circlets or crowns of flowers, or olive and myrtle, or silver and gold were used. However, the crowning of the bride (and groom) was restored and given a Christian interpretation—i.e., the couple were crowned as victors in a spiritual struggle over the temptations of the flesh during their betrothal. The crowning began the marriage ceremony. If the couple had not won the spiritual struggle, then the crowning was omitted. (It is interesting to note that when the "care cloth" was used in the medieval English church, if one of the couple had been married before, the cloth was not held over that person's head.) After the reading of Psalm 128 and other preliminary discourse, the priest lifted the crowns from the altar and put one on the groom's head and the other on the bride's, with the words, "This servant of the Lord hereby crowns this handmaid of the Lord in the name of the Father, and of the Son, and of the Holy Ghost, world without end. Amen." On the eighth day after the consummation of the marriage, the couple revisited the church and the crowns were removed by the minister with the prayer:

O Lord our God, who crownest the year with Thy blessing, and hast given these crowns to be placed upon the heads of those united to one another by the law of marriage, rewarding them thus for their continence, because they have come pure and clean to marriage instituted by Thee, do Thou bless their union, now that they lay aside their crowns, keep them inseparably united, that in everything they may give thanks to Thy most holy name, Father, Son and Holy Ghost, now and ever world without end. Amen. (James 1933)

Bridal headdresses come in many shapes and sizes, ranging from simple headscarves to veils to very elaborate headdresses that show off family wealth. The brides of the Minangkabaus people of Indonesia wear a horned headdress on the day of the marriage. The name "Minangkabaus" signifies "victorious buffalo," and the buffalo horn motif is also found on the roof of the house, where the couple receive the congratulations of the guests. The bridal headdress is passed down from mother to daughter and symbolizes the position of women in this matrilineal society—land is held by the women who pass it from mother to daughter. The marriage is not consummated until a few days after the wedding following a sumptuous reception known as the *basandiang*, which elevates the couple to the status of royalty for the day. The bride wears a very elaborate golden headdress.

See also Christian Weddings; Greek Weddings; Scandinavia; Veil

References

Baldizzone, Tiziana, and Gianni Baldizzone. 2001. *Wedding Ceremonies: Ethnic Symbols, Costume, and Rituals.* Paris: Flammarion.

James, E. O. 1933. *Christian Myth and Ritual.* London: J. Murray.

Lovett, Richard. 1885. *Norwegian Pictures.* London: Religious Tract Society.

Murphy, Brian M. 1978. *The World of Weddings: An Illustrated Celebration.* London: Paddington.

Scott, George Ryley. 1953. *Curious Customs of Sex and Marriage.* London: Torchstream.

Van Nespen, W., ed. 1975. *Love and Marriage: Aspects of Popular Culture in Europe [exhibition], Antwerpen.* Brussels: Ministerie van Nederlanse Cultuur en Nationale Opvoeding.

Customs

Customs in marriage are difficult to define but can be described as events or practices commonly observed that are not part of the official or statutory ceremony. However, they are often essential and part of the community's involvement and recognition of the marriage. It is often the case that those taking part in a customary activity do not regard it as anything other than the normal actions of everyday life associated with an event, occasion, or even a time of year. It is often the outsider who recognizes and labels a custom as some form of exotic other. In weddings there are many customary activities that may appear strange and exotic to the outsider but for the participants are as much part of the wedding celebration as the exchange of vows and the signing of the register. In some cases the nonobservance of a custom may cast doubt in the mind of friends and family of the validity of the marriage. Among the Turkish Cypriots of Cyprus if there is no feast or reception after the wedding it is not considered a proper wedding, although the marriage would be lawful. During a BBC television program in 1984, an interviewee, in commenting on the prewedding "ribbon girl" event filmed by the filmmakers, considered this ritual almost as important as the wedding itself.

The customs of a wedding were obviously important in the sixteenth and seventeenth centuries. It was customary, for example, for gloves to be distributed at a wedding and was an important signifier of a wedding, so that Ben Jonson in his play *The Silent Woman* (1609) has one character remarking: "We see no ensigns of a wedding here, no character of a brideale—Where be our scarves and our gloves?" Custom can also indicate social inclusion. Of the industrial prewedding ribbon girl custom, one bride wrote that "even though it was a little embarrassing we would have hated to miss it" (Monger 1996).

Although customs may appear quaint, exotic, anachronistic, or pointless, they often fulfill one or more of the following three functions: First, they can be a part of a public show to announce to the community that a new family unit has been established, for example, "barring the way," where the gates of the church are tied up, usually by the children or young adults in the community. The custom of making "rough music" outside the house of the bride and groom or outside the reception venue was a form of welcome into the community of the married. And the motorized procession, sounding horns, in Ireland, Portugal, and other European countries announced and drew attention to the new marriage.

Second are customs to help the couple set up home as an independent economic unit. These include the bridal shower, the giving of presents, penny weddings, and biddings in Wales and the north of England. The Bulgarian Gypsy tradition of having a big show of the girl's dowry before the wedding is known as her *čeiz*. She sits among all her presents and receives visits from her friends, neighbors, and family. Similarly, the practice of pinning money onto the clothes of the bride and groom by the guests is intended to help the couple to begin life together.

Third, customs are observed to bring luck and good fortune to the couple and the new family unit. These include throwing confetti over the newlywed couple, or tying boots, shoes, or tin cans behind the going-away car. The bride having a gold or silver coin in her shoe—walking on gold or silver—is a way of hoping for good fortune and plenty.

Customs may be continued after their apparent function has ceased to be relevant because they become embedded in the psyche and they are simply fun and provide a contrast on a day of celebration to the solemnity of the official and legal part of the event. The observance of local and regional customs provides a form of reminder of the marriage event for members of the community, and the distribution of gifts such as favors, gloves, or almonds provides a physical memento. Today the wedding memento is often photographs (or videos) that are shown to friends and workmates unable to attend the wedding.

See also Barring the Way; Greek Weddings; Photographs; Premarriage Customs; Ribbon Girl; Rough Music/Rough Band; Walking on Gold

References

Huddleston, Mary. 1973. "A Yorkshire Miscellany." *English Dance and Song* 35, no. 1: 24.

Monger, George. 1996. "Pre-Marriage Ceremonies: A Study of Custom and Function." *Lore and Language* 14: 143–155.

Dances

Dancing, drinking, and eating are usually all included in marriage celebrations. Dance can also be used to initiate one or both of the couple into their new role in society, be an opportunity for those at the function to help the couple set up home or help pay for the celebrations, or be part of the competition between males and females.

Ceremonial dancing is integral to the Zulu wedding, with the bridal party dancing into the kraal of the groom's family. This dance, performed by the bride's party, indicates to the groom's ancestors that she is joining his family group. There is also a dance performed by the bride alone and a dance performed by the groom and his party before a gift of cattle is made to the groom's family. This is followed by the legal registration of the marriage (which appears as an intrusion into the traditional elements), and then everybody, except the bride who goes alone to a hut assigned to her and eats food that she has brought with her, joins in with feasting, singing, and dancing. Thus, in the Zulu wedding, formal dancing is part of the serious ceremonial business as well as the social.

In most Western countries, the dancing is less ceremonial and more social and not generally part of the actual act of marriage; however, some forms of ritual have developed.

For example, in the "first dance" at the wedding reception, the bridal couple will lead off the dancing, often with a waltz. This dance was introduced into European society from Vienna during the seventeenth century. Often considered vulgar and sinful, it did not manage to break into English society until the beginning of the nineteenth century, to much disgust and moral outrage. Apparently, the waltz was danced for the first time in the United States in Boston in 1834. The close-hold dance known today began to gain a place in the repertoire of dances for the upper class in the late eighteenth century. Although not specifically associated with weddings, it is a dance where the basic stepping is not difficult to master so that it was an easy dance for the bride and groom to lead off the dancing. And the partner can be held quite closely—appropriate for the beginning of married life. The newlyweds being first on the dance floor signals that the next stage of the festivities can begin and also gives some reinforcement that they are now a couple. This does not apply to all cultures—in some, notably in Islamic and Orthodox Jewish cultures, men and women dancing together in public is still strictly taboo. Gregor (1881, 95) wrote that in the nineteenth century, in northeast Scotland, it was usual for the bride, her groom, "the best young men," and the bride's maidens to dance the first dance, called the *shaimit reel:*

> The music to which it was danced was called the *shaim-spring,* and the bride had the privilege of choosing the music. The male dancers then paid the musician his fee. Another dance was performed by the same six, after which the floor was open. In some districts the *shaimit-reel* was danced by the bride and her best maid, with the two *sens* [young men who had accompanied the bride to the church] as partners. After it was danced the bride fixed a marriage favour on the right arm of her partner in the dance, and the best maid fixed one on the left arm of her partner. The two *sens* then paid the fiddler. Frequently the bride and her maid asked if there were other young men who wished to win favours. Two jumped to the floor, danced with the bride and her maid, and earned the honour on the left arm. Dancing was carried on far into the morning with the utmost vigour, each dance being begun and ended by the partners saluting each other.

Etiquette rules for weddings in the United States by the late twentieth century stipulated that the newly married couple lead off the dancing. The bride's father then claims his daughter and dances with her, and the groom dances with his mother-in-law; then the best man dances with the bride, and the groom with the maid of honor. In many societies and cultures there are specific wedding dances, and in some societies these are not performed by mixed groups. In many Muslim countries, the sexes are not allowed to mix socially, so that the men dance with each other and the women likewise will dance together in their separate celebration rooms.

Hassidic Jews have a variety of specific dances for weddings, including the first dance after the ceremony, the *knussen-kaleh mazel tov* (bridegroom and bride, good luck); the *patch tants* (clap dance), an initiation dance for the bride; and the *koilitch* dance. The *knussen-kaleh mazel tov* is a farandole, danced in a snake-like line with the male rel-

atives holding the bride's veil, one on each side of her. In the other hand, they hold a handkerchief to which the other guests hold, forming a line. This dance is also known as a *mitsveh* (precept) dance. The *patch tants* is performed by the married women, who circle around the bride with the handkerchief held downward; during a grand chain (a right and left chain movement), the bride joins in, thus becoming one of them. Although dancing at weddings is generally a communal activity, there were also some solo or display dances performed for the couple, such as the *koilitch* dance—the dancer holds a loaf of white braided bread *(khaleh)* to signify that the couple's home should never be without bread—and a dance performed by a beggar, who is specially invited as the couple's first charitable act. The dance of the *kazatskies* features the oldest male relative dancing to express his joy at the wedding and to demonstrate that he still has the strength to do so. During his performance, a female dancer, waving a handkerchief, dances a circle round him. The mothers-in-law may also dance the *beroiges tants.* At Orthodox Jewish weddings, the celebration room is divided into male and female halves so that the sexes do not actually dance together.

In a Greek wedding, we find a dance for the guests to show their support for the couple by making donations to help them begin their new life together and, perhaps, to help pay for the celebrations. The guests pin money to the dancing couple's clothes. In some parts of England, notably Devon and Kent, the "broom dance" was performed at weddings. This dance, performed over and with a broom, was often performed at weddings in pairs, with the "competing" couples facing each other, and it was sometimes said that it would determine who would have the upper hand in the household. It is probably not significant that the dance was performed with brooms—it was also sometimes danced during slack periods on a farm or in a mill when, for example, sweeping the barn was a cause for entertainment.

See also Bidding; Breakfast, Wedding; Bride-Ale; Jewish Weddings; Penny Weddings; Zulu Weddings
References
Gregor, Rev. Walter. 1881. *Notes on Folklore of the North East of Scotland.* London: Folklore Society.
Humphries Family. 1954. "A Broom Dance from Devon." *English Dance and Song* 18, no. 6: 204–205.
Seid, Marsha. 1972. "Introduction to Hassidic Dancing." *Viltis* 30, no. 6: 8–9.
Smart, Marion. 1954. "The Broom Dance." *English Dance and Song* 19, no. 1: 26.

Dancing in a Hog (Pig) Trough

The expected order of marriage within a family was for an elder sister to be married before the younger. This order has been followed, or expected, across many cultures. In the Old Testament story of Jacob wanting to marry Rachel, the younger daughter, he was told that "it is not our custom to give the younger daughter in marriage before the older one" (Gen. 29.26). This practice was observed well into the twentieth century. In 1978, the *Times* (London) reported a case from Kostalexi, a village north of Athens, where a peasant family had locked up one of their daughters because her love affair with another villager had threatened the tradition that her elder sisters should be married first. The woman was locked in a basement for twenty-nine years (8 November 1978).

If for any reason this rule was not followed in Britain and North America, there was a tradition for the elder sister to dance in a pig's trough on the wedding day. In some places she would be barefoot and in others she had to wear green stockings (green is often believed to be an unlucky color). This may have been seen as a sign of shame or may have been an act to demean herself in order to break her bad luck. Similarly, an unmarried elder sister served barefoot at her sister's wedding in order to change her luck. A variation of the custom, from northeast Scotland, was for the younger sister to present her older sister with a pair of green garters if she married first. This custom was not always confined to the females in the family. There is an account of a brother having to perform the dance and of the dancers breaking the trough to pieces from being too vigorous. This practice was well known in the time of Shakespeare. In *The Taming of the Shrew* (act 2, scene 1), Katharina says to her father, regarding her younger sister:

> She is your treasure, she must have a husband;
> I must dance bare-foot on her wedding-day,
> And for your love to her lead apes in hell.

The line concerning leading apes in hell refers to a belief that if a woman dies unmarried, or an old maid, she would be destined to leads apes in hell as a punishment for willfully opting out of marriage and childbearing. A twenty-seven-year-old unmarried woman, worrying about her unmarried status, wrote to the *Tatler* of London, 12 August 1710: "I become weary and impatient of the derision of gigglers of our sex, who call me old maid and tell me I shall lead apes" (Ratcliff 1969, 11).

According to Clarke (1972), the expression "to dance in a hog trough" was still being used by people in Kentucky well into the latter half of the twentieth century as a teasing remark to an unmarried woman, or to a woman whose younger sister was likely to be married first. Many using or familiar with the expression were unaware of the origins of, or the custom associated with, the phrase.

See also Garter; Shoes
References
Clarke, Mary Washington. 1972. "To Dance in Hog Trough: A Folk Expression." *Kentucky Folklore Record* 18, no. 3: 68–69.
Dyer, T. F. Thiselton. 1906. *The Folklore of Women.* London: E. Stock.
Glyde, John Jun. [1872] 1973. *Folklore and Customs of Norfolk.* Facsimile publication. Wakefield, Yorkshire: E. P. Publishing.
Gregor, Rev. Walter. 1881. *Notes on the Folklore of the North East of Scotland.* London: Folklore Society.
Porter, Enid. 1974. *The Folklore of East Anglia.* London: B. T. Batsford.

Ratcliff, Rosemary, ed. 1969. *Dear Worried Brown Eyes*. London: R. Maxwell.

Days for Marriage

In many societies, the important step of marriage, with its many pitfalls, needs to take place at a propitious time. For Turkish Muslims, a marriage is an alliance, a contract between two families, with the couple involved having no say or choice. An auspicious day is chosen for the wedding feast, preferably a Friday, with Monday as second choice. Zoroastrians consult astrologers to determine a favorable day for the betrothal ceremony. In the province of Atjeh, in northern Sumatra, the best day and month for a wedding is carefully calculated, and the Chinese also ensure that a lucky day is chosen for the marriage. In Greece, the ideal day for a wedding is a Sunday; Monday is usually avoided. The Greek word for Monday, *deftéra*, means "second day," and this is considered an omen of a second marriage with the implication of the death of one of the couple. Similarly Tuesday, *tríti*, meaning third, may indicate that one of the couple will be married three times (the Greek Orthodox church allows up to three church marriages). Thursday (*pémpti*, meaning fifth) is also avoided because the folk version of the day name, *péfti*, sounds the same as "it falls,'" which is something negative.

Similarly in Britain, there were times that couples would avoid. It was said that St. Thomas' Day, 21 December—the shortest day of the year, would "make a wife a widow 'ere long." The church in medieval times spoke against practices of celebrating marriage, or undertaking other events, when the moon was waxing. Before the Reformation in England, the usual and preferred day for marriage was a Sunday, and the brides in Elizabethan dramas were usually married on this first day of the week. There were many regional differences concerning the best day for marriage and there are a number of traditional rhymes that outline the properties of each day:

Monday for wealth,
Tuesday for health,
Wednesday the best day of all,
Thursday for losses,
Friday for crosses,
And Saturday no luck at all.

Wed on Monday, always poor,
Wed on Tuesday, wed once more,
Wed on Wednesday, happy match,
Wed on Thursday, splendid catch,
Wed on Friday, poorly mated,
Wed on Saturday, better waited.

Monday for health
Tuesday for wealth
Wednesday the best day of all,
Thursday for losses
Friday for crosses,
And Saturday no luck at all.

Evans (1914) noted that at St. Monans in Fife, Scotland, although Fridays were considered ominous, it was rare to see a wedding on any other day. The evil associations for Friday may have come from the church. The day was dedicated to the Germanic goddess Frija, who, in her Norse incarnation Freyja, was the wife of Odin, a revered wife and mother and, as consort to the high god, the queen of heaven. Several writers have noted that Fridays, and sometimes Thursdays, were considered lucky days for marriage in northern Scotland and the Isles of Orkney and Shetland, and sometimes the explanation is associated with the day being linked to Good Friday and hence holy. However, this could equally explain beliefs that it is an unlucky day, since it was the day of the crucifixion.

Although Thursdays, in the above rhymes, were not considered good for marriage in Shropshire and Northamptonshire in England, it was a lucky day. However, the worst day of all, Saturday, became the most usual day for marriages in Great Britain, as the most convenient for working people. But the trend seems to be changing again with changing work patterns, and with changes in the law allowing venues other than places of worship and registry offices, such as hotels, museums, and stately homes, to be licensed for marriages.

See also Factory Customs; May, Marriage in
References
Edwards, T. B. 2002. "Unlucky Times for Weddings." *FLS News: Newsletter of the Folklore Society* 36 (February): 14.
Emrich, Duncan, ed. 1970. *The Folklore of Weddings and Marriage.* New York: American Heritage Press.
Evans, John Ewart. 1914. *County Folklore 7: Fife Clackmannan & Kinross.* London: Folklore Society.
Gutch, Mrs. 1899. *County Folklore. Vol. 2. Concerning the North Riding of Yorkshire, York, and Ainsty.* London: Folklore Society.
Polson, Alexander. 1926. *Our Highland Folklore Heritage.* Dingwall, Inverness: G. Souter (*Northern Chronicle* office).
Radford, E., and M. A. Radford. 1969. *Encyclopaedia of Superstitions.* Edited and revised by Christina Hole. London: Hutchinson.
Thomas, Keith. 1988. *Religion and the Decline of Magic.* Reprint. London: Penguin.

Divinations

The desire to know the outcome of future events is deep-seated. In many societies a wise man or wise woman may be employed to determine auspicious days for undertaking important events—such as marriage. And there are many personal and private quasi-magical rites to determine the identity or initial of one's future partner, or even to determine if one will be married at all. Many of these divinations are still commonly known and some are still used. A writer to the *Daily Mirror* (London) for 3 August 1971 said that she had put her shoes in the shape of a T, said "goodnight" aloud seven times, and then had climbed into bed backward with her eyes shut, a ritual that is supposed to bring a dream of the future husband. That night the writer dreamed about Douglas Fairbanks Jr. Ten years later she married a man who, her friends said, was his double. To sleep with a mirror, a silver spoon, a ladder made of sticks, or a piece of wedding cake under the pillow will make the sleeper dream of her (or his) future spouse. The reason for the wedding cake is obvious; the mirror, spoon, or stick ladder may seem more obscure. Mirrors are used in other marriage divinations, and the spoon may represent a distorted mirror image. The ladder may be representative of an elopement. A refinement to the wedding cake tradition, and probably to enhance its efficacy, involves passing the piece of cake three (or nine) times through a wedding ring and then sleeping with it under the pillow. Sometimes divinations involve rituals—adding to the mysticism. In Yorkshire, for example, a woman may sit on top of a gate and look at the first new moon of the year through a silk handkerchief, reciting:

> All hail to thee new moon,
> All hail to thee;
> I pray thee, new moon,
> Reveal to me this night
> Who shall my future husband be.

She then hopes to dream of her future husband. Additionally, the number of moons seen through the handkerchief would indicate the number of years that must pass before she marries. St. Agnes Eve (20 January) was a magical night and had a few divinations, mentioned by John Keats in his poem "The Eve of St. Agnes":

> They told how upon St. Agnes Eve,
> Young virgins might have visions of delight,
> And soft adorings from their love receive
> Upon the honey'd middle of the night,
> If ceremonies due they did aright;
> As, supperless to bed they must retire,
> And couch supine their beauties, lilly white,
> Nor look behind, nor sideways, but require
> Of heaven with upwards eyes for all that they
>   desire.

Some divinations required a great deal of determination to perform, such as this St. Agnes Eve one: Hard-boil an egg, remove the egg and fill the shell with salt, and then eat the shell and salt without taking a drink. Then go to bed backward, saying:

Sweet St. Agnes, work thy fast,
If ever I be to marry man,
Or even man to marry me,
I hope this night to see.

The future husband would then be dreamed of. Divinations were not necessarily only for women. A Tyneside (north of England) St. Agnes Eve divination for a man was to eat a raw herring whole in order to dream of his future wife. Another magical time was Midsummer Eve. A girl fasts on Midsummer Eve, and at midnight she lays a cloth on the table, sets out bread, cheese, and beer, and sits down as if to eat. The door of the room is left open and the image of her future husband will appear at the doorway.

A divination, found in the United States, is the "dumb supper," usually done by a group of girls. The food is prepared late at night. The place settings at the table and the chairs are all backward, and everything is prepared in absolute silence and darkness. The girls then wait until midnight, when the apparitions of their future husbands will supposedly walk toward them. Similarly a "dumb cake" may be prepared on Christmas Eve. The cake had to be prepared while fasting; the girl would prick her initials in the cake, place the cake on the hearth, and leave the room door open. At midnight the apparition of her future husband would enter the room and prick his initials beside hers. A variation was for two girls to prepare the cake, divide it equally, walk backward to their bedrooms, and eat the cake before getting into bed. They would dream of their future husbands.

All Hallows' Eve (Halloween) has long been associated with the supernatural. As a time when the barriers between the world of the living and that of the dead briefly fell, many divinations were performed on this night. A girl would wet a shirtsleeve with water and hang it up by the fire to dry. She would then go to bed and watch the sleeve until midnight, when the apparition of her future husband would enter the room and turn the sleeve. If a girl sat in front of a mirror in a room lit only by a candle and either comb her hair or eat an apple, she would see the face of her future husband looking over her shoulder. Another means to see the apparition of a future husband was for the girl to go to the churchyard at midnight and sow hempseed over her shoulder while reciting: "Hempseed I sow, / Hempseed grow, / He that is to marry me, / Come after me and mow." She is then supposed to see the form of her future husband following her with a scythe as if mowing the hemp. If nothing happens, she will either not be married within that year or not be married at all. If an apple is peeled so that the peel is removed unbroken and the peel thrown over the left shoulder, the peel will form the initial of the future spouse. In the United States, the peel should be first swung three times around the head before being thrown over the shoulder. Similarly, if a string of beans is made and thrown into the air, the initial letter of a future spouse is formed upon landing.

Not surprisingly, St. Valentine's Day also attracts divinations. If on this day a girl pins bay leaves to each corner and to the middle of her pillow, she will dream of her future husband. Another divination was to write the names of possible husbands on slips of paper, enclosing each slip in a clay ball. These are dropped into a bowl or bucket of water, and the first name to rise to the surface will be the spouse. If the first person a single girl meets on St. Valentine's Day is a man, she will be married within three months. If she meets a woman first, she will not marry during that year. In the United States and not associated with any particular day in the year, a girl wears a four-leaf clover in the heel of her left shoe, and she will then marry the first man she meets.

Some divinations are associated with particular areas or landscape features. If a person walks three times, backward, around the well at Kelsey, Lincolnshire, England, on St. Mark's Eve (24 April) and then goes on hands and knees to stare into the water, the future loved one will smile from the water. Also on St. Mark's Eve, if a girl puts a flower in the church porch during the day and returns for it at midnight, she would see a wedding procession as she returned home that included the form of her future husband.

The bride's throwing her bouquet as she leaves the wedding party determines who among the unmarried people is to be married first. And there are other methods. One can prepare a syllabub or posset—a drink made from milk, wine, and sweet cake—and drop a wedding ring into the preparation. The unmarried person who receives the ring when the posset is served will be the first married. A more potentially humiliating practice was to prepare a flat cake with water, flour, currants, and other fruit in which a ring and a sixpence were baked. Near the end of a wedding celebration, the cake was broken and distributed among the unmarried women. The one who found the ring would soon be married, and the one who received the sixpence would be an old maid.

See also Posset; Rings, Wedding and Betrothal; Valentine's Day

References

Emrich, Duncan. 1970. *The Folklore of Love and Courtship.* New York: American Heritage Press.

Hole, Christina. 1941–1942. *English Custom and Usage.* London: Batsford.

Porter, Enid. 1969. *Cambridgeshire Customs and Folklore.* London: Routledge and Kegan Paul.

Divorce

An English saying, "Marry in haste, repent at leisure," reflects the draconian nature of divorce law, or lack of it, in England from about the tenth century until a softening of the law in the nineteenth century. According to British law, marriage is "the union of one man with one woman voluntarily entered into for life to the exclusion of all others." Marriage is therefore considered irrevocable.

This view comes from that of the Christian church, which imposed a rule of monogamy as a part of its moral foundation. The church viewed marriage as a sacrament, representing the union between Christ and the Church, and as such was indissoluble. The Council of Trent (1545–1563), which reformed the Catholic church and brought about the establishment of the Protestant faith, suppressed divorce as a legal practice. Consequently in Roman Catholic societies, such as Spain, Portugal, and Italy, although a husband could demand a judicial separation—a "divorce *a mensâ et thor*"—the marriage contract could not be dissolved. Westermarck (1894, 526) states that "in all Protestant countries divorce is allowed. In every one of them, a man may be divorced from a wife who has committed adultery, but the other legal grounds on which a divorce, in most of them, may be obtained, vary in different States."

Until about the tenth century, there were means of easy divorce in northern Europe, conforming to the general pattern in many human societies where there are systems of divorce, and compensation payments were negotiated in the marriage agreement. But at that time in England, the church imposed a new marriage regime that did not allow easy divorce or remarriage. This state of affairs continued until 1857, when the Matrimonial Causes Act made civil divorce possible. But it was not until the latter half of the twentieth century that divorce could be said to have become easy. Before the 1857 act and the establishment of divorce courts, couples, or an aggrieved party, would have to get an act through Parliament to annul the marriage—not an option for most of the population. There were very few grounds for divorce, and the wife had little or no power to instigate proceedings should she be the aggrieved party. The judgment of Judge Maule in his address to a prisoner accused and found guilty of bigamy at the Oxford Assizes in 1855 illustrated the impossibility of the situation for the majority of the population before the 1857 act:

You had no right to take the law into your own hands. . . . Now, listen to me, and I will tell you what you ought to have done. Immediately you heard of your wife's adultery you should have gone to an attorney and directed him to bring an action against the seducer of your wife. You should have prepared your evidence, instructed counsel, and proved the case in court. . . . Having proceeded thus far, you should have employed a proctor, and instituted a suit in the Ecclesiastical Courts for a divorce *a mensâ et thoro*. Your case is a very clear one, and I doubt not you would have obtained your divorce. After this step your course was quite plain: you had only to obtain a private Act of Parliament to dissolve your marriage. This you would get as a matter of course, on the payment of the proper fees and proof of the facts. You might then have lawfully married again. . . . I see you would tell me that these proceedings would cost you £1000, and that your small stock-in-trade is not worth £100. Perhaps that may be so. The law has nothing to say to that. If you had taken these proceedings you would have been free from your present wife, and the woman whom you secondly married would have been a respectable matron. As you have not done so, you stand there a convicted culprit, and it is my duty to pass sentence upon you. You will be imprisoned for one day. (Jeaffreson 1872, 2: 343)

In the case of this man and many like him, there was no possibility of obtaining a legal divorce; most people would therefore either continue to live with their spouse, desert their spouse, or resort to a wife sale, a form of plebeian divorce that was illegal. In his novel *The Mayor of Casterbridge* (1866), Thomas Hardy described a wife sale taking place at a fair as a drunken, spontaneous action on the part of the husband. But this was not normally the case. Generally, wife sales were more sober and deliberate affairs and usually involved the husband leading his wife, with a halter around her neck, to a marketplace, sometimes along a set route or passing a set number of turnpikes or over a set dis-

tance, where she would be sold by auction. The woman would go with the winning bidder and they would live together as husband and wife. Although this seems to be a cruel, humiliating, and degrading performance, this would only happen if both of the couple were willing. It would be very rare for the winning bidder to be a complete stranger to the woman and would most likely be her lover. In some respects, this represented a public change of household and was almost considered a remarriage. This form of divorce seems to have developed in the seventeenth century and was still evolving during the eighteenth century.

There were apparently other odd forms of divorce practiced. Simson (1865) suggested that Gypsies would divorce over a sacrifice of a horse. It is sometimes difficult to be entirely sure about Gypsy customs and ceremonies—there are variations, claims, and counterclaims from different writers and collectors—and it is difficult to generalize about this divorce procedure. It may be confined to a particular group, or groups, of Gypsies. Braddock (1961) describes the ceremony, after noting that divorce is rare among Gypsy communities. The woman would lay her head on an "unblemished" horse, and this animal was allowed to roam free for a time; the horse was carefully observed, and from its behavior, an indication of the degree of the woman's guilt could be discerned. One of the group was appointed as a form of priest. The horse was brought before this person, charged with the crimes, and, after a mock trial, was sacrificed by being stabbed through the heart and allowed to bleed to death. The couple to be divorced stood, one on each side of the corpse, joined hands, and recited words repudiating each other, after which they separately walked three times around the carcass, crossing each other en route, and finally meeting at the tail, where they shook hands and then turned and walked off in opposite directions. After the divorce, the woman had to wear a cast-iron token as a symbol of her divorced status and was not allowed to marry again, risking death if she was ever caught pretending to be unmarried.

As mentioned above, the situation in England became easier after the 1857 Matrimonial Causes Act that established the divorce courts. The Matrimonial Causes Act of 1937 eased the situation further by providing for divorce or judicial separation on the grounds of adultery, desertion (for three or more years), cruelty, or incurable unsoundness of mind lasting over five years. In all cases, the act allowed either of the husband or wife to apply for a divorce on any of these grounds. Additionally, the wife could apply for the termination of the marriage if her husband was found guilty of rape, sodomy, or bestiality. In the second half of the twentieth century, the law relaxed further, so that grounds for divorce are adultery by one of the couple, unreasonable behavior, separation for at least two years—in this case both of the couple have to agree to a divorce, separation for more than five years—in this case no agreement for divorce proceedings is necessary from the partner, or desertion for at least two years.

There has been tacit acceptance of plebeian and unofficial forms of divorce when an annulment by an ecclesiastical court along with an act of Parliament was financially out of the question, and in 1857 legal divorce was taken out of the hands of the church authorities. The stigma often associated with divorced women remained well into the second half of the twentieth century. The Christian church generally discourages divorce, and, indeed, many Church of England clergy will not allow remarriage of divorced women in church. This has been a subject of controversy during the last part of the twentieth century—a fact that is somewhat ironic, since Henry VIII founded the Church of England, breaking away from the Roman Catholic church because the pope would not let him have a divorce from his first wife, Catherine of Aragon. The Archbishop of Canterbury eventually declared the marriage null

and void, and Henry went on to have five other marriages, one of which was ended by divorce in 1540. Even today there are clergy in the Church of England who refuse to even bless a marriage if one of the couple has been divorced, even if they were the innocent party.

It was not until 1884 that divorce was reintroduced into France. In Spain, divorce was introduced during the brief period of the Republic, from 1931 to 1936, but was repealed during General Franco's reign on the insistence of the church authorities. In the United States, the divorce laws differ from state to state, with some being very lax. But there has long been a greater acceptance of the rights to divorce and remarry in the United States. In Britain many thought that the 1857 Matrimonial Causes Act would cause an epidemic of divorces. Although it did allow more divorces, the numbers were very low compared to those of the United States; in 1886, for example, there were 708 divorces in Great Britain, whereas there were more than 25,000 in the United States, with a population only twice that of Great Britain.

The religious versus the civil view of divorce can be an uneasy topic, even in societies where the concept and acceptance of divorce is considered within the marriage contract. Muslims, for example, ensure that the woman has some sort of support in the event of a divorce. In Egypt, at the time of the engagement, a divorce settlement is agreed upon. If the wedding does not proceed, with the groom pulling out of the arrangement, he has to pay 50 percent of the settlement. In ancient Egypt, divorce, or the breakdown of the marriage partnership, was a recognized possibility, though to be discouraged—not for religious reasons, but to promote a stable society and a property and inheritance infrastructure. A heavy fine could be imposed on a man for divorcing his wife. The woman had to leave the family home, whether or not she instigated the divorce, making her and her children homeless and placing a burden on the wider society, which took pride in the collective care given to widows, divorced women, and children. Although there were clauses in the marriage contract to provide financial compensation upon divorce, such settlements were not particularly generous and would still leave the woman facing economic problems.

Generally, in Islamic societies, if the man divorces the woman, she takes the remainder of her dowry and the household goods that she brought to the marriage. If she wants a divorce from her husband, she forfeits her household goods and dowry. Both men and women may divorce, and a reconciliation is allowed twice. If they divorce a third time, then it becomes final and irrevocable. This is where the idea of saying "I divorce you" three times comes from.

In the Jewish wedding, the marriage contract, the *ketubah,* is read out (usually in Aramaic and with a translation into the language of the couple being married) and includes details of the settlement that the husband would give his wife in the event of him divorcing her (a previously married woman would receive half the amount that would be paid to a virgin). However, in Jewish divorce, although the couple can obtain a legal divorce in the civil courts, which is binding and does separate the couple, the ex-husband and ex-wife also need to grant each other a religious divorce known as a *get.* If this is not granted, then the spouse is "chained." It is more often that an ex-husband refuses his divorced wife a *get,* and this has grave implications for the "chained" women or *agunot,* who are unable to remarry within the Orthodox faith because the marriage would be viewed as adulterous and any children deemed illegitimate. However, the man may remarry in the Orthodox faith and his children would be considered legitimate, as long as his new wife is not herself "chained."

In Chinese tradition, divorce is permitted, which has caused problems in China because of the one-child family policy, coupled with the desire of Chinese men to have a son. If a woman bore a female child, it was quite common for her husband to abandon his wife and child for another woman in the hope of getting a son. At one time, having a female child was cited as grounds for around one-third of Chinese divorces. In 1991, the law was changed to prevent a child's sex from being grounds for divorce. Many husbands ill-treated their wives to cause the woman to file for divorce on the grounds of cruelty.

In general, in societies where there is free choice of partner and usually a period of courtship followed by an engagement period, once married it is difficult to undo the contract. But in societies where marriage is arranged between two families, and perhaps there is not such a possessive exclusiveness, there tends to be divorce by consent and a more permissive attitude toward adultery, concubinage, and polygamy.

See also Besom Weddings; Bigamy; Wife-Selling

References

Braddock, Joseph. 1961. *The Bridal Bed.* New York: John Day.

Depla, Annette. 1994. "Women in Ancient Egyptian Wisdom Literature." In *Women in Ancient Societies,* edited by Léonie J. Archer, Susan Fischler, and Maria Wyke. London: Macmillan.

Gillis, John R. 1985. *For Better, For Worse: British Marriages, 1600 to the Present.* Oxford: Oxford University Press.

Jeaffreson, John Cordy. 1872. *Brides and Bridals.* 2 vols. London: Hurst and Blackett.

Lane, Edward W. [1836] 1994. *The Manners and Customs of the Modern Egyptians.* Everyman Edition. London: J. M. Dent

Macfarlane, Alan. 1986. *Marriage and Love in England, 1300–1840.* Oxford: Basil Blackwell.

Menefee, Samuel Pyeatt. 1981. *Wives for Sale.* Oxford: Basil Blackwell.

Pearsall, Ronald. 1971. *The Worm in the Bud: The World of Victorian Sexuality.* Harmondsworth, Middlesex: Penguin.

Scott, George Ryley. 1953. *Curious Customs of Sex and Marriage.* London: Torchstream.

Simson, Walter. 1865. *A History of the Gipsies.* London: Sampson, Low, Son, and Marston.

Tegg, William. 1877. *The Knot Tied: Marriage Customs of All Nations.* London: William Tegg.

Westermarck, Edward. 1894. *The History of Human Marriage.* 2d ed. London: Macmillan.

Dowry

The dictionary tells us that a dowry is either a widow's share for life of her husband's estate or property, or money brought by the wife to her husband on marriage. This is a simplification that leads to some confusion about the purpose of the dowry. The dowry is part of the "business side" of the marriage arrangement and is sometimes outlined in law. It is often confused with the bride-price—a payment by the groom's family to the bride's family as compensation for the loss of the labor or earning power of the woman leaving the family unit—and is also sometimes seen as the father paying for his daughter to be married. Indeed, among the landed classes in sixteenth- and seventeenth-century England, a woman was expected to bring a substantial amount of cash, a marriage portion, with her to marriage; this money went to the bridegroom's father (who often used it to provide a dowry for his own daughters). In return the bride was guaranteed an annuity, called a jointure, in the event of her outliving her husband. The marriage portion was usually seen as the woman's share of the parents' estate, provided as an advance payment. Sons would receive their share at the parents' (or just the father's) death.

In earlier times, and in some parts of Britain, the dowry was goods or land given to the bride by the groom. This could be property or goods that she could use as she saw fit and functioned as a form of pension or insurance for the woman and her children. For example, in Anglo-Saxon law, the husband gave his new wife the *morgengifu,* "the morning-gift," which could be quite a substantial amount of land or money. This was paid to her and was hers to do with what she wished. It was not paid to her family, as was a bride-price. Similarly, in Byzantium, a woman acquired her own property in her dowry and gifts from her husband. These belonged to the woman (these assets were controlled by her husband, but he could not do anything with the dowry without her permission, al-though it was not unknown for a woman to be defrauded of her property). She had the right to dispose of her dowry as she wished, affording her some security if she were to be widowed.

In about the twelfth century in England, the endowment, which a groom would give to his bride, would be announced in a betrothal ceremony held in the church porch. The wedding itself was basically a repetition of the vows taken at betrothal, but moved inside the church, and included the blessing of the wedding ring and the confirmation of the groom's dowry to his wife, symbolized by coins placed on the service book. This was referred to as the dow-purse. By the eighteenth century, this had disappeared from the marriage ceremony (and among the upper classes was confined to the lawyer's office) in most parts of England. However, in parts of northern England, a vestige of the dow-purse was still practiced in the nineteenth century. The groom placed coins or a handful of money onto the prayer book held by the priest during the ceremony. The priest took out his fees, and those of other officers of the church, and passed the rest of the money to the bride—symbolic, it is said, of the dowry or of the sharing of wages.

That there is some confusion concerning the dowry can be seen by the marriage business arrangement outlined in the ancient laws of Ireland. At the marriage of a spouse who would be the "chief wife" (a *cétmuinter*), the "business aspect," of which the details would differ with social rank, was in three parts. The *coibchei,* the principal dowry of the bride, was a sum paid by the bridegroom to the father of the bride. This was to be paid each year for twenty-one years. The first payment was divided between the father and the head of the tribe or clan. In the second year, the woman kept a third of the payment, and her father and his superior divided the remainder. As the years passed, the woman kept a greater and greater proportion of the payment. By the end of the twenty-one years, the woman would have acquired enough to be independent if the husband transferred his affections to a younger woman. The *tinól* was a form of wedding present given to the bride by her friends, usually consisting of cattle. This she shared with her father, keeping two-thirds of the gift. The *tinnscra* was paid to the father of the bride in the form of items of gold, silver, copper, and brass.

The provision of a dowry was not confined to the landed English. Among eighteenth-century Romanian nobility, a dowry was essential to ensure a marriage. In 1785, the wife of a nobleman, Zmaranda Zalariu, wrote to Prince Alexandru Ioan Mavrocordatos, begging for a special dispensation of Gypsies (as a dowry) so that her only daughter would be "saved from spinsterhood." The prince granted her four Gypsy families. In about 1844, the niece of Prince Constantin Brâncoveanu of Romania was given, by the prince, "Mogosoaia village together with the land; the vineyards, the lakes and the mills, and 19 Gypsy families." (European nobility considered that they had ownership of the people on their lands.)

Lower down the social scale, in families without great assets of land or other income, the dowry was a contribution which the woman would bring to the marriage for setting up the home and establishing the family unit. In England it was not unusual for charitable endowments to be established in wills to provide dowries for girls from poor families. A girl would save money from her earnings to provide a dowry for herself or would collect household goods and linen for her marriage—known as her "bottom drawer." Often a girl would be expected to make or prepare household items, such as linen tablecloths, for her bottom drawer.

In some cultures, notably nomadic peoples, it was customary to have an ostentatious show of the dowry. The Romanian Kalderash Gypsies kept valuables in a wearable gold form so that a girl could wear her dowry around her neck and in her hair. Similarly, a Bedouin girl wore coins given to her by her father that constituted part of her dowry. Her husband had no claim to this money, as in the Byzantium and Anglo-Saxon examples. The dowry was her insurance against divorce. A Bulgarian Gypsy girl's dowry, known as the *čeiz*, was displayed, with the bride and groom, in the girl's parents' house for a few days before the wedding feast. The dowry was made up of gifts of mainly household items presented to the couple by family and friends.

Today, a girl or woman is not expected to provide a dowry as such on her wedding, but wedding presents are given to a couple to help set up the home. Although this may be related to the provision of a dowry, in the context of a woman's dowry helping to establish the new household, it is also analogous to a number of other practices where the community help to establish the couple as an independent unit. The American "shower," a party attended most often only by women at which household items are given to help furnish a house, has similarities with the tradition of a woman collecting for the bottom drawer and with the provision and show of a dowry, as in the example of the Bulgarian Gypsy *čeiz*.

See also Bidding; Gloves; Presents; Shower

References

Fell, Christine. 1984. *Women in Anglo Saxon England and the Impact of 1066.* London: Colonnade Books, British Museum Publications.

Fonseca, Isabel. 1995. *Bury Me Standing: The Gypsies and Their Journey.* London: Chatto and Windus.

Gillis, John R. 1985. *For Better, For Worse: British Marriages, 1600 to the Present.* Oxford: Oxford University Press.

Henderson, William. 1866. *Notes on the Folklore of the Northern Counties of England and the Borders.* London: Longmans, Green.

Herrin, Judith. 1994. "Public and Private Forms of Religious Commitment among Byzantine Women." In *Women in Ancient Societies,* edited by Léonie J. Archer, Susan Fischler, and Maria Wyke. London: Macmillan.

Power, Patrick C. 1976. *Sex and Marriage in Ancient Ireland.* Dublin: Mercier.

Stone, Lawrence. 1990. *The Family, Sex, and Marriage in England, 1500–1800.* Abridged and revised ed. London: Penguin.

Dress, Wedding

Bridal dress is a matter of folklore and fashion. In many countries the couple may be dressed in what is considered national dress and may wear special or new clothes to demonstrate their status as the bridal couple. The Norwegian bride will normally wear the national dress, the *bunad,* an outfit presented to her during her confirmation years. Each region has its own distinctive style, but generally this outfit comprises a long woolen skirt, an apron, a linen shirt, a cap, a waistcoat, and sometimes a shawl. A matching purse may also be included. The outfit is heavily embroidered with traditional regional designs and is embellished with silver brooches and/or silver squares on a leather belt.

Some brides wear their dowry, or are heavily decorated with jewelry on the wedding day to show wealth. Styles of dress, decoration, and, in some cultures, the crowning of the bride suggest that the bride is elevated to the status of a queen or princess for the day. For example, traditionally a bride from the Fassi people of Morocco would wear seven bridal garments over the course of the wedding. However, modern marriage ceremonies in Morocco last just a few days, so that a bride may wear only five or even only three outfits during the celebrations. One of these is a gold brocade gown, with a crown and a hanging pearl headdress. With only her face showing, she sits cross-legged on a platform that is carried at shoulder height in a procession. Western-style wedding clothing is now, however, found throughout the world. Japanese brides will sometimes choose a Western-style wedding and wedding costumes according to the fashions in the United States and Great Britain. At the mass weddings held in Seoul, Korea, by the Unification Church (the

Lapp bride and bridegroom. (Michael St. Maur Sheil/ CORBIS)

"Moonies"), the couples wear the current Western-style costumes.

The fairy-tale white wedding, traditional in Britain and the United States, is a relatively recent custom. It was not until the mid-nineteenth century that a specific fashion for the wedding dress was introduced into Britain and America, although the bride would wear favors and ribbons to indicate her bridal status. A description of a multiple wedding in the poorer part of Manchester in the first half of the nineteenth century by Head (1840) commented that all the parties were poor people, "and as to the brides and bridegrooms, as few were dressed in special costume, and all were very generally attended by friends and relatives, it was not easy to say which was which." Women would normally wear a best dress, and it would only be the well-off who could afford a new outfit, and not necessarily white. At the wedding of Jane McKinney, the second eldest child of a prosperous Ulster farming family, near Newtownabbey, Belfast, in 1855, the bride wore "a dark silk dress with white ribbon braclets and belt, ribbon and bow, a little opera cloth of a beautiful shade between lavender and drab, with white lining and ribbon on the hood, and a splendid white bonnet and veil" (Walker 1981, 31). The white wedding dress did not become fashionable or usual in Britain until the mid-eighteenth century, when it became symbolic of purity and virginity. But it was the "wedding industry" that dictated fashion and established the white wedding dress as *the* bridal outfit. This developed in the mid-nineteenth century, with etiquette books outlining behavior (prescribing where people should sit at the wedding breakfast, the order of speeches, and what should be worn) and fashion magazines, women's magazines, and magazines specifically aiming at prospective brides. There is a great deal of myth concerning the "traditional" use of white in British weddings. Jeaffreson (1872, 1: 167) wrote: "From ancient of days our maidenly brides have arrayed themselves in robes of lustrous whiteness for the marriage ceremony." In *The Good Natured Man* by Oliver Goldsmith (1768), one of the characters says: "I wish you could take the white and silver to be married in, it's the worst luck in the world in anything but white." The significance of different colors for the dress are outlined in rhymes, and most of the eighteenth- and nineteenth-century wedding dresses in museum collections are in colors other than white.

White is traditionally worn by the groom at a Buddhist wedding, and the Japanese wear white at commencement ceremonies, so that a Japanese bride in traditional costume will wear white beneath a robe of red and gold—the colors of festivals and rejoicing. The wedding color for the Russian Orthodox church is white, and after the death of Stalin, brides would wear white wedding dresses as a form of dissident activity. In a similar way, during the American Revolution, brides in the United States wore red outfits as a sign of rebellion. During the 1970s in Great Britain, the fashion for colored wedding dresses reemerged. Often in subtle pastel shades, the style ignored the dictates of traditional color symbolism, and pink and green were among the colors.

Many brides in Great Britain and the United States wear "something old, something new, something borrowed, something blue." Other superstitions have come to be associated with the wedding dress. For example, the bride should not make her own wedding dress nor should she try on the complete, finished outfit before the wedding day, and, most well known of all, it is bad luck for her future husband to see her in her wedding dress before the wedding.

See also Bridegroom; Colors; Crowns; Dowry; Veil

References
Baldizzone, Tiziana, and Gianni Baldizzone. 2001. *Wedding Ceremonies: Ethnic Symbols, Costume, and Ritual*. Paris: Flammarion.
Cunnington, Phillis, and Catherine Lucas. 1972. *Costume for Birth, Marriage, and Death*. London: Adam and Charles Black.
Head, Sir George. 1840. *A Home Tour through the Manufacturing Districts and Other Parts of England, Scotland, and Ireland*. London: John Murray.
Jeaffreson, John Cordy. 1872. *Brides and Bridals*. 2 vols. London: Hurst and Blackett.
Lansdell, Avril. 1983. *Wedding Fashions, 1860–1980*. Aylesbury, Bucks: Shire Publications.
Monger, George. 1991. "Colour in Marriage." In *Colour and Appearance in Folkore*, edited by John Hutchings and Juliette Wood. London: Folklore Society
Walker, Brian. 1981, 2003. *Sentry Hill: An Ulster Farm and Family*. Belfast: Blackstaff Press.

Dunmow Flitch

The ceremony of the Dunmow Flitch Trials, in mid-June every leap year, at Great Dunmow, Essex, England, is held to reward couples who can swear to having been happily

The winners of the 2004 Dunmow Flitch Trials being carried through the streets of Dunmow, Essex. (Courtesy of the Dunmow Flitch Trials)

ownership of Sir Thomas May, the custom was revived and the present form of the custom was developed, with a judge and a jury to test the claimants' worthiness to receive the flitch. After the trial, the claimants would kneel on two pointed stones near the church door and the oath would be administered:

> You doe swear by custom of confession
> That you ne're made Nuptiall Transgression,
> Nor since you were married man and wife,
> By household brawles or contentious strife
> Or otherwise in bed or at boarde
> Offended each other in Deed or in Word
> Or in a twelve moneths time and a day
>   Repented not in any way
> Or since the Church Clerke said Amen
>   Wish't yourselves unmarried agen,
> But continue true and in desire,
> As when you joyn'd hands in Holy Quire.

After the oath the sentence was pronounced:

> Since these Conditions without any fear,
> Of your own accords you do freely swear,
> A whole Flitch of Bacon you doe receive,
> And beare it away with love and good Leave,
> For this is the Custome of Dunmow well
>   known,
> Tho' the Pleasure be Ours, the Bacon's your
>   own.

married for at least a year and a day without even a day's regret, sleeping or waking, or ever wishing themselves unwed. The couples are awarded with a flitch of bacon (a side of bacon). The origins of the custom are obscure, but it is said that it dates back to 1104 when Lady Juga Baynard founded the Little Dunmow Priory, to encourage people to get married in the church rather than by such practices as handfasting or other trial marriages. However, it has also been suggested that it was instituted by Robert Fitzwalter in the thirteenth century.

The Dunmow Flitch custom was well known in the time of Chaucer and is alluded to by the wife of Bath in *Canterbury Tales* (first published 1387): "The bacon was not fet for him, I trow, / That som men have in Essex at Dunmow." The custom fell into disuse after Henry VIII dissolved the priory. In 1701, when the Dunmow Priory came under the

In 1751, the flitch was awarded to Thomas and Anne Shakeshaft in one of the earliest and most detailed of the recorded flitch trials, and it was at this time that the practice of carrying the winning couple in procession through the streets of Dunmow began. However, the public custom apparently died out soon after. There is an account of a couple, one John Gilder and his wife, who, in attempting to claim the prize in 1772, arrived at the priory with their supporters, only to find the gates locked. In 1851, the flitch was claimed by a couple from nearby Felstead, but the lord of the manor refused to award it on the grounds that the custom had been dormant for too long. However, the villagers of Great Dunmow decided that the couple deserved to be awarded the flitch and did so, with an imitation of the old ceremony and administration of the oath, at a fete.

The custom was revived in 1855 after the publication of a romantic novel by a popular writer of the time, William Harrison Ainsworth, *The Flitch of Bacon, or the custom of Dunmow, a Tale of English Home Life* (published in 1854). The novelist transferred the action from Little Dunmow to Great Dunmow, where the custom continues today. Ainsworth gave a great deal of assistance to the revival by donating two flitches of bacon. The custom was interrupted by the two world wars, but after the Second World War, the custom was revived, in 1949, as reported in the *Times* (London), 19 August 1949, made possible by the provision of a flitch through the Commonwealth Gift Scheme since Great Britain was still subject to rationing restrictions. The Dunmow Flitch today takes the form of a mock trial, with celebrities acting as counsel and with a jury of six spinsters and six bachelors. Dunmow is not the only place to have offered a flitch as a prize for marital fidelity and happiness. It was said by some antiquarian writers that at the Abbey of St. Melaine, near Rennes (the old capital of Brittany), a flitch of bacon hung for more than six centuries, still quite fresh, for the first couple who for a year and a day had lived without dispute and grumbling and without repenting their marriage. A flitch was also said to have been hung in the "old Red Tower of Vienna." Underneath was a rhyme that translated as:

Is there to be found a married man
That in verity declare can,
That his marriage him doth not rue,
That he has no fear of his wife for a shrew,
He may this Bacon for himself down hew?

And there is a tale of a claimant for this bacon who, when the ladder was brought for him, asked that someone should cut it down for him because, if he got a grease spot on his best clothes, his wife would scold him. Needless to say he was refused the flitch. At Wychnor, near Lichfield, in Staffordshire, England, the lord of the manor in around 1337 (Sir Philip de Somerville) offered a flitch for marital fidelity. The flitch was to be laid on a quarter of wheat and a quarter of rye and the applicant would have to go on one knee and pronounce the oath:

> Hear ye, Sir Philip de Somervile, lord of Whichenoure, maintain and giver of this Bacon, that I, *A,* syth I wedded *B,* my wyfe, and syth I had her in my kepying and at wylle, by a Yere and a Daye after our Marryage, I would not have changed for none other, farer ne fowler, richer ne pourer, ne for none other descended of gretter lynage, sleeping ne waking, at noo time, and if the said *B* were sole and I sole, I would take her to be my wyfe before all other wymen of the worlde, of what condytion soevere they be, good or evyle, as helpe me God, and Seyntys, and this flesh and all fleshes.

In 1780 it was noted that the flitch had "remained untouched from the first century of its institution to the present."

References

James, E. O. 1953. "New Information on the Dunmow Ceremony: Correct Form of Oath and Sentence." *Folklore* 64: 355.

Robertson-Scott, J. W. 1909. *The Strange Story of the Dunmow Flitch*. Dunmow, England: D. Carter.

Steer, Francis W. 1951. *The History of the Dunmow Flitch Ceremony*. Essex Record Office Publications No. 13. Chelmsford: Essex County Council.

Egypt

Egypt is an Islamic country and follows Islamic traditions concerning marriage. But it is a cosmopolitan country and consequently subject to outside influences that alter traditional practices. There exist many variations on the details of weddings, depending upon the religion, social status, outlook, and location of the family. There are also differences between city-dwelling Egyptians and those living in the rural areas. Although the arrangements between the families are carried out in private, wedding celebrations are very public.

In accordance with Muslim practice, the man and woman should not see each other before being married. Indeed, the practice in Muslim communities is for girls to be veiled at puberty and usually to be married soon after. It was therefore usual for a young man intending to marry to ask a matchmaker to find him a wife, or inquire if there was a family with marriageable girls so that the father could be approached. Today, Muslims in the city may meet socially; if they meet via an intermediary, a matchmaker, this is referred to as a "salon marriage." The young man does not approach the woman's father himself to offer marriage but sends one of his female relatives. The fathers of the couple have an initial meeting to assess each other's family

circumstances and social standing. If the fathers agree, the young man, with his mother and father, go to the young woman's house to meet her and her parents. In the case of a salon marriage this will be the couple's first meeting. Again, after this meeting, the families and the couple consider whether to proceed with the marriage, and if all decide to go ahead, there is another meeting at the young woman's house, this time with members of the extended family.

Once the entire family has given approval, the couple will become engaged a few months later. It is during this time that the two families make the financial arrangements. A marriage agreement has two parts—the *mahr,* a monetary payment from the husband-to-be to the prospective bride's family to help them prepare and obtain the furniture and other household goods that the bride will take to the marriage, and the *shabka,* a gift, usually of jewelry, that the man gives to his fiancée. The financial details include the amounts to be spent on the celebrations. After the agreement is completed, a date is set for the engagement party; the date for the wedding is set only when a home for the couple is ready. At the engagement, the man gives his fiancée a present as a token of his love. At one time this would have been gold jewelry but today is more likely to be a diamond ring—by custom, the more expensive the ring, the greater his love for her. The couple, along with their mothers, shop for this present together.

The engagement party is paid for by the bride's family and is similar to the wedding celebration but on a smaller scale. The couple may exchange rings, which are worn on the right hand, there is a cake, and the bride wears colorful clothes. It is after this party that the mothers start to make the arrangements leading up to the wedding. During this period, the couple have a chance to get to know each other (for a salon arrangement) or have family approval to get to know each other better if they had met socially before. The young man visits the woman's home, taking gifts each time, and they may be allowed to go out together, sometimes alone but often with a chaperone. This is a time for preparation and for the buying of the household goods for their future home (the amounts to be spent and who provides what having been previously agreed upon).

At some point during the time before the wedding, the ceremony of *katb el ktab* (the writing of the book) is performed. Performed by a sheikh, either in a mosque, at the bride's home, or in a special office that is similar to a theater, with those taking part on a stage, this is a formal agreement between the two fathers (or the groom's father and the bride's approved agent) that seals the arrangement. The two join right hands and press their thumbs together. Their hands are covered with a white cloth. If the woman is divorced or widowed it is the woman who performs this ceremony with the groom-to-be. In rural areas, the *katb el ktab* takes place on the same day as the wedding.

The young man now gives to the woman an agreed-upon sum of money, and they agree on a divorce settlement in the event of the man divorcing the woman. From this point, if she wishes to divorce him, or pull out of the wedding before the final ceremony, she will have to pay him back the money given at this ceremony. If the young man decides to pull out of the wedding, he has to give her half of the agreed-upon divorce settlement. The fathers act as the two witnesses to these arrangements, and five copies of the arrangement certificate, with the couple's photographs and thumbprints, are prepared. The groom, before the wedding, signs an inventory, *ayma,* of all the furniture and household goods supplied for the home. This is a form of promissory note indicating that he is now responsible for these items for life. The gold and jewelry that he has bought are also displayed.

Between one and three days before the wedding, the relatives and friends of the bride gather to celebrate with her at a henna party where they will dance and sing, paint henna designs on her hands and feet, and remove all her body hair. Traditionally, part of the bride's preparation would be a visit to the bathhouse. She would process through the streets, covered completely with a red cashmere shawl, wearing a small cap or even a crown, under a silk canopy open only at the front, and accompanied by musicians and her friends. After the bride and her party have visited the bathhouse, they return to the bride's house, again in procession, where she and her companions continue to celebrate the henna party. A large quantity of henna is made into a paste, and the bride holds a lump of it in her hand. Each of her guests sticks a coin into the lump; when it is covered, she scrapes it off her hands onto the edge of a basin of water. Once all her guests have contributed, more henna is applied to her hands and to her feet, which are then bound with linen and left overnight. By the next morning, her hands and feet have become a deep orange-red. The guests dye their own hands and feet with the remainder of the henna. A similar preparatory party is held at the groom's house, where he is bathed, shaved, and fed a lot of protein. In the city, the bride and groom visit a photographer for a wedding photograph to be taken before going to the ceremony.

The marriage contract is signed and registered the next day, and after sunset the wedding party begins. Traditionally the bride processes, again with her friends, family, supporters, and musicians, to the groom's house, but this time on a camel or a saddled ass, or in a closed carriage completely hidden from view. The procession may take the most circuitous route possible and the procession may last several hours. At the bridegroom's house, a feast is held, and then the bridegroom goes to the mosque to pray. On returning from the mosque, he is introduced to and left alone with his bride. After giving her money, he lifts her veil and sees her for the first time. Her garments are removed, during which she is expected to offer as much resistance as possible.

In cities today, parents hire a venue for the wedding, which, depending on their wealth, may be a ballroom, an entire five-star hotel, a hotel nightclub, or other nightclub or restaurant. Rarely is the party held at home. The bride and groom will arrive either by car or by horse-drawn transport (the *caleche*). The bride and groom are led from the transport by a group of musicians and dancers to thrones on a dais in the main celebration room. This part of the event is called a *zaffa*. Middle-class, less expensive weddings may not include the *zaffa* and the thrones. This journey may take quite some time to complete, as the couple will be stopped on the way for photographs and for the guests to dance. Throughout the evening, the guests take turns in approaching them with their congratulations. After the meal there is usually a band and a singer, and the bride and groom lead off the dancing. A belly dancer and her band will be included in the evening's entertainment. The night sometimes ends with a disco. During the evening the bride and groom may cut a cake, in the center of the dance floor, and exchange rings. If the wedding is celebrated at a nightclub or restaurant, the bride and groom might not sit on thrones, but they are likely to be called up on stage to dance and

be congratulated; even complete strangers will join in with the congratulations.

Variations occur according to social standing and wealth. In the poorer urban areas and city outskirts there may be a party at the groom's house before the engagement party at the bride's house, where she will be publicly given gifts of gold jewelry. The wedding celebrations are carried out in the street, which is decorated with lights. Rows of canopies and chairs are set up. The thrones are set up to one side of the street and a stage is prepared for the musicians. Men and women sit apart, and soft drinks and cake are served to the guests. In rural areas the partying may last for up to a month after the wedding, with sacrifices of sheep and cows, readings from the Koran, recitation of prayers, music, and dancing. Here, again, the sexes are segregated.

In rural areas, proof of virginity is sometimes displayed. The bride's mother and her female relatives serve breakfast to the couple in the bridal chamber on the morning after the wedding, again containing a lot of protein. Proof of virginity is sometimes required and is displayed on a handkerchief rather than on a sheet. Additionally, sometimes, the newly married woman will be checked for pregnancy after the first month.

Marriage centers on the church for members of Coptic Christian sects. Priests know the families intimately—he receives confessions, makes regular house visits, and organizes Coptic Clubs where young people can meet. If a couple wish to be engaged they are free to make the agreement themselves, but they do involve their families, who check the status and respectability of the other family before undertaking negotiations. Once a verbal agreement has been reached, the priest is informed of the engagement. The church retains records of all marriages and engagements, and the priest checks that neither of the couple has been married or engaged before (if the church has been informed of the breaking of any previous engagement then the couple may proceed). Copts do not allow divorce (the only exception being the case of adultery)—if the previous marriage has been terminated at a government office, this is not recognized by the church and the couple may not be married in the church—but could marry in a register office. The young woman's family pays for the engagement party, the church fees, and other expenses, and the man buys the cake and gifts of gold for his fiancée. (If she breaks off the engagement, she is obliged to return all the gifts; if he breaks it off, they are not returned.)

On the day of the engagement, the bride usually goes to the hairdresser, afterward meeting the groom. The couple go to have their photograph taken and then to church where they sign a contract, just inside the church, before the engagement ceremony. This contract has to be witnessed. If the family is poor, the engagement ceremony takes place at the home. Prayers are said, and the priest gives the couple their rings and blesses them by marking the sign of the cross in holy oil on the couple's foreheads, chins, and wrists. After the service, congratulations are received, more photographs are taken, and a party is held with the couple seated on thrones. In the period between the engagement and the wedding, the household is prepared, with the man responsible for all the furnishings except kitchen equipment and bedroom furnishings. He also has to provide gifts for his fiancée. Before the wedding, the couple each have all body hair removed, and they each have a prewedding celebration with friends. The bride has her henna night (henna is not usually used, except in rural areas—this is a Muslim tradition) with singing and dancing, and the groom has an evening out with his friends.

On the wedding day, usually a Sunday and never a Wednesday or Friday because these are days for fasting, the priest begins to prepare the marriage contract before the bride arrives at the church, continuing to write it during the ceremony of prayer. The groom meets the bride at the church, where she is given away by her father. Once the contract is signed and witnessed the priest gives each a ring and then anoints them with the holy oil as he did during the engagement. Each is given a red sash, gold cloak, and gold-colored crown, so that they are dressed like a king and queen, and they kneel before the altar for prayers. After the priest has offered advice, the sashes, cloaks, and crowns are removed and they leave the church. The wedding party is paid for by the bridegroom. The day after the marriage, the bride's mother prepares their breakfast. In some rural areas, proof of virginity may be displayed, again on a handkerchief. A very religious couple, a small minority, will fast, abstain from everything, or even go to a monastery, for three days after the wedding.

The ceremony in the Coptic church has changed over time. Descriptions from the nineteenth century have some variation from the contemporary description above, which may have incorporated elements of Western Christian tradition. In earlier accounts, the couple processed to the church together but, once in church, were separated, the groom sitting with the men in the choir and the bride with the women. After the priest had recited and led lengthy prayers and hymns and read more prayers over the groom, signing with the cross at the beginning and end of each prayer, the groom would sit on the ground facing east, a silver cross held over his head, as more prayers were read. The priest led the bride and one of her nearest relatives to chairs placed by the choir. The bridegroom was then dressed in a long white robe, with a girdle around his waist and a white cloth on his head, and led to the bride. The priest would cover both their heads with the cloth and anoint their foreheads and wrists with oil. Joining their right hands, the duties in their new lives together were read to them. After more prayers and a communion mass, the ceremony was complete.

See also Arabic Weddings; Bathing; Betrothal; Canopy, Bridal; Henna; Islamic Marriage

References

Contemporary account, personal communication, with Sara Farouk Ahmed, Cairo, 19 October 2002.

Lane, Edward W. [1836] 1914. *The Manners and Customs of the Modern Egyptians.* Everyman Edition. London: J. M. Dent.

Wood, Edward J. 1869. *The Wedding Day in All Ages and Countries.* 2 vols. London: R. Bentley.

Elizabethan Wedding Party

A commonly quoted account of a wedding during the time of Queen Elizabeth I of England (1558–1603) comes from *The History of John Newchombe, the Wealthy Clothier of Newbery* by Thomas Deloney (1633).

It was thus that John Newchombe's spouse was led to her marriage by two dainty urchins, bravely decked with laces and sprigs of rosemary. The bride being attired in a gown of sheep russet, and a kirtle of fine worsted, her head attired with a filament of gold, and her hair, as yellow as gold, hanging down behind her, which was curiously combed and plaited according to the manner of those days. She was led to the church between two sweet boys, with bride-laces and rosemary tied about their silken sleeves. Then was there a fair bride-cup of silver-gilt carried before her, wherein was a goodly branch of rosemary gilded very fair, and hung about with silver ribands of all colours; next there was a noise of musicians that played all the way before her. After her came the chiefest maidens of the country, some bearing bride-cakes, and some garlands of wheat finely gilded, and so passed to church; and the bridegroom finely apparelled, with the young men, followed close behind. (quoted in Jeaffreson 1972, 1:185)

The wedding procession provided inspiration for the poet Edmund Spenser (1552–1599) in his poem "Wedding of the Medway and the Thames":

Her godly locks adown her back did flow
Unto her waist, with flowers bescattered,
The which ambrosial odours forth did throw
To all about, and all her shoulders spread
As a new spring; and likewise on her head
A chaplet of sundry flowers she wove,
From under which the dewy humour shed

Did trickle down her hair, like to the hoar
Congealed little drops which do the morn
  adore.
On her two pretty bride-maids did attend,
One called the Theise, the other called the
  Crane,
Which on her waited, things amiss to mend,
And both behind upheld her spreading train,
Under which her feet appeared plain—
Her silver feet, fair washed against this day;
And her before there paced pages twain,
Both clad in colours like, and like array,
The Doun and eke the Frith, both which
  prepared her way.

The wedding celebrations of the rich or well-off during this period often lasted several days, and the poor and servants benefited from these celebrations. When Lady Jane Grey (1537–1554) was married, the poor were provided with bread, beef, and ale for three days. The celebrations were usually uproarious and coarse and included a great deal of music and dancing. Bishop Coverdale (1488–1569), translator of the Bible into English, denounced the "shameful pompe and vaine wantonness" and the drunkenness and gluttony of marriage banquets and feasts. He railed against "bridal-feasters" who went to church the worse for drink and who paid no attention to the wedding sermon. They entered the church with a great clamor and then, returning to the feasting house, continued to drink and feast and behaved offensively. Bedding practices and customs in the bedchamber to put the couple to bed, with such practices as throwing the bride's stocking, outraged a clergy that had only been allowed to marry since the Reformation in the sixteenth century. Clergy tended to be embarrassed by their own marital states and were expected to keep their wives in private lodgings and not in their official residences, on the insistence of Queen Elizabeth.

See also Confetti; Epithalamium; Garter; Gloves; Rosemary

References

Deloney, Thomas. 1597. *History of John Newchombe, the Wealthy Clothier of Newbury.* N.p.

Jeaffreson, John Cordy. 1872. *Brides and Bridals.* 2 vols. London: Hurst and Blackett.

Monsarrat, Ann. 1973. *And the Bride Wore . . . : The Story of the White Wedding.* London: Gentry.

Elopement

According to the *Oxford English Dictionary,* to "elope," with reference to a woman, means to run away from a husband or a home with a lover or paramour. The word brings images of a romantic escape from parental disapproval by a young couple in love and determined to marry. Fortune hunters would elope with heirs and heiresses to be married by unscrupulous priests at such places as the Savoy and Fleet prisons in London and at certain known churches at various places in England. For example, entries in the parish records of St. Mary's Church, North Stifford, Essex, England, suggest that the incumbents were not too fussy about observing ecclesiastical law:

> 1658: Octobr ye 28 were married Grace Heath and Thomas Ffish, strangers both, by Mr. John Stone, Ministr of Greyse, ye banns not published
>
> 1709: July 25 Edward Horniblew and Rose Holman banns thrice published and married the same day
>
> 1709: October 16 William Roberts and Elizabeth Nelson banns 3 published and married the same day

The 1658 entry is interesting because this date was during the Commonwealth Period in England when marriage was considered a civil act and ceremonies were conducted by a justice of the peace. However, some couples did go to a church for religious services, and it may be that these two "strangers" felt the need to have the religious service in private to make sure that their marriage was proper, without getting in trouble with the local authorities for having done so. Elopements and clandestine marriages were part of the reason for the enactment of Lord Hardwick's Marriage Act of 1754. In essence the act declared that

all marriages solemnized from and after March 25, 1754, in any other place than a church or such publick chapel, unless by special license as aforesaid, or that shall be solemnized without publication of banns or license of marriage from a person or persons having authority to grant the same first had and obtained, shall be null and void to all intents and purposes whatsoever.

This did not totally prevent elopements, but it made matters more difficult. In addition to Jewish people and Quakers, nonconformists and Catholics were also badly served by this legislation, in that their places of worship were not licensed for marriages. After 1754, couples would elope to the Isle of Man or Guernsey, until the Isle of Man parliament enacted a special statute in 1757 that brought Isle of Man law into line with England and Wales. Lord Hardwick's act did not apply to Scotland, so lovers would travel to Scotland, initially to Edinburgh, where they could marry in the Cannongate district, and then later to Gretna Green, the nearest place over the Scottish/English border.

In the Ceiriog Valley in North Wales where there was a tradition of strong family authority and a tradition of besom weddings (a form of irregular marriage), elopements were common in the later nineteenth century. Courting strangers was strongly discouraged, and parents would frequently intervene to try to stop a marriage even if the girl was pregnant. In this situation a couple would run away "over the mountain." The couple would eventually return to the bride's home, where she would show her wedding ring. After much scolding and weeping, there would be forgiveness.

A similar practice is found among Bulgarian Gypsies. A couple may elope for a night and have intercourse, returning with the evidence of the girl losing her virginity, which is tested to ensure that it is human blood. After a show of disapproval, the couple are considered married and a public wedding follows, after the usual negotiations of settlements between the two families.

Elopement among the Australian Aborigines was not so amicably and quickly settled. An eloping couple had to stay away for many years or they would be punished and any children killed. They could rejoin their families only after several years and with gifts of food for the man's parents.

See also Aborigines (Australian); Besom
   Weddings; Fleet Weddings; Gretna Green;
   Gypsy Weddings; Lord Hardwick's Marriage
   Act

References

Fonseca, Isabel. 1995. *Bury Me Standing: The
   Gypsies and Their Journey.* London: Chatto and
   Windus.
Gillis, John R. 1985. *For Better, For Worse: British
   Marriages, 1600 to the Present.* Oxford: Oxford
   University Press.
Gwynn, Gwenith. 1928. "Besom Weddings in the
   Ceiriog Valley." *Folklore* 39: 149–166.
Jeaffreson, John Cordy. 1872. *Brides and Bridals.* 2
   vols. London: Hurst and Blackett.
Monger, George. 1975. "Was North Stifford the
   Gretna Green of Essex?" *Essex Countryside* 23,
   no. 225: 26–27.

Endogamy/Exogamy

Endogamy refers to marriage within a tribe or clan group, and exogamy refers to the practice of marrying outside of the tribe, kin-group, or clan. Guichard (1977) suggested that one of the six points that differentiate Eastern marriage structures from Western structures is the different degrees of endogamy and exogamy inherent in the marriage structure. The Asian system strongly favors endogamy, with the preferred marriage to the father's brother's daughter. It is or was seen as dishonorable to give a wife to another lineage, and "wife-takers" are considered superior to "wife-givers." Arab society is not exclusively endogamous—"out marriage" or exogamy is allowed and may be undertaken to cement a political alliance. Islamic society is less strict than Hindu society, where endogamy is practiced in its true sense of marrying within the clan, or caste, group.

Among immigrant or ethnic groups, endogamy is often the preferred or accepted practice, so that Orthodox Jews will usually marry within the Orthodox Jewish community and Greek Cypriot immigrants (whose marriages are usually arranged) generally within the Greek Cypriot community. The Gypsy traveler community also presumes endogamy—that young people will choose partners from the Gypsy community. A woman who marries outside the Gypsy community is likely to be ostracized by her group, but a non-Gypsy woman marrying into the group, as long as she conforms, is likely to be tolerated and later accepted. This seems to support Guichard's analysis of endogamous societies, that it is more honorable to be a "wife-taker" than a "wife-giver."

In Western society, the tendency is towards exogamy. Wife-giving is seen as superior to wife-taking—marriages outside the immediate circle of family or community brought goods and honor and cemented often useful and political alliances. Guichard commented that endogamy is also found in European cultures, but for economic rather than social reasons. However, there may be other reasons, such as a restricted social circle, that may result in endogamous cousin marriage. As in Asian societies, exogamy is an aspiration rather than a rule or obligation, as it was frequently said to be in African societies. (There are some notable exceptions to this rule, such as among the Kgatla people of Botswana, South Africa, who prefer endogamous marriage, with the partner chosen by the parents from the children of close relatives or near neighbors. Polygyny was allowed and a man would be allowed to choose his second wife himself.)

In Western societies, obligations for exogamy became the rule imposed by the church authorities, and in 1560 tables of forbidden marriage alliances were published. In Britain, these became law in 1835 in Lord Lyndhurst's Act.

See also Consanguinity

References

Goody, Jack. 1983. *The Development of the Family and Marriage in Europe.* Cambridge: Cambridge University Press.

Guichard, P. 1977. *Structures sociales 'orientales' et 'occidentales' dans l'Espagne musulmane.* Paris: N.p.

Schapera, Isaac. 1940. *Married Life in an African Tribe.* London: Faber and Faber.

Engagement

There are subtle differences among the terms "engagement," "betrothal," and "spousal." The latter two have more legally binding implications for both of the couple and there is more public ceremony involved in betrothal and spousal (in some cultures, such as Jewish, the betrothal is an integral part of the wedding ceremony). However, all three could be, and can be, private agreements.

In reviewing wedding traditions from around the world, it becomes clear that in many societies, including European and American, marriage is a process that is achieved in a number of stages. Sometimes these stages are only really clear to the people within that society, and sometimes the major stages of the transition from single unmarried to married are very clear. In societies with a free choice of marriage partner, this transition is from single to courtship to engagement to marriage. In societies without free choice, there is no courtship, and the engagement is properly termed a betrothal because of the more binding nature of the agreement. The loosening of terms surrounding the agreement to marry began around the late-eighteenth to early-nineteenth centuries. In the eighteenth century, couples generally entered into engagement as the first stage of matrimony when they determined that they were able to establish their own home. By the Victorian period, couples were beginning to become engaged and then work toward getting married when they could afford to do so. However, by this time betrothals were not blessed by the church nor were engagements considered as legally binding as a betrothal. Jeaffreson (1872, 1:86) commented on the lax view of engagement/betrothal:

> Though the engaged girl of the present period is the modern social equivalent of the virginal spouse of feudal England, her position is seen to differ considerably from that of the espoused damsel. She enjoys greater liberty than the maiden of former time. She may retract any number of lightly given matrimonial promises; and after promising herself with interchangement of rings and holy close of lips to half-a-dozen different suitors, she may become the wife of a seventh admirer, and ask her jilted lovers to be spectators of her wedding. . . . The law that allows her to trifle with a bevy of lovers, also permits men to jilt her. And it sometimes happens that the frivolous beauty, after playing falsely and cruelly with a true man's passion, receives appropriate, though terrible punishment from a masculine trifler, who wins her love only to show his disdain of it.

The etiquette of engagement has further changed over the past hundred or so years, changes that have reflected changing social mores, age of consent, age of majority, and family patterns. As with spousal, the couple are in a no-man's-land between being single and being married, although in contemporary Western societies those boundaries are becoming more and more fuzzy. Unlike *espousal de futuro* (a contract to marry in the future but with the status of being virtually married), which could be undone by mutual consent unless the couple were having sexual relations, in which case it would be a binding contract that neither could break, an engagement may be broken off at any time, whether or not the couple were having sexual relations.

The giving of a ring by the man to the woman is still an important part of the engagement ritual. A diamond ring is usual, but some etiquette books suggest that the woman's birthstone is the most auspicious gem for her engagement ring. The man still sometimes goes through the ordeal of asking the woman's father for his daughter's hand in marriage, although it is probably rare for the father to demand details of the young man's prospects or of his savings account, often the case until the last quarter of the twentieth century. In Britain, a couple can marry without parental permission at age eighteen, and data suggest that many young Britons are delaying marriage until their late twenties or early thirties. Parents are more likely to be told of the couple's decision to marry than be asked. The period of engagement is a preparatory time—the couple prepare for the wedding (the bride-to-be and her mother do most of this) and start to save money and collect items for the new home. Etiquette books advise that they should exchange small, inexpensive personal gifts, have an engagement photograph taken, put an announcement in the local newspaper, and hold a small engagement party.

Either of the couple has the option of calling off the engagement, although the nearer the wedding, the more likely the party calling it off will be expected to compensate for wedding expenses. The couple may return gifts that they had given each other, and the woman would be expected to return the ring.

See also Betrothal; Courtship; Spousal

References
Dobson, Sue. 1981. *The Wedding Day Book.* London: Arrow.
Gillis, John R. 1985. *For Better, For Worse: British Marriages, 1600 to the Present.* Oxford: Oxford University Press.
Heaton, Vernon. 1986. *Wedding Etiquette Properly Explained.* Rev. ed. Kingswood, Surrey: Elliot Right Way.
Jeaffreson, John Cordy. 1872. *Brides and Bridals.* 2 vols. London: Hurst and Blackett.
"Two Ladies of England." 1932. *The Bride's Book or Young Housewife's Compendium.* London: Gerald Howe.

Epithalamium

A song or poem to celebrate a wedding, an epithalamium differs from fescennine songs or verses in that the epithalamium is a praising verse, while fescennine songs may be lewd and insulting. But there may be some link between the two verse forms. In the Russian wedding of the past, epithalamium verses were often insulting. The epithalamium, or wedding hymn, was common in classical Greek and Roman weddings where it was sung outside the bridal chamber (the *thalamos* in Greek) by young men and maidens, usually accompanied by soft music. The two best proponents of the epithalamium verse form were the Greek poetess Sappho (said to be born at Mytilene in the island of Lesbos around 612 B.C.) and the Roman poet Catullus (who lived from 87 to 54 B.C.), known to be a great admirer of Sappho's work. These poets were often commissioned to write marriage poems for aristocratic families.

Poets have often written nuptial songs or poems, such as "A Nuptial Song, or Epithalamie, on Sir Clipseby Crew and his Lady" from the seventeenth-century writer Robert Herrick. He was vicar of Dean Prior, near Ashburton, Devon, from 1629 to 1647 and then from 1662 to 1674, and was known to have been influenced by the classical poets, including Catullus. Herrick's verse suggests contemporary wedding practice, the sprinkling of wheat over the bride and the scattering of rose petals and other flowers in her path, for example:

> Glide by the banks of Virgins then, and passe
> The Shewers of Roses, lucky-four-leav'd
>   grasse:
> The while the cloudes of younglings sing,
> And drown yee with a flowrie Spring:
> While some repeat
> Your praise, and bless you, sprinkling you
>   with Wheat:
> While that others doe divine;
> *Blest is the Bride, on whom the Sun doth shine;*
> And thousands gladly wish
> You multiply, as doth a Fish.

The last two lines seem to destroy the romanticism of the verse. In a later verse he mentions traditions concerning the bride's garter and points (favors):

> To bed, to bed, kind Turtles, now and write
> This the short'st day, and this the longest
>   night;
> Yet too short for you: 'tis we,
> Who count this night as long as three,
> Lying alone,
> Telling the Clock strike Ten, Eleven, Twelve,
>   One.
> Quickly, quickly then prepare;
> And let the Young-men and the Bride-maids
>   share
> Your Garters; and their joynts
> Encircle with the Bride-grooms Points.

A further verse refers to the blessing and drinking of sack posset by the bride to give her strength at the end of a long day:

> If needs we must for Ceremonies-sake,
> Blesse a Sack-posset; Luck go with it; take
> The Night Charme quickly; you have spells,
> And magicks for to end, and hells,
> To passe; but such
> And of such Torture as no one would grutch
> To live therin for ever: Frie
> And consume, and grow again to die,
> And live, and in that case,
> Love the confusion of the place.

A number of Herrick's verses in this poem refer to the bedding of the bride and groom, and this is in keeping with the traditional epithalamium of Sappho and others (not forgetting that they were recited or sung outside the nuptial chamber). A surviving fragment of one of Sappho's verses is:

> Bride, full of rosy love-desires;
> Bride, the most beautiful ornament of
>   Aphrodite of Paphos,
> Go to your marriage-bed,
> Go to the marriage-couch whereon you shall
>   play so gently
> and sweetly with your bridegroom;
> and may the evening star lead you willingly
>   to that place,
> for there you will be astonished at the silver-
>   throned Hera.

The American poet Walt Whitman (1819–1892) briefly revived this tradition when he wrote an epithalamium "A Kiss to the Bride" for President Ulysses Grant's daughter Nellie on her wedding in 1874.

See also Confetti; Favors; Fescennine Songs;
    Garter; Posset
References
Braddock, Joseph. 1961. *The Bridal Bed*. New
    York: John Day.
Herrick, Robert. 1961. *Selected Poems*. Edited by
    John Hayward. Harmondsworth, Middlesex:
    Penguin.

Espousal

See Spousal

Etiquette

Etiquette lays out rules of behavior in society and the form and order of ceremonies and celebrations. Wedding etiquette has evolved through custom and social mores, and wedding etiquette books have become instructional manuals about what to do, how things should be arranged, and when they should be arranged. The major difference between customary practice and etiquette is that the former allows for regional (or family) variations, whereas etiquette standardizes behavior and social procedures.

There seems to be a great difference between etiquette developed in an organic manner through customary practice and that developed in the laying down of the rules for "polite" society. Increasingly over the nineteenth and twentieth century, in Britain, rules of behavior were laid out in etiquette books that were the manners and conventions of the moneyed and ruling classes, to be used as a template for the aspiring classes to follow.

There is a long history of books and articles that prescribe how to conduct oneself in society and what should and should not be worn, going back to the early nineteenth century. These followed fashion and were written in a very didactic way, so that, for example, in the 1860s, a fashion writer rebuked gentlemen for wearing black at weddings, noting that black frock coats were not proper for the occasion of marriage, except in the case of the weddings of clergymen. The advice was for grooms to wear blue, mulberry, or claret frock coats. However, by the end of the century, etiquette demanded that the groom and his best man wear black frock coats (faced with silk) with a light-colored, double-breasted waistcoat with a dark tie, or a dark waistcoat with a light tie.

Rules of etiquette often become very entrenched and difficult to break. Seligson (1974, 95) reported a wedding musician being concerned about breaking the etiquette of the order of the first dance, which dictated that the bridal couple should start, then the bride's father should break in and dance with the bride while the groom danced with his mother-in-law, then the best man should dance with the bride and the groom with the maid of honor. His worry was that there were so many divorces that the order of precedence was quite confused: "I've been to weddings where there are so many fathers-of-the-bride and step-fathers-of-the-groom that the first dance goes on for an hour." In any case, although rules of etiquette are laid out in instructional books and appear immutable, they do in fact change in detail over time as dictated by fashion and changing social mores.

See also Cards, Wedding; Dances
References
Monsarrat, Ann. 1973. *And the Bride Wore . . . : The Story of the White Wedding.* London: Gentry.
Seligson, Marcia. 1974. *The Eternal Bliss Machine: The American Way of Wedding.* London: Hutchinson.

Evil Eye, Protection from

The notion of the "evil eye" suggests that there are malevolent influences that will bring bad luck, or even worse, to people, and that there are specific times when these forces can be most active and effective. Transitional times are believed to bring specific vulnerability, and a wedding is certainly a transitional time. The evil eye or evil influences range from malevolent spirits that will enter and do harm to the newly married couple to simple bad luck. There are, according to tradition, three main methods of protection from the evil eye: deceiving the malevolent spirits; using protective amulets, charms, or clothing; and frightening the spirits by firing guns or making a huge noise.

Veils to hide the bride and dressing the bridesmaids in a similar way to the bride are used to protect the bride from bad luck, malevolent spirits, or magicians. The Berbers of Morocco keep the marriage time secret for fear of witchcraft. Canopies used in some marriage ceremonies are sometimes seen as a form of protection from the evil eye (although the Jewish *huppah* is said to be derived from the bridal chamber, or tent, wherein the marriage would be consecrated).

According to Chinese legend, rice is thrown at a wedding not as a symbol of fertility or prosperity but to distract a malevolent bird-spirit. The ancient Romans sang unchaste and lascivious songs at weddings, fescennine songs, in the belief that they would avert the evil eye. It was thought that the more abominable, the more certain the effect. At marriage ceremonies among the Jews of Tunis, after the religious ceremony, the bride is taken into an upper room, accompanied by all her friends, who remain with her. The bridegroom retires with his friends, without taking the slightest notice of the bride. She is seated on a chair placed upon the usual divan. Her mother-in-law now comes forward, unveils her, and with a pair of scissors cuts off the tips of her hair. This last ceremony is supposed to be of great importance in driving away all evil influences that might do harm to or come between the newly married pair.

Pearls form the main element in the traditional bridal outfit of the Fassi of Morocco. The costume is known as *el-jawbar,* the "dress of pearls" because it is believed that the shiny surface offers a defense against the evil eye. The bride's head and chest, vital parts of her body, are covered with pearl decorations. The extremities are considered by some to be very susceptible, and hands and feet are to be protected by decoration with henna. In Germany, the wedding is a civil ceremony carried out by a registrar, often followed by a church ceremony on the next day. On the evening of the first day, a party is held in the old tradition of *Polterabend*—neighbors drink, dance, and make a great deal of noise breaking crockery, banging saucepans, and cracking whips to drive away evil spirits. This goes on until the early hours of the morning.

There are suggestions that traditions such as "firing the anvil," firing guns into the air, and "rough bands" at weddings may also be related to practices to scare away evil spirits.

See also Anvil, Firing of; Fescennine Songs; Henna; *Polterabend* Party; Rough Music/Rough Band

References

Baldizzone, Tiziana, and Gianni Baldizzone. 2001. *Wedding Ceremonies: Ethnic Symbols, Costume, and Rituals.* Paris: Flammarion.

Crawley, Ernest. [1902] 1932. *The Mystic Rose: A Study of Primitive Marriage and of Primitive Thought in Its Bearing on Marriage.* 4th ed. Revised and enlarged by Theodore Besterman. London: C. A. Watts.

Elworthy, F. T. 1895. *The Evil Eye.* London: J. Murray.

Murphy, Brian M. 1978. *The World of Weddings: An Illustrated Celebration.* London: Paddington.

Exogamy

See Endogamy/Exogamy

Factory Customs

Wedding customs in factories and in industry are mainly before the wedding and by women workers, although it is not unknown for men to have a prewedding celebration. It is likely that these factory customs arose during the twentieth century and were particularly practiced when married women did not work outside of the home. Upon marriage a woman was expected to leave paid employment and the premarriage celebration was a farewell from her workmates. Men's events noted by Monger (1975) were analogous to the customs associated with an apprentice completing his training. Just as the apprentice changes from one who is learning the trade to one considered able to practice the trade, the young man changes his status from being a boy to being a man.

There is one nineteenth-century account (possibly dated around 1836) of a factory marriage custom from a printing establishment in London from Smith (1857). The ceremony involved parading the newly married man through the workplace, accompanied by a mock bride and groom, while the workers banged the benches to make a form of "rough music."

See also Ribbon Girl; Rough Music/Rough Band; Shower; Stag Night

References
Monger, George. 1996. "Pre-Marriage Ceremonies: A Study of Custom and Function." *Lore and Language* 14: 143–155.
———. 1975. "Further Notes on Wedding Customs in Industry." *Folklore* 86: 50–61.
Smith, Charles Manby. [1857] 1967. *The Working Man's Way in the World.* London: Printing Historical Society. Reprinted from the 3d issue.

Fantasy Weddings

In Japan, many couples have a Western-style wedding, with the bride wearing a white bridal gown and the groom in tails, in addition to the civil ceremony. This style of wedding is often referred to as a "fantasy wedding," probably because it resembles fairy-tale events from stories and film, and is often an amalgam of this style of wedding with Japanese tradition. In Japan, as in many countries, a wedding is a civil arrangement with little or no religious connotation so that the actual ceremony has no bearing on the legality of a marriage as long as the union is correctly registered.

See also Japan
References
Monger, George. 1991. "Colour in Marriage." In *Colour and Appearance in Folklore.* Edited by John Hutchings and Juliette Wood. London: Folklore Society.

Murphy, Brian M. 1978. *The World of Weddings: An Illustrated Celebration*. London: Paddington.

Favors

Sir George Head (1840), in his description of a multiple wedding of poor couples in Manchester, England, during the first half of the nineteenth century, described one couple arriving by horse-drawn carriage and noted that the coachman and his companion wore a white favor. A wedding favor was usually a ribbon tied with a lover's knot; these were distributed among the guests, as well as given to friends and relatives who did not attend the wedding. Samuel Pepys, the seventeenth-century London diarist, complained in his diary from about 15 to 22 February 1667 that, despite the fact that Sir William Penn, a work colleague at the Admiralty, had borrowed kitchen items to prepare the wedding dinner, he did not receive his wedding favor until a few days after the wedding. Pepys recorded that Penn had been distributing the favors around town before he had been given one to wear in his hat (which he did reluctantly).

Perhaps the practice of distributing favors found its way to England from Holland and seems to have been widespread in fashionable circles in continental Europe at one time. But by the end of the seventeenth century and early eighteenth century, the custom had dropped out of fashion. A French Protestant traveler in England, Francis Misson (1698), was disparaging about the English distributing favors, stating that in France formerly they had given out a "Knot of Ribbands," or *Livrées de Nôces,* which were worn on the arms of the guests, but that this practice was now carried out only by peasants. He went on to note that the custom continued among the English noblemen and that favors were distributed not only to those at the wedding but also "to five hundred people besides." *The Newgate Calendar* (Rayner and Crook 1926, 4), an account of notorious prisoners held and executed at Newgate prison, when describing the biga-mous marriage of the countess of Bristol to the duke of Kingston, for which she was tried in the House of Lords in 1776, said that wedding favors were worn by persons of the highest distinction in the kingdom.

The distribution of favors is often said to have originated in Denmark in pre-Norman times when little ribbon bows were given and worn as pledges. The Danish word *trulofa* translates as "I plight my troth." Thus, the word *trulofa* became transformed into "true-love," and the knots of ribbons became "true-love knots." Favors are also known as "points," as in Herrick's *Hesperides* (1648):

Let the young Men and Bride-Maids share
Your garters; and their joynts
Encircle with the Bridegroom's points.

"Points" were ties worn in the young men's hats. "Bride laces"—also ribbons—were also given out as favors, and sometimes ribbons were cut up and the pieces distributed as favors. In later years, favors were usually white, as in the nineteenth-century example from Manchester, above, and at Queen Victoria's wedding in 1840. Women generally wore white favors, although these do not appear to have been a simple true-love knot but were more like elaborate rosettes with orange blossoms with some silver decorations in the center, or with lace mixed in with the ribbon. In earlier times the colors of the favors were chosen with great care. Colors were often given symbolic meanings associated with character traits, emotions, and luck, so that, for example, yellow favors expressed jealousy but also honor and joy, while blue signified religion and was considered too serious (even though there was a saying that the bride should wear "something old, something new, something borrowed and something blue"). Green was associated with wantonness. Gold, silver, and white were often used. Other colors and shades were sometimes problematical.

The distribution and wearing of favors continued into the nineteenth century. Wedding favors were distributed to guests and servants after the wedding. The bridesmaids pinned white knots to the lapels of the groomsmen, and the men pinned them to the women's bodices. In some districts of Scotland, it was traditional for the bride to place a favor on the minister's right arm after the service. The bride and her "best maid" pinned favors on the right and left arms of partners after a reel. In the United States, wedding favors were used to decorate the ears of the horses and the coats of the servants. The bridegroom wore a boutonniere of natural flowers. It is now traditional at weddings in Great Britain and the United States for the male members of the bridal party to wear a boutonniere, usually a white carnation, and this can be related to the tradition of the wearing of ribbon favors. The favors distributed at weddings were not always ribbon knots, but could also be plain ribbons, gloves, or garters. There were games at weddings that involved vying for the bride's garter, worn in the hat as a wedding favor. Today, favors, or other mementos of the wedding, are distributed by the bride, usually to the female guests. These may be bags of sugared almonds, decorations from the cake (extra cake decorations are made), or small flowers. In contemporary continental Europe, the cars of wedding guests are decorated with a ribbon bow, often white, attached to the antenna. The favor is often left on the antenna for weeks after.

See also Almonds; Flowers; Garter; Gloves; Racing

References
Charsley, Simon R. 1991. *Rites of Marrying: The Wedding Industry in Scotland.* Manchester and New York: Manchester University Press.
Cunnington, Phillis, and Catherine Lucas. 1972. *Costume for Birth, Marriage, and Death.* London: Adam and Charles Black.
Gillis, John R. 1985. *For Better, For Worse: British Marriages, 1600 to the Present.* Oxford: Oxford University Press.
Gregor, Rev. Walter. 1881. *Notes on the Folklore of the North East of Scotland.* London: Folklore Society.
Head, Sir George. 1840. *A Home Tour through the Manufacturing Districts and Other Parts of England, Scotland, and Ireland.* London: John Murray.
Jeaffreson, John Cordy. 1872. *Brides and Bridals.* 2 vols. London: Hurst and Blackett.
Misson, Francis. [1698] 1719. *Memoirs and Observation in His Travels over England.* Translated by J. Ozell. London: Printed for D. Browne.
Monsarrat, Ann. 1973. *And the Bride Wore . . . : The Story of the White Wedding.* London: Gentry.
Rayner, J. L., and G. T. Crook. 1926. *The Complete Newgate Calendar.* 4 vols. London: Privately printed for the Navarre Society.

Feet

A tradition mentioned in Radford (1969) stipulated that it was unlucky for a bride to enter her new home for the first time after the wedding with the left foot foremost. Beginning a journey with the left foot was also said to be unlucky (one wonders what this implies for an army marching left-right-left-right). A bridegroom from the Zoroastrian faith will enter the bride's family compound on the wedding day with the right foot first (and without touching the threshold). The feet, and also the hands, are sometimes seen as being vulnerable to evil influences as exposed extremities—the henna decoration applied to the feet and hands of a bride in Islamic countries is sometimes said to have a protective function. However, the feet have a particular focus in some marriage traditions, found from the United Kingdom to the Indian subcontinent. There exists an interesting parallel with decoration of feet with henna that is found in the wedding preparations of the Tuaregs of Niger and the Fassi of Morocco. In Scotland it was a well-known tradition, which continued well into the latter half of the twentieth century, for the feet of people about to be married to be blackened. A prewedding custom observed in Kingston-upon-Hull in the 1970s was for the group of people celebrating with the prospective bride and groom before the wedding day to kiss the bride-to-be on the foot. This was noted to be a family custom and consequently not widespread.

There appears to be another coming together between the East and the West with a practice of washing the feet. In the past in some parts of the north of Scotland, on the evening before the wedding, the bridesmaids attended the bride and washed her feet (from a letter from a "Gentleman in Northern Scotland," 1754, quoted in Heseltine 1951, 172). The bathing of feet appears in wedding ceremonies among several groups of people. In Hindu ceremonies, the bridegroom's feet may be washed by the bride's father; in the Zoroastrian wedding, the bride and groom's feet may be washed; and in parts of Europe there were feet-washing customs, with the washing water being afterward sprinkled over guests, cattle, and parts of the house. At the Hindu ceremony of the Tamils of South India, after the ceremony of the *saptapadi* where the couple circle the sacred fire seven times together, the groom places the bride's right foot on a stone to represent the steadfastness of their marriage. Earlier in the ceremony the bride's mother may have placed a few ochre and saffron-yellow rice balls at the bride's feet to ward off malevolent influences.

The feet are seen as a gateway to the person. Feet, like hands, leave an impression on the world. There are beliefs that the life essence of a person can linger within their shoes, which may account for the tradition of throwing old shoes after a person embarking on a journey, for luck, and the related practice of throwing old shoes after a newly married couple as they leave the reception (and later tying old boots behind the car taking them away from the reception). This is in contrast with Muslim tradition, where to throw a shoe at someone or their image, or to hit someone with a shoe, is the highest insult.

In Chinese tradition, if a betrothed girl died before the wedding day, her prospective husband would ask for a pair of her recently worn shoes. These he would take to his home, calling her to follow him at every street corner. On arriving at his home, he would inform her where they were, and the shoes would be placed either on or under a chair arranged at the table with incense burning on the table. Finally, a tablet was placed in her memory with the other family ancestral tablets. The shoes, having been in contact with her feet, retained her spirit, her essence, her impression.

One way to break a witch's spell was to stab a knife into her footprints, causing lameness in the witch. The Berber people of Morocco believe that witchcraft may disrupt the couple's married life, and the date and venue of the wedding is kept secret until the last moment, and, further, the bride's henna-decorated feet must not touch the ground on her wedding day.

See also Bathing; Henna; Hindu Weddings; India; Shoes; Zoroastrian Weddings

References
Braddock, Joseph. 1961. *The Bridal Bed.* New York: John Day.
Crombie, James E. 1895. "Shoe Throwing at Weddings." *Folklore* 6, no. 3: 258–281.
Heseltine, G. C. 1951. *A Bouquet for a Bride.* London: Hollis and Carter.
James, E. O. 1933. *Christian Myth and Ritual.* London: J. Murray.
Murphy, Brian M. 1978. *The World of Weddings: An Illustrated Celebration.* London: Paddington.
Radford, E., and M. A. Radford. 1969. *Encyclopaedia of Superstitions.* Edited and revised by Christina Hole. London: Hutchinson.

Fescennine Songs

A wedding is often considered a dangerous time for the bride and groom. Couples were thought to be particularly vulnerable to bad influences and evil spirits at this important turning point in life. Consequently, in many cultures, efforts are made to ward off these bad spirits and bad luck with various talismans (lucky black cats or horseshoes, for example). In ancient Rome the performance of fescennine songs was used to avert the evil eye. These songs were shocking or lascivious, invoking Nemesis (a Grecian avenging goddess), Cunina, and Priapus (Greek gods associated with sexuality), accompanied by obscene gestures and expressions. It was believed that the more shocking and abusive the songs and gestures, the more effective they would be. The poet Horace (65–8 B.C.) noted the performance of these songs, and the natural philosopher Pliny (A.D. 23–79) remarked that walnuts were used along with the fescennine songs at nuptials as a "symbol consecrated to marriage" and a protector of offspring.

Crawley (1902) noted that "amongst the Kaffirs [peoples from northeastern Afghanistan] the bride insults the groom," which was said to show that her moment of submission had not yet arrived. Crawley also noted that in the Punjab there was a general custom for the bride's relatives to be abusive to the bridegroom, and that this was often supposed to be related to or be a vestige of "marriage by capture." (But in Hindu tradition, marriage by capture is not a recognized and lawful form of marriage.) It is more likely that these were tactics to divert the attention of malevolent spirits away from the couple.

It is, however, the very nature of the wedding and the traditional implication of the first night (the beginning of the sexual relationship) that can also give rise to ribaldry and innuendo aimed at the couple. In the West, the speech given by the best man and the suggestive graffiti written on the going-away car represent this. It would be inaccurate to make a link between the ribaldry and sexual innuendo in speeches and graffiti and the fescennine; these songs are more related to the joking and general hilarity associated with customs of seeing the newlyweds to bed—throwing the stocking, the custom of the hot pot, or the French custom of *la rôtie* (otherwise known as *la soupe*) where the "friends" of the couple invade their bedchamber to force them to drink a disgusting concoction of wine, champagne, and leftover food from a chamber pot.

See also Bed, Marriage; Epithalamium; Evil Eye, Protection from; France; Hot Pot; *Soupe, la*
References
Crawley, Ernest. [1902] 1932. *The Mystic Rose: A Study of Primitive Marriage and of Primitive Thought in Its Bearing on Marriage*. 4th ed.

Revised and enlarged by Theodore Besterman. London: C. A. Watts.
Elworthy, F. T. 1895. *The Evil Eye*. London: J. Murray.

Fiancé(e)

Fiancé(e) is a French word that has been taken up by English-speaking people to refer to the person to whom they have become engaged or have promised to marry. The word simply means "one's betrothed" or "engaged." Fiancé refers to the male partner and fiancée to the female partner and is derived from the French word for betrothal, *fiançailles* and *fiancer*—to become engaged. In seventeenth century Normandy, *fiançailles* formed binding contracts, in much the same way that the spousal was regarded in England. The contract was confirmed and cemented by payments of money or gifts. The church marriage could follow after a considerable time, and it was accepted and agreed, even by the ecclesiastical authorities, that the couple should share a bed after the *fiançailles*. A hundred years later, the *fiançailles* disappeared as a distinct contract. Popular tradition retained some of the spirit of *fiançailles* and spousal, in the practice of bundling and in what is sometimes termed common-law marriage. However the word *fiançailles* continues to be used for "engagement to marry."

The word fiancé is today commonly used in England and the United States, but earlier in the twentieth century this was considered an ugly and coarse word in fashionable society. In a footnote to their use of the word fiancé, the "Two Ladies of England" (1932, 25) wrote: "The well-disposed reader will have noticed that we have done everything in human power to avoid using this *horrid* word, but with the best will in the world it is not always possible to find a substitute."

See also Betrothal; Bundling; Engagement; Spousal
References
Goody, Jack. 1983. *The Development of the Family and Marriage in Europe*. Cambridge: Cambridge University Press.

"Two Ladies of England." 1932. *The Bride's Book or Young Housewife's Compendium.* London: Gerald Howe.

Finland
See Scandinavia

Fleet Weddings

Before Lord Hardwick's Marriage Act of 1754, the Fleet area of London, England, was renowned as a place to go for a quick wedding or to find someone (a "clergyman") who would perform a marriage with no questions asked. This Fleet area, or Fleet Ditch, was the location of the notorious Fleet Prison, which held debtors and those jailed for contempt of court. Conditions in British prisons during the seventeenth and eighteenth centuries were terrible, but arrangements could be made by prisoners from the middle and upper classes to take lodgings outside the prison. In 1686, a Mr. Elliott was suspended by the ecclesiastical authorities for conducting weddings without calling the banns the requisite three separate Sundays or without the couple having obtained a special license. This was against ecclesiastical law but not civil law. The Reverend Elliott was suspended from his church, St. James's, Duke's Place, London, for three years. But he only served about fifteen months of his suspension. It was during this fifteen months that furtive weddings were performed at the Fleet Chapel. After Elliott's reinstatement at Duke's Place, clandestine marriages continued to be performed over the next fifteen years at the Fleet Chapel by the Reverend Jeronimus Alley. The Bishop of London, after visiting the prison, put a stop to this and suspended the Reverend Alley, who disappeared from the diocese. However, there were many left behind to carry on his work. By these suspensions the authorities drew attention to the fact that, as Jeaffreson (1872, 2: 130) put it:

> though the canons required ordinary weddings to take place in the parish churches and between certain hours of the day, a marriage might be solemnized at night, and in a secular building, and even without the assistance of a clergyman, and yet be as valid a union, for all civil purposes, as any wedding performed with banns or license by half-a-dozen bishops in a cathedral.

This knowledge, along with a tax placed on marriage licenses and the £100 fine for clergymen found guilty of conducting irregular or clandestine marriages, sent many couples to the Fleet parsons, who would marry a couple in their own home or at one of the many taverns that established marriage rooms in the Fleet area. Some of these "marrying houses" became very well known and many employed touters to find clients for the wedding trade. The Hand and Pen was one such marrying house. This establishment managed to convey some form of respectability and became very popular, so popular that several other establishments adopted the same name. Some of these were not even inns or taverns—one was a barber shop in the Fleet quarter.

It is thought that during the heyday of the Fleet as a wedding location there were approximately one hundred Fleet parsons. The records suggest that there were not less than seventy such clergy between 1700 and 1754. However, there were probably not more than around fifty practicing at any one time. Jeaffreson (1872, 2: 150–151) wrote of them:

> Most of the Fleet parsons were miserably indigent. Their earnings were as irregular as their practices; and it often happened that a marrying minister, living with a wife and children "in the liberties," was in arrears for the weekly rent of his squalid lodging, and had not tasted brandy or bread for twenty-four hours. The bachelors of this strange brotherhood of clerical black-sheep could usually provide for their wants by acting as the salaried chaplains of the tavern-keepers, if not by the independent exercise of their profession; but the unlucky married Fleet clergymen passed their lives in abject penury.

The case was very different with the few leaders of the profession who were aided by insinuating address and gentlemanlike appearance, and had aristocratic patrons in the fashionable quarters of the town.

Lord Hardwick's Marriage Act of 1754 put a stop to the Fleet wedding business, but similar irregular marriages continued to be performed elsewhere—the Fleet area was not the only place where couples could obtain a quick and secret wedding, with no questions asked, for a small fee. The act proclaimed that any marriage performed after that date that was not solemnized in a church or public chapel, unless by special license, without the due publication of the banns, should be null and void. This bill had a very stormy ride through Parliament, and some concessions had to be made on the way, one of which was an exemption for Scotland from the provisions of the act. There was little reason for this exemption, but a side effect was that it led to the establishment of the wedding trade at Gretna Green, the first village on the Scottish side of the border with England.

See also Gretna Green; Irregular Marriage
Reference
Jeaffreson, John Cordy. 1872. *Brides and Bridals.* 2 vols. London: Hurst and Blackett.

Flowers

Many cultures use flowers as decoration, worn by people, and sometimes to decorate a space or to signify a celebration. Flowers play a big part in the decorations at the church or wedding venue in Great Britain and the United States—they are sometimes carried in baskets by the bridesmaids or attendants, are carried by the bride in her bouquet, and are often used as a decoration in the back window of the bridal wedding car and to decorate the reception. One guide to wedding planning (Dobson 1981) counseled brides that the flowers are "an integral and important part of the wedding day." How-

ever, it was not until the nineteenth century that it became fashionable to decorate the church with flowers and for the bride to carry a bouquet.

Brides in ancient Rome apparently carried three ears of corn at the wedding ceremony, but it would be a stretch to claim that there is a direct link between this and the modern bridal bouquet. The plant or flower that seems to have had the longest association with weddings is rosemary. Orange blossoms are often used to decorate wedding cakes and are often included in bridal bouquets. The orange blossom is said to have been introduced into Britain from Spain around 1820, perhaps as an emblem of fruitfulness, and has had associations with a prosperous marriage because the orange tree is able to bear ripe fruit and blossom at the same time. Thus orange blossom is symbolic of good luck, fertility, and happiness. Oranges are said to be the golden apple that Jupiter gave to Juno on their wedding day. Saracen women were also said to wear the orange blossom in their hair on the wedding day, and crusaders were said to have brought the practice to the West. This is probably a myth. The introduction of orange blossoms into weddings in the United States is said to date from about 1838. This French fashion started with a goodwill shipment of orange blossom from the south of France. Before this time, American brides were more likely to wear a wreath of white roses, following English fashion, so that June, the time when most roses are in bloom, became the best time to marry.

Roses have long been associated with love, affection, and beauty, but also with secrecy and with Venus. Culpepper, in *Complete Herbal* (1649/52), stated: "Red rose are under Jupiter, damask under Venus, white under the moon." Jeaffreson (1872, 1: 190–192) wrote that the model bridesmaid:

displayed her cleverness and industry in preparing decorations of flowers for the adornment of the wedding guests and the rooms in which they will be entertained.

Besides making a wreath—of purple and white, or of white, and green, and gold—for the bride, she knotted yards upon yards of floral rope, to be hung in festoons upon the walls of the banqueting-chamber and galleries. She tied with silver lace dozens of little sprigs of rosemary, arranged that there should be an abundance of sweet rushes to cover the road from the bride's house to the church, and gathered a brave store of wild flowers to be sprinkled on the rushes as the newly-wedded bride returned from the sacred building to her father's dwelling. If the gardens near at hand would not yield her roses enough for her artistic purposes, she sent messages out to scour the country in search for more of the flowers that she specially needed; for in the seasons when roses were procurable no rooms were thought to be suitably dressed for bridal festivities unless the flower of love and secrecy glowed in every nook and perfumed every corner of them.

Of course, not all brides and bridesmaids in the nineteenth century, and earlier, were able to get flowers, roses in particular. However, in the twentieth century, manufacturers produced paper rose petals to be showered over the bride and groom as confetti, in the same way that flower petals were scattered in the pathway of well-to-do newlyweds in earlier centuries.

Myrtle, a plant associated with love and peace, was most likely introduced into wedding flowers by Queen Victoria, who carried myrtle in her bouquet at her wedding in 1840. (Many old-established myrtle bushes are said to have grown from a sprig of the myrtle carried by Queen Victoria.) But myrtle was associated with weddings long before Queen Victoria. In *Herbal from the Bible* by Lævinus Lemnius (1587), with English translation by T. Newton, we are told that it is dedicated to Venus and:

for that, at brideales, the houses and chambers were wont to be strawed with these odoriferous and sweete herbes [*myrtle and rose*]; to signifie that in wedlocke all

pensive sullenness and lowering cheer, all wrangling strife, jarring variance, and discorde, ought to be utterly excluded and abandoned, and that in place thereof al mirth, pleasantness, cheerfulness, mildness, quietness, and love should be maintained, and that in matters passing between husband and the wife all secresy should be used. (quoted in Jeaffreson 1872, 1: 192)

Brand (1777) wrote that "nuptual garlands" have been worn in many parts of the world ("equally used by the Jews and heathens") since remote antiquity, and that those used in the Eastern churches were sometimes made from myrtle, which, being sacred to Venus, was an emblem of love. Although before the nineteenth century, brides may have carried bouquets or posies of wildflowers at their weddings, it was not fashionable to have flower carriers—bridesmaids carrying small baskets of flowers—and arranged bouquets until the nineteenth century. Consequently, the tradition of the bride throwing her bouquet to the gathering of unmarried women (the one catching it being destined to be the next married) can only date from the nineteenth century. But this can be seen as a continuation of other throwing and scrambling traditions, such as throwing the bride's stocking.

The boutonniere often worn by the male members of the wedding party (as well as the corsage for the mothers of the bride and groom) have a link with wedding favors, which were once distributed at and after the wedding. But the buttonhole flower appears to have become fashionable during the nineteenth century; the buttonhole in a suit jacket made for holding a flower was not tailored into suits until the 1840s.

See also Bouquet; Divinations; Favors; Rosemary; Stockings, Throwing of

References

Brand, John. [1777] 1900. *Observations on the Popular Antiquities of Great Britain.* Revised and enlarged by Sir Henry Ellis in 1841 and 1848. 3 vols. London: G. Bill and Sons.

Charsley, Simon R. 1991. *Rites of Marrying: The Wedding Industry in Scotland.* Manchester and New York: Manchester University Press.

Culpepper. [1649/1652]. *Culpepper's Complete Herbal.* London: Milner and Sowerby, Paternoster Row.

Cunnington, Phillis, and Catherine Lucas. 1972. *Costume for Birth, Marriage, and Death.* London: Adam and Charles Black.

Dobson, Sue. 1981. *The Wedding Day Book.* London: Arrow.

Jeaffreson, John Cordy. 1872. *Brides and Bridals.* 2 vols. London: Hurst and Blackett

Monsarrat, Ann. 1973. *And the Bride Wore . . . : The Story of the White Wedding.* London: Gentry.

Vickery, Roy. 1995. *A Dictionary of Plant Lore.* Oxford: Oxford University Press.

France

Weddings in France, certainly, have a lot in common with those in the rest of Europe. As happened in England, the French Revolution in 1789 broke the power of the church over marriage in France. But the changes in France have been longer lasting than they were in England after the revolution in the mid-seventeenth century. After the English revolution, marriage was declared a civic event. However, upon the Restoration of the monarchy, the power of the church was reinstated. In France, the Republic has lasted much longer (today is the Fourth Republic). The Revolutionary Council established a new civic ceremony for marriage in which the local magistrate would read appropriate passages from the laws and remind the couple of duty to each other and to the state. Wedding ceremonies were held between set hours and tended to follow one after the other in quick succession. Weddings became a form of popular entertainment and occasionally got very rowdy.

Napoleon I gradually reintroduced the church into French life, and religious wedding ceremonies began to be accepted. The civic ceremony came to be followed by a church ceremony (for many fashionable people, the church ceremony would take place at night). It was usual for marriages to be arranged between families, especially among higher-class families, although love matches and courtship were known in preindustrial France. Marriage was largely an economic agreement between the two families, but also was seen as in the interests of the larger social and economic community. French proverbs cast doubt over the wisdom and longevity of love matches. One counsels that "who marries out of love has a good night and a bad day." Another warns that a "love-match brings disappointment after six months."

Young people did mix and socialize, especially after church on Sunday or at communal events and fetes and fairs, so they were able to get to know each other and no doubt develop alliances. Gifts were exchanged, but generally only after the couple had developed an understanding. The family of the man proposed marriage to the young woman through her family. This involved meeting at each other's houses and negotiating and agreeing on the dowry to be given to the couple. Once the agreement had been made, a banquet was held where the contract was signed and sealed and presents exchanged. The dowry usually included essential furniture for setting up a new home—a bed, linen chest, linens, and clothing. The young husband was expected to provide tools, agricultural equipment, and his personal clothing. The guests to the wedding also brought gifts. Godparents and members of the wedding party usually gave useful items, such as a hearth plate (a cast-iron plate that went at the back of the hearth), a kettle, or other kitchen equipment, sometimes inscribed with names and dates.

The bridal party processed to the village hall for the civic ceremony, followed a few days later by the church ceremony. As the guests left the church, they sometimes fired guns into the air to make noise. Today, guests are more likely to throw confetti or rice over the couple, but the drivers in the procession to the reception sound their car horns along the way. Traditionally, the party walked in procession, often led by a fiddler, to the reception, perhaps stopped on the way by barriers put in their pathway by the local children. The wedding feast might last until the early hours of the morning, with close family and friends continuing to celebrate for a couple more days. During the feast, the bride's garter may be removed (sometimes a boy goes under the table to ceremonially retrieve the garter), to be cut up and sold to the guests. An alternative garter tradition, from Normandy, is for the guests to urge the bride to dance on the table wearing a garter, and during the dance the guests put money into the garter. In some regions of France, the bride was given an engraved "wedding cup," a two-handled cup from which the bride and groom drank during the day.

Eventually the bridal couple retire to the wedding room, or bedroom, and it is here that, after a time, their friends find them and invade the room carrying a chamber pot (sometimes inscribed with words such as "to the bride"), which is filled with seasoned food and milk or wine to be served to the couple, called *la saucée, la soupe,* or *la rôtie.* Today, this is an unpalatable mixture of cake, wine, cheese, and vegetables, and whatever else, which the couple is obliged to taste.

See also Barring the Way; Bed, Marriage; Bridesmaid; Confetti; Dowry; Garter; Rice; *Soupe, la*

References

Lamotte, Françoise, ed. 1984. *Du berceau à la tombe: Les rites de passage.* Tome 26: Revue du Département de la Manche.

Segalen, Martine. 1975. "France." In *Love and Marriage: Aspects of Popular Culture in Europe [exhibition], Antwerpen.* Edited by W. Van Nespen. Brussels: Ministerie van Nederlanse Cultuur en Nationale Opvoeding.

Van Gennep, Arnold. 1932. *Folklore du Dauphiné.* Vol. 1. Paris: Librairie orientale et américaine.

Garter

Blue garters are often worn by brides in Britain, and wedding garters, along with black cats, foil-covered horseshoes, and miniature silver shoes, are often for sale among wedding cards and novelties in card shops. These elastic garters are often frilly and lacy items that the bride wears around the thigh. But the traditional wedding garter was very different and the subject of races and trophy hunting by the guests at the wedding. The bride's garter was an important tradition during the seventeenth and eighteenth centuries and consisted of a ribbon tie fastened just below the knee. The garter may have had long ribbons because of the practice for the "bride-men" to pull off the garters and wear them in their hats for luck, usually before she retired to the bedchamber. The bride would often loosen her garter to "prevent a curious hand from coming too near her knee" (Misson 1698). In some areas of northern England, the scramble for the garter began immediately after the wedding ceremony, with the winner parading the garter around the church in triumph. To protect herself from being hurt in the confusion, it was not unusual for the bride to distribute her garter herself. Bridal garters were prized as love tokens with magical properties—probably a magic by association and suggest-

ing that a gift of a garter that had been worn by a bride would ensure that the receiver of the gift would also be a bride, specifically the gift-giver's bride. In Normandy, France, the bride would bestow her garter upon a particular young man, although there were occasions when it was fought for. Garters were distributed as wedding favors at the weddings of the richer classes. Tegg (1877) mentioned this practice in his description of "An Old English Wedding": "An English wedding, in the time of good Queen Bess, was a joyous public festival; among the higher ranks the bridegroom presented the company with scarves, gloves, and garters of the favourite colours of the wedding pair."

The distribution of the garter persisted into the nineteenth century, especially among the European nobility. In 1821, at the wedding of the princess royal and the prince of Bavaria in Berlin, a garter custom was observed. After the ball, the royal family went into the apartment of Frederick I, where the grand mistress, countess of Norda, distributed the garter of the bride.

In the north of England, where the practice of racing for the bride's garter seems to have been vigorously observed, a ribbon, donated by the bride, replaced the garter. Atkinson (1841), the parish vicar, described the customs from Danby-in-Cleveland,

Yorkshire, England. After the wedding, the guests went into the field adjoining the church, and there they ran footraces for the ribbons donated by the bride. Atkinson further noted that earlier the races had been run on horseback cross-country to the bride's house, with the winner earning the right to remove the bride's garter. In Atkinson's parish, every bride was expected to donate at least one ribbon as a prize. If she refused, the local people expressed their displeasure by "firing the anvil," although this custom was also, usually, used to celebrate the marriage. The groomsmen, and even the groom, might also wear garters. The bride would usually have a blue garter (still the color used for bridal garters in the novelties shops), the color associated with the Virgin Mary, or even red or white. Those of the groomsmen would usually be white.

In North Yorkshire, during the seventeenth and eighteenth centuries, garters were popular gifts given as tokens of love. Sometimes the initials of the young man were stitched onto it, and the woman was expected to wear the garter above the knee of the left leg. The garter was supposed to help the couple be true to each other. The binding power of love gifts was not limited to garters, but they were often used in this way. Again from North Yorkshire, there was a practice for a young woman to weave barley straw and wheat straw, taken from the shock during the harvest moon, to make a garter that she fastened around her left leg. The number of strands that she used represented the number of children she hoped for, using wheat for boys and barley for girls. She should do this in secret, not let her intended know of it or see it, and wear the garter from Friday evening until Monday morning. It had to be fastened in place as she recited a charm that reportedly invoked the straw upon which the baby Jesus lay when sleeping in the manger. If the garter broke during the prescribed time of wearing, the charm lost its power. Only a

"true maiden" could wear this—it was considered a badge of virginity—as it would bring evil to any child born in wedlock if the girl "ever left the path of virtue" (Gutch 1899).

A report in Burne (1908) described how, in the area of Balmoral, Scotland, when a younger sister married before an older sister, the latter was forced to wear green garters at the wedding. Any young man who removed them was destined to become her husband. A vestige of the practice of claiming the bride's garter, which also has elements of the distribution of wedding favors and of the penny wedding tradition, is the custom from Orleans, France, of holding an auction of the bride's garter at the wedding reception. The highest bidder is allowed to remove the garter. A modern variation is to cut the garter into small pieces, which are then sold to guests for a small amount. These are pinned onto lapels.

See also Dancing in a Hog (Pig) Trough; Favors; Racing; Tokens

References

Atkinson, J. Canon. 1841. *Forty Years in a Moorland Parish*. London: Macmillan.

Burne, Charlotte. 1908. "Wedding Customs." *Folklore* 19, no. 5: 339–340.

Cunnington, Phillis, and Catherine Lucas. 1972. *Costume for Birth, Marriage, and Death*. London: Adam and Charles Black.

Furnborough, Peter, and Elizabeth Atkins. 1973. "Traditions and Language in Orleans and the Val de Loire." *Lore and Language* 1, no. 9: 16–19.

Gillis, John R. 1985. *For Better, For Worse: British Marriages, 1600 to the Present*. Oxford: Oxford University Press.

Gutch, Mrs. 1899. *County Folklore. Vol. 2. Concerning the North Riding of Yorkshire, York, and Ainsty*. London: Folklore Society.

Jeaffreson, John Cordy. 1872. *Brides and Bridals*. 2 vols. London: Hurst and Blackett.

Misson, Francis. [1698] 1719. *Memoirs and Observations in His Travels over England*. Translated by J. Ozell. London: Printed for D. Browne.

Monsarrat, Ann. 1973. *And the Bride Wore . . . : The Story of the White Wedding*. London: Gentry.

Tegg, William. 1877. *The Knot Tied: Marriage Customs of All Nations*. London: William Tegg.

Germany

Marriage, across Europe, is quite similar from one country to the next, with some variation in localized customs. In Germany, the influence of the church is very strong even today, although German law states that a wedding is a civil ceremony that must be conducted by a registrar and specifically not a priest. Before reunification, in both West Germany and East Germany, and today, in the reunited Germany, marriage was and is a civil ceremony since the nineteenth century. In West Germany, a religious ceremony was allowed as an additional ceremony. In East Germany, of course, religious services were strongly discouraged. Couples were allowed to follow the civil ceremony with a church marriage, but only the registry office marriage was/is valid.

Historically, both parts of Germany have shared common wedding traditions. The celebrations usually began at the official engagement, a formal ceremony before witnesses, at which the couple exchanged gifts to mark the event on the day before the first announcement of the banns. The usual gift from the woman to the man was a wedding shirt and embroidered handkerchief; he would give her a pair of decorated slippers (apparently a symbol of her subjugation to her husband). The trousseau or dowry brought to the new household would consist of household articles, such as furniture, linen, and tools—the spinning wheel and distaff for holding the wool. These might be elaborately carved and decorated. As in other cultures, the trousseau was displayed and perhaps added to by well-wishers, perhaps during the formal procession for taking the items to the new home. Some documents suggest that the government laid down rules for the trousseau, telling people of different social classes to what degree of goods and finery they were entitled. In some regions, the conveying of the trousseau to the new home was the beginning of the wedding. But before the trousseau or dowry was arranged, the banns had to be called in the church. The actual wedding would take place a few weeks after the reading of the banns. After the banns had been announced, the couple would choose a friend to act as the "inviter" to the wedding. This person, generally a young man, would decorate his coat and his walking stick with ribbons and flowers and go to each house to invite the inhabitants to the wedding and the feast. As it was usual for each household to give the inviter a drink, it was not unusual for him to fail to complete his circuit. All knew that they were invited anyway. The inviter had other duties at the wedding—much the same as the best man in Britain and the United States, he acted as a master of ceremonies at the wedding feast.

The night before the wedding, a party known as the *Polterabend*, "noisy evening," was held. This was a feast put on by the relatives of the bride, at which the bridesmaids presented a myrtle wreath to the bride that they had bought or made. This would be her bridal crown, although some churches owned a bridal crown that could be borrowed. The local townspeople brought out old crockery, pots, and pans and around midnight threw them at the door of the house. (In parts of Great Britain and the Galician area of Spain, there were similar traditions of the local population making noise, but this usually happened on the wedding day itself. In Finland, the *Polterabend* party differs in that the bride-to-be is paraded around the town, with a collection being taken, on the day before the wedding.) Today, in Germany, the *Polterabend* retains some of the flavor of the historical tradition but usually takes place during the wedding celebrations. The church wedding usually takes place the day after the civil ceremony, and the *Polterabend* usually takes place on the evening of the civil marriage, with the neighbors drinking and dancing and making a great deal of noise, including breaking crockery, banging saucepans, and cracking whips to drive away evil spirits. This party goes on until the early hours of the morning.

On the day of the wedding, the bride would wear a special dress, not necessarily white, but perhaps decorated with ribbons and flowers (elaborately decorated dresses only really developed in the second half of the nineteenth century). In fact, often the preferred and traditional dress for a bride was black. When the groom arrived at the bride's house to take her to church, depending on the local tradition, he might have found that his bride appeared to be a burly man, with a beard, in bridal array, or perhaps she was surrounded by her bridesmaids all dressed identically, or she was hidden from him by her friends and he would have to undertake a vigorous search. Such customs are said to be symbolic of her reluctance to leave her family home and leave her childhood but may also have been a mechanism, seen in other cultures, to deflect ill-wishes, bad luck, and evil spirits. The couple would lead a procession, in a cart, to the church. On the way the path would often be blocked by the young men of the village using a rope or a chain. The groom would have to pay a toll before the wedding party was able to proceed.

At the church, the couple walked down the aisle close together to prevent evil spirits from coming between them. While kneeling before the priest, the groom tried to ensure that he had the upper hand in the household by kneeling on the hem of her dress while the bride would try to stand on his foot when they rose to stand in front of the priest for the same purpose. Similar traditions are found in the Jewish wedding, where the position of the feet beneath the *huppah* and of the hands during the cutting of the wedding cake is important. After the ceremony, the couple again led the procession, again in a cart, to their new home. The groom carried the bride over the threshold as a beer stein was thrown over the roof to prevent him from drinking too much. Once inside, they would share a piece of bread, and then the bride went into the kitchen and symbolically took up the housewifely role by adding salt to the soup.

All the guests, except the honored, head-table guests, paid entrance to the feast with a small gift. After the first course, the "inviter," who now assumed the role of master of ceremonies, toasted the couple, finished his drink in one gulp, and then threw his glass over his shoulder, ensuring that it smashed to bring the marriage good luck. He would then call on each guest by name to present their gift to the couple, for which they were rewarded with a drink. The bride would then pay the musician with a coin that she had in her shoe, and the dancing would begin, led by the bride and groom. The feasting and drinking would resume, but only after the cook, with her hand bound up in a cloth, was paid "for medicine." At midnight the bridesmaids removed the bridal wreath from the bride's head and a piece of the myrtle from the bridegroom's buttonhole. The bride was blindfolded and her wreath placed in her hand, as the unmarried girls danced around her and she attempted to put the wreath onto the head of one of them. The one who received the wreath would be married within a year. A similar ceremony was performed with the bridegroom and the unmarried men.

A white muslin cap was now placed on the bride's head, prepared by the bridesmaids, a sign that she was now a "dame" or "Frau." Similarly, the bridegroom was given a white cotton nightcap, with a tassel at the crown. The party continued eating and drinking, and at some time during the evening one of the men slipped under the table and removed a garter from the leg of each of the women (which they wore for this purpose). These ribbon garters were cut into pieces and each man wore a piece in his buttonhole. Eventually, the bridal couple was accompanied to the bridal bed, in which pieces of bread and coal had been put for good luck, symbolic of plenty and warmth. After much suggestive humor, the couple were left alone.

At one time a "pay wedding" was very common, similar to the penny weddings and bridewains in Great Britain, where at the feast the bride would sit at a table with a large bowl in front of her into which the guests put money or some other article of value, such as jewelry or gold or silver. Sometimes, however, each guest would pay a fixed sum for the refreshments. Until 1839, when it was abolished by law, it was a common practice for the bridegroom to give his new wife a gift on the morning after the marriage—known as the *Morgengale* (morning gift)—which became her sole property and was said to have been to compensate for her lost virginity. The bride was allowed to choose the gift, which could be money or, more often, jewelry. But a law limited the size of the gift because of abuses, and exorbitant gift demands eventually led to the end of the tradition.

During the Nazi period in Germany, efforts were made to remove the religious elements from weddings and introduce a neopagan form of marriage. Heinrich Himmler expected members of the S.S. to repudiate the church. He tried to establish a so-called Order of Germanic Clans, and in 1936 he made it clear that it was the duty of members to marry and have a family. Couples had to be medically examined, show proof of their pure Aryan origins, and submit a photograph of themselves in bathing costume. If they were accepted the couple was allowed to marry and their names were entered in the S.S. clan book; the ceremony had to be a civil one and was attended only by close relatives. After the civil ceremony, the couple had a ceremony conducted by the S.S. commander. Supposedly based on pagan ritual, this included the couple swapping iron rings and eating bread and salt in front of witnesses. It is ironic that bread and salt feature in some Gypsy marriage ceremonies—also victims of the Nazi Holocaust.

Today the wedding in Germany is both a civil and a religious event. By law the ceremony has to be performed by a registrar who cannot be a priest. When the couple become betrothed, they are almost considered man and wife, and from the day of their engagement are referred to as the "bridegroom" and the "bride." Instead of exchanging handmade or personally embroidered gifts, they exchange rings, usually a plain gold band worn on the fourth finger of the left hand. Many couples have a religious ceremony on the day after the civil ceremony. On the evening before the church ceremony, the *Polterabend* party is often held, which may go on until the early hours of the morning. For the church wedding, brides today usually wear white wedding dresses, and grooms wear dark suits. As they enter the church, they are preceded by children scattering flower petals in their path. As they process from the church, young people are likely to barricade the path, allowing the bridal party to pass only on payment of sweets and coins. The wedding reception is likely to take place in the home of the bride's parents or perhaps a restaurant, during which toasts to the couple are drunk and speeches made. The celebrations usually continue until well into the night.

See also Banns; Dowry; Garter; Penny Weddings; *Polterabend* Party; Rough Music/Rough Band; Trousseau

References

Murphy, Brian M. 1978. *The World of Weddings: An Illustrated Celebration.* London: Paddington.

Scott, George Ryley. 1953. *Curious Customs of Sex and Marriage.* London: Torchstream.

Van Nespen, W., ed. 1975. *Love and Marriage: Aspects of Popular Culture in Europe [exhibition], Antwerpen.* Brussels: Ministerie van Nederlanse Cultuur en Nationale Opvoeding.

Giving Away

It is customary in the Western Christian wedding for the bride to be "given away" at the ceremony by either her father or the nearest male relative. The wording in the service is "who giveth this woman to be married to this man." Her father, or other male relative, passes the bride's hand to the officiant, who then passes it to the bridegroom's hand. In many cultures, marriage arrangements between families are negotiated by the fathers of the couple involved, and in Jewish weddings the bride may be escorted to the *huppah* (the canopy) by her father, although traditionally she would be escorted by her mother and future mother-in-law.

In Britain during the sixteenth and seventeenth centuries, fathers did not usually give their daughters away; the father's role was completed with the negotiations between the families at the time of betrothal. The bride would be given away by a brother or friend who accompanied her to church. In the eighteenth and nineteenth centuries, wedding ceremonies for the poorer laboring classes would take place during a break in the working day, and it was rare for the bride's father to escort her to church because he would lose earnings. The best man at the wedding was a relative, who would also give the bride away. A clergyman correspondent to Chambers (1863), from Suffolk, England, noted that at a laborer's wedding the attendants were only three: "the official father, the bridesmaid and the groomsman, the latter two being, if possible, an engaged couple, who purpose to be the next pair to come up to the altar on a similar errand upon their own account."

Some brides today object to the very notion of being "given away," and some ask a female friend or relative to perform this task. There is some precedent for this. Charlotte Brontë was given away by a woman when her father refused to attend her wedding in a temperamental outburst. There were other accounts of fathers who for one reason or another refused to give their daughters away. An account in the "Family Life and Work Experience before 1918" Oral History Archive at the University of Essex, Colchester, England, tells of a Preston father refusing to give his daughter away because he objected to the bridegroom taking one of his best lasses; her sister gave her away at the ceremony. The "Two Ladies of England" (1932) wrote that the bride had to be given away by some person as part of the ritual. But in the Quaker marriage service, no one person gives the bride away, and in a civil wedding ceremony

there is no necessity for the bride to be "given away." And in the remarriage of a widow, it is not usual for the bride to be given away. Sometimes the "giving away" is interpreted as being derived from a time when the bride was sold to the groom. However, there is little evidence of bride-sale in the Christian tradition in which the overt "giving away" is found, and it is probably not valid to make a connection between the payment of a dowry, by the bridegroom, and the concept of a sale transaction.

See also Dowry

References

Chambers, Robert. 1863–1864. *The Book of Days.* Vol. 1. Edinburgh: W. and R. Chambers. Philadelphia: J. B. Lippincott.

"Family Life and Work Experience before 1918." Oral History Archive. University of Essex, Colchester, England.

Gillis, John R. 1985. *For Better, For Worse: British Marriages, 1600 to the Present.* Oxford: Oxford University Press.

"Two Ladies of England." 1932. *The Bride's Book or Young Housewife's Compendium.* London: Gerald Howe.

Wrightson, Keith. 1982. *English Society, 1580–1680.* New Brunswick: Rutgers University Press.

Gloves

A handwritten list titled "gloves given at our wedding January 26th 1748" unfortunately does not name the bride and groom or the location of the wedding, but does give the names of fifty-two people, who, all together, were given eighty-three pairs of gloves. This is evidence of a once-common tradition, which appeared to have died out by the nineteenth century, whereby gloves were distributed to the guests at a wedding. It is recorded, for example, in 1560, that one hundred pairs of gloves were distributed at the wedding of the daughter of a merchant, Henry Machyn. In sixteenth-century France, too, gloves were distributed, as suggested by the mock marriage in Rabelais' *Pantagruel,* published in 1532, where as soon as the marriage contract was signed, "on one side was

Partial list of gloves presented to guests at a wedding, 26 January 1748. (Author's collection)

brought [wine, comfits, and favors]; on another gauntlets [gloves] privately handed." The distribution of gloves was considered an important signifier of a wedding. In Ben Jonson's *The Silent Woman,* from 1609, one character remarked: "We see no ensigns of a wedding here, no character of a brideale— Where be our scarves and our gloves?" And in a poem published in 1648, "To the Maids to walke abroad," Robert Herrick wrote:

> And talke of Brides; and who shall make
> That wedding-smock; this Bridal-Cake;
> That Dress, this Sprig, that Leaf this Vine . . .
> What Poses for our Wedding Rings;
> What Gloves we'l give, and Ribanings.

Gloves were once a common form of gift among friends and were often given as special presents on such occasions as New Year's Day and other solemn gift-giving occasions. In this context, gloves may be symbolic of extending a hand of friendship. They may also be presented as tokens and reminders of the marriage in the same way that favors and ribbons would be given. The paying of fees with gloves or the giving of gloves as a token of investiture into high office or upon taking possession of land was well established in European countries, and it has been suggested that the presenting of gloves at a wedding began as fees paid to the bridesmaids and the groomsmen for services rendered. In the 27 June 1863 issue of a weekly journal edited by Charles Dickens, *All the Year Round,* an account is given of a wedding in Wrexham in 1785. The houses in the street where the bridegroom lived had been decorated with boughs cut from trees and hung with ribbons and white paper cut to the shape of women's gloves. Dickens wrote:

> The Belgic custom at weddings is odd. The priest asks the bridegroom for a ring and a pair of gloves; red gloves, if they can be had; with three bits of silver money inside them. Putting the gloves into the bridegroom's right hand, he joins this with the right hand of the bride, and then, dexterously loosing them, he leaves the glove in the bride's grasp; as a symbol, doubtless that she is taken possession of, bought and paid for and conquered like any other vassal.

I am not sure that I agree with Dickens's explanation. It appears more analogous to the presenting, symbolically, of a dowry to the bride. In any case, the gloves given at weddings were often white, representing a clean hand and innocence. At the funeral of a young unmarried woman, a garland with a white glove (real or cut from paper) hanging from the middle was carried (and sometimes hung in the church), and there was a custom of presenting a pair of white gloves to a judge if there were no criminal cases for him to try. Gloves were also given as a sign of affection. In Devonshire if a woman was interested in a young man, she would approach him on Valentine's Day with the words:

Good-morrow, Valentine, I go today
To wear for you, what you must pay,
A pair of gloves next Easter day.

The young man was expected to send her a new pair of gloves on Easter Eve (sometimes he would send the gloves without encouragement). If she wore the gloves to church on Easter Day then the signs were good for the courtship. However, a gift of gloves is also sometimes considered to break up a friendship. Opie and Tatem (1989) have recorded, as late as 1984, a belief that gloves are given to a friend when that friendship will be broken. Some believe that a token payment for the gloves will prevent this happening.

See also Dowry; Favors; Shoes

References
Cunnington, Phillis, and Catherine Lucas. 1972. *Costume for Birth, Marriage, and Death.* London: Adam and Charles Black.
Herrick, Robert. 1961. *Selected Poems.* Edited by John Hayward. Harmondsworth, Middlesex: Penguin.
Monsarrat, Ann. 1973. *And the Bride Wore . . . : The Story of the White Wedding.* London: Gentry.
Opie, Iona, and Moira Tatem, eds. 1989. *A Dictionary of Superstitions.* Oxford: Oxford University Press.

Greek Weddings

The Greek wedding is essentially a secular event with a blessing by the church added.

Details of the event vary among regions. The practices of Greeks living in other countries also vary. The major elements of the wedding in Greece include public displays of the betrothal/engagement, the showing of the dowry, the crowning of the bride and groom, the public procession of the bride with her possessions to the groom's house, including a ritual for her threshold crossing, and public feasting and dancing.

The parents of a couple have a say in the choice of marriage partner, although marriage is no longer arranged. Sometimes the parents make all the marriage arrangements, but the young people "suggest" the name of a suitable partner. Once an agreement has been made and the dowry settled, the couple exchange rings in a ceremony in front of family and friends, followed by toasts and feasting. Sugared almonds may be distributed to those attending this event (American Greeks sometimes have a table set aside with sugared almonds and the wedding rings and an icon. A priest may also be invited to bless the rings and almonds, and small net bags of sugared almonds may be distributed to the guests.) The engagement rings are worn on the left hand and transferred to the right hand at the wedding. The engagement is considered to be as binding as marriage, but gives the couple an extra chance for getting to know each other better. The couple spend the time between the engagement and the wedding preparing to set up home together—collecting additional items for the woman's dowry.

The wedding itself is a mixture of secular custom to which has been appended a church blessing. The formal marriage usually takes place on a Sunday. The days leading up to the event, starting on the Wednesday, are spent in celebration and preparation. In some parts of Greece, married women go around the village carrying a basket of sugared almonds, pomegranates, a mixture of walnuts and almonds, and a bottle of ouzo, inviting people to attend the wedding. In the homes of the bride and groom, a ritual of "starting the leaven" may be taking place whereby a boy and a girl sieve some freshly milled flour watched by the relatives. When the sieving is finished, the watchers toss coins into the sieve and call "good luck." The flour is mixed with pure water to make a dough, and three shots may be fired into the air to announce this stage of the proceedings. Dough is smeared on the faces of the bride and groom, and the guests in each house eat a meal, after which the groom's family goes to the bride's house for a joint celebration with much dancing and drinking. The following day is spent quietly. On Friday, the dowry is laid out, and female friends and neighbors visit. The visitors bring small gifts of basil, cotton, and rice. The dowry is then packed into a sack, with the bride's mother beginning the packing with a copper saucepan. While the bride-to-be is packing up her dowry, the guests throw coins among the items. The woman's bed linen is also stacked up, and her friends throw rice and pin herbs to it. All her goods, including furniture and jewelry, is taken to the groom's house, where the bed is made up by two young girls whose parents are alive, and a baby boy may be tossed onto the bed to ensure that the couple, too, will have children. American Greeks roll a male child on the bed and then toss sugared almonds, money, and rice onto it.

The groom-to-be, meanwhile, will have sent a pitcher of wine to his friends and relatives in the village with a written invitation to the wedding. The bride's father does likewise. The bride, accompanied by a group of friends, spends Saturday morning inviting the girls of the village to her wedding, giving them sweets or sugared almonds. The wedding itself takes place after the usual church service on Sunday. After church, the girls go to the bride's house to dance as she prepares herself for the wedding, and the boys go to the groom's house. An escort is sent from the groom's party to collect the sponsor *(koumbaros),* usually the groom's godfather. After the sponsor has arrived, the groom's party processes to the bride's house, led by a young man carrying a white flag decorated with herbs and apples. When they reach the bride's home, the flag is flown from the roof,

and the flag bearer is rewarded with a ring biscuit (a shortbread-type biscuit baked in a ring shape, containing nuts and decorated with icing). The groom is greeted at the doorway by the bride's mother, with wine and a buttonhole of herbs. He kisses her hand and she kisses him on both cheeks. After he has drunk the wine, the bridal party processes to the church with the bride on the arm of a male relative leading the way.

The religious ceremony combines the betrothal with the wedding. The priest blesses the rings and touches the couple on the brow with the rings three times, saying, "The servant of God is betrothed," each time. The rings are placed on the couple's fingers and the rings changed back and forth between the couple three times. Psalms and prayers are chanted. In a cathedral wedding, large choirs sing, hidden behind a grill, while the service is chanted by the archimandrite. The couple is crowned with two crowns (or garlands of flowers) joined with white ribbon. The crowns are swapped from head to head three times, and then the couple each take three spoonfuls of wine. This is seen as one of the defining moments of the marriage—"to be crowned" means to be married—and many older people refer to couples who have been married in a registry office as "uncrowned," that is, not properly married. The crowning is followed by the "dance of Isaiah." The couple, with the groom holding the hand of the priest and the bride holding the hand of the *koumbaros,* walk around the altar three times, stopping four times on each circuit. Sometimes at this point sugared almonds are thrown on the couple. Once the dance of Isaiah has been completed, the couple face the altar for scripture readings and the priest's blessing. The couple may also be showered with sugared almonds as they leave the church, and guests may be given a small net bag of sugared almonds *(bononiéra)* or they may take a large handful from a basket.

When the bride arrives at the groom's house after the wedding, the flag is displayed over the house and she throws a piece of iron onto the roof. At the door, her mother-in-law will give her a ring biscuit, which she breaks into four pieces; one piece she eats, she puts two in her breasts, and the fourth piece is given to her mother-in-law, for which she receives a glass of wine. After making the sign of the cross with the wine, she returns it to her mother-in-law. There are a number of different ceremonies for the bride's crossing of the threshold of the groom's house. In Cephalonia, a Greek island, the bride may be met at the door by her mother-in-law with a plate of *kouphéta,* a mixture of rice and almonds, from which she takes a handful and throws it three times back and front for good luck and fertility. She is then embraced by her mother-in-law and enters the house. In other regions, the bride may have to throw a ripe pomegranate at a patch of honey in the middle of the door, hoping to make some of the seeds stick to the honey. The groom offers her bread and salt, which she eats outside. After touching oil and water, she is carried over the threshold and placed in a corner with her back to a wall. The dowry is unpacked and displayed and the feasting and dancing begin. The father of the groom pays the musicians and names a dance, which he will lead, to honor the bride. This is followed by the bride's closest male relative doing the same to honor the groom and then the bride; the *koumbaros* will next honor the couple, followed by other members of the wedding party. During the dancing, money may be pinned to the clothing of the bride and groom.

See also Almonds; Betrothal; Crowns; Dances;
    Dowry
References
Edwards, Thornton B. 1996. "The Sugared
    Almond in Modern Greek Rites of Passage."
    Folklore 107: 49–56.
Murphy, Brian M. 1978. *The World of Weddings: An
    Illustrated Celebration.* London: Paddington.

Gretna Green

Gretna Green in Scotland is the first town over the border with England and has be-

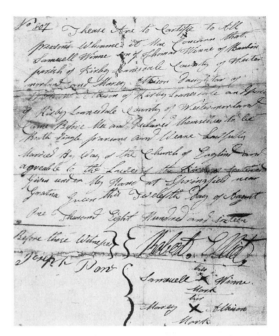

Gretna Green marriage certificate from 1816. (Courtesy of the Ilfracombe Museum)

come famous as the site for elopements. Before the 1754 Lord Hardwick's Marriage Act, there were many places where a couple could be married clandestinely (without prior reading of the banns, without the consent of the parents, and without a special license), and there were many priests willing to officiate at such marriages. Some places, such as the Fleet Prison in London, had become well known for irregular marriages. But the 1754 act made such clandestine marriages illegal and eliminated the trade in irregular marriages, with the intention, among other things, of trying to protect young women from being married for their money and being defrauded by their new husband. But the act did not apply in Scotland where a couple could declare themselves husband and wife before two witnesses.

By tradition, couples would be married "over the anvil" and by a "blacksmith priest." But these folks were neither priest nor blacksmith, and most of the marriages during the heyday of Gretna Green (approximately 1738 to 1856) took place in the inns or marriage houses, where a bedroom was handy for the consummation of the marriage (considered a vital element of the marriage—up to that point the marriage could be stopped or annulled). The couple usually received a certificate. Joseph Pasley, one of the early "priests," worded his certificates:

> This is to sartfay all persons that may be concerned at *A.B.* from the parish of *C.* in the County of *D.* and *E.F.* from the parish of *G.* and in the county of *H.* and both comes before me and declaryed themselves both to be single persons and now mayried by the forme of the Kirk of Scotland and agreible to the Church of England, and ginie ondre my hand this 18th day of March 1793.

In a book of memoirs, *The Gretna Green Memoirs,* Robert Elliot claimed to have married 7,744 people between 1811 and 1839, and he gave the form of marriage service used by him and, he claimed, his predecessors:

> The parties are first asked their names and places of abode; they are then asked to stand up, and inquired of if they are both single persons: if the answer be in the affirmative the ceremony proceeds. Each is next asked, "Did you come here of your own free will and accord?" Upon receiving an affirmative answer the "priest" commences filling in the printed form of the certificate. The man is then asked "Do you take this woman to be your lawful wedded wife, forsaking all other, keep to her as long as you both shall live?" He answers, "I will." Then the woman is asked the same question, which being answered the same, the woman then produces the ring which she gives to the man, who hand it to the "priest"; the "priest" then returns it to the man and orders him to put it on the fourth finger of the woman's left hand, repeating these words, "With this ring I thee wed, with my body I thee worship, with all my worldly goods I thee endow, in the name of the Father, Son and Holy Ghost, Amen." They then take hold of each other's right hand, and the woman says, "What God joins together let no man put asunder." Then the "priest" says, "Forasmuch as this man and this woman

have consented to go together by giving and receiving a ring, I therefore declare them to be man and wife before God and these witnesses, in the name of the Father, Son and Holy Ghost, Amen.

It is difficult to determine when the idea arose that Gretna Green marriages were performed by a blacksmith using the anvil as an altar, although the use of the expression "blacksmith wedding" or "blacksmith marriage" to describe any marriage of doubtful authenticity was known in the fifteenth century and may have originated from continental Europe. There is no record of the Gretna "priests" being blacksmiths. And, most likely, it was not until around 1907, when a blacksmith's shop was converted into a shop for marriages and for the sale of curios and souvenirs, that anyone was actually married in a blacksmith's shop at Gretna Green. In 1927 the Laird of Gretna Green employed a certain Dick Rennison to act as a "priest"—however, his activities were curtailed in 1940 when these marriages were declared illegal. Marriage activities at Gretna Green continue to this day. Some romantically minded couples still get "married" over the anvil at Gretna Green, but the marriage proper has to be performed by the village registrar. The town now mainly attracts tourists.

There were other places along the Scottish border where couples could be married. One such place was the Lamberton Tollbar, Berwickshire, on the eastern side of the British Isles. Gretna Green is on the west. Until as late as the middle of the nineteenth century there were at least eight or nine "toll priests."

See also Anvil, Firing of; Fleet Weddings; Irregular Marriage; Lord Hardwick's Marriage Act

References

"Claverhouse." 1934. *Irregular Border Marriages.* Edinburgh: Moray Press.

Elliot, Robert. *The Gretna Green Memoirs.* London: N.p.

Milne, F. A. 1901. "Border Marriages." *Folklore* 12: 352.

Groom

See Bridegroom

Gypsy Weddings

It is first necessary to clarify who and what we mean by Gypsy and Romany, two terms that are used interchangeably and often together to describe a person or group (Romany Gypsy). However, Gypsy properly refers to one of the itinerant peoples who call themselves Roma or Romany, which literally means man or husband and is related to Sanskrit and modern Indian words for a tribe or group of people who have similar physical characteristics (Fonseca 1995, 100). The word Gypsy is said to have originated in sixteenth-century England from the belief that these groups originated or came from Egypt. These people were referred to as *gipcyan*, meaning Egyptian (*Concise Oxford Dictonary,* 1972). Confusingly, in many parts of the world, many Gypsy or Romany families have settled in, but still proudly hold onto their traditions and are still unassimilated into the larger society. In many places in Europe today the Gypsy peoples are still discriminated against and persecuted.

The weddings of Gypsies are veiled in a certain amount of myth. Gypsy peoples often absorb and assimilate traditions and practices of the "host" populations but are also very secretive to outsiders. Often Gypsies not only assimilate the settled population practices but also take them to extremes, so that, for example, at a wedding of a couple from an Irish Gypsy family and an English Gypsy family, in Lincolnshire, England, in 2002, the bride's dress had a fifty-foot train. The church doors had to remain open to accommodate it. Similarly, cakes may have many tiers. These are intended to show opulence, wealth, and status. It is probably because the Gypsies are seen as outsiders and as transient (even where they are settled Roma) that they are viewed with suspicion. In Great Britain in the sixteenth century, legislation was enacted that outlawed intermarriage between Gypsies and the settled population. Romany tradition also discouraged marriage outside of the community. A Gypsy woman marrying a non-Gypsy man was likely to be excluded from her group, she might be held in great contempt, and her husband would not be able to become part of the group. A non-Gypsy woman marrying a Gypsy man—if she blended into Gypsy traditions, submitted to Gypsy laws, and, especially in many East European Gypsy societies, submitted absolutely to her mother-in-law—was more easily accepted.

The Gypsy marriage is said to be achieved by one of three methods—by abduction (through force or consent), by purchase, or by mutual consent. But it is difficult to categorize marriages into one of these types. Among Bulgarian Gypsies, a couple may elope for a night, have sex, return with the evidence of the girl losing her virginity (the blood-stained sheet), and be considered married; however, they would still be publicly married with the usual ceremony after settlement negotiations are completed between the two parties. The ceremony and style of marriage depends on the location or "tribe" of the couple. Wood, in his autobiography (1973), described the marriage of Gypsies in Britain. He noted that he knew of two forms of ceremony: jumping the broomstick and mingling of blood (interestingly, Clébert [1963] said that Gypsies are silent on the subject of "blood marriage" and concludes that this is a myth).

If a young man wishes to marry a girl, he would give her his neckerchief. If she wore the neckerchief as a headscarf, then his proposal had been accepted. If she does not, he would know that he had been rejected. Similarly, in the Balkans, upon the girl accepting a red handkerchief from a young man, they become betrothed. If the girl accepts the proposal from the young man, he approaches her father, who would refuse his request without any consideration. The couple would then elope and live together for a time, eventually returning to the tribe (if they are from two

A relative of the groom, holding a knife in his hand, performs the wedding rite between Marusca and Rosario Porado in 1953. The marriage rite is solemnized in the union of the bleeding wrists, followed by singing, dancing, and merry drinking. (Bettmann/CORBIS)

different groups they return to her tribe). After arguments and recriminations, the girl's family begins the arrangements for the wedding. The Gypsy wedding is brief and usually involves the mingling of blood. The young man's right wrist and the girl's left wrist are pierced and squeezed so that they bleed slightly. The wrists are then together to mingle the blood. In the broomstick wedding variation, the couple, holding hands, jump over a besom, made from flowering gorse or thorn, in front of their families. According to Clébert (1963), the mar-

riage in Britain can be even quicker when an elder of the tribe simply asks the couple to join hands. Most couples marry for a second time within a few weeks at a church or registry office.

Wood (1973) recounted an old Romany story concerning a king of the Gypsies. A marriage ceremony lasted two and a half hours (Wood noted that modern Gypsies would get restless after ten minutes). The couple sat, facing an elder of the tribe, while he recited a long sermon about marriage, during which the groom had to give set answers to questions. At certain points in the sermon, the elder threw flower petals onto the couple. They then had to jump over a broom besom, a toolbox, a musical instrument, and a set of fortune-telling cards. Next, the couple faced the elder, the man to the right and the woman to the left and holding hands. An unmarried girl stood to each side of the elder, one holding a silk cord and a sharp pointed knife and the other holding a bunch of twigs from seven different types of tree. With a magical recitation, the twigs were broken one at a time and thrown to the winds, followed by a sermon on the meaning of marriage—how it should not be broken until death and that they would have to share and give and take. The bride would then fetch some bread, salt, and a bucket of water. When she returned, the groom produced a small cup and filled it with water from the bucket, which they both drank, the groom drinking first. The cup was then smashed. Then their blood was mingled. Cuts were made on their wrists and the two wrists were tied together with the cord, with three knots made in the cord—one for constancy, one for fertility, and the last for long life. The cord was untied. The elder took the bread, broke it in half, squeezed some of the groom's blood onto one half, and gave it to the bride, and the same for the groom. The couple had to eat the bloodied bread—the remainder was broken over their heads. They then threw some of the salt over their left shoulder. The elder gave them each half of the silk cord, stained with their blood, which they had to keep for two years (if they wanted to part, the same elder could divorce them by burning the two halves of cord before witnesses). The elder also gave them a kettle-iron (used to hold a kettle over a fire). The bucket of water that the bride had collected was set to boil over the fire, and, when it came to the boil, the couple leapt over it and departed. When the couple had left, the bucket was beaten flat, and guests began the feasting and celebrating. As Wood sug-gested, we see in this story elements that have been adopted by various Romany tribes around the world to be their marriage ceremony—although, as he also noted, they may also go through the religious or civil marriage of the settled population.

Simson (1865) gave a long account of the marriage ceremony of the Scottish Gypsy community of the nineteenth century, which, he wrote, "are historical gems of the most antique and purest water." Simson's account described the wedding, which was led by a "priest" (probably an elder). When all of the wedding party had assembled, a wooden bowl of about one-gallon capacity was passed to the bride, who had to pass urine into the bowl. It was then passed to the groom who did likewise. The bowl was passed back to the "priest," who added some earth from the ground and sometimes a quantity of brandy; this he would stir with a ram's horn or a spoon made from ram's horn. The priest would then present the bowl and mixture to each of the couple, in turn, calling on them to separate the mixture in the bowl, if they could. Obviously, they could not. The couple were then told to join hands over the bowl and were pronounced man and wife, saying that, as none can separate the mixture, so they in turn cannot be separated till death dissolved the union. The couple then retired to the nuptial bed. After some considerable amount of time, close family members might enter, where they examined proof of the bride's virginity. The bride would then be given a handsome present as a mark of their respect. The couple could then dress and join the rest of the wedding party for the feasting, dancing, and singing. The mixture from the bowl was bottled and marked with the Romany equivalent of an M and kept in the house or tent or else buried in a field.

Borrow, in his account of the Zincali Gypsies of Spain (1924), noted that they married in church, but that the procession to church was led by a man holding a long pole, at the top of which was a pure white cambric handkerchief as a symbol of the bride's purity. He was followed by the bride and groom and then a "rabble" of Gypsies, shouting and screaming and firing off guns. At the church gate, the pole was stuck into the ground to a great cheer from the assembly as they entered the church. During the day, there was a great deal of dancing, drinking, and feasting, and in the evening "the most singular part of the festival" took place. A great quantity of sweetmeats had been prepared, of all sorts, but mainly *yémas,* egg yolks with a crust of sugar. The sweetmeats were strewn on the floor of a room to a depth of about three inches, and at a given signal, the bride and groom entered and began dancing a *romális.* They were soon followed by all the company, so that in a very few minutes the sweetmeats were reduced to a form of mud and the dancers were covered to their knees with sugar, yolk, and fruit. The "dancing" became even more frenetic, with the men jumping high into the air and shouting, while "the Gitánas snapped their fingers in their own fashion, louder than castanets, distorting their forms into all kinds of obscene attitudes, and uttering words to repeat which were an abomination."

Among the Turkish Gypsies, the betrothal is marked by the couple drinking from the same cup (this is usually a taboo and would be the one and only time the couple would do this). A Kalderash Gypsy girl who is betrothed wears a gold coin on her neck, but the girl is still not allowed to visit or talk to her betrothed, even with a chaperone. In some respects this illustrates the dichotomy of views and taboos within the worldwide Gypsy community. There is a taboo preventing the free association of young men and women; yet, in a number of Gypsy cultures, the consummation of the marriage comes before the actual ceremony and in some cases even causes the family to arrange the wedding. Even if there is no elopement, in some Gypsy groups, the consummation came before the ceremony.

A French journalist, Jean Didier, reported on a French Gypsy marriage in the early 1960s (quoted by Clébert [1963, 172]). Didier was known for the accuracy of his writings about Gypsy culture. The girl was thirteen years old and the boy fifteen. The groom's father asked the bride's father for her hand in marriage and, both agreeing to the match, gave a large dowry. Invitations were sent out to family traveling all over Europe. About one hundred and twenty came for the wedding. The bride, wearing a white wedding dress, was introduced to all the guests. The groom was not with her. His education about married life was being conducted by some of the elders. The guests danced and feasted and drank French wines all night, the bridegroom joining them around midnight. At dawn, the groom's father asked permission to take the young bride to his son's tent, and she, wearing a necklace of twenty gold dollars, went with her husband to his tent. Around eleven that morning, the couple went to the marriage ceremony where the couple, kneeling, received bread and salt from an elder. The "bread and salt" ritual involved the leader of the tribe breaking the bread in two, putting a pinch of salt on each half, and giving one to each of the couple, telling them that when they are tired of this bread and this salt they will be tired of each other. Among the Kalderash Gypsies, the expression "to take bread and salt" means to get married.

The age of this couple suggests that Gypsy children were expected to marry soon after puberty, much the same as Muslims. And the whole celebration involves an ostentatious display of wealth, often important in Gypsy cultures. The Bulgarian Gypsy people have a big show of the girl's dowry before the wedding, known as her *čeiz* (pronounced chay-eez). She sits among her new goods and receives visits from her friends, neighbors, and family. The Bulgarian wedding will often occur after the couple had eloped and produced the evidence of their having had successful sex. A couple who eloped would spend at least one night away and have sexual intercourse and would return to their families with the bloodied sheet as evidence of the girl's virginity (and the young man's ability). On returning from their elopement, the couple first visits the man's home, where the women of the house, after clearing the men from the room, test the blood on the sheet by sprinkling *rakia,* a plum brandy, over the stains. If the *rakia* caused the blood to move into the shape of a flower, all was well (if the couple had tried to fool the parents by using pig's blood to stain the sheet in the event of the girl not being a virgin or the young man unable to perform, the shape would be different). Inevitably, there are rows between the parents and the young people, but these are for show.

However, the young man still has to ask her parents, specifically her mother (the grandmothers and mothers arrange all the marriages). He would be turned down several times, the message being that his family should increase "appreciation" of their daughter, that is, increase a settlement that will be paid to the bride's parents. During this period, however, the family would be gathering the presents and money for her *čeiz*. In the period leading up to the wedding, the young bride sits, dressed up, among her presents for a day. She will be feted and have a week of dancing and a ritual bathing with her girlfriends and acquaintances. Her hands will be decorated with henna, used to "cleanse" the bride. But henna stains are also said to be symbolic of the bloodstained sheet from her elopement, which had been displayed as a flag around the community. The wedding includes a week of celebrations and dancing. The girl's shoes are likely to be stuffed with money. At the wedding banquet, after processing to her new home and crossing the threshold carrying a child in her arms (as a wish for her own fecundity), she is likely to be covered with money pinned to her dress. Finally she is washed by her mother-in-law and given a small glass of *rakia* to toast her virginity.

Perhaps elopement became the norm because the purchase price of brides became prohibitive. It is difficult to determine whether the transaction between families was ever a simple financial transaction or whether there were subtleties of which the outsider was not aware, and which over the years Gypsies have forgotten. In other cultures, we see the financial transaction being part of setting up the home, paying for the celebrations, and providing some form of insurance in case the girl returns to her parents widowed or divorced. Clébert (1963), in mentioning marriage by purchase, gives examples—one of a fortune-telling family from the Balkans who settled in Wales in 1942 who claimed that the price was arranged between the parents without the knowledge of the couple. Clébert also noted that the practice continued in the United States but was falling into disuse because girls, being warned, threatened to run away and thus reduce their market value. Another example he gives is from Asia Minor. A father, approached for his daughter in marriage, asked for money. When money was offered he wanted more; not having more, the young man ran away with the daughter. The father followed but could not find them or catch up with them. The father was again offered the same money, which he accepted. When the couple returned, her father welcomed them into the family.

See also Besom Weddings; Betrothal; Broom, Marriage over the; Consummation; Dowry; Purchase, Marriage by

References

Borrow, George. 1924. *The Zincali: An Account of the Gypsies of Spain.* New York: E. P. Dutton.

Clébert, Jean-Paul. 1963. *The Gypsies.* Translated by Charles Duff. London: Vista Books.

Fonseca, Isabel. 1995. *Bury Me Standing: The Gypsies and Their Journey.* London: Chatto and Windus.

Simson, Walter. 1865. *A History of the Gipsies.* London: Sampson, Low, Son, and Marston.

Wood, Manfri Frederick. 1973. *In the Life of a Romany Gypsy.* London: Routledge and Kegan Paul.

Handfasting

Handfasting originally referred to the act of betrothal but came to mean a form of trial marriage that was common in Scotland. The sixteenth-century Swiss church reformer Heinrich Bullinger (1541) made it clear that handfasting was the betrothal ceremony and the first stage of the marriage procedure: "After the handfastynge and making of the contracte, the church-goyng and weddyng shuld not be differed to long." This could take place when the couple was very young, some years before the actual wedding. The betrothal—handfast—was a time for the payment of any bride-price settlement or the announcement of a promise of the dowry. Vows, which were much like the vows of the contemporary Anglican church service, were taken and were as binding as the coming marriage. The betrothal was normally a public ceremony (often in the church porch) presided over by the bride's father or other male relative of the bride and, in Scotland and the north of England, included the joining of hands and the exchanging of vows or "plighting the troth." Sometimes this would take place at some local ceremonial site—a plighting stone, betrothal stone, or bridal stone, where the couple would join hands through an opening in the stone.

The practice of handfasting in Scotland is sometimes said to have been suppressed after the Reformation in Europe (1563), only lingering in the highland areas. However, it seems to have carried on in isolated areas and the lowland border country well into the late seventeenth century, where it is clear that large numbers of the poor were not getting married in church. In an effort to suppress the practice, the Aberdeen Kirk Sessions of 1562 decreed that all people cohabiting under handfasting agreements should be married forthwith.

The handfasting agreement was, as noted, a form of trial marriage whereby the couple would agree at a public fair to cohabit for a year, or, in the sixteenth-century in the Lake District of England, a year and a day. Similar time limits were used in Wales and the Isle of Portland. After the year was up, the couple could either marry or separate and resume their single status as if nothing had occurred. A child born under this arrangement was not considered a bastard, whatever the outcome. It is unlikely that many who came together under a handfasting arrangement underwent any further formal ceremony. For many people, an exchange of promises before witnesses, followed by cohabitation, was considered binding. This was especially true of remote communities, and, as noted above, few people in remote lowland areas bothered to be married in church well into the seventeenth century. It was common for monasteries to send friars out into these remote areas to find handfasted couples and offer to formally marry them; in the Esk valley, the Abbacy of Melrose, which owned the land, regularly sent out a priest, who became known as "book-i-the-bosom," to confirm these irregular marriages.

James Browne, a nineteenth-century Scottish historian, wrote that the highland chieftains used a form of handfasting to ensure their lineal descent by handfasting the son of one chieftain with the daughter of another and that they would cohabit for a year and a day. If the woman had a child, or became pregnant, the marriage was said to be sealed; if there was no child, the couple were free to marry or handfast with another (Browne 1853, 398).

Giraldus Cambrensis, an early Welsh chronicler, reported that in ancient Wales, parents would "let" their daughter to a prospective husband, who would put down a sum of money. If the couple decided to part and not be married, he would have to pay a further fee to the parents (Scott 1953, 95). This is very similar to a formal betrothal and trial marriage.

See also Besom Weddings; Betrothal; Bundling; Common-Law Marriage; Temporary Marriage

References
Browne, J. 1853. *A History of the Highlands and of the Highland Clans.* N.p.: n.p.
Bullinger, Heinrich. 1541. *The Christian State of Matrimony.* Translated by Myles Coverdale.
Gillis, John R. 1985. *For Better, For Worse: British Marriages, 1600 to the Present.* Oxford: Oxford University Press.
Rogers, Charles. 1869. *Scotland Social and Domestic.* London: C. Griffin.
Scott, George Ryley. 1953. *Curious Customs of Sex and Marriage.* London: Torchstream.
Stone, Lawrence. 1990. *The Family, Sex, and Marriage in England, 1500–1800.* Abridged and revised ed. London: Penguin.

Hen Night

This is an all-female, usually drunken, celebration of the bride-to-be and her friends on the eve of, or a few days before, the wedding, in Britain. These parties developed during the last quarter of the twentieth century and are the female equivalent of the stag party.

See also Stag Party

Henna

Henna (or *hinnâ* in Arabic) is a dark, reddish-orange plant dye derived from the shoots and leaves of the Egyptian privet (*Lawsonia alba* or *Lawsonia inermis*), used as a cosmetic and for decorative purposes. Although some medicinal properties have been claimed for the dye, it has not traditionally been used in healing. The leaves are crushed into a green powder, and water is added to make the paste. It is applied to the body as a paste and left for, usually, up to two hours to dye the skin a deep orange color. This will fade over two to three weeks. (It is also used for dyeing hair.)

Black henna is also sometimes used, but only on the soles of the feet and on the hands. It is interesting to note that in Scotland there is a tradition of blackening the bridegroom's feet on the day/night before his wedding. The black henna is prepared by adding to the henna a paste made from powdered lime and powdered crystal ammoniac. This causes the orange coloring to turn black. The resulting markings will remain on the skin for twenty or thirty days. Henna is considered very sensual in some societies and is used as a beautifying agent to decorate the hands and feet of brides, with often intricate patterns. In Afghanistan, henna is said to bring good luck and happiness. The Bulgarian Gypsies use henna to ritually "clean" the bride during a week of celebrations. In this culture, henna was said to be emblematic of the blood-stained sheets of the virgin bride after consummation of the marriage, and it is also said that the longer the henna stays on the girl's hands, the longer her husband will love her.

See also Afghanistan; Arabic Weddings; Egypt; Feet, Gypsy Weddings; Hindu Weddings; India

Reference
Kjeilen, Tore. "Henna." In *Encyclopaedia of the Orient.* Oslo, Norway. Available at *http.www.*

The ritual of mehndi *on the night before a Sikh wedding, in which the hands and feet of the bride are decorated with henna. (Richard Olivier/CORBIS)*

webeverything.co.uk/directory/53197.html (accessed 4 May 2004).

Hindu Weddings

In the epic heroic poem of the Brahmin culture, the *Mahabharata* (dating from the beginning of the Christian era), the origins of marriage are explained. According to the poem, women were independent and roved about freely and thus could go astray from their husbands. (In Hindu tradition, women were considered naturally libidinous, and therefore if a girl was not married by puberty she would soon find a lover.) Swêtakêtu, son of Rishi Uddâlaka (the Rishis are the "mind-borne" sons of Brahma, deities that preexisted the gods and demons who are sometimes credited with some parts of the creation), did not like this practice and ruled that henceforth wives should remain faithful to their husbands and husbands faithful to their wives. But in the *Mahabharata* there is a great emphasis on love and beauty and on the idea that the best motive for marriage is love.

But the Laws of Manu (Manu is considered the ancestor of the human race), which outlined the basic rules for society, disapproved of the voluntary union of a couple (the *Gandharva* mode), although this mode was legalized for members of the king and warrior castes in later laws. The Laws of Manu cited eight forms of marriage; four of these forms—*Brâhma, Ârsha, Daiva,* and *Prâgâpatya,* in which the father gives his daughter away— were considered blessed, and from these marriages, sons with a knowledge of the *Veda* would result, who would be honored by good men and would live a hundred years. The other four systems, condemned as "blamable" unions, were by forcible abduction of a maiden from her home with her house being broken into and her kinsmen slain or wounded *(Râkshasa);* by stealth; by purchase *(Âsura),* which the Laws of Manu forbade, stating that a man who, through avarice, accepted a gratuity for his daughter, was guilty of being a seller of his offspring; and by voluntary union *(Gandharva),* a marriage chosen by the daughter, which Manu condemned as coming from desire and having sexual intercourse as its purpose. The sons of such marriages would be untruthful and hate the *Veda* and the sacred laws. (Ancient Persian culture also viewed a marriage contracted by a woman against her parents' wishes as the worst type of marriage.)

Although the *Mahabharata* suggested that marriages were made for love, and that this was the best motive for a marriage, a love match needed the approval of the girl's parents; perhaps this was how the reservations expressed in the original Laws of Manu were overcome. Manu said that in an ideal marriage the bride should be one-third the age of the groom so that a man of twenty-four should marry a girl of eight. But it was also decreed in Hindu writings that a man of thirty should marry a girl of twelve and that it would be sinful for a man to break this rule. Early Hindu religious writers said that a girl should be married by the age of ten or twelve years old, and if she was not married by then she should be immediately married, even in the prohibited married season. However, intercourse before puberty was forbidden. If a girl was betrothed as a child and her prospective husband should die before she had reached the age at which she could marry him, she was treated as a widow, given the low status of a widow, and not allowed to "remarry" later. In 1846, the Indian Penal Code, in an attempt to reduce the problems of child marriage, made it a criminal offense for a marriage to be consummated before the girl had reached the age of ten. In 1891 this age was raised to twelve. However the Joshi Report of 1929 (the Report of the Age of Consent Committee) found that few people knew of the 1891 legislation.

When a Hindu woman married, her husband was considered to be her earthly god to whom she was totally subservient. She could not choose another husband if he should die

before her. At one time, a Hindu wife was not even permitted to mention the name of her husband. If she dreamt of his name, it was believed that this sin would lead him to an untimely end. Widows in Hindu communities were (and in some cases still are) not accorded any status and were not allowed to remarry, thus leaving a widow with essentially no support. However, it was considered that a son's first duty must always be to his mother.

Within Hindu tradition, even today, the ideal wife is *pativratā,* meaning she whose vows *(vrata)* are to her husband *(pati).* She is expected to devote her life to her husband. Ideally, she should die before he does, but if by some mistake he dies first, she should kill herself on his funeral pyre. *Suttee,* as this practice is called, dates back to at least the tenth century and has its origins in the Hindu belief that a woman who sacrifices herself on her husband's funeral pyre will achieve a divine status and become a manifestation of the god Shiva's consort. A widow's failure to commit *suttee* would subject her to perpetual infamy. In the *Padmapurana,* a series of ancient religious poems, which are a form of Hindu equivalent of the Bible, the duties of the wife are outlined:

> A wife must eat only after a husband has had his fill. If the latter fasts, she shall fast too; if he touch not food, she also shall not touch it; if he be in affliction, she shall be so too: if he be cheerful, she shall share his joy. . . . She must, on the death of her husband, allow herself to be burnt alive on the same funeral pyre; then everybody will praise her virtue.
>
> If her husband flies into a passion, threatens her, abuses her grossly, even beats her unjustly, she shall answer him meekly, shall lay hold of his hands, kiss them, and beg his pardon, instead of uttering loud cries and running away from the house. (Braddock 1961, 187)

According to the Laws of Manu, marriage is a religious duty incumbent upon all men and women. According to the *Brahmadharma,*

The bride and groom at a Hindu wedding in 1997. (Bob Krist / CORBIS)

a man is not whole until he finds a wife. An unmarried man, unless he is a religious celibate and therefore honored, is regarded as a useless member of society. (It is interesting to compare this with Irish and other European traditions, in which an unmarried man was treated as a child by his family, regardless of his age.) It was considered important for Hindus to have male children as soon as possible to provide sacrifices so that the souls of the ancestors could stay in heaven. Similarly, the woman's role was to marry. The laws and scriptures considered that a woman was meant to be subservient to the wants and pleasures of men. According to the Laws of Manu, the father, or husband, should be regarded as the Rajah of the household, his word was law, and he was the master of his wife, his sons, and his slaves. Manu declared that a wife, son, or slave had no wealth of his or her own and that everything they earned

was passed over to the man—husband, father, master—to whom they belonged. However, it was also clear in the *Rig-Veda,* the early Indian religious texts, that he could only maintain his role as head of the household for as long as he could be protector and maintainer of the family.

Hindu tradition promoted child marriage; once a girl had lost her virginity she would be considered unmarriageable (and consequently a disgrace and an economic liability). However, at one time in the valley of the Ganges River, virgins were compelled to offer themselves before marriage in the temples dedicated to Juggernaut (or *Jăg'gănăth,* a form of Vishnu that represented the trinity of the dark Krishna, the fair Balarama, and Subhadra, their sister). Although in Hindu tradition a woman may be married only once and for life, a man may marry up to four times. (In the Punjab he was not permitted to marry for the third time. To get around this, the third marriage would be to a babul tree or an akh plant.) It was not uncommon for a man with a wife and child to bring up a young girl to become his second wife when she reached the desired age.

As with many marriage traditions, the Hindu marriage can be divided into three elements—betrothal, marriage, and consummation—which may be spread over a matter of years. Although details may vary from region to region, there are a number of fixed features. Offerings are made on a sacred fire. The couple are joined by tying their garments together and circling the sacred fire either seven times (clockwise) or three times, but taking seven steps each time. The groom applies the *bindior* (the spot in the center of a married woman's forehead that indicates her married status). The groom hangs a silk cord with a gold pendant (the *mangalustra*) around his bride's neck, a symbol of the marriage itself. Once the *mangalustra* (sometimes called a *tali*) has been tied around her neck, the marriage is irrevocable. However, Wood (1869) suggested that the marriage becomes irrevocable after the seventh step in the perambulation of the sacred fire. Lastly, at the end of the day of the wedding, when night has fallen, the couple go outside together to contemplate the polestar as an emblem of stability. (The symbolic tying of the couple, either with their clothing or with some form of cord, occurs in other marriage ceremonies around the world, such as the Thai Buddhist wedding, and the symbolism of the number seven is very strong in Indo-European cultures. For example, in the weddings of followers of the Zoroastrian tradition, the couple's right hands are bound together with twine, which passes seven times around their hands, then seven times around the couple, and seven times around the knot, joining the ends of a cloth encircling the seated couple.)

When a family agrees to a union, the horoscopes of the couple are usually consulted to ensure that the two are compatible. Omens are also observed. A young man would choose an auspicious day to approach the woman's parents with the appropriate gifts and the request to marry their daughter. If during his journey to her home he should encounter any bad omens, such as a cat, fox, jackal, or snake crossing his path, he would turn back. To see a mongoose, however, would be considered a good omen. Marriages are usually solemnized during the hot months of March, April, May, or June. A rainy day is considered very bad luck for a wedding. Some will test the prospects using divination by melting a gold coin. If the metal appears to be shiny, the signs are good; if the metal appears dull, the omens are bad, and the marriage possibility should be abandoned.

See also Child Marriage; India; Rice; *Suttee*
References

Braddock, Joseph. 1961. *The Bridal Bed.* New York: John Day.
Mair, Lucy. 1971. *Marriage.* Harmondsworth, Middlesex: Penguin.
Murphy, Brian M. 1978. *The World of Weddings: An Illustrated Celebration.* London: Paddington.
Scott, George Ryley. 1953. *Curious Customs of Sex and Marriage.* London: Torchstream.
Sumner, William Graham. [1906] 1940. *Folkways.* New York: Mentor Books.
Wood, Edward J. 1869. *The Wedding Day in All Ages and Countries.* 2 vols. London: R. Bentley.

Home, Setting Up

Upon marriage, a couple is usually establishing a new unit within a community, unless the couple is moving in with one of the sets of parents—in which case the bride usually becomes part of the groom's extended family, the case in Japan, China, and among Eastern European Gypsy communities, where the couple may be established as a separate unit within the man's family compound. In Japan, it was customary for the woman to take nothing into the marriage. In Britain, couples would delay marriage until they could set up a home, and the busiest marriage seasons in the seventeenth and eighteenth centuries were in early spring and autumn when people were paid at the end of a contracted year's work or after the harvest. Traditions have developed to help couples in the community, the penny wedding, the bridewain, and bidding (in Wales).

A couple in setting up a home must collect furniture and items for cooking and eating to be able to function as an independent unit. In many Muslim communities, the provision of the household items is included as part of the financial negotiations in the marriage arrangements, so that usually the groom gives the bride-to-be money to buy household goods, which she then brings to the marriage. In many European countries, a girl will begin to collect items, referred to in England as her "bottom drawer" or in the United States as the "hope chest."

The Rev. Walter Gregor (1881) gave a list of the items that a new bride among the well-to-do fishing communities of northeast Scotland had to collect and take to her new home. Included were a chest of drawers, a *kist* (a chest for storing meal or clothes), a feather bed, four pairs of white blankets, two bolsters, four pillows, sheets, one dozen towels, a tablecloth, the kitchen hardware, and wooden milking buckets and tubs. All of these items she began collecting from a young age, beginning with the feathers for mattress and pillows. Her contribution to the new household was known as her *providan* or *plinisan* and was taken to her new home in procession with some ceremony. Two carts were used. In the first was the chest of drawers, with the bed with the blankets over this and the bolster and pillows on top. The second cart carried the *kist*, tubs, and other hardware. The husband provided the furniture and all the fishing gear. It was also generally agreed that the husband made the living. This personal collection of items was often supplemented with gifts from friends and community.

In Britain and America, wedding presents are given to the bride and groom. The bridal shower in the United States (and other countries) is said to have started in Holland when a friend of the bride was unable to give a present to the bride that she felt was worthy of their friendship. Finding other people in the same predicament, she arranged for them to all give together at a party before the wedding. In the Welsh *stafell*, the married women in the community help the couple set up home, with the household items being transported to the couple's new home the day before the wedding. In some parts of Wales, the *stafell* also came to be a term for the practice of giving gifts of household goods to the couple on the eve of the wedding. Guthrie (1885) described the custom in Scotland of *thrigging*, in which the couple were allowed to go to each house in the community and choose one piece of furniture or household item.

The setting up of the home for the couple is often a community affair, and in some cultures, especially in Muslim communities, the display of the goods is an essential part of the celebrations. The European Gypsy girl, along with her groom, sits among the displayed items, and family and friends visit and view the wedding gifts. All cooperating to help the couple get started avoids the couple becoming a burden to the community.

See also Bidding; Bottom Drawer; Gypsy Weddings; Presents; Shower; *Stafell*

References
Fonseca, Isabel. 1995. *Bury Me Standing: The Gypsies and Their Journey.* London: Chatto and Windus.
Gregor, Rev. Walter. 1881. *Notes on Folklore of the North East of Scotland.* London: Folklore Society.
Guthrie, E. J. 1885. *Old Scottish Customs.* London: Hamilton, Adams.
Owen, Trefor M. 1961. "A Breconshire Marriage Custom." *Folklore* 72: 372–384.

Honeymoon

The idea of the honeymoon began near the end of the eighteenth century and became an institution associated with weddings among the aristocratic and very wealthy classes in the early part of George III's reign in Britain (1760–1820). The honeymoon once simply referred to a period of approximately one month following the wedding, which was characterized by goodwill and sexual passion between the couple, although the *Oxford English Dictionary* suggests that the word is a compound of approximately sixteenth-century origin of the words honey and moon, indicating a waning of a period of affection or sweetness, and not necessarily of one month.

Others have written that the honeymoon refers to the time when marriage was by capture. The woman's tribe would pursue the couple to attempt to rescue her, so that it was necessary for the man to take his bride into hiding for about a month until tempers cooled, during which time the couple got to know each other in every way, drinking a lot of mead—wine made from honey—which is associated with sweetness and sensuality. According to Brewer's *Dictionary of Phrase and Fable,* the honeymoon is the month after the marriage, or at least as much of it as was spent away from home, derived from the ancient Teutonic practice of drinking honey-wine for thirty days after the marriage. However, this appears to be a myth, probably derived from the ideas and theories put forward in the writing of the nineteenth-century writer, Sir John Lubbock, who seemed to be particularly enthusiastic in showing dubious connections between the wedding practices of his day and those of distant history, particularly to the supposed custom of "marriage by capture." He suggested that the honeymoon was a period when the bridegroom kept the bride away from her relatives and friends in seclusion. He even suggested, as others had done, that the throwing of a slipper or shoe at the bridal couple was done in mock anger, as her relative would have done to prevent the girl from being abducted. However, there are many flaws in this argument, not least of which was the fact that, until the honeymoon trip became fashionable, the bridal couple were only allowed enough secluded time by their friends and relations to consummate the marriage. The honeymoon, or bridal tour, did not become fashionable until around the end of the eighteenth century. In the United States, there was no tradition of honeymoon until toward the end of the nineteenth century, when the English wedding began to set the fashion for American weddings. The aristocratic bridal tour became fashionable among persons claiming any degree of gentility or "respectability." Jeaffreson (1872, 2: 273) noted:

> The change of usage was, however, so agreeable to lovers of both sexes that the new fashion became yearly more general; so that, by the end of the last century, it was unusual for a bride, having the slightest claim to gentility, to pass the evening of her wedding-day under her father's roof.

Jeaffreson (1872, 2: 274) outlined the type of honeymoon trip that a couple of "gentle quality" would take at the beginning of the nineteenth century. Whereas the bridal tour of an aristocratic or landed family might involve travel to the continent and would last at least a month, those aspiring to emulate aristocratic classes would be much more modest:

> The honeymoon trip of a married couple, who, though of gentle quality, were too busy or thrifty to think of spending much time or money on a romantic excursion, seldom exceeded ten days or a fortnight. The London merchant or lawyer took his London bride to Bath or Tunbridge Wells or Brighton for seven or eight days, and on returning to town she entered her new home … feeling herself to have seen much of her native land. The country clergyman or provincial doctor took his spouse for as short a time to London to see parks and theatres, St. Paul's and the Tower; and on crossing the threshold of her future abode, the young wife felt she had seen as much of the world . . . as she ought to wish to see for the next twenty years.

The honeymoon holiday did not permeate all levels of society until around the middle of the twentieth century. In the eighteenth and nineteenth centuries, the wedding ceremony for the laboring classes would take place during some small break in the working day, and the bride and groom would usually be given time for the actual wedding celebrations but no time for any holiday. Those that did have time off would have little more than a single day, perhaps spent at the seaside. Some couples who were able to take the time might visit relatives. Ballard (1998), in describing wedding traditions in Ireland, recounted the story of a Ballymoney couple who married in the early 1860s whose honeymoon was spent at the farm of the bride's sister, about seven miles distant. The groom helped his new brother-in-law on the farm, and his wife helped her sister in the house. The honeymoon is now part of wedding ritual in Britain and the United States. It is common for couples to honeymoon at some exotic destination—perhaps one that specializes in honeymoons.

See also Capture, Marriage by; Cards, Wedding; Shoes

References

Ballard, Linda May. 1998. *Forgetting Frolic: Marriage Traditions in Ireland.* Belfast and London: Institute of Irish Studies, Queens University, Belfast, and Folklore Society, London.

Brewer E. C. *Dictionary of Phrase and Fable.* London: Cassell.

Jeaffreson, John Cordy. 1872. *Brides and Bridals.* 2 vols. London: Hurst and Blackett.

Seligson, Marcia. 1974. *The Eternal Bliss Machine: The American Way of Wedding.* London: Hutchinson.

Stone, Lawrence. 1990. *The Family, Sex, and Marriage in England, 1500–1800.* Abridged and revised ed. London: Penguin.

Hope Chest

See Bottom Drawer

Hot Pot

After the vestry scene, the bridal party having formed in procession for leaving the church, we were stopped in the porch by a row of five or six women, ranged to our left hand, each holding a large mug with a cloth over it. These were in turn presented to me, and handed by me to my wife, who, after taking a sip, returned to me. It was then passed to the next couple, and so on in the same form to all the party. The composition in these mugs was, mostly, I am sorry to say, simply horrible; one or two were very fair, one very good. They were sent to the church by all classes, and are considered a great compliment. (Tegg 1877, 294)

The above account is an eyewitness report of this custom, which was observed in the north of England at least until the late nineteenth century. The hot pot was a concoction of spiced and sweetened ale prepared by the friends and neighbors of the bridal party, which was expected to be tasted on the journey away from the church after the wedding. The quality, and taste, varied greatly, depending on the abilities of the people preparing the brew and the ingredients available. In the above account, the makers of the hot pot took their preparation to the church. In other accounts, the makers would wait by their house for the wedding party to come to them. The wedding party had to drink the preparation at each house they passed, which could result in the couple drinking a consid-erable quantity of spiced and sweetened ale before they arrived home.

Just as the health, future happiness, and good fortune of the couple are toasted with champagne or wine by the friends and family attending a wedding reception, so a similar rationale appears to be associated with the hot pot custom—that of the makers offering their good wishes. It was thought a bad omen if any of the contents of the first hot pot were to be spilled, because the couple would have let slip away from them the first kindly wish for their health and happiness.

See also Posset

References

Gutch, Mrs. 1899. *County Folklore. Vol. 2. Concerning the North Riding of Yorkshire, York, and Ainsty.* London: Folklore Society.

Robinson, F. K. 1875. *A Glossary of Words Used in the Neighbourhood of Whitby.* London: N.p.

Tegg, William. 1877. *The Knot Tied: Marriage Customs of All Nations.* London: William Tegg.

Huppah (Chuppa)

The use of the *huppah* in the Jewish wedding ceremony is the best known of the many traditions that use a canopy in weddings. The *huppah* is said to represent the new home, the basis of Jewish life. The open sides represent hospitality. The fact that there is no floor beneath the *huppah* symbolizes that it is not material things that will make for a happy marriage. According to many writers, especially early Jewish writers, the *huppah* was originally the groom's house or a room or building other than the bride's parental home. By entering the *huppah,* she cut her ties with her family and came under the protection of her new husband.

The seclusion of the bride and groom (*yichud* or *yihud*) is the last part of the wedding ceremony, and today there is a separate room in the synagogue for the couple to break their fast in privacy. It is likely from early writings that the *huppah* was originally the place for seclusion for the *yichud.* However, there was considerable confusion among medieval writers on Jewish religious law about what was being referred to in the Talmud when the *huppah* was mentioned. A twelfth-century rabbi—Rabbi Isaac ben Abba Mari—said that it was customary to decorate the room for the seclusion—which was designated the *huppah*—with colorful tapestries and cloths, or with myrtle leaves and roses. Rabbi Isaac also mentioned with disapproval the practice of holding a cloth, or *talit,* over the couple while marriage prayers and blessings were recited. So there seems to have been a definite difference between the *huppah* and other forms of canopies. It was not until the sixteenth century that the familiar four-posted canopy came to be used, albeit with reluctance on the part of the rabbis.

But there was great reluctance even for weddings to take place within the synagogue—because they involved actions inappropriate for a sacred place that should be used only for religious study and prayer, i.e., at a wedding the clothing of the congregation is not always suitable for a sacred place, and the free mixing of the sexes is also a problem. And traditionalists saw the synagogue wedding as an imitation of the Christian practice. Consequently, many authorities believed that the *huppah* should be set up outside, and there was a custom in Ashkenazic communities to hold weddings in the synagogue courtyard. The *huppah* set up outside, under the heavens, further symbolizes the hope that descendants will be as plentiful as the stars in heaven.

See also Canopy, Bridal; Jewish Weddings
Reference
Segal, Eliezer. 1999. *Why Didn't I Learn This in Hebrew School?* Northvale, NJ: Jason Aronson.

Inca

See South America

India

The major religion in the Indian subcontinent is Hinduism. There are also significant numbers of Muslims, the majority of northern Indians are Sikhs, and there are Buddhists, Christians, and Zoroastrians. Details of marriage ceremonies differ among these groups and regions, but the overall form of the marriage ceremony remains the same within Hindu groups. In Hindu tradition, a woman marries for life. If her husband should predecease her, she is not permitted to remarry. (According to ancient Hindu tradition, she should commit *suttee*—throwing herself on her husband's funeral pyre—but this was outlawed in the nineteenth century.) A man may marry up to four times. Polyandry, a woman marrying more than one man, occurred in the Himachal Pradesh area of India, but this is a rarity. The practice of polyandry tends to occur in places where it takes the work of at least two men to support a family.

The fact that a man may marry more than once has led to some scandal in Indian society with the accusations of dowry deaths. On 11 October 1975, the *Times* of London reported that the Punjab state government had or-

dered an investigation into a spate of suicides and fatal accidents involving young brides; the suspicion was that young brides with small dowries were so badly treated by their in-laws that they were driven to suicide so that the husband could remarry and obtain another dowry. In some areas of India, to get out of paying a dowry, a girl's family may kidnap a likely young man and forcibly marry him to their daughter. If he refused, he could be threatened with violence. Within Hindu tradition it is considered imperative for young people to marry. Girls should be married as soon as possible, with the marriage arranged by the parents. Beginning at the end of the twentieth century, there has been a significant move away from the imperative for marriage, due to greater education and more independence.

The Hindu marriage rite usually takes place beneath a wooden canopy called a *mandap*, which is specially constructed for the event. One form of the marriage rite involves the couple sitting on the floor while a sacred fire, from the wood of a consecrated tree, is lit between them by the priest, who will then recite prayers. This is carried out to the accompaniment of prayers and the chanting of hymns. The couple are then united by their garments being tied together with a piece of consecrated cloth (in some areas the

A wedding ceremony in India in 1985. (Jerry Cooke/CORBIS)

bride and groom were bound together with grass). The couple then join hands beneath the cloth and walk three times around the sacred fire, always in seven steps (making the *sapta-padi,* or "seven steps," together), which symbolizes everlasting friendship.

The full Hindu wedding ceremony consists of ten elements. During the first part, the *Pani-Gradana,* a parent of the bride offers his or her daughter's hand to the bridegroom, asking him to accept the woman as his wife; the groom takes her hand, accepting the bride as his wife, and gives her presents of jewelry and clothing. It is during this period that the sacred fire is lit and invoked; the fire *(Agni)* represents the mouth of Vishnu and symbolizes the illumination of the mind, of knowledge, and of happiness. Oblations are poured into the fire. In the next stage, the *Shilarohana,* the bride puts her right foot onto a stone, implored by the groom to stamp as hard and as firmly as she can to symbolize that they will be strong and firm together to face the onslaught of enemies and the difficulties of the future together. During the *Laja Homa* (putting parched rice in the sacred fire), the bride's brother puts some parched rice into the bride's hand, half of which slips through into the groom's hands, and three oblations of rice are tossed into the sacred fire. The bride prays to the god of death, Yama, for long life, prosperity, and happiness for the bridegroom.

The next parts of the ceremony are related to the Hindu belief that the bride is under the protection of the moon for the first seven years of her married life—the following seven years are overseen by the sun and the following seven by fire. (In many societies seven is a mystical number.) The couple therefore walk around the fire *(Agni Parokrama)* four times. The first three times, the bridegroom leads, and the fourth, the bride leads; she approaches the fire with seven steps. The couple each take seven steps around the sacred fire *(Saptapadi),* and at each step they ask to be granted the blessings of food, prosperity, happiness, family, strength, and lifelong friendship. The groom then blesses the bride *(Saubhgya Chinha)* by smearing *kumkum* or *sindur* (vermilion powder) at the parting of her hair or on her forehead and also by giving her a sacred necklace *(Mangle-sutra)*. It has been suggested that this marking with red powder originated with a practice of the bridal couple marking each other with their blood. The groom takes his bride to look at the sun, accepting her as his wife in the presence of the sun. If the wedding is at night, they look up at *Dhruva,* the star of steadfastness, or *Arundhati,* the star of devotion. The bride tells him that she is looking and promises to be as steadfast and devoted as the stars. They touch each other's hearts *(Haridaya-Sparsh),* each vowing: "I touch thy heart unto mine. God has given thee as my husband [wife]. May my heart be thine and thy heart be mine now. When I talk to thee, please listen to me with perfect attention." The bride then feeds the groom *(Anna-Prashana)* with sweet food, saying that by feeding such sweet food she binds her heart to his with a "thread of truth, sincerity, and love." The ceremony is completed with the *Purnahuti*—further oblations are poured onto the sacred fire with a blessing from the priest, and rice and flower petals are distributed to the guests, who shower the couple with them with blessings.

In the Punjab area of India (northwestern region), weddings have their own characteristics but are based on Hindu traditions. The agreement for the marriage is followed by the engagement ceremony *(roka)* where the groom's family goes to the bride's family home and the two families exchange presents. The bride's family gives the groom an auspicious sum of money, and his family presents the bride-to-be with a sari and a gold chain. Money and presents are also exchanged between the parents of each family. The couple are then officially engaged and the wedding date is fixed.

As the wedding day approaches, the couple take part in the *sagan* ceremony, a cere-mony of acceptance of the wedding by both families. At the groom's home, the bride's father marks the groom's forehead with a *tikka* of saffron, rice, and flower petals. The bride's relatives offer him blessings, along with money and sweets *(mithai),* and then take the groom to a common place where he will meet his bride-to-be, after she has undergone a ceremony known as *chunni chadana,* which involves the groom's sister presenting a red item of clothing (perhaps a sari or a shawl). The bride is dressed in this clothing, along with the jewelry they had brought, and is led back to the common place. At this place, the groom's mother feeds the bride with boiled rice and milk, after which the couple exchange rings, and further gifts of clothing, sweets, and toiletries are given to the bride-to-be. The *sagan* is followed by nightly parties *(sangeets)* of singing and dancing.

On the wedding day, the couple are separately prepared for the wedding but both at the bride's family home. The bride's ceremony is called a *chuda* ceremony and the groom's is known as the *seant* ceremony. The *chuda* ceremony refers to a set of red and white ivory bangles that the bride wears for the ceremony. The holy man *(pandit)* leads prayers and then each guest touches the set of bangles, blessing the bride as he or she does so. The bride, with the help of the *pandit,* puts the ivory bangles on, along with the rest of her jewelry and an iron bangle for luck. The bride's oldest aunt and uncle, who have fasted until this ceremony, tie gold and silver jewelry, *kaliras,* to her wrists. As she leaves for the wedding ceremony, the bride hits one of her female relatives with the *kaliras*—she will become the next to wed. Meanwhile, the bridegroom is prepared for the wedding at his *seant* ceremony, which is preceded by prayers from the *pandit.* The groom is bathed, dressed, and a pink turban is tied on his head by his father. In a similar way to the bride's ceremony, everyone present touches the turban. The groom's father then ties a veil, decorated with flowers and gold, to his face; all present touch this covering. The groom will go to the wedding on a horse, which has been fed lentils. The groom's sisters and cousins have braided the horse's mane, for which they are given gifts of money. The groom and his entourage process to the wedding venue, where they are welcomed by the bride's family with garlands of flowers and presents.

The groom begins the wedding ceremonial by chanting mantras, during which the bride's female relatives try to remove his shoes, which he has to buy back later. The bride then joins her groom, accompanied by the parents of the couple, and a prayer is offered. The groom is given a ring by the bride's father, which symbolizes the giving of his daughter to the groom. The wedding ceremony follows that of the general Hindu ceremony, except that the couple are bound together with a cloth called a *chunni*. On one end is a knot holding a silver coin and a lump of sugar. Tied together, they walk around a ceremonial fire seven times, and then they are married. The couple begin their married life at the groom's house. On her first day, the bride must cook a sweet dish for her new family, marking the beginning of her domestic duties.

The Gujarati wedding (west India) follows elements of the Hindu ceremony, especially in the betrothal and the time leading up to the wedding day. However, on the wedding day, the groom is welcomed into the *mandap* (canopy) by the bride's mother, who, as she welcomes him, will try to grab his nose (to remind him that during courtship he came "rubbing his nose at the family door," asking for the daughter in marriage). His feet are then ritually washed *(madhurparka)*, during which his shoes are likely to be stolen by the bride's sisters (and which he will retrieve, for a fee, after the ceremony). The bride is carried in the *mandap* by her mother's brother, where the couple are seated facing each other but separated with a curtain. After the holy man begins the ceremony with prayers, the curtain is raised, and the couple put garlands on each other. What follows in the Gujarati wedding ceremony is similar to that of the Hindu ceremony, but with a few changes. The elders, for example, tie cords around the necks of the couple to ward off evil spirits. The groom will help his bride touch seven betel nuts with her right toe instead of the couple taking seven steps northward, and after the main ceremony, the married women pass by the couple, each one whispering into the bride's right ear. As the bride's mother passes, the groom tugs on her sari, which was once the way the groom asked for the gifts or dowry he was owed. After the celebrations, at the groom's home, the couple often play a game known as *aeki-beki*. A pot of water containing a ring and some coins is tinted with milk and vermilion; the bride and groom each have seven chances to find the ring. The first to find it four times is said to be the one who will rule the household.

Followers of Jainism have similar rituals. Before the wedding day, gods and goddesses are called upon to take up temporary residence in the homes of the bride and the groom. At the *amtruka sthapan* ceremony, goddesses are called into the bride's home. At the *kulkar sthapan* ceremony, the seven gods are called upon to take up residence in the groom's home. This ritual is to ensure fertility, happiness, and maintenance of family tradition. Seven days after the marriage, in another ceremony, the deities are sent off from the homes. In the days leading up to the wedding day, the bride and groom are prepared and beautified with massages of perfumed oil, turmeric, and other ingredients. During this time prayers will be offered for the couple in the temple. Also in this period, the *mandap* is prepared, usually at the bride's house; it is then taken to a hired hall for the ceremony. An altar *(vedi)* for the sacred fire is also prepared. On the wedding day, the groom's party arrives in procession at the marriage hall, traditionally with the groom on horseback, but today by car and then walking the last part. As the groom's party arrives at the hall, the Brahmin, who will conduct the ceremony, chants a mantra for him.

Here he is greeted by his bride with a garland of flowers. He then stands on a stool while his soon-to-be mother-in-law and the other women welcome him by waving a lamp in front of him and offering him a length of red cloth, after which he enters the *mandap*, stepping on two earthenware bowls as he does so to protect the ceremony from evil spirits. There are two chairs in the *mandap*. The groom sits on the chair to the left, and his bride, who enters after him led by her mother's brother, sits on the other. A series of prayers are spoken to ask for the blessing and protection of the gods. The joining ceremony follows *(hasta melap)*. The Brahmin places a cloth garland around the necks of the couple; the groom's feet are washed by the bride's parents and then dried and decorated with flowers. He is given a number of auspicious items to hold, including sandalwood paste, and the priest puts the bride's hand into the groom's, linking them together with a prayer. After the *hasta melap*, the *toran pratishtha* ceremony takes place to honor the goddess Lakshmi. The bride's parents are given rice, sandalwood, and flowers by the priest with a prayer; they throw this mixture on the top of the *mandap*, and the couple are anointed with holy water as another prayer is spoken. This is followed by a prayer to honor the gods of *Ksetras* (fields and directions), known as *vedi pratishtha*, after which a sacred fire is lit in a small vessel on the altar; this, too, is accompanied by a prayer.

Offerings of ghee, betel nuts, and grain are made to the fire god (with a request that he pass them on to the other gods, the planets, and heavenly bodies). The couple are anointed again with holy water as the priest recites words declaring that the couple are bound together (the first *abhisheka* ceremony). After this ceremony, the couple's lineage is read out in the *gotrachar* ritual, and then the declaration of marriage is read by the priest. The couple are given incense, rice, flowers, and sweets to offer to the fire god. The bride's brother gives each of the couple a handful of rice, which they give to

the priest as they circle the sacred fire four times; the priest offers the rice to the fire. As they circle the fire, a different mantra is recited at each perambulation. Before the couple starts the fourth perambulation, the bride's father formally offers his daughter to the groom and the groom accepts her in the *kanya dan* ceremony. The fire is circled for the fourth time as the priests reads a fourth mantra. After this perambulation, the bride and groom exchange seats. The *vakshepa* ritual follows, in which the heads of the two are sprinkled with water and tel (oil), and the bride's father gives the groom water and tel, saying, "Please take this." The groom replies, "I have taken it, I have accepted it," and the mixture is sprinkled on the bride's head by the priest. During the final part of the ceremony, the second *Abhisheka* ceremony, the couple are addressed by the priest, giving them a blessing, followed by the *kar-mochan*, where the couple's hands are released as the priest chants a mantra and the bride's father presents the groom with a symbolic gift. The ceremony finishes with another blessing from the priest. The couple leave, going first to the temple and then to the bride's home.

In contrast, the Buddhist ceremony is much simpler. After the marriage has been arranged by a matchmaker and the dowry settled, an auspicious day is chosen for the wedding. In the days leading up to the wedding, monks may visit the homes of the couple to give blessings. On the wedding day, each goes separately to the temple to ask for blessing from the Buddha. At the auspicious time, the two meet in the shrine room, or other hired hall, equipped as a shrine to Buddha, with candles, flowers, incense, and a statue of Buddha. The ceremony begins with those gathered reciting from Buddhist writings. The couple lights incense and candles around the Buddha image and offers him flowers. There are no set marriage vows, but the couple will make vows to each other and they may exchange rings. If there are monks present (not required), the vows are preceded and followed with chants. After this ceremony the couple and their guests celebrate with a huge feast.

See also Bangladesh; Canopy, Bridal; Hindu Weddings; Islamic Marriage; Polyandry; Polygyny; Rice; Sikh Weddings; *Suttee;* Zoroastrian Weddings

References

Detailed descriptions of wedding ceremonial traditions in Asia can be found at *http://www.clickwalla.com.*

Murphy, Brian M. 1978. *The World of Weddings: An Illustrated Celebration.* London: Paddington.

Westermarck, Edward. 1894. *The History of Human Marriage.* 2d ed. London: Macmillan.

Indonesia

Indonesia comprises a large group of islands, including Sumatra, Java, and Timor, in which many different styles of marriage ceremony are found. The majority of the population of the islands is Muslim, and the underlying traditions are Islamic, although some of the wedding practices found here vary from strict Islamic tradition. Young men and women are usually allowed to make their own choice of marriage partner, but the young man will inform his parents of the intentions of the couple. His parents, in turn, make the marriage proposal via the headman of the group to the girl's parents. If they agree to the marriage, the man will give them a token of the betrothal, usually consisting of gold ornaments and cash.

The day before the wedding, the bride's house, the venue for the wedding, is decorated with gold hangings and palm leaf decorations. These are usually quite elaborate—the designs often symbolize the cosmos. In North Sumatra, in Aceh, large woven reed mats, decorated in deep rose, green, black, red, and yellow, decorate the walls and floors of the wedding venue. A decorated throne for the bride and groom is prepared. The bride is considered a queen on her wedding day and is decorated with golden hair combs, an ornamental collar, an ornate headdress, bracelets, earrings, ankle decorations, crescent-shaped breastplates (three on a chain),

and hairpins mounted on springs so that they shimmer with the light. Her decoration is inspired by queenly regalia, and she is usually dressed by a professional dresser. In West Java, the bride's crown (called a *siger*) includes jasmine. Thus richly dressed and ornamented, she is expected to sit perfectly still for many hours during the celebrations. During this time, female attendants, often dressed like nymphs from Islamic and Hindu legend, cool her with fans. The groom, too, is highly ornamented and is considered as royalty for his wedding day. He is adorned with gold jewelry, belts, and buckles with a *kris*—a dagger—in a bright scabbard. All this despite Islam's disapproval of gold jewelry for men. Many of the gold adornments for the bride and groom are rented for the occasion and may be imitations.

Gold and silver jewelry are given by the groom's family to the bride's family, who, in turn, present handwoven cloths to the groom's family. There is a certain amount of symbolism within this exchange of gifts—the cloth is soft and considered to be associated with the female, and the cold, hard metal symbolizes the male. In the Nasa Tenggara island group, also known as the Lesser Sunda Islands, of eastern Indonesia, which includes Timor, Sumba, and Flores, when the gifts are exchanged between the families the bride's family is likely to present beads or beadwork—beads are considered to be female goods. The bride in the Sumbian region (one of the Javanese islands group) may give, as part of the dowry, cloths with tufts of ornamental thread and decorated with split shells and glass and ceramic beads. In South Sumatra, cockerel-shaped containers *(kendi)* are used at weddings to symbolize the new life of the couple as they take on their new adult roles and identities. The cockerel welcomes the new day after the frightening darkness of the night and is therefore representative of new life.

The groom's party processes to the bride's home, where they are welcomed by the bride's party reciting suitable poems to the

A Minangkabau bride dressed in elaborate wedding clothes made of songket, *sits in the carved windowsill of a* rumah gadang, *a Minangkabau home in Padang, West Sumatra. (Lindsay Hebberd/CORBIS)*

groom's party, who recite an answering poem. Eventually the groom's group is allowed in, and the groom joins the bride. They go before the Muslim cleric and witnesses. The cleric recites verses from the Koran and requires the couple to declare that they both consent to the marriage; the marriage certificate is then signed. The dowry would have been previously arranged between the two families, and the bride may have exercised her right to impose certain conditions upon the marriage. This agreement, the *ta'lik,* can be either written or oral but has to be made before witnesses. After this ceremony the couple are installed on their wedding thrones in all their gold finery as the center of attention. The wedding feasting and celebrations now proceed around them.

The people on the island of Sumba believe in the existence of three worlds, that of the human being, that of the ancestors, and that of the gods, and it is the ancestors, the souls

of the dead, that have particular control of a wedding. The Sumbanese are grouped into clans, and clan members are expected to marry outside their clan, but there are restrictions about which clan a person can marry into. Another obstacle for a prospective bridegroom is raising the dowry he is expected to pay, which may be very high and may include horses, water buffalo, cattle and pigs, clothing, ivory, gold jewelry, and cash. An alternative to providing the dowry was for a young man to "kidnap" the woman; her father and male relatives immediately attempted to find the couple and take them back to the village where they would be officially married. In this case, the young man had to work for his father-in-law until it was judged that he had worked off the value of the dowry.

On the island of Sumba, marriage is usually arranged between the two families by the young man telling his father whom he would like to marry and his father sending a messenger to the young woman's father with gifts to propose the marriage. If the proposal is accepted, the bride-to-be's family presents a sarong for the groom, and there is a ceremonial chewing of betel at the meeting of the two families. The wedding itself begins at the bride's home, with the groom and his relatives presenting any outstanding balance of the dowry. After prayers are offered up to the souls of the ancestors and to the gods for their blessing, the groom is taken to meet his bride, who has been sitting in a separate room. They ceremoniously chew betel leaves, and his hands are rubbed with chalk by the bride. The celebrations, with musicians and dancers, proceed well into the night. The following day, friends and relatives arrive to escort the bride to the groom's home. But she is guarded by her relatives, who will not let her go until a payment is made to them. After a great deal of bargaining, she is allowed to go, but she makes a show of her sorrow at leaving her home by crying as she is led away on horseback completely covered with a cloth. When she arrives at her new home she is welcomed with a celebration.

The Chinese ethnic group in Java have a different set of traditions, which seem to mingle Chinese practice with the modern Western wedding. After an agreement has been made to marry, and a date set, the family of the groom-to-be goes to the house of the bride about a week before the wedding, taking gifts arranged in red baskets or boxes. The groom does not accompany this group. The baskets or containers contain different gifts, fruit in one, clothes in another, and jewelry for the bride in yet another. These are carried by male members of the family. Once presented, the gift baskets are taken to another room, where the gifts are sorted and about half returned, with the basket returned to the family member who brought it. About three days before the wedding, the bride's family takes gifts in red baskets to the groom's home; again the gifts are sorted and about half returned. Baskets containing the

bride's personal belongings are also taken, the acceptance of which symbolizes the family's acceptance of the bride into their home. This also ensures that her personal belongings are waiting for her when she moves into the groom's house on the wedding day.

On the morning of the wedding day, the groom's parents symbolically help him to get dressed, helping him put on his jacket and putting the flower in his lapel. This can be seen as a symbolic action recognizing his transition from being a dependent child to his adult status. The groom and his parents then go to the bride's house where the bridal couple, on their knees, serve tea to their parents. This symbolizes the couple asking for permission of the parents to marry. Following this, the couple travel in a decorated car to church for the wedding ceremony, which normally only the family of the couple attends. Before going to the reception that follows, the important event, the couple go to the photographer to have pictures taken in twenty different poses. It is expected that they will show the photographs to their children in twenty years time. The reception is for the wider family and friends to be able to offer their congratulations to the couple. Usually the reception does not include a sit-down meal, but at more elaborate weddings there may be a meal, which might consist of nine or ten courses.

The reception is presided over by a master of ceremonies, who makes a speech of welcome to all the guests, followed by the cake-cutting ceremony. The wedding cake is usually a layered cake and sometimes very large—the layers represent the ladders the couple will have to climb for success. Often the cake is cut by the bride and groom together from the bottom layer upward. The couple then feed cake to each other with arms entwined and then cut cake for their parents and grandparents together, feeding the cake to each of these immediate relatives. Sometimes a toast to the couple follows. Music is played to entertain the guests, and the bride and groom and their parents stand on a stage to greet all their guests one by one.

The contemporary wedding ceremony of the Sundanese in West Java is designed to suggest to the couple that they need to work together for their household and that this is a new beginning. The proceedings are overseen by a female companion of the bride, much like a maid of honor. The wedding ceremony consists of two main parts—the welcoming of the bridegroom and the wedding ceremony, which consists of six parts—beginning with the veiling of the couple and the asking for their parents' blessing, followed by a series of actions known as the *sawer,* the *nincak endog, buka pintu, huap lingkung,* and *patarik-tarik bakakak.*

On arrival at the wedding site, the bridegroom is welcomed with a specific form of decoration known as an *umbul-umbul,* which indicates that a marriage ceremony is taking place. A procession of women carrying candles pray for a blessing and no hindrances for the ceremony. Dancers shower the bridal couple with flowers (to symbolize the fragrant future for the couple). An umbrella is held over the heads of the couple—for protection and as an indication of esteem and respect. The bridegroom's future mother-in-law presents him with a garland of flowers to welcome him and demonstrate his acceptance into the family and gives him a *keris,* a hidden message, to encourage him if he should become discouraged while working for his family. The wedding ceremony begins with the couple sitting together with their heads covered with a veil (or *selendang*), symbolic of the couple being two people but with one mind. The couple then bend forward and kiss the knees of their parents, asking for their blessings and forgiveness for any wrongdoings and making a promise to continue to serve them. This ceremony usually takes place in front of a gargoyle. Water flowing from the gargoyle is suggestive of the continuous flow of parental love for their children. The bride and groom, still seated in front of the house beneath the umbrella, are serenaded with a song, called a *kidung,* sung by a man and woman, which asks a blessing

on the couple and advises them to treat each other well and to live in harmony.

The couple are then showered with the *sawer,* consisting of turmeric rice (the yellow color symbolic of everlasting love and the rice of prosperity), coins (to remind the couple to share their wealth with the less fortunate), and candy to indicate sweetness and fragrance throughout the marriage. A betel nut is also set down near the couple as a reminder that their different customs should not spoil their marriage. The next part of the ceremony is the *nincak endog,* the egg-breaking ceremony. This is conducted by the woman who was in charge of the bridal make-up and begins with the bride being given a *harupat,* seven broomsticks, which are burned by the bridegroom lighting them with seven candles *(ajug).* The fire is extinguished, and the remainder of the sticks broken and thrown away (this is to symbolize that the couple discard old bad habits that may compromise their future harmony). The groom then breaks an egg with his right foot; the bride washes his foot with water from an earthenware jug *(kendi),* which she then throws in order to break it. The couple is escorted to the house, the bride stepping over a log (unmarried girls are not allowed to cross over logs), and the bride enters the house as her bridegroom waits outside to perform the *buka pintu* ceremony. This is a dialogue between the bride and groom in which the groom requests permission from the bride to enter the house. However, the dialogue is carried out by a couple of singers; they knock three times at the door and then make the request. The bride allows him in after he confirms his Muslim faith.

The *huap lingkung* is symbolic of the last time that the daughter is fed by her parents. She prepares a dish consisting of turmeric sticky rice with yellow spiced chicken. Finally, in the *patarik-tarik bakakak,* the couple are presented with a barbecued spiced chicken which, on the word "go" from the woman overseeing the ceremony, they pull apart. The one who gets the larger part will bring in the majority of the family income, but this ceremony reminds the couple to work together.

See also China
References
Baldizzone, Tiziana, and Gianni Baldizzone. 2001. *Wedding Ceremonies: Ethnic Symbols, Costume, and Rituals.* Paris: Flammarion.
Murphy, Brian M. 1978. *The World of Weddings: An Illustrated Celebration.* London: Paddington.
Richter, Anne. 1993. *Arts and Crafts of Indonesia.* London: Thames and Hudson.

Irregular Marriage

The laws governing marriage differ from place to place and country to country, and sometimes these differences have been exploited. The more lenient requirements for marriage in Las Vegas in the United States has led to numerous chapels being set up for quick marriages. In Great Britain, the tightening of marriage laws by Lord Hardwick's Marriage Act in 1754 led to the establishment of Gretna Green in Scotland as a spot for quick marriages. An irregular marriage occurs when there is a discontinuity between religious and civil authorities and in situations where they both claim authority over marriage. Thus, irregular marriages do not really include Las Vegas "quickie" marriages or such practices as Israeli couples going to Cyprus for a civil marriage rather than having a religious ceremony as stipulated by legislation of 1948. Irregular marriages do not include common-law or popular forms of trial marriage (such as besom weddings).

The church canons of 1604 stipulated that church weddings had to be performed between 8 A.M. and noon at the church in the place of residence of one of the couple, after the banns had been called three times over successive weeks; however, a marriage outside of those hours in, for example, a tavern or private house without the proper calling of the banns or special license, and far away from the residence of both of the couple, although illegal, was still binding. It was the officiating clergyman who would face punishment, usu-

ally from the ecclesiastical authorities. Therefore, in a state where a marriage that had been conducted by a priest without observing the due process was legally binding in the eyes of the civil authorities, there is ample scope for subverting the system. And this was the case in England until 1754. The church authorities could take action against priests who performed irregular weddings, but they could not declare such unions null and void. Thus, a substantial business developed for such marriages, and venues for irregular marriages were well known and openly advertised. An advertisement in a London newspaper of 8 September 1716 read:

> Sion Chapel, at Hampstead, being a private and pleasure place, many persons of the best fashion have lately been married there. Now as a minister is obliged constantly to attend, this is to give notice that all persons bringing a license, and who shall have their wedding-dinner in the garden, may be married in the said Chapel without giving any fee or reward whatsoever, and such as do not keep their wedding-dinner in the gardens, only five shillings will be demanded of them for all fees. (Jeaffreson 1872, 2: 147)

The 1754 Marriage Act in England and Wales, which to a great extent brought ecclesiastical law and civil law together, brought an end to these irregular weddings in England, and, since the law did not apply in Scotland, moved the trade to Scotland, famously to Gretna Green, but also to such places as Edinburgh, Coldstream, Lamberton, and Glasgow. Irregular marriages occur for a variety of reasons: convenience, the inability to afford a special license or provide the accompanying marriage bond, or the wish for privacy, sometimes for nefarious reasons.

See also Banns; Besom Weddings; Fleet Weddings; Gretna Green; Israel; Temporary Marriage
References
"Claverhouse." 1934. *Irregular Border Marriages.* Edinburgh: Moray Press.

Jeaffreson, John Cordy. 1872. *Brides and Bridals.* 2 vols. London: Hurst and Blackett.

Stone, Lawrence. 1990. *The Family, Sex, and Marriage in England, 1500–1800.* Abridged and revised ed. London: Penguin.

Islamic Marriage

The Koran states that men have authority over women and that Allah has made the one superior to the other because men "spend their wealth to maintain them." The Koran further states that "good women are obedient. They guard their unseen parts because Allah has guarded them. As for those from whom you fear disobedience, admonish them and send them to beds apart and beat them. Then if they obey you take no further action against them."

In Arab countries it has been the practice to veil a girl at puberty and, according to Sharia law, to arrange her marriage soon after. But the Koran also states that marriage is a partnership to be shared between the man and the woman, based upon love, respect, and consent. Marriage is seen as a joining of two families, and parents have a great deal of say about the choice of marriage partner. Any contact between girls and boys is prohibited by Islam, and there is no courtship to allow young people privacy to get to know each other. In some Muslim cultures, the sexes do not mix even during the wedding celebration. The prophet Muhammad said that when a man and woman are alone together there is a third among them—*Shaytan* or Satan. At all times a Muslim is taught to follow the command in the Koran that he or she should "lower their gaze and guard their modesty" (24: 30–31). Islam does not allow sex outside of marriage, and efforts are made to protect young people from temptation.

Muslim marriages are arranged by the parents of the couple who, after considering potential partners for their children, arrange a chaperoned meeting for the two. The parents investigate the prospective bride and groom by talking to religious leaders, friends, colleagues, and other family members, and the couple pray for guidance in their choice of partner, because they cannot be forced into a marriage. After this process has been completed satisfactorily, the couple might agree to the marriage or agree to not proceed.

Islamic law allows a man to have up to four wives (usually with the proviso that he have the financial ability to keep them all to the same standard and with the permission of previous wives) and allows for divorce and for concubinage. However, if a man engages in polygyny, he is expected to treat each of his wives equitably. The Koran instructs that "you may marry other women who seem good to you: two, three or four of them. [B]ut if you fear that you cannot maintain equality among them, marry one only or any slave girls you may own—this will make it easier for you to avoid injustice" (4: 3). The practice of polygyny is, of course, regulated by the laws of the country in which any particular Muslim community lives.

A young man who has fallen in love or who wishes to marry may tell his mother, who will make inquiries about the woman and her family. If his family are satisfied, they will approach the girl's family with an offer of marriage. The Koran spells out degrees of relationship that would forbid marriage: a man may not marry his mother, daughters, sisters, paternal and maternal aunts, the daughters of his brothers or sisters, foster sisters, the mothers of his wives, stepdaughters in his charge born from his wives with whom he has consummated the marriage, and the wives of his sons. Nor may he marry two sisters at the same time or married women, unless they are slaves acquired as captives. The Koran says that it is unlawful for a man to inherit the women of his dead kinsmen against their will, nor may a widow be prevented from remarrying in an effort to make her repay anything (money, goods) that her deceased husband's kinsmen may have given her. Traditionally, Muslim women are veiled when they reach puberty. This is when a girl is considered to have achieved womanhood and is therefore marriageable. However, in the latter half of the twentieth century not all Muslim women took the veil. Where tradition is followed, a prospective husband is not likely to see his proposed bride before the wedding night. The marriage offer and arrangements are likely to be arranged through an intermediary, either a relative or a matchmaker. However, the young woman has to agree to the marriage before the parents set a date and go to the mosque to mark the beginning of the engagement period. This is a time for preparation and for the couple to set up the home. The bride-to-be begins to collect items to take into the marriage, including gold, clothes, household items, and wool to produce mattresses. The young man meanwhile buys presents for his bride and her mother as a sign of respect and love. But he may also pay a dowry (called a *mahir* in Egypt) to help with purchase of the household goods as part of the marriage preparations. The Koran instructs him to give the woman the dowry as a free gift (but adds that if she chooses to give some of it to the man, he may accept that portion and it is lawfully his).

The wedding ceremony can be conducted by anyone learned in Islamic law (Sharia) and must take place in the presence of two male witnesses who must be Muslims. The couple have to publicly consent to the marriage, and the bride receives the promise of the dowry. The celebration *(walimah)* follows to publicize the marriage to the whole community.

At the wedding, the Imam at the mosque explains the Islamic moral code, which the couple is expected to follow. The couple's responsibilities are also clearly defined; generally, the husband and wife are equal partners in the marriage so that the husband, while being expected to provide for, and protect, the family, has no rights to ruling the family. The woman is required to care for the children and run the household; however all decisions should be by mutual agreement between the couple (this is not entirely spelled out in the Koran).

The actual ceremony of marriage may vary from community to community but always involves elaborate feasting and community involvement in the preparation of the bride—bathing her and decorating her with henna (a separate and integral part of the wedding ceremonial in some societies) and processions to the bridegroom's house.

Divorce is allowed, although a man divorcing a wife in order to marry another will forfeit the dowry that he had given her. The notion that saying "I divorce you" three times makes the separation irrevocable comes from the fact that a reconciliation after divorce is allowed twice. Divorcing for a third time is final.

The position of a widow in Islamic society has been difficult, since, by custom, a woman is not allowed to work outside the home. The prophet Muhammad sanctioned a temporary marriage—*sigheh* in Iran and *muta'a* in Iraq—which is a form of prostitution for widows and divorced women, especially during times of war, to enable them to provide for their families. The Sunni Muslims do not follow this practice—they consider it outdated and subject to abuse. However, the Shia Muslims consider this view blasphemous because the practice was sanctioned by the Prophet, and they still practice temporary marriage.

See also Arabic Weddings; Dowry; Egypt; Henna; Temporary Marriage
Reference
Dawood, N. J., trans. 1974. *The Koran.* Harmondsworth, Middlesex: Penguin.

Israel

Israel is probably the only country where its citizens do not have the choice between a religious or a civil wedding ceremony. In Israel, Jews, Christians, and Muslims are all required to be married by their own clergy; this requirement holds even for those of a secular persuasion or those who wish to marry a person not of their own religion. Thus many Israelis marry in another country, usually nearby Cyprus, or do not formally marry but set up home together. Some Israeli couples who do not adhere to Jewish Orthodox traditions fly abroad for a civil ceremony and then have a Jewish wedding in Israel, perhaps performed by a reform rabbi to please their parents. The wedding ceremony is similar for Jewish people around the world.

Israel was established in 1948, and these restrictive marriage laws were passed in 1953, supported by Orthodox Jewish authorities as being necessary to preserve Israel's essential Jewishness. The rabbis argued that God only recognizes Jewish marriages performed according to the traditions of the Orthodox faith. The biblical traditions of the Orthodox Jewish faith are continued in that only a man can seek a divorce from the marriage. The biblical injunction for the brother-in-law of a childless widow to marry his sister-in-law to produce children in the deceased husband's name is still technically followed. However, he had, and still has, the right to refuse to marry her, but had to do so publicly, which could bring shame on his family (Deut. 25.4–10). Today, the brother is under less of an obligation, but this right has led to some abuses where the man may forego his "right and obligation" if the widow pays to be released from the bonds of obligation.

See also Divorce; Jewish Weddings

Reference

Chu, Henry. 2003. "Where 'I Do' Meets 'No, You Don't.'" *Los Angeles Times,* 30 May, A1.

Jamaica

Jamaica in the West Indies was a British possession from 1670 until independence in 1962. Until the Emancipation Act of 1833, the majority of the population were slaves working on the plantations. Plantation owners did not allow their slaves to marry. This caused insecurity among the slaves because they could be sold at any time. Slave owners did not want slaves to settle into family groups, which could complicate moving the slaves between plantations. Slave owners in the United States seem to have been more flexible regarding slave marriages, although the weddings seem to have been regarded as entertainment for slave owners and their families. Plantation owners were often asked to officiate. And slave owners did sometimes cooperate in arranging with other slave owners to sell or buy a slave when the couple were from different plantations so that the couple could be reunited.

After the 1833 Emancipation Act, marriage was often an aspiration among the former slaves. But for many people, since there was no societal or cultural tradition for marriage, this was not a priority, and many opted for a loose family arrangement—cohabitation or common-law marriages—a situation the church and the moral establishment tried to change. For example, a 1938 Royal Commission Report referred to promiscuity and disorganization in family life. Responding to this, in 1944–1945, the governor's wife, Lady Huggins, tried to establish a "mass marriage movement" to help couples that were cohabiting to reduce the costs of getting married, identifying this as being a bar to marriage for many people. An underlying objective was "normalizing" family life on the islands. This was a curious twist from the earlier policy of the white plantation owners and governors in discouraging the slaves from establishing family units but at the same time encouraging procreation (to provide more slaves). This effort tried to impose a European civilization cultural norm on an established social milieu that was previously imposed by the Europeans. This effort was, not surprisingly, a failure.

Those that did aspire to a legal, church-sanctioned wedding followed European traditions. Wedding presents were usually given to the bride and groom by those attending the wedding. It was the tradition for the presents to be taken to the wedding and received by an old woman, charged with displaying and taking the presents. The presents would be displayed in one of the bedrooms set aside for the purpose, where the bed was draped with a pretty bedspread and details of each present were noted in a book. During the reception the guests would view the presents. It is now customary, partly because of the difficulty of finding someone willing to remain behind to look after the presents, to hold a shower or for the presents to be sent in advance. There is also a story of the guests at a London Jamaican immigrant wedding (in 1971) getting so drunk at the reception that they took their gifts back, some even taking someone else's present instead if they liked it better.

The wedding itself is divided into three sections—the church service, the table, and the party. The church service is probably seen as the least important and is the least well-attended part of the wedding. The table, probably the heart of the event, involves feasting, with speeches and the cutting of the cake. This is held in the home of one of the couple or at a friend's house; in country areas, a bower is made from palm trees. The feast centers around curried goat and rice, bread, baked green bananas, and most likely a pudding of corn or cassava meal boiled in bluish banana leaves served with homemade ice cream. The feast is presided over by a master of ceremonies, who coordinates the toasts, prayers, and speeches, which sometimes include advice to the couple for a happy marriage and wishes for them to have children. The party, as the name suggests, features music and dancing. Traditionally, couples do not go away on honeymoons, due to the expense and the fact that they may have been living together for some time before the wedding.

See also Shower; Slave Weddings

References
Newall, Venetia. 1983. "Love and Marriage Customs of the Jamaican Community in London." *London Lore and Language* 3, no. 9: 30–43.
Sides, Sudie Duncan. 1974. "Slave Weddings and Religion." *History Today* 24, no. 2: 77–87.

Japan

In Japan, marriage is a civil rather than a religious ceremony, and, consequently, followers of both the Shinto and the Buddhist religions use similar ceremonies. Marriage is an arrangement between families but not a joining or alliance of families as found in Western cultures. The choice of partner was dependent upon social, political, and economic rank; social status was, and to some extent is, very important. Marriage in Japan still reflects a rigid social structure.

Elaborate ceremony and show are often important parts of wedding practices around the world, but there is little ceremony in the traditional Japanese wedding, which is mostly a private affair. Like most Asian countries, marriages in Japan are still arranged through an intermediary, a matchmaker, but, increasingly, young people are seeking to make their own choice of marriage partner. This has been a slow social change. In the 1950s, Japanese parents made concessions to Western thought so that a young girl might be shown a photograph of a prospective spouse and asked if she would like to marry him. Or a young couple might be allowed to meet and go on one date before getting married. In Japan there has been a move, in fashionable circles, and among those who wish to emulate such circles, to have costumes and ceremonies mirroring the Western form of wedding. This form of event is sometimes referred to as the Western "fantasy wedding" and is a mixture of European and Japanese tradition. However, couples having a Western-style ceremony will often follow it with a traditional Shinto ceremony.

The bride's preparations for the Shinto wedding start early on the wedding day—she puts on her kimono, arranges her hair, and puts on the *tsunokakushi,* a square-shaped hood. The bride's facial make-up also takes a great deal of time and care to apply. The Japanese bride wears white beneath a red and gold robe. White is a symbol of purity and is worn at all commencement ceremonies, and red is the color of fraternity and harmony. White is also a color for mourning and death, and traditionally the woman, when she married, was parted from her birth family as though she were dead. The bridegroom's tra-

A bride and groom in Japan during their wedding ceremony, c. 2000. (Peter M. Wilson/CORBIS)

ditional costume consists of a *montsuki*, a crested coat, over his kimono, which is worn with a pleated skirt, a *hakama*. Today in Japan, the groom often wears a morning suit or a business suit.

The actual ceremony is private, with only the couple's immediate family members present, and is often performed at the bride's home, sometimes at night. The influence of Western culture has led the Shinto and Buddhist sects to emulate the Christian church by holding wedding ceremonies at their shrines. The ceremony may also take place at a hotel or sometimes at the bridegroom's house. The matchmaker leads the bride to a seat beside the groom, and the couple exchange ritual gifts, which are intended to reflect the social status of both the bride and groom.

A central part of the ceremony is for the bride and groom to sip *saké* (rice wine), ex-

changing cups nine times (the *san-san-kudo*, or the three-times-three ceremony) to symbolize the marriage bond: A container of *saké* is placed on a table, along with an empty pitcher and three lacquered cups graded in size so that they fit in each other. Wine is poured from the full pitcher into the empty one. Some is poured back from the second pitcher to the first, symbolizing union, and then a little wine is poured from the first pitcher into the smallest, and uppermost, cup. The bride takes three sips from this and passes the cup to the bridegroom to do likewise. He moves the cup to the bottom of the three, holds out the middle cup to be filled, and takes three sips, before passing it to the bride to do the same. When she has drunk from the middle cup, she places it below the small cup and holds the largest cup to be filled with wine; again she takes three sips before passing the cup to the groom to take three sips. He places the largest cup beneath the middle cup so that the three cups are once again stacked in order. Thus the marriage is completed. The couple may be blessed by a priest and make a pledge to build a happy home. A religious ceremony is not required by law, but the wedding has to be registered with the civil authorities. After the ceremony the bride changes from her kimono for the reception, which may be a very elaborate celebration attended by the couple's families and friends.

Women have few rights in marriage. The man is allowed to take mistresses and concubines (the children of whom have the same legal rights as those of a legal wife), whereas she is expected to not even talk in private to any man. She may be divorced for being barren, too talkative, or too idle, and in 1921 the Reverend Walter Weston noted that one in three or four marriages ended in divorce.

In about 1639, François Caron, a director of the Dutch East India Company in Japan, noted that the Japanese "have a common saying that a Woman hath no constant dwelling, living in her youth with her parents, being married with her Husband, and when she is old with her Childe." The bride took nothing to the marriage—no dowry, no gifts, no household goods, and, in much the same way as the Chinese bride, left her birth family behind and joined her husband's family. She was completely dependent on other people throughout her life. However, this statement is not true for today's Japanese women, and in fact there is a great deal of deference given to a woman by her children. Of whatever age, she is the matriarch in her family.

In traditional societies, the purpose of marriage was to perpetuate the family name, and to this end there was a tradition for a family with no sons to "adopt" a husband, whereby a man is taken into the family by marrying the eldest daughter and taking the family name.

See also China; Colors; Fantasy Weddings
References
Murphy, Brian M. 1978. *The World of Weddings: An Illustrated Celebration.* London: Paddington.
Scott, George Ryley. 1953. *Curious Customs of Sex and Marriage.* London: Torchstream.
Westermarck, Edward. 1894. *The History of Human Marriage.* 2d ed. London: Macmillan.
Wood, Edward J. 1869. *The Wedding Day in All Ages and Countries.* 2 vols. London: R. Bentley.

Jewish Weddings

It is said that the Jewish nation has the oldest recorded rites of marrying because of accounts in the Bible of Adam and Eve as the first "married" couple. However, there are no descriptions of marriage in the Old Testament, except for the story of Laban marrying his eldest daughter Leah to Jacob, instead of Rachel, his youngest, as promised. When Jacob found that he had been fooled, Laban said, "Finish this daughter's bridal week: then we will give you the younger one also, in return for another seven year's work" (Gen. 29.27). This suggests that the early Jewish wedding involved a celebration lasting a whole week. In justifying his deceit, Laban said, "It is not our custom here to give the younger daughter in marriage before the older one" (Gen. 29.26–27).

Jewish marriage, traditionally, is largely monogamous. However, there are accounts of leaders such as Moses and Solomon having more than one wife and of the Jewish "nobility" taking concubines. In the above account, Jacob could apparently have two wives. The Tunisian Jews in the nineteenth and early twentieth centuries practiced polygamy if the first wife was unable to have children. Continuity of the tribe or family has been very important to Jewish people everywhere, and the choice of a marriage partner for a young man has often been arranged by a go-between—usually a rabbi. Rabbis were asked for their help because of their knowledge of the families and tribes. A donation to the synagogue was often made for this help.

In time, the professional matchmaker, the *shadchan,* came into being who would be commissioned to find a wife for a young man. The *shadchan* would extol the virtues of a prospective bride to the young man and arrange the contracts. It was customary for the bride and groom to not see each other before the wedding day, and if the wedding was arranged by a matchmaker, the couple may have seen very little of each other. Certainly they would not have been able to get to know each other.

The contemporary Jewish wedding ceremony combines the betrothal ceremony, the marriage ceremony, and a public joining of the couple to become an individual family unit. Judaism prescribes that a marriage be a community event and should not take place in private. Indeed, if a bride or her family are not able to afford a large wedding, a collection may be taken from the community to ensure that the celebrations are carried through properly. To help with the expense and arrangements, the groom's friends are expected to send gifts of money to the groom. Those donating help were entitled to eat and drink with the groom during the week of wedding celebrations. These friends and acquaintances were referred to as *shoshbins.* The

The wedding of actor Nitsan Hess at an Orthodox Jewish wedding in Jerusalem in 1998. After living a secular life, he returned to his Orthodox Judaic roots. (Koren Ziv / CORBIS SYGMA)

shoshbin was also traditionally the groom's confidant, analogous to the best man at a Gentile wedding. The word in Aramaic has the sense of a close friend. The bride, too, has her *shoshbin* to attend and support her through the wedding.

There are nine elements in the Jewish wedding: the *huppah* (canopy); the signing of the *ketubah;* the *bedeken,* the veiling of the bride; the seven circuits; the *kiddushin,* the betrothal ceremony; the *nissuin,* the marriage ceremony; the breaking of the glass; the signing of the civil register; and the *yichud,* the time of seclusion or privacy. There are questions concerning when they were introduced and disputes concerning whether or not the wedding should take place inside a synagogue because a ceremony held inside a building is reminiscent of Gentile practice. The *huppah* or *chuppa* (canopy) symbolizes the new home, the basis of Jewish life, and is open on all four sides to represent hospitality. It is bare to indicate that it is not physical or ma-

terial things that make a good marriage but the love and affection and sacrifice of each partner and the spiritual richness with which they invest their home.

Before the ceremony the groom reads and accepts all the terms of the marriage contract, the *ketubah.* This outlines the duties and responsibilities of the husband to provide food, clothing, and conjugal rights. The groom, by accepting this contract, allows the rabbi to read this to the bride at a later stage of the ceremony. The *ketubah* is then witnessed.

Bedeken, or the veiling of the bride, comes from the Hebrew word meaning to check and recalls the story of Jacob being tricked into marrying Leah, Rachel's older sister. The groom is escorted to the bride's room where he confirms that the woman is the right one. After lifting the veil over the bride's face, the rabbi blesses the bride with words from the blessing given to Rebekah on her marriage to Isaac: "Our sister, may you become the mother of thousands of ten thousands" (Gen. 24.60), and adds, "The Lord make you as Sarah, Rebekah, Rachel and Leah." The bride and groom are conducted to the *huppah* by the couple's parents. This is considered to be a *mitzvah*—a privilege and an honor. The bride wears no jewelry or other ornament, signifying that the couple are equal at the beginning of their new life together. On their wedding day the couple is viewed almost as royalty, and it is usual for the bride to stand to the right of the groom to reflect the words of Psalm 45.10: "At thy right hand doth the queen stand." It is also a tradition that the guests should tell the groom how beautiful the bride is. Ancient rabbis, worried that in some cases this could result in the guests bearing false witness, decreed that every bride was beautiful on her wedding day and in the groom's eyes she is without equal.

Under the *huppah,* the bride makes seven circuits of the groom, representing the seven days of creation. This is said to remind the couple and the witnesses that marriage is a reenactment of the creative process—an opportunity for the couple to create a new world, create a new life together, and become a new unit within the community. The number seven also corresponds to the seven marriage blessings. Seven is often considered a mystical number. One of the central symbols and artifacts of Judaism is the seven-branched candelabrum, the *menorah.* (Among the Fassi of Morocco, the number seven also recurs throughout the wedding, symbolic of a complete cycle, with seven days of celebration, seven evenings spent on ritual cleansing, and seven wedding garments worn by the bride at the wedding.)

Next is the betrothal ceremony, the *kiddushin.* The bride and groom sip from a cup of wine to remind them that they are now going to share the same "cup of life." The rabbi recites the two betrothal blessings, and the groom says, in Hebrew, "You are now consecrated to me with this ring according to the law of Moses and Israel." He places the ring on the index finger of her right hand. The *ketubah* is then read aloud in Aramaic, with a translation.

The marriage ceremony, *nissuin,* follows. Seven blessings are recited over a cup of wine to seal the union—blessings that allow the couple to live together as husband and wife, with such themes as the "wondrous" nature of the marital state, the inclusion of Jerusalem as a partner in the happiness and joy of the bride and groom, the wish that the couple will be as happy as Adam and Eve in the Garden of Eden, and the wish that the marriage will be blessed with happiness.

The end of the ceremony is marked by the breaking of the glass under the heel of the groom to symbolize the destruction of the Temple in Jerusalem. Jews are taught to put Jerusalem above their greatest happiness, and this is said to remind the couple of the sorrows of Israel. However, some have interpreted this act as one to ward off evil spirits. Everyone present shouts *mazal tov,* which means "good fortune." The rabbi then blesses the couple.

In Great Britain, the legal aspect of the marriage is the signing of the civil register, witnessed by two friends or relatives. This takes place on the *bimah* where they are given the *ketubah* and their state marriage certificate.

After the ceremony the couple return together to the bride's room where they have some moments of privacy—*yichud*—and they break their fast. It is customary for the bride and groom to fast on their wedding day—it is considered their own Yom Kippur. After the ceremony, the guests will join in the celebrations and enjoy themselves as an obligation to make the bride and groom happy on their own special day. Money is scattered among the crowd as a reminder, that the guests had been present at the wedding; and barley also is thrown before the newly married couple, symbolizing their wish for many children.

See also Almonds; Canopy, Bridal; Dowry; *Huppah (Chuppa);* Israel; Matchmaking; Veil

References

Fraser, John Foster. 1911. *The Land of Veiled Women.* London: Cassell.

Michals, Andrea. 1973. "Jewish Ceremony." *Viltis* 31, no. 6: 11–12.

Segal, Eliezer. 1999. *Why Didn't I Learn This in Hebrew School?* Northvale, NJ: Jason Aronson.

Seid, Marsha. 1972. "Introduction to Hassidic Dancing." *Viltis* 30, no. 6: 8–9.

Tegg, William. 1877. *The Knot Tied: Marriage Customs of All Nations.* London: William Tegg.

Kuwait

In Kuwait, an Islamic country, marriage is still arranged between the parents, with the woman sometimes having no say in the choice of partner. Parents sometimes obtain the relevant marriage certificate from the magistrates before telling the prospective bride that she is to be married.

On the morning of the wedding, the bride is prepared for the marriage by her mother and other female relatives, who bathe her, braid her hair and make it shine with oils, and decorate her hands and feet with a black dye or black henna. Her eyes are made up, using kohl and powdered antimony, which is applied to the eye using a small stick soaked in olive oil, and her lips are reddened with rouge prepared from safflower (*Carthamus tinctorius*) or from the red roots of the plant *Arnebia decumbus.* These preparations take some time, and when complete, she must sit quietly—the henna designs on her hands and feet should not be disturbed for up to six hours for them to set. The bridegroom, accompanied by his male relatives, processes to the bride's house. The relatives carry lanterns and sing and clap to the music of drummers who bring up the rear of the party. It is not unusual to see the wedding guests processing in cars with a truckload of drummers following. During the wedding night, the women of the house usually sit in a room adjacent to the bridal chamber listening for noises emanating from therein. This is a social event and considered part of the wedding entertainment.

As with many Arab weddings, over the next three days the bride and groom sit in separate rooms of the house, entertaining guests of their own sex who have come to congratulate them. Observers have noted that over this period the bride may make a spectacular change in appearance from a diffident and scared young woman to becoming a self-assured married woman. She is likely to be wearing a great deal of borrowed gold jewelry and ornaments, such as a gold plaque on the crown of her head with a fringe of gold coins and loops of gold attached to her braids of hair at the back. She may also be wearing a nose ring, earrings, necklaces, and gold bangles and bracelets.

Again, as in most Middle Eastern countries, weddings have become very expensive, including the dowry, payments to the family, feasts, the setting up of the home, and, increasingly, honeymoons. A wedding might cost sixty thousand dollars. Consequently, many Kuwaiti men either marry foreign women or remain bachelors. In an attempt to reverse this trend, in 1999, a religious charity, the Othman Zakat Committee, organized the first mass wedding in the country for twenty-eight couples. The couples were also given a free hotel suite for their honeymoon.

See also Arabic Weddings; Henna; Islamic Marriage; Mass Weddings

Reference

Braddock, Joseph. 1961. *The Bridal Bed.* New York: John Day.

Lapland

See Sameh People

Leap Year

According to the Gregorian calendar, the year is divided into 365 days. But every fourth year an extra day must be added, 29 February, to reconcile the calendar with the solar year, which is approximately 365¼ days long. In Western marriage tradition, it has become usual for the man to make the first move in the courtship and marriage proposal. However, the extra day in leap years allowed a certain license—an unusual event often prompts the suspension of some aspect of life. A woman is allowed to break with convention and propose marriage to the man of her choice on this day. If the man turns her down, he is obligated to give her new gloves on Easter Day.

As with many traditions and beliefs, there are differences of interpretation in different areas, so that in some places a woman could propose marriage at any time during the leap year. But it was more usual for this practice to be limited to leap day, sometimes called Bachelor's Day.

> **See also** Gloves
> **References**
> Dunkling, Leslie. 1988. *A Dictionary of Days.* London: Routledge.

Kightly, Charles. 1987. *The Perpetual Almanack of Folklore.* London: Thames and Hudson.

Lord Hardwick's Marriage Act

This pivotal piece of legislation was passed in England in 1753 and came into effect in 1754. It was designed to prevent irregular and clandestine marriages, especially those of heiresses and young men of good family being married for their fortunes, against the wishes of their family and sometimes against their own wills. The law gave the established Church of England a great deal of control of the institution of marriage. It followed earlier acts of William III of 1695, which taxed all bachelors and childless widows over the age of twenty-five and also imposed a heavy tax on marriage to raise money to fight the French Wars. The effect of this was to increase the market for clandestine marriages.

Lord Hardwick's Marriage Act was a very contentious issue at the time because of the control it gave the Church of England and because it made it more difficult to avoid the taxes on marriage by employing the services of priests willing to marry couples in taverns, backrooms, and "marriage houses" without the publication of the banns. The act required that all marriages should be solemnized only after the publication of the banns or the issuing of a special license, and only in the parochial church or chapel where the banns of matrimony had been published. Additionally, any clergyman convicted of contravening the law would

> be deemed and adjudged to be guilty of felony, and should be transported to some of His Majesty's plantations in America for the space of fourteen years. . . . All marriages, solemnized from and after March 25, 1754, in any other place than a church or such publick chapel, unless by special license as aforesaid, or that shall be solemnized without publication of banns or license of marriage from a person or persons having authority to grant the same first had and obtained, shall be null and void to all intents and purposes whatsoever.

The consent of the parents or guardians was required before the marriage of or promise to marry of "minors," and there was a clause that allowed for capital punishment for anyone convicted of destroying, forging, or falsifying, "with evil intent," an entry in a marriage register. The act did have some exclusions. It did not apply to Scotland and was instrumental in the development of the clandestine marriage market at Gretna Green and other border towns in Scotland. And it did not apply to Jews and Quakers:

> That nothing in this Act shall extend to the part of Great Britain called Scotland, nor to any marriages among the people called Quakers, or among the persons professing the Jewish religion, where both the parties to any such marriage shall be of the people called Quakers, or persons professing the Jewish religion respectively, nor to any marriage solemnized beyond the seas.

The act was cruel, inconsiderate, and insulting to all sincere nonconformists who were not Quakers or followers of other non-Christian (for example, Jewish) religions. During the passage of the bill through Parliament, the Catholic and non-conformist Protestant groups made representations against the act that would compel them to be married by clergy of the established church (Church of England) in the parochial church. It is obvious why the Jewish community should be exempt—because of their quite different religious practice and the fact that their marriage practices, and those of the Quakers, made it unlikely that members of these communities would have a clandestine marriage, which would not be recognized by their communities. The exemption for Scotland had no other reason than that the opponents of the bill tabled many amendments to destroy the bill including the exclusion for Scotland. This exclusion was one with which Lord Hardwick complied to ensure that his bill passed into law.

See also Fleet Weddings; Gretna Green; Irregular Marriage

Reference

Jeaffreson, John Cordy. 1872. *Brides and Bridals.* 2 vols. London: Hurst and Blackett.

Love Spoons

Love spoons are elaborately carved wooden spoons, given by a prospective suitor to a girl to indicate his interest in courtship. It is sometimes said that the offer of a carved spoon by a young man and its acceptance or rejection constituted a rite of betrothal, but there is little evidence for this. It is merely a token and symbol of affection and perhaps a prelude to courtship. There is some suggestion that some of the spoons may have been made and given anonymously, much like a Valentine greeting of today. The earliest known surviving love spoon dates from the latter part of the seventeenth century and is in the Museum of Welsh Life, St. Fagans, Cardiff, Wales.

Making spoons was a common winter pastime, and it was quite natural for young men to carry that a step further and elaborately decorate a wooden spoon to present to a young woman who interested him. It is a common tradition for utilitarian items to be decorated and presented by a young man to a young woman. In the Dales of Yorkshire, where there is a strong knitting tradition, knitting sheaths, to hold the needles, may be decorated as love tokens, and, similarly, in bobbin lace-making districts, young men made and inscribed lace bobbins for their sweethearts. In some cultures, the production and carving of household items by a young man, to be given to a young woman, serves to demonstrate his skills as a provider. In Finland, for example, young men carved spinning wheel distaffs and reel holders to give to their prospective brides.

A spoon was sometimes decorated with the initials of the maker and the date it was given, but there was symbolism in other designs carved on the spoons. A spoon with two bowls coming from the same handle was considered to represent "we two are one"; occasionally spoons were carved with a third, smaller, bowl protruding from the handle, indicating the child that would complete married bliss. Chains were sometimes carved as part of the handle, the number of links indicating the number of children the maker hoped for. A wheel carved on the handle was a promise that the carver would work for his sweetheart. Spades conveyed the same message. A heart, or two hearts together, have the obvious symbolism of "my heart is yours" or that both the giver and receiver feel the same about each other. Houses, keyholes, or keys symbolize setting up home together. A clever design was to carve the handle as a cavity with free rolling balls within to symbolize that the woman had captured the man's heart—trapped by his love for her, only the return of affection will free him. However elaborate the designs were, remarkably they were always carved from a single piece of wood.

Love spoons are still carved in Wales, but usually only for the tourist market. Miniature love spoons are also being produced as refrigerator magnets to distribute to wedding guests as wedding favors.

See also Courtship; Tokens

References

N.a. *Love Spoons from Wales.* 1973. Swansea: Celtic Educational Services.

Owen, Trefor. 1968. *Welsh Folk Customs.* 2d ed. Cardiff: National Museum of Wales.

M

Maori Weddings

Marriage among the Maori was a flexible thing—there was a great deal of sexual freedom, sexuality was enjoyed, and partners were chosen of either sex for pleasure (same-sex relations were not condemned). Monogamy was not the norm for the Maori, and polygyny was allowed (indulged in usually by high caste men—but aristocratic women also sometimes indulged in polyandry). Families would sometimes use marriage arrangements to cement or develop political alliances among families. To bring peace between warring families, a marriage would be arranged between them, accompanied by the exchange of gifts of treasured possessions. The Maori generally married very young, and a girl may be promised in marriage at a very young age. However, anthropologists and travelers noted that a woman was often able to choose her marriage partner. Endogamy was expected— "great opposition is made to any one taking, except for some political purpose, a wife from another tribe" (Yate 1835)—and marriage generally took place between relatives.

European observers have reported (Taylor 1870) that the favored method of marriage was to capture a bride and that marriages usually occurred after sunset or at night, apparently because there were so many relatives to be consulted, some of whom would be upset if their consent was not obtained. It was simpler and quicker to simply get a "war-party" together and abduct the woman. Often the abduction and defense was just for show.

But this does not seem to fit with the idea of marriage being used to cement alliances, and, according to Crawley (1902), mock fights took place when groups met. It may be that European observers misunderstood what they were observing; often there are puzzling discrepancies in the accounts observed by travelers and missionaries. For example the Reverend R. Taylor noted that if a girl had two suitors with equal claims to her as a wife they would have a "pulling match," a form of tug of war, where each man grabbed one arm of the woman and pulled her in opposite directions, the stronger being the winner. However, he also wrote that the ancient and most usual way of obtaining a wife among the Maori was for the man to get together a party of his friends and carry off the woman by force, apparent or actual. It is also often noted that a Maori girl was able to have her choice of marriage partner.

Divorce was allowed, but only disaffection between the two was a good enough reason. Sometimes the two simply moved apart. It was only if there were issues of property and alliances that there were problems, in which case there would be rituals of confrontation and retribution involving claims, payment, or even the forcible taking of compensation in the form of goods such as weapons, textiles, or ornaments.

Missionaries introduced the concept of Christian marriage to the Maori. Yate (1835) gave a short account of a Christian Maori marriage in which the bride's mother expressed her anger at the wedding even though she was pleased that her daughter was to be married:

> On returning with the bridegroom and the bride the procession was met by her. She began to assail us furiously. She put on a most horrific countenance, threw her garments about, and tore her hair like a fury; then said to me "Ah, you white missionary you are worse than the devil; you first make a slave lad your son by redeeming him from his master, and then marry him to my daughter. I will tear your eyes out!" The old woman, suiting the action to the word, feigned a snatch at my face, at the same time saying in an undertone, that it was "all mouth" and that she did not mean what she said. (Yate 1835)

Today, the Maori wedding ceremony is available to couples getting married, but it seems to owe more to the Christian Maori tradition than to native Maori tradition. Illustrations on the Internet (among other places, www.maoriweddings.co.nz) show the bride wearing a white wedding dress and veil. The ceremony is in six parts: *Te Karanga* (the welcome call)—a traditional Maori welcome call invites the bride and groom onto the sacred land where the ceremony will be performed; *Te Powhiri*—the local tribe performs a traditional song and dance for the bridal party; followed by the touching noses *(Hongi),* a gesture of friendship and goodwill between the couple; the couple exchange vows in a ceremony conducted by a Maori priest *(Te Marena);* after which they are serenaded with a Maori love song, "Po kare kare ana." The *Te Manaakitanga* follows, a blessing

from the priest on the marriage, followed by the presentation of a gift *(Taonga)* to the couple that symbolizes new beginnings and happiness. This part of the ceremony is completed with the *hongi.* This formal part of the ceremony being over, the wedding feast *(Te Hakari)* begins, with music, dancing, and feasting through the night, where the groom is honored as a chief. Finally, when the bridal couple departs, they are seen off with traditional Maori songs and dances *(Te Haere Atu,* the departure).

See also Aborigines (Australian); Capture, Marriage by; Polygyny

References
Crawley, Ernest. [1902] 1932. *The Mystic Rose: A Study of Primitive Marriage and of Primitive Thought in Its Bearing on Marriage.* 4th ed. Revised and enlarged by Theodore Besterman. London: C. A. Watts.
Information is available at *www.maoriweddings.co.nz* (accessed 1 June 2004).
Starzecka, D. C., ed. 1996. *Maori Art and Culture.* London: British Museum Press.
Taylor, R. 1870. *Te Ika a Maui; or, New Zealand and Its Inhabitants.* London: W. Macintosh.
Westermarck, Edward. 1894. *The History of Human Marriage.* 2d ed. London: Macmillan.
Yate, William. [1835] 1970. *An Account of New Zealand.* London: R. B. Seeley. Reissued, Shannon: Irish University Press.

Mass Weddings

Mass weddings are associated with the Unification Church (the "Moonies")—thousands of couples being married in a stadium in Seoul, Korea, with marriage partners arranged or chosen by the leader and founder of the church, Reverend Sun Myung Moon. These events began in 1982 and occurred every three years until 1995. The rationale of these mass weddings was that they were part of a spiritual journey through which world peace would prevail. The Unification Church taught that the greatest problems in the world have roots in the breakdown of family and that these problems can be solved by the purification and sanctification of the family through marriage.

A crowd of excited brides at a mass wedding of the Unification Church. Approximately 25,000 couples were married by Reverend Sun Myung Moon and Hak-ja Ha Moon in the Seoul Olympic Stadium. (Gideon Mendel/CORBIS)

This use of family, and the perception of the role of the family in bettering society, seems to be reminiscent of other mass marriage movements and events. Mass weddings have been used (though never before on the scale of the Unification Church) by the Church of England to "legitimize" cohabiting couples, often in a misguided attempt to get the couples to conform, but with little appreciation of the social and historical backgrounds of the people involved. Church records from the East End of London in the latter part of the nineteenth century and the early twentieth century showed that the clergy arranged for mass weddings for the poor who were unable to afford individual wedding ceremonies. These mass ceremonies were carried out in an effort to eradicate the high incidence of cohabitation and common-law marriages, which were one of the social consequences of the industrial revolution.

The Reverend Arthur W. Jepherson of St. John's Church, Walworth, London, officiated at many multiple weddings, and it is said that sometimes he married forty couples at once. The practice continued in London into the twentieth century. There is a photograph from 1903 of five couples being married at the same time in St. John's Church, Hoxton (in Scott 1953, 226).

Head (1840) described a mass wedding in the Manchester Parish Church. Fees charged at this church were very low so that it was a popular marriage venue, often with several couples married at once, especially on Easter Monday. Head noted that the couples were all poor people: "As to the brides and bridegrooms, as few were dressed in special costume, and all were very generally attended by friends and relatives, it was not easy to say which was which." He also described one couple trying to be of a higher class than the other couples by arriving by horse-drawn carriage. There is a story regarding one of the priests who officiated at these group marriages who accidentally married the wrong pairs. He enjoined: "Pair as you go out; you're all married; pair as you go out."

It happened that a couple would consider that it was sufficient for them to exchange simple vows to be married, and it was not unusual for couples to attend a marriage service and follow the responses and exchange vows in order to be surreptitiously "married by clergy in church." (The vows should be before witnesses, and thus this would not be recognized as a proper and legal marriage in the eyes of the law.) Mayhew (1861–1862) noted that the costermongers (hawkers of fruits and vegetables) disliked putting money in the parson's pocket unnecessarily by paying his fees for a wedding and would only be married in church when it was free of charge.

After a Royal Commission Report in 1938 that referred to promiscuity and the "disorganization" of family life in Jamaica, Lady Huggins, the governor's wife, in 1944 and 1945, attempted to launch a "mass marriage movement," hoping to overcome the problem of the wedding costs. But an underlying motive would have been to "normalize" family life on the islands. The movement failed.

In 1999, a religious charity in Kuwait, the Othman Zakat Committee, organized the first mass wedding in that country for twenty-eight couples who were given the use of a honeymoon suite at a hotel for taking part. The charity was trying to encourage Kuwaiti men to marry Kuwaiti women by lowering the cost of marriage. It was estimated that the average cost of getting married, including wedding party expenses, honeymoon, payments to family, dowries, and setting up of the home, was around sixty thousand dollars, and many Kuwaiti women were unmarried because men either married foreign women or decided to remain bachelors. Mass weddings are common in Shia Muslim villages in the eastern parts of Saudi Arabia, and officials of the United Arab Emirates have also promoted mass weddings to cut the costs of weddings for individual families.

In Iraq in October 2002, to celebrate his new term in office, Saddam Hussein not only released thousands of political prisoners of his regime, a much-publicized event, but also had the state pay for over five hundred weddings across the country. In Baghdad, 155 couples were married in a mass wedding. Interestingly, as with the Unification Church mass weddings, the brides wore white wedding dresses and the grooms dressed in suits.

See also Common-Law Marriage; Jamaica

References
Gillis, John R. 1985. *For Better, For Worse: British Marriages, 1600 to the Present.* Oxford: Oxford University Press.
Hawley, Caroline. 2002. "Mass Weddings Mark Saddam's New Term." *BBC News Online.* (21 October). Available at *http://news.bbc.co.uk/1/hi/world/middle_east/2348205.stm* (accessed 6 June 2004).
Head, Sir George. 1840. *A Home Tour through the Manufacturing Districts and Other Parts of England, Scotland, and Ireland.* London: John Murray.
"Kuwait Holds First Mass Weddings." 1999. *BBC News Online.* (5 December). Available at *http://news.bbc.co.uk/1/hi/world/middle_east/551292.stm* (accessed 6 June 2004).
Mayhew, Henry. 1861–1862. *London Labour and the London Poor.* London: Griffin and Bohn.
Newall, Venetia. 1983. "Love and Marriage Customs of the Jamaican Community in London." *London Lore and Language* 3, no. 9: 30–43.
Scott, George Ryley. 1953. *Curious Customs of Sex and Marriage.* London: Torchstream.

Matchmaking

In many societies, the choice of marriage partner was not necessarily made by the couple involved, and social mores prevented meeting and approaching members of the opposite sex. Therefore a go-between was used to bring marriageable men and women together. There are basically three forms of matchmaking: The first and most well-known is for a person to act as a go-between.

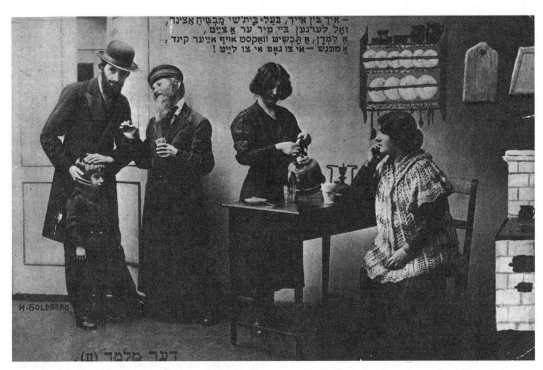

- אִיךְ בִּין אֵיךְ, בַּעֲלֵי־בָּתְּ'שִׁי מִבְטִיחַ אֲצִינְך,
זָאל לערנען בֵּיי מִיר עֶר אַ צַיִּט,
אַ לַמְדָן, אַ תַּכְשִׁיט וואֵקסְט אוֹיף אֵייעֶר קִינד,
אַמְפֶּנְשׁ — אִי צוּ גָאט אִי צוּ לֵייט!

דֶער מְלַמֵּד (ח)

A shadchan *and another man have a conversation while a woman pours from a teapot. The* shadchan, *or marriage broker, was traditionally an essential part of a Jewish marriage. (Hulton-Deutsch Collection/CORBIS)*

Secondly, an event might take place for the specific purpose of bringing marriageable young people together. Or, third, agencies and newspaper columns might be devised where single people are able to advertise or be brought together. The first type of matchmaker may be a friend or relative or a "professional" who knows all the young women of marriageable age in an area or community and has knowledge of family backgrounds and social standings and who charges a commission for performing the service. The duties of the matchmaker range from being a go-between taking messages between the couple and bringing them together to being part of the negotiation of the marriage settlement and contract.

The second type is likely to occur within a widely scattered community, where there is a problem of where to meet prospective life partners. Matchmaking events—dances and fairs—develop so that young people can meet others outside their immediate family groups. The Guizhou Miaos from the highland area of western Guizou in the Liupanshui region of China have an annual love festival known as the *Tiaohuapo,* or "dance on the flowery meadow." About forty thousand people attend this festival, some as spectators. But unmarried young men and women meet others and flirt and "seduce"—through music, song, dance, smiles, and furtive glances—members of the opposite sex with the hope of finding a marriage partner. Similarly, matchmaking is a feature of the annual fair held in the town of Lisdoonvarna in Northern Ireland in September. In this town it is still possible to engage a matchmaker to help in finding a marriage partner; but it is well known and accepted that the social events and dances are strongly geared toward allowing couples to meet to establish courtships and eventual marriage.

The third type of matchmaking agency, the "marriage bureau" or dating agency, is sometimes considered to be a twentieth-century phenomenon. But, in 1797, an advertisement appeared in a London newspaper that announced "A New and Original Grand Matrimonial Intercourse Institution." This grand institution boasted a "mode of accelerating and promoting the union of the sexes in the bands of holy matrimony, without exposure of either person or character." In the nineteenth century, offices were established for the negotiation of marriage. These marriage brokers regularly advertised in the newspapers. In 1839, the following publication was announced:

> Portfolio for the inspection of ladies, and which will contain certain copies of the letters, without name or address, from gentlemen of rank and fortune, gentlemen of private fortune, officers in the army and navy, and other professional gentlemen of high respectability and fortune, who are sincerely desirous of uniting themselves in marriage with ladies of respectability.

On 1 April 1889, the *Belfast Newsletter* printed an advertisement for the *Matrimonial Herald and Fashionable Marriage Gazette,* which claimed to be the "largest and most successful Matrimonial Agency in the world." Most advertisements for wives that appeared in the eighteenth century required the women to have money.

Matchmakers are familiar because of such popular shows and films as *Fiddler on the Roof* and *Hello Dolly,* but he or she is an important figure in marriage traditions. In many societies there is a great emphasis on the purity or virginity of the bride—the reason in many Islamic countries that betrothal and marriage is expected to occur soon after a girl reaches puberty, ensuring that children belong to the husband, a factor deemed important for issues of family inheritance. Consequently, children and young adults are allowed little chance to meet and get to know each other and court, as generally accepted and understood in Britain and the United States, so that the only chance of finding a marriage partner is through the offices of a matchmaker.

In Jewish tradition, the matchmaker is known as the *shadchan.* Originally he would have been the head of a school established to keep alive and develop Judaism after the destruction of the second temple in 70 A.D. As a leader in the community and knowledgeable in religious and legal matters, he would know the families in the vicinity and their circumstances and would have been approached for his help and advice concerning who should marry whom. The fathers of the couple would express their gratitude by making a donation to the school. Rabbis were also approached for their help and advice, and again donations would be made to the synagogue for the service rendered. In time, the *shadchan* became more like a traveling peddler. This person would often be not very successful as a rabbi or be one holding only a minor post in the synagogue. With a good knowledge of religious observance and custom, he would be welcome in any Jewish home and would arrange marriages on a commission of 2 or 3 percent of the dowry, depending on the amount of travel involved. Not surprisingly, since the *shadchan* worked by commission and was paid upon a successful marriage, there are stories of the overselling of the attributes of each of the couple.

Lane (1836), in a nineteenth-century description of life in Egypt, related how the mother of a young man who wishes to marry may employ one or more matchmakers, known as a *khát'beh* or *khátibeh,* who would report back on the girls available, describing their looks and attributes. The man's mother and other female relatives would help in the choice of bride. Once a choice was made, the *khát'beh* would take a present from the young man to the girl's family and extol his virtues to the girl.

The matchmaking tradition still exists in parts of Ireland, notably the rural areas where the population is scattered and it is difficult to meet members of the opposite sex. Country fairs, such as that at Lisdoonvarna, have developed a reputation for making matches. The matchmaker may be unofficial, known as a "blackfoot," or an officially recognized matchmaker who charges a fee for services. Again, the job of both of these is to extol the virtues of their client (usually a man) to the woman of their choice, or to find an eligible woman for the man. The couple often have the opportunity to express agreement or disagreement to the marriage, although the parents may overrule or bring pressure to bear on the dissenting party. In some societies, although the parents make the decision about their child's marriage partner, the young woman's (or man's) views are taken into account and she (or he) can object.

In Tibet, the wife has a great deal of authority over her husband, but she has no choice in marriage partner. When a man achieves marriageable age, his parents look for a suitable wife for him. When they find a suitable girl they communicate with her parents via a middleman, and all arrangements are made between the parents. The couple usually only find out that they are to be married on the wedding day.

In the late twentieth century and the early twenty-first century, the Internet has become part of the matchmaking market, with Internet sites developed for unmarried people to advertise as available for marriage.

The tradition of the fair or event designed for couples to be able to meet and get to know each other is also continued through "speed dating" events, at which the participants have a short time in which to talk to participants in turn, judge whether they would like to meet again, and, if so, arrange another, more leisurely meeting.

See also Arranged Marriage; Contracts; Egypt; Islamic Marriage; Jewish Weddings; Tibet
References
Baldizzone, Tiziana, and Gianni Baldizzone. 2001. *Wedding Ceremonies: Ethnic Symbols, Costume, and Rituals.* Paris: Flammarion.
Ballard, Linda May. 1998. *Forgetting Frolic: Marriage Traditions in Ireland.* Belfast and London: Institute of Irish Studies, Queens University, Belfast, and Folklore Society, London.
Lane, Edward W. [1836] 1994. *The Manners and Customs of the Modern Egyptians.* Everyman Edition. London: J. M. Dent.
Murphy, Brian M. 1978. *The World of Weddings: An Illustrated Celebration.* London: Paddington.

May, Marriage in

Many folklore books say that the month of May is considered unlucky for a wedding and quote the couplet, "Marry in May, you'll rue the day." Although given as a superstition in Great Britain in general, most of the reports regarding this observation are from the north of England and Scotland. Another couplet, from Scotland, also warned of May marriages: "Of marriages in May, the bairns [children] die of decay." And there is a story that the novelist Sir Walter Scott dashed back from London in 1820 after receiving his baronetcy so that he could ensure that his daughter married before May began. She married on the 29 April, but her firstborn died from "decay" at the age of ten; the end of April came within the orbit of the maliciousness of May. In Ayrshire, Scotland, it was thought that the firstborn from a May marriage would be born an idiot. Another punishment for marrying in May was thought to be that the wife would not be thrifty.

Research in parish registers in England suggests that the May taboo may not have been particularly observed. This is one of the few superstitions for which the widespread observance can be tested over a long term, because Thomas Cromwell instructed parishes to maintain records of births, marriages, and deaths from 1538. The superstition perhaps dated to the ancient Romans because their feast of the dead—Lemuralia—occurred during this month and mourning clothing was worn. The women's festival of Bona Dea at which no man was allowed to be present also occurred in May, and within Catholic traditions, May was dedicated to Mary and thus had associations with chastity and virginity. (This would seem to conflict with May Day traditions that celebrate the renewal of life and fertility. However, some in the Christian churches associate the May queen tradition with the celebration of the Blessed Virgin Mary.)

This association of May with women is found in France, where it was thought that May was a month when women were powerful (perhaps also referring to the link with the Virgin Mary). The belief was that a May bride would keep her husband in yoke all year round, and thus marriages were not frequent in May. In Greece, people will not marry in May as it is believed to be a month "for donkeys to get married." This taboo is said to be related to the fall of Constantinople, which occurred in May, and with the third of May feast of St. Maura, whose name means "black."

See also Days for Marriage
References
Edwards, T. B. 2002. "Unlucky Times for Weddings." *FLS News: Newsletter of the Folklore Society* 36 (February): 14.
Hole, Christina. 1941–1942. *English Custom and Usage.* London: Batsford.
Monger, George. 1994. " 'To Marry in May': An Investigation of a Superstition." *Folklore* 105: 104–108.
Parsons, Coleman O. 1964. *Witchcraft and Demonology in Scott's Fiction, with Chapters on the Supernatural in Scottish Literature.* London: Oliver and Boyd.

Mexico

Mexico was formerly inhabited by the Aztecs and, like the rest of South America, was conquered and settled by the Spanish. Spanish settlers intermarried with the Aztec Indian population, and missionaries brought Christianity to the area. Consequently, the contemporary marriage rite is that of the Catholic church. The marriage beliefs of the Aztec Indians (and their descendants) were observed by early missionaries and travelers, sometimes with variations.

Girls married between the ages of eleven and eighteen. It was expected that she would be a virgin. Westermarck (1894) noted that among the central tribes of Mexico girls generally married before the age of fourteen or fifteen. A young man would be married by the age of about twenty-two unless he intended to become a priest. The Aztecs were brought up to honor and obey their parents without question, and even adults treated their parents with great deference. Marriage rarely took place without the consent of the parents, with the marriage partner usually chosen by them. A young man who did not marry with the consent of his parents and kinsfolk would be regarded as ungrateful and ill-bred. An account of an Aztec Indian wedding was contained in a privately published book, *Matrimonial Ceremonies Displayed* (1880), believed to be by Louis de Gaya, which seems to paraphrase an account from 1588 by Joseph Acosta:

> The Mexicans, before they received the Christian faith, married in this manner: they both presented themselves to their priest; who, taking them by their hands, asked them many questions; and lastly, of their desire to be married together. Then taking the skirt of the woman's veil, and that of the man's garment, tied them together, and led them so fastened to the bride's house, where was a great fire kindled; they went seven times round this fire and sat down together; which ended all the ceremonies, and the marriage was complete.

Aztec civilization was organized on a clan basis, and usually marriage partners were sought from outside the parents' own clan. When the parents had chosen a partner, the priests would be consulted to ensure that the couple's birthdates were harmonious and to determine the lucky or unlucky days for holding the ceremony. Once the priests had given a favorable report, the man's parents would get his tutors to release him from his education so that he could marry. Two older women would then approach the girl's father, with gifts so that they would be welcomed, and ask for his daughter in marriage. By convention he would refuse, several times. Each time they made the request, they would take ever more valuable gifts. Eventually the father would agree to seek the approval of the girl's clan, and if they agreed, the most auspicious day for the wedding would be established by the priests.

The wedding began around midday on the chosen day, with a banquet at the girl's home. Presents were given to the bride by married women; this was followed by the bathing of the bride. Her hair was washed and arranged, and she was dressed in a heavily embroidered dress with the legs and arms decorated with red feathers. Older members of the groom's family now visited her and welcomed her to their family, and at nightfall they escorted the bride to her new home. She was carried there by an older woman and escorted by her friends and relatives and numerous well-wishers, in a procession lighted by flaming torches.

The wedding ceremony was performed by the family hearth. The couple sat side by side on mats, and the groom's mother presented the bride with new clothes. The bride's mother gave a similar present to the groom. The two women who arranged the marriage on behalf of the groom's family then tied the cloaks of the bride and groom together, after which the couple shared a maize cake. The couple then sat and listened to orations and instructions from their elders about married life and about their obligations. Before the marriage was consummated, the couple separated for four days, during which they fasted and prayed. The marriage was consummated on a bed of piled mats and feathers, with pieces of jade interleaved, the latter to ensure that the couple managed to have many children. After the consummation, the couple went for a ritual bath and a blessing and purification from the priest.

With such a ritual and the fact that weddings were generally arranged by the parents, it is difficult to believe reports that in some parts of Mexico a man wishing to be married would go to the priest at the temple, where, before an idol and in front of the congregation, part of his hair would be cut off, and the priest would announce that he required a wife. He was expected to accept the first unmarried woman he should meet after leaving the temple as his wife.

See also Spain
References

Gaya, Louis de. 1685. *Matrimonial Ceremonies Displayed*. English translation, 1704. London: Privately printed.
Scott, George Ryley. 1953. *Curious Customs of Sex and Marriage*. London: Torchstream.
Westermarck, Edward. 1894. *The History of Human Marriage*. 2d ed. London: Macmillan.

Middle East

The countries of the Middle East—Iran, Iraq, Palestine, Jordan, Oman, Kuwait, United Arab Emirates, Bahrain, Yemen, Oman, Jordan, Syria, and Saudi Arabia—are Islamic countries and have similar marriage traditions. In many of these oil-rich countries, women have been delaying marriage in order to follow careers—the average age of marriage had risen from around eighteen in the 1980s to the mid- to late-twenties or even thirty by 2000. Additionally, dowry demands upon the man's family have become so excessive that governments have had to intervene either to limit the size of dowry or to organize mass marriages to help with the costs. And families have become more and more extravagant in the celebrations. Traditionally, the more spent on the wedding, the greater the status of the family in the community, and weddings have often been an ostentatious show of wealth.

In 2000, it was estimated that 80 percent of the United Arab Emirates consumer credit market was generated by weddings and that young, newly married men would have to use around two-thirds of their annual incomes to repay the loans. Thus, men in the United Arab Emirates were marrying foreign women to avoid the high dowry demands of Arab women. To counteract this, in 1992 Sheikh Zayed, the ruler, established a "marriage fund" to provide dowry and wedding costs in order to encourage young men to marry Emirate women. In 1998, laws were introduced to limit dowries to less than $10,000.

In recent years, couples have been helped by governments holding mass weddings. Mass weddings were promoted in the United Arab Emirates to cut wedding costs. Mass weddings are common among the Shia villagers in eastern Saudi Arabia. And mass weddings have been used to celebrate special events. In 2002, to mark Saddam Hussein's new term in office, over five hundred couples were married at the same time (155 of them in Baghdad) at state expense, although the Ba'thist Party regime (overturned in 2003) suppressed the traditional Muslim celebrations involving firing of guns into the air.

Middle Eastern marriage generally follows traditional Muslim practices but is also influenced from the outside world, as women gain more control of their lives. Among wealthier families, the costs of weddings are rising as families strive to outdo each other.

See also Afghanistan; Arabic Weddings; Egypt; Henna; Islamic Marriage; Kuwait; Mass Weddings; Morocco

References

Barwig, Andy. 9 November 1997. "Weddings: A Sanaani Experience." *Middle East Times.* Available at *http://metimes.com/issue45/reg09ltryemen.htm* (accessed 6 June 2004).

Hawley, Caroline. 21 October 2002. "Mass Weddings Mark Saddam's New Term." *BBC News Online.* Available at *http://news.bbc.co.uk/1/hi/world/middle_east/2348205.stm* (accessed 6 June 2004).

Murphy, Brian M. 1978. *The World of Weddings: An Illustrated Celebration.* London: Paddington.

Thomas, Karen. July 2000. "What Price a Wedding? The Middle East Mosaic." IP Publications. Available at *http://www.africasia.com/archive_index.html* (accessed 6 June 2004).

Mormon Church

The Mormon church, or the Church of Jesus Christ of the Latter Day Saints, is well known for the practice of polygyny, that is, for a man to be able to marry more than one wife. This practice was considered an essential part of the religious system, which was based upon revelations in the Book of Mormon. Indeed, it was said to build upon the biblical practice of polygyny of Solomon and others.

Mormons place great emphasis on family life, with a strict law of chastity that allows sexual relations only within marriage. Couples are required to preserve fidelity to ensure that children are born in wedlock to parents who completely honor the marriage vows. (However, those who break these laws can gain forgiveness.) The Mormons also have a belief in the concept of "eternal marriage" or "celestial marriage," and a marriage in the temple is recorded both in heaven and on earth. A marriage performed in the Holy Temple is not just "til death do you part," as in the Christian marriage service, but continues eternally, based upon the words of Jesus to Peter: "And I will give unto thee the keys of the kingdom of heaven; and whatsoever thou shalt bind on earth shall be bound in heaven" (Matt. 16.19). According to an account in Scott (1953, 88), quoting from an 1891 book entitled *Mormonism Unveiled,* the concept of eternal marriage was used as a method to gain obedience among followers—part of a woman's endowment robe included a cape covering her face that had to be lifted by her husband. When she died she would be buried in her endowment robes, with this cape covering her face. She could not be resurrected until her husband lifted the cape. He could threaten to not lift the cape at the time of resurrection unless he was obeyed.

The Mormons refer to the marriage ceremony as a "sealing," and it is carried out in the temple and lasts for about twenty minutes. The event is witnessed by the family and close friends. Non-Mormons are not allowed into the sealing room in the temple, but wait in the temple foyer. They are allowed to join in the photographs on the temple grounds. Before the couple can be "sealed" in the temple they must both have a card known as a "Temple Recommend" that verifies that the holder is a baptized and confirmed member of the Mormon church and is of good standing.

The couple must be appropriately dressed, with the man in a suit and the woman's dress

Alex Joseph, who claims to have thirteen wives, is surrounded by seven of them, two of his children, and the sister of one of the wives, in this photo taken recently at Glen Canyon City, Utah. Along with his wives, Joseph, an excommunicated Mormon who claims to have started his own church, recently abandoned disputed southern Utah homesteads with some more followers and moved down the road to build a city. (Bettmann / CORBIS)

conforming to a strict dress code. The dress must be white and simple in design, with sleeves, a long skirt, and a high neckline, and sheer fabrics must be lined.

The ceremony is conducted by someone who has been given the priestly authority to act as the "sealer." The couple kneel on each side of the altar. The sealer gives guidelines and advice about marriage and the new life together. The couple then individually and jointly make promises to God and then individually and then jointly receive blessings. After this they are considered to be joined in a celestial marriage. There are further blessings for children from the marriage. The sealing must be witnessed by two holders of the Melchizedek priesthood.

Throughout the nineteenth century, and to the present day, the biggest controversy surrounding the Mormon church was, and is, the practice of polygamy. In 1835, the Mormon church issued an article on marriage, decreeing that, "according to custom, . . . [m]arriage is regulated by laws and ceremonies . . . that all marriages . . . be solemnized in a public meeting or feast prepared for that purpose, and that the solemnization should be performed by a Presiding High Priest, High Priest, Bishop, Elder or Priest. . . . we declare that we believe that one man should have one wife and one woman but one husband." However, despite this pronouncement, church leaders and elders such as John Smith and Brigham

Young continued to practice and encourage selected followers to practice polygamy.

Despite signing an antibigamy law that prohibited polygamy in all of the territories of the United States in 1862, Abraham Lincoln chose to turn a blind eye to the practices of the Mormons. However, several cases were brought to court against Mormons in polygamous marriages. The law was strengthened in 1882, but the church president, John Taylor, claimed that he was told in a revelation that all the priesthood should live in plural marriages.

In 1890, Mormon church president Wilford Woodruff received a revelation telling him that church leaders should abandon the teaching and practice of plural marriage. But the practice continued well into the twentieth century. In 1998, the president of the Church of Jesus Christ of the Latter Day Saints issued a statement setting out the church's position on plural marriage, stating that the church rejected polygamy, and that if members of the church were found to be practicing plural marriage they would be excommunicated, since they were violating not only state law but also the law of the church.

See also Polyandry; Polygyny
References

Porter, Perry L. 1998. "Chronology of Federal Legislation on Polygamy." 4 January. Available at *http://www.1dshistory.net/pc/chron.htm* (accessed 1 June 2004).

Scott, George Ryley. 1953. *Curious Customs of Sex and Marriage.* London: Torchstream.

Statements on Mormon Internet site. Available at *http://www.mormon.org* (accessed 1 June 2004).

Morocco

Morocco is an Islamic country that does not practice polygamy, but cousin marriage is common. Superstition and the fear of witchcraft dictate that weddings take place either after sunset or at night. Or, as among the Berber people, the date and time of the wedding is kept secret until the last minute. Marriage is an alliance between two families, and thus arranged between them, but today this does not mean that the couple have not met before, especially as the two may be cousins. However, as virginity at marriage is considered extremely important, the meetings during a courting period only occur in the open field where the couple can talk privately without being accused of any impropriety.

The marriage involves three days and nights of ceremony and feasting, but, as is generally true of Islamic marriages, the bride undergoes a great deal of preparation for the wedding. Her hands and feet are painted with henna designs. Her fingers are wrapped with a skein of white wool. Thus unable to do much for herself, a friend, or witness (the *wazira*), looks after her welfare during the wedding events. She is made up with black kohl around her eyes, her lips are reddened, her hair is oiled to make it shine, she is dressed in her white muslin bridal chemise and pantaloons *(serwal)*, and she is festooned with jewelry lent to her by female friends and relations, who hope that by the time it is returned, her good luck will have been absorbed by it. Her head is covered with the *abroc*, a red silk, two-pointed hood covering her face, which she will wear throughout the wedding events. Once so covered, a Berber bride is fitted with a heavy, twelve-pronged silver bracelet on each wrist (the *asbig n iquzzain*), associated with matrimony. The ring shape symbolizes the female, and the silver is thought to protect the wearer from bad luck.

There was a custom for the husband-to-be to place a silver coin underneath the mill to be used to grind the grain for the wedding feast. This may have been to drive away bad spirits, but it may also have been to ensure abundance. A silver coin is often also dropped into the bride's slipper, usually by her brother, after the henna ceremony. (In European traditions, the bride may have a silver or gold coin in her shoe to ensure prosperity in married life.) At Amzmüz, in the Atlas Mountains, after the bride's brother has placed a silver coin in one of his sister's slippers and put them on the bride's feet, he taps her three times with his own slipper. The bride has to be escorted from the house and is accompanied by a shrill ululation of the women in the house courtyard. The bride's feet should not touch the ground and her brother will usually carry her to the back of the car that will take her to the bridegroom's house. In times past, she would ride on the back of a mule, sometimes with a tower structure with thin veils to obscure the bride. A wealthy or important bride would have been taken to her bridegroom on the back of a camel. The bridal party follow behind the transport, banging drums *(tellunt),* chanting and singing to bring her good luck in her new life and to say farewell to her father's house.

On arrival at the bridegroom's home, the bridal party circumambulates the house three times, accompanied by drum banging, ululation, and fireworks. Some beat on the house or, in the past, on the bridegroom's tent, three times with a cane to expel evil spirits and to protect the domestic animals from death. If a child or domestic animal died soon after the bride's arrival into the family, the death was associated with her arrival and life would be very difficult for her thereafter.

Once this is complete, the bride is escorted to a specially prepared chair set against a wall. During all of this, the bride remains silent with her face covered (and her eyes closed). Sometimes the groom remains silent too. The bride has been given a red, white, and black woollen rope, used for tying bundles to the back of a mule, by her father. This is another symbol of marriage and is also said to help her in childbirth. It is used for hanging items from her dowry as a form of display in the area where she is sitting.

All await the most important part of the wedding event, the "night of virginity," or "wedding night," where the couple consummate the marriage—she has to prove her virginity and he his virility. The relatives wait expectantly to see the bloodstains on her *serwal.*

The morning after the wedding night the bride, still wearing the bloodstained *serwal,* receives guests for several hours, who offer gifts and congratulations. Now the bride, with the help and support of her *wazira,*

throws handfuls of almonds to the children (the almonds are considered to be endowed with the good fortune of the bride).

Toward nightfall, the groom appears, and this signals the beginning of the dancing. Women break into a loud song to the accompaniment of the *tellunt,* and the young people line up for the dance of the *abidus.* The boys line up opposite the girls, who wear embroidered black veils. They hold hands with each other, their hands crossed in front of their bodies, and they stamp to the beat of the drum. The men and women vie with each other in songs about love and beauty, sometimes including village anecdotes.

The bride and groom eventually join the group and dance the *abidus* just once. The chanting eventually ceases, and the guests and relatives accompany the couple to the matrimonial home. It is here that, by the light of a single lantern, the groom lifts the *abroc* to reveal his bride's face.

As an Islamic country, Moroccans can, in theory, practice polygamy. But, in 2003, King Mohammed VI reviewed laws governing women's rights—polygamy was outlawed, the legal age for marriage for a woman was raised from fifteen to eighteen, divorce laws were simplified, and women were given greater protection should their husbands leave them.

See also Almonds; Islamic Marriage; Veil; Walking on Gold
References
Baldizzone, Tiziana, and Gianni Baldizzone. 2001. *Wedding Ceremonies: Ethnic Symbols, Costume, and Rituals.* Paris: Flammarion.
Crawley, Ernest. [1902] 1932. *The Mystic Rose: A Study of Primitive Marriage and of Primitive Thought in Its Bearing on Marriage.* 4th ed. Revised and enlarged by Theodore Besterman. London: C. A. Watts.
Scott, George Ryley. 1953. *Curious Customs of Sex and Marriage.* London: Torchstream.
Westermarck, Edward. 1894. *The History of Human Marriage.* 2d ed. London: Macmillan.

Muta'a
See Temporary Marriage

N

Native American Marriage

Generalizations about Native American courtship and marriage traditions are difficult to make, but there are similarities among tribes and groups of peoples. Courtship is by the couple's choice, and couples are able to get to know each other before deciding to become partners. "Courting in a blanket" was a way of providing privacy. A girl would stand in front of the family tepee with a blanket and would wrap the blanket around herself and her suitor, completely covering them both. They could then get to know one other. Being covered in the blanket meant that they "were not there" and were considered unseen by those around them. A girl could see several prospective husbands in an evening in this way. However, this did not occur in all tribes. In some, a grandmother would act as a go-between for a couple, and they would pay her with a horse.

Initial meetings could be difficult to arrange—Indian men were bashful and had trouble expressing their feelings for a woman. Flutes were used in courtship, and only in courtship, and could convey a range of feelings and messages. The Sioux Indians had a form of love magic, the "Big Twisted Flute," with which a young man was supposed to be able to entice the young woman of his choice. The flute was a flageolet made from cedar wood and decorated with a figure of a horse (which was considered the most ardent of all animals) by a shaman, who would also compose the music and then instruct the young man in the music to be played on the flute. The flute was only effective with the magical music, which was conveyed to the shaman in a dream. If played correctly, the woman would find the music irresistible and would go with the young man.

And there were other ways that a young man could meet and express an interest in a girl. He would know that at certain times of day she would collect water, and he could by chance be on the same path. Or she would be returning from collecting vegetables at a certain time with her female companions, so that he and his companions would meet them and have a play battle to try and get the vegetables from the girls. A girl could signal her liking for a young man by making it easy for him to "capture" the vegetables.

A Plains Indian woman looked for a man who would be a good hunter and a brave warrior. Men would seek young women who were modest, virtuous, and skilled in beadwork and tanning. Both would look for someone attractive, and both young men and young women spent a great deal of time on their appearance.

Before a marriage could take place, the two families would meet to decide on the arrangement—couples would not usually marry without parental consent. However, in some instances, it was not unknown for a couple to elope, taking a horse and going away for a few days by themselves. They would return and set up home. The elopement would be accepted by the families and the couple accepted as married. The groom often gave gifts of horses and other items to the bride's family to show his respect for the woman and to show that he was a good provider. However, if he could not supply any horses or could not afford such gifts, he might hunt for the family. The bride's family might also give gifts to the family of the groom.

The marriage ceremony itself was simple. Among the Cheyenne, for example, the woman would be wrapped in a blanket and delivered, with gifts, to the tepee of the young man's father. The Sioux wrapped the couple together in a blanket, holding a sacred pipe, with their wrists bound together with a length of red cloth. The ceremony was led by a medicine man.

The Wabanaki proposal of marriage involved the young man sending wampum (beads of polished shells used as money, pledges, and decoration) to the woman's father, via one of the old men of the tribe as an intermediary. If the wampum was returned, the proposal was rejected; if not, the proposal was accepted. On the day of the wedding, the couple prepared a feast and invited all of the tribe. At the feast, traditional Indian dances were performed. Early in the twentieth century, a wedding was one of the few times these traditional dances would be performed.

If able, the parents of the couple would provide the couple with a tepee. Otherwise, the couple would start their married life in the wife's parents' lodge. If the woman was from another tribe, the man would be adopted by that tribe. The woman was responsible for the tepee and everything to do with the home, and the man's role was to provide for the new family by his hunting. Although the society appears very patriarchal—the men concerned themselves with hunting and village politics and polygamy was practiced—the women owned property and did the work that held the tribal group together, and a woman who was so inclined could also ride into battle with the men.

During the twentieth century, it became more and more common for Native American couples to be married in a church or a marriage bureau. However, they often did not feel married until they had been joined together in traditional Indian fashion by a medicine man. Sioux medicine man John Fire (Lame Deer) (1972, 144) wrote:

> At home, when I marry a boy and girl the Indian way, there's more to it. More talk, more medicine men, a tipi, an altar, a big open space under the sky, singers and drummers, a big feed outdoors, a give away of presents and afterwards, when it is dark, everybody dresses up for the big dance. But one ceremony is as good as the other. Its only a few main things that count.

See also Arranged Marriage; Bundling; Courtship

References

Curtis, Natalie. [1907] 1968. *The Indians' Book.* New York: Dover.

Erdoes, Richard. 1972. *The Sun Dance People: The Plains Indians, Their Past and Present.* New York: Alfred A. Knopf.

Fire, John (Lame Deer), and Richard Erdoes. [1972] 1980. *Lame Deer: Sioux Medicine Man.* New York: Quartet Books.

Netherlands

Since the seventeenth century, weddings in the Netherlands have been civil ceremonies, which may be followed by church ceremonies. Although the civil ceremony has been compulsory for about four hundred years, many still consider the church ceremony as being the real ceremony. There was, and is, a considerable degree of free choice in marriage partner, although, in the past, the family and the community would have had their say on the suitability of the match.

The courtship process was very prescribed. In the Frisian district, the man would visit the house of the girl's family on a Saturday or Sunday evening. He would greet her parents first, and then the young woman. If she was interested, she would adjust her cap or make other movements. If she sat calmly and still, he would know that he need not bother calling again.

In the Zaanstreek area, young people would meet at a central place to play games and sing. The boys would call for the girls at exactly nine o'clock (if he called later, it would indicate that he had been turned down elsewhere). The girl would first have a conversation with him through the closed door. Eventually he might be admitted, and they would agree to go to the gathering together. It was important for the young man to call upon her on three successive Sundays. However, if on the third Sunday he was not admitted, he knew that he had been turned down. If his courtship was accepted he would be admitted much quicker on the third Sunday. From this point on, the courtship would be allowed to develop in a more public way—going for walks together or the man escorting her to church. In southwest Netherlands, it was a tradition that the young man was allowed to kiss the girl as they walked past a bridge.

The next stage was the engagement. The formal asking for the girl in marriage fell to the young man's father, who approached her father. In Friesland, the engagement was sealed by the young man giving the young woman a coin in a knotted shawl. The parents discussed the dowry and the bride's trousseau, much of which she was expected to make, prepare, or embroider herself. The centerpiece of the trousseau was a linen cupboard that was filled with the linen and clothes that she had prepared. She also made shirts and trousers for herself (her mother made the same for the groom) and shrouds for herself and for her future husband. The

linen cupboard had to be filled and it had to be packed in a specific way. The cupboard was finished off with two decanters, one with red gin and the other with ordinary gin, and two glasses. This cabinet was kept in the "best room" when the couple established their new home together, and the preparation was closely watched by the neighboring women. A cupboard filled mainly with linen was a sign that the bride came from a good family.

The engagement period, usually short, was followed by a period of preparation known as the bridal days. These followed the couple registering their intention to marry at the town hall. This was a period when the couple prepared for their wedding and was a festive time. The bride was given a finely carved pair of wooden shoes, decorated with their initials, which she wore during this time and then kept carefully afterwards. Traditional presents were given, such as decorated mangle boards (for ironing) and wooden boxes. On their return from registering their intention to marry, the groom was given a long decorated pipe, and his bride-to-be served wine or brandy mixed with sugar and plums. They held parties with their own age group, who gave the couple presents—usually tableware.

The wedding day itself followed a few weeks after the registration. The groom arranged for the bride's bouquet, often of artificial flowers (the pipe and the bouquet were often kept in a glass case afterward). The civil marriage was performed at the town hall, with the couple accompanied by their parents, close relatives, witnesses, and friends. All might then return home and carry on with normal workdays, even including the bride and groom. The church wedding took place a few days later and was often considered the real wedding. But in the province of Friesland, the civil wedding and the church wedding took place on the same day. Here the couple went to the town hall in procession in decorated carts. The couple signed the wedding contract after it had been read out by the clerk, and then the burgomaster (mayor) addressed the couple officially, before all went in procession to the church.

See also Cars; Civil Ceremonies; Dowry
Reference
Van Nespen, W., ed. 1975. "Netherlands." In *Love and Marriage: Aspects of Popular Culture in Europe [exhibition], Antwerpen*. Brussels: Ministerie van Nederlanse Cultuur en Nationale Opvoeding.

Niger

Niger, in Africa, encompasses part of the Sahara Desert and includes tribes that display differing marriage rites. The nomadic Tuaregs observe different customs according to the status of the couple and the region that they travel. At one time marriages were arranged between the parents, but this has changed. Although endogamous marriage is still usual within the clan, the young woman is allowed to refuse any suitor.

A young man interested in a girl sneaks up to the tent in which she is sleeping with her parents and wakens her by tickling her ear. If she wakes and pulls the covers over her head, he has been rejected. If, on the other hand, she moves her mat away from her parents, he may stay but must answer riddles that she whispers into his ear. If he answers these correctly, he is likely to be accepted by her as her husband and wears a pendant that she gives him as a token. Courtship negotiations take place to determine the amount of dowry, sometimes referred to as a "bride-price," for the groom to pay. This payment is properly termed a dowry, since the goods that make up the payment become the woman's exclusive property after the marriage. This dowry may include camels, goats, silver bracelets, and leather sandals.

The bride's family pays for the ceremony and provides the bride's trousseau, which includes a tent, carpets, and blankets for the couple to establish their new independent unit. The ceremony itself takes place in the woman's encampment and lasts over several days at a time considered auspicious and at a full moon. A tent is erected, after the sacrifice of a goat to purify the site, away from the main encampment, and here she is prepared for the wedding, with her female friends, usually by the wife of the blacksmith, who has a knowledge of plants and the natural products of the desert to prepare the bride's make-up. Her face is decorated with small, pale-red crosses and pastel-colored dots on her cheeks. Her hands and feet are decorated with henna (as are the hands and feet of the groom), a sign of purity and fertility.

All this time she is in the bridal tent, where the marriage will be consummated, and where all the tools required for a nomadic existence are hung, including the most important one, an iron-tipped tool called an *ahula*, used for digging the holes to fix the tent. This tool symbolizes the security of the woman and, being made of iron, also protects against bad spirits (important as the couple are considered particularly vulnerable to attack from malevolent spirits during the marriage ceremony). The *ahula* is presented to the bride by the blacksmith who, as a worker with metals, is considered to have occult powers and was always invited to the wedding celebrations. The guests arrive dressed up. The women usually arrive on asses, sitting on blankets and surrounded by cushions and adorned with jewels. The men wear a veil called a *tagelmoust* and silver amulets and arrive on camelback. The marriage itself is officially signed and sealed by the two families before the *marabout*, who recites sections from the Koran to ensure that the marriage has divine blessing.

The celebrations culminate in a dance of camels. The women sit together and play a drum called a *tende*, while the men on the backs of their camels circle around the women, their animals moving with a rhythmic amble. The groom watches this performance until the sun goes down and then goes to join his new wife in her tent.

By contrast, the Peulh Bororo people, nomadic herding tribes in Niger, put much effort into courtship and the art of seduction. The young man is the one made up, and, through dances and the rolling of eyes and facial expressions, he attempts to attract the woman of his choice. Although families usually choose marriage partners for their children at a young age, they are still taught the tribal arts of seduction. The Bororo practice endogamy, marrying within the clan, which will keep the family and the family's wealth together. But the kinship cannot be closer than the fourth degree.

Engagement is sealed when the boy's family gives presents of money and bottles of milk to the girl's family. The marriage is finalized at the annual gathering of the nomadic clans at the end of the rainy season (the *worso,* where members of the same bloodline meet to exchange news and arrange marriages) with the sacrifice of a bull, the meat of which is distributed in a ritualized system. The tripe and intestines are given to the women as symbols of fruitfulness. The testicles, representing procreation, go to the men. The old men receive the hooves.

If a woman is unhappy with her marriage, she has the possibility of eloping with a man from another clan. The woman quietly follows her chosen man to his own camp, where an animal is quickly sacrificed to seal the new marriage before her legal husband and family have realized that she has gone. At the gathering known as the *geerwol,* new alliances are developed and marriages are arranged with members of other lineages. At this gathering, young men are heavily made up to accentuate the profile of their faces, the whites of their eyes, and their teeth. They dance to attract women who have decided to leave their husbands. The women critically assess the dancing men. A woman who makes a choice surreptitiously touches the robe of the man and wanders off into the bush, followed quietly by her chosen man to establish a new alliance.

See also Consanguinity; Dowry; Endogamy/ Exogamy; Trousseau

Reference

Baldizzone, Tiziana, and Gianni Baldizzone. 2001. *Wedding Ceremonies: Ethnic Symbols, Costume, and Rituals.* Paris: Flammarion.

Norway

See Scandinavia

Nuer Weddings

The Nuer people of southern Sudan in Africa are a cattle-owning society, and marriage was accomplished through a payment of cattle by the groom's family to that of the bride. This was not a form of purchase, and the anthropologist E. E. Evans-Pritchard (1940) used the term "bride-wealth" for the transaction, as opposed to "bride-price," because he wanted to avoid implications of buying and selling. The kinsmen of a bride would expect to receive twenty or thirty cattle, but because cattle circulated as the main currency among the Nuer, bride-wealth was not a method by which a man would gain wealth. Bride-wealth gained from the wedding of a daughter in the household would be used for the bride-wealth for a son to be able to marry.

The Nuer marriage was in three parts, the betrothal, the marriage, and the consummation. When a marriage was agreed to, the bridegroom pressed for a date for the rituals to take place at the same time as the bride's family requested more cattle. To seal the betrothal, the first installment of the bride-wealth cattle was driven to the bride's home, where an ox was sacrificed to the ancestors; the meat was cooked by the bride's family and eaten by the groom's party. The couple was now considered husband and wife, and the man showed the formal behavior to his new in-laws expected from him. It is interesting to note the similarity with the early European practice of betrothal and spousal, whereby after this public promise to marry the couple were practically considered as husband and wife.

The bride-wealth negotiations were concluded at the actual wedding, with the ancestors called upon to witness the marriage, after which the young men danced the whole night. Later the consummation ceremony took place. The husband gave the bride's mother a small present and asked if he could take the bride away. The bride was taken to the husband's village (she showed reluctance, but Evans-Pritchard [1940] noted that she was rarely a virgin in the sexual sense and that maidenhood was "a social, not a physical state"). The girls who had accompanied the bride to the husband's village gave bracelets to the husband's kinsmen. The bride's head was then shaved, and she removed all her old ornaments and was given new ones by her husband's family, thereby symbolically showing her change of status and family. She did not immediately live with her new husband in his house but moved in with him only after her first child had been weaned. When she eventually did leave her parent's home, she was given a porridge spoon and a gourd for drinking milk by her parents.

Only when a man was married and had children, and therefore had an established and independent household and herd, was he considered an elder of the village. It was also seen as important for the husband to have sons to carry on his name and ensure his place among the ancestors. If a man was unable to do this, there was a system of "ghost-marriage." If a man died unmarried or with no male children (or if the male child had died), a close kinsman married his wife "to his name." The children from this marriage would be considered to be the dead man's children and consequently could keep his name among the ancestors. However, the man who stepped in in this way could not take another wife (that is, have a wife of his own who would have *his* children). Thus, when he died, one of his kinsmen would have to make a "ghost-marriage" on his behalf.

Because of the levels of bride-wealth paid over a period of time, and the fact that the bride-wealth may have been used to pay the bride-wealth of a son, it was very difficult to dissolve a Nuer marriage since the bride-wealth would have to be returned. The higher the bride-wealth, the more difficult it was to dissolve the marriage.

See also Betrothal; Bride-Price; Consummation; Spousal

References

Evans-Pritchard, E. E. 1951. *Kinship and Marriage among the Nuer.* Oxford: Oxford University Press.

Mair, Lucy. 1971. *Marriage.* Harmondsworth, Middlesex: Penguin.

Open Marriage

During the 1970s, "open marriage" was much discussed as an alternative to monogamous marriage. It was argued that life as a couple, rather than encouraging growth as people, was stifling, and that eventually boredom would set in. An open marriage would afford each of the partners the freedom to explore other ways for developing and growing so that a freshness could be brought to the marriage. The philosophy arose from the notion that partners change during the marriage, but in different ways and at different rates. In an open marriage, neither would be allowed to stifle that change, but both would be striving to develop the relationship with mutual respect and understanding, free from jealousy and with the knowledge that all needs may not be met within the marriage. To some couples, this meant having other relationships outside of the marriage, which flew in the face of the Western marriage vows and philosophy and the expectation that the couple would form an exclusive partnership.

This was not an entirely new idea. Historically, many couples of the European landed and gentry classes, whose marriages may have been arranged for dynastic purposes, may have led separate lives and even practiced concubinage or had lovers outside the marriage. Spouses and society turned a blind eye to what was going on unless something happened to draw attention to the man's or woman's behavior to cause a scandal. In society, the couple would be expected to maintain the appearance of being a close and exclusive couple, as demanded by their wedding vows.

See also Concubine

References
Macfarlane, Alan. 1986. *Marriage and Love in England, 1300–1840.* Oxford: Basil Blackwell.
O'Neill, Nena, and George O'Neill. 1975. *Open Marriage: A New Life Style for Couples.* London: Abacus, Sphere Books.
Stone, Lawrence. 1990. *The Family, Sex, and Marriage in England, 1500–1800.* Abridged and revised ed. London: Penguin.

Palestinian Weddings

Weddings among Palestinian people in the late twentieth century are an amalgam of traditional Muslim practice with some elements of Western celebration. Traditionally the groom's family pays for the wedding celebrations and makes all the arrangements. The celebration is a big event and everyone is invited, even those from nearby villages and travelers in the area. The groom's family personally invite guests to the wedding, going from house to house issuing the invitation with an offering of a mixture of nuts and seeds called *makhloota*. For several days leading up to the wedding, the family and friends of the couple meet for a *sahra*, a night of singing and dancing. These celebrations normally take place in a field or open space to accommodate large numbers of people. It is usually only the men who dance the *el debka*, in which the participants join in a line and step to the heavy beat of the *al tabla*, a form of drum. The women usually do the singing. The night before the wedding, as is common in many Muslim cultures, the women hold the "henna night." They meet for dancing, eating sweets, and decorating the bride's hands with henna.

On the wedding day, the groom's female relatives prepare the food for the wedding celebrations and the groom is paraded around the village, traditionally on horseback, wearing the traditional Palestinian black and white head covering called a *kafiyeh* and a cloak decorated with gold trimmings. He is followed by a procession of his friends and relatives, who sing and clap and are likely to fire guns into the air as part of the celebration. In late afternoon they return to the groom's family home to eat. The groom's family will have sent a meal to the bride's home, and after this has been eaten, the bride, dressed in a traditional Palestinian dress called a *thobe* (a long dress with long sleeves and embroidered with gold, silver, and red designs, the color and design depending on the area the bride is from), leaves home in procession. Traditionally, she would have been seated on a horse, but today she may walk. On her way, friends, neighbors, and passers-by may give her gifts. The bride and her party usually process to the groom, but among some people it has been the tradition for the groom to go and collect his bride. At the groom's house, she takes her seat on an elevated platform with the groom beside her, and the two families begin to celebrate. At the end of the night, the bride sits with a scarf on her lap, and the guests put gifts of money or gold into the scarf to wish the couple luck and prosperity.

The political situation for the Palestinian people has caused a marked change in weddings in the last part of the twentieth century and the early twenty-first century so that many of the traditions mentioned above have disappeared. Instead of the large noisy celebration, the wedding guests are usually just the close relatives (and not all invited relatives attend because of fear of attack). The songs are sung in a subdued manner. Instead of the several days of celebration leading up to the wedding day, the event now lasts just a few hours, beginning after afternoon prayers and finishing before sunset. The bride's dress has changed. Many Palestinian girls now want to wear the white wedding dress associated with the contemporary European and American wedding, rather than the traditional Palestinian dress, the *thobe*. Military roadblocks and checkpoints have also curtailed and created problems for bridal processions to the groom's home. It is even more difficult or impossible for the groom to process to meet his bride without endangering his life. Palestinian weddings today are subdued and surreptitious events.

See also Islamic Marriage
References
Hasan, Aida. 1999. "Palestinian Weddings—America vs. Traditional (Part 2)." *Arab Culture and Identity.* 17 December. Available at *http://www.suite101.com/article.cfm/arab_culture_and_identity/30303* (accessed 1 June 2004).
Qineeta, Itidal. 2003. "Palestinian Weddings Now Clad in Black." *IslamOnline.* Summer. Available at *IslamOnline.net/English/news/2002-06/04/article74.stml* (accessed 6 June 2004).

Paper of Pins

I'll give to you a paper of pins,
That's the way our love begins.
If you'll marry me, me, me,
If you'll marry me.
I'll not accept your paper of pins,
That's not the way our love begins.
I won't marry you, you, you,
Oh, I won't marry you.
("Paper of Pins," traditional folksong)

A paper of pins was a gift of many, some say hundreds, of long pins arranged on a decorated paper and was a typical Appalachian love token, given either as an indication of an intent to court or as a marriage proposal, as suggested in the traditional folksong. Pincushions, with pins and sometimes decorative beads arranged to give messages of love and affection, were well-known love tokens. Sailors often made pincushions for their sweethearts, such as a carved wooden acorn that opened to reveal a padded cushion studded with pins.

Pins may seem to be insignificant as a token of love, but before about 1817, when an all-in-one process of pin manufacture was developed in America, pins had to be individually made by hand. This process did not become common in Britain until around 1840.

See also Tokens
References
Asch, Moses. 1964. *104 Folk Songs as Recorded on Folkways Records by Famous Folk Song Singers.* New York and London: Robbins Music Corporation.
Roith, Cynthia. 1972. *Bygones: Love and Marriage Tokens.* London: Transworld.

Penny Weddings

Penny weddings, sometimes known as "beggars' weddings" or "public bridals," were events by which the guests helped the couple pay for the wedding celebrations and the setting up of the home. This community help enabled couples to marry who might not otherwise have had the means and resources to do so. In Cumberland, England, these events were known as "bridewain." Originally bridewain referred to the wagon used by the bride to transport her goods to her new home. On the way, folks would make contributions to her goods from their own homes. However, in time, the bridewain came to be a collection taken up by the bride, with a pewter dish on her knee, to which all those present contributed. In Wales, the system of mutual assistance, known as "bidding," was quite formalized. Contributions were documented and were repayable at some future date at another bidding.

Generally a penny wedding was organized by the family of the couple or other members of their community. If one or both of the couple were servants, sometimes the event would be set up and sponsored by the employer. For example, a letter from a "Gentleman in the North of Scotland," dated 1754 (quoted in Heseltine 1951), noted one such event:

> They have a Penny Wedding, that is, when a Servant-Maid has served faithfully, and gained good Will of her Master and Mistress they invite Relations and Friends, and there is a Dinner and Supper on the Day the Servant is married, and Musick and Dancing follow to complete the evening.
> The Bride must go about the Room and kiss every Man in the Company, and in the End every Body puts Money into a Dish. According to their Inclination and Ability.

Similarly, Samuel Pepys, the seventeenth-century London diarist, recorded attending such an event on 15 November 1660:

> To Sir W. Battens to dinner, he having a couple of servants married today; and so there was a great number of merchants, and others of good quality, on purpose after dinner to make an offering, which, when dinner was done, we did, and I did give ten shillings and no more, though I believe most of the rest did give more, and did believe that I did too.

The "Gentleman in the North of Scotland," above, went on to explain that by this method the couple were able to begin their married life comfortably, for people in "their low condition"; he also pointed out that the cost of the feast and of the musicians was also met from the contributions of the guests and that this was a custom "all over the Lowlands of Scotland." Another well-known example of this practice, from Essex, England, is described in a book published in 1687, *The Famous History of Sir Billy of Billericay:*

> Now in most parts of Essex (where the wedding was kept) it is the common custom when poor people marry to make a kind of dog hanging, or money gathering, which they call a wedding dinner, to which they invite rag and tag, all that will come; where after dinner, upon the summons of the fiddler, who setteth forth his voice like a town crier, a table being set forth, and the bride set simpering at the upper end of it, the bridegroom standing by with a white sheet overthwart his shoulders, as if he did penance for the folly he had committed that day; whilst the people invited to it, like soldiers of a country train band march up to the bride, present their money and wheel about. After this offering is over, there is a pair of gloves laid on the table, most monstrously bedaubed about with ribbons, which by way of auction, is set to sale, at who gives most, and he whose lot it is to have them shall withall have a kiss of the bride.

Prior to the seventeenth century, churches often provided "wedding houses," with a room for the wedding celebrations and, perhaps, as at the house at Braughing in Hertfordshire, England, a bedchamber with a bridal bed. At Theyda Garnon, Essex, England, the "Old Priests House," which stood near the tower of the church, and which was probably a wedding house, was used for wedding feasts and appears to have been used for penny weddings. Penny wedding customs differ from the Welsh bidding customs in that no account seems to have been taken of who gave what, nor does it seem that the donations were returnable or repayable at some later date.

Some authorities disapproved of penny weddings and attempted to suppress them, because it was said that they led to disorder and licentiousness. Indeed, there does seem to have been fairly substantial amounts of money collected at these events—a poor couple could probably collect half a year's wages, and, since some of the money went toward the food, drink, and music, this could lead to a substantial celebration. Although authorities had trouble suppressing these events they did try to limit the amount of money that could be given.

See also Bidding; Garter; Gloves
References
Gillis, John R. 1985. *For Better, For Worse: British Marriages, 1600 to the Present.* Oxford: Oxford University Press.
Heseltine, G. C., ed. 1951. *A Bouquet for a Bride.* London: Hollis and Carter.
King, Frank A. 1957. "Essex Wedding Customs and Superstitions." *Essex Countryside* 5, no. 19: 96–97.
Monger, George. 1974. "A Note on the Similarities between Some Wedding Customs in England and France." *Lore and Language* 2, no. 1: 36–37.

Peru. *See* South America

Petting Stone

In some places, for example, the north of England, the wedding party and guests had to jump or stride over some obstacle outside the church immediately after the ceremony, the "petting stone." This custom at Holy Island, County Durham, England, was described in Brand (1777, 397): "Whenever a marriage is solemnized at the church, after the ceremony, the bride is to step upon it [the petting stone], and if she cannot stride to the end thereof, it is said that the marriage will prove unfortunate." The petting stone was usually a makeshift obstacle, perhaps a stool or a bench or, as sometimes described, three upright stone flags set on edge with another laid flat on the top. Sometimes the obstacle would be improvised on the spot, as described in an account from a wedding in 1868 in the north of England (Dyer 1891, 125): "It was proposed to have a petted stone. A stick was therefore held by two groomsmen at the church door for the bride to jump over."

Sometimes the bride would be lifted over the petting stone by two young men on either side of the bride. The groom would leap over the stone after her and then drop a coin into the hands of the "bride-lifters." Etiquette demanded that the bride should show some reluctance in jumping over the stone. This, it was considered, showed an appropriate degree of modesty. If she was too eager to jump

the stone, it was thought that she displayed too much independence. At Belford, Northumberland, England, a stool was placed at the church door as a petting stone. When the bride had stepped or leaped over the stool, complimentary verses about the bride and groom were recited. This was called "saying the noning." The "noning sayer" was rewarded with silver.

The most common explanation for this practice was that in her leaping the bride would leave all her "pets and humors" behind her, that is, that she would leave behind her youthful obstinacies and become an obedient wife. Others have suggested that it represented a leap forward into a new life for the bride and groom as a married couple. If the woman was reluctant to jump over the stone or stool, had difficulty observing the practice, or stumbled and fell as she leaped or stepped over the barrier, negative conclusions about her temperament would be drawn. The groom would usually also have to leap the barrier, and sometimes the couple would be followed by the guests.

See also Barring the Way; Creeling; Fescennine Songs; Threshold, Carrying over
References
Brand, John. [1777] 1900. *Observations on the Popular Antiquities of Great Britain.* Revised and updated by Sir Henry Ellis in 1841 and 1848. 3 vols. London: G. Bill and Sons.
Crooke, W. 1902. "The Lifting of the Bride." *Folklore* 13: 226–251.
Dyer, T. F. Thiselton. 1891. *Church-Lore Gleanings.* London: A. D. Innes.
Gillis, John R. 1985. *For Better, For Worse: British Marriages, 1600 to the Present.* Oxford: Oxford University Press.

Photographs

Perhaps the twentieth-century development with the most impact upon weddings has been the greater availability of the camera. During the nineteenth century, it became fashionable for the wealthy to have a photograph of the wedding, and, by the end of the century, some well-off couples would engage a photographer for the day. Some also had an

The wedding portrait of Muriel Vanderbilt and Frederick Church Jr., July 1925. (Bettmann/CORBIS)

engagement photograph taken. With the advent of the twentieth century, less well-off couples would visit the photographer's studio for a wedding photograph, often a few days after the wedding so that all concerned would have to get into their wedding outfits again. Toward the middle of the twentieth century, when photography started to become quicker, the bridal party would visit the photographer's studio on the way to the wedding reception, a practice that continued in some places into the 1950s. But, by this time, photographic equipment had become more portable, and it became popular to have the photographer record more of the moments of the wedding (such as the arrival of the bride at the church). The clergy were still reluctant to allow photography in the church at this time, but by the 1960s clergy were

more willing for photographs to be taken within the church, at a distance.

A similar development appears to be occurring in contemporary Egyptian cities where, among both the Muslim and Coptic communities, the bride and groom go to the photographer before the wedding ceremony for an official photograph. But today, as a Muslim couple go into the marriage ceremony, people take photographs, and after Coptic weddings, time is allowed for the taking of photographs. The Coptic church still does not allow photography in the church.

Over time, the church, probably through gentle pressure from couples who wanted to have a photographic record of all that happened on the wedding day, has gradually relented and allowed more photographic freedom. It is now common to have a video made of the ceremony. And, today, disposable cameras are sometimes on the guests' tables at the wedding reception so that photographs by the guests can be taken to add to the official photographs. Today, photography is part of wedding tradition in Britain and North America. Seligson (1974) described a mother of a bride in Milwaukee who recounted all the details of her daughter's wedding and said that she could not wait for the pictures to arrive so that she could "live it all again." Wedding photography has become a way to earn a living for many.

See also Egypt
References
Ballard, Linda May. 1998. *Forgetting Frolic: Marriage Traditions in Ireland.* Belfast and London: Institute of Irish Studies, Queen University, Belfast, and Folklore Society, London.
Dobson, Sue. 1981. *The Wedding Day Book.* London: Arrow.
Seligson, Marcia. 1974. *The Eternal Bliss Machine: The American Way of Wedding.* London: Hutchinson.

Polterabend Party

The *Polterabend* party (the "noisy party") is held on the night before the wedding in Germany and in Finland. It resembles other customs that seek to draw attention to the wedding party, such as honking car horns or "rough music." However, the "rough band" and the blowing of car horns takes place on the day of the wedding, and these noisy events function to draw the attention of the entire community to the wedding to gain wide recognition of the marriage. The south German *Polterabend* party combines a family get-together with communal recognition of the wedding, although today the event probably does not go to the lengths of the past.

Traditionally, the *Polterabend* was a feast, or dinner party, put on by one of the bride's relatives, during which her bridesmaids presented her with a myrtle wreath to wear as part of her bridal crown. Toward midnight the party was disturbed by members of the village or town throwing crockery against the

front door of the house. By morning, there would be a pile of broken crockery littering the path outside the house. Crockery throwing occurred at every marriage, as a means of wishing good luck. (In the Jewish wedding, a glass is stamped underfoot to smash it. In parts of England, a piece of wedding cake on a plate was thrown over the heads of the bride and groom, making sure that the plate smashed.) Perhaps these customs were meant to prevent domestic strife between the couple in the future—with the crockery-smashing symbolic of the "disturbances" that are likely to come between the couple in later life. It could probably also be used to express disapproval, as can the "rough band." According to a story of the *Polterabend* of the fiancée of a drunkard saddle-master, who had a bad reputation, the whole community turned out to throw things at the door. So bad was his reputation that the crowd kept throwing things at the door for several hours, so that the door eventually broke and the walkway was completely blocked with debris.

The contemporary *Polterabend* is tame compared to this. In Germany, marriage is a civil ceremony conducted before a registrar, often followed the next day by a church service. The *Polterabend* party is usually held the night before the church service and involves much eating, drinking, dancing, and a great deal of noise of the breaking of crockery, the banging of saucepans, and the cracking of whips, said to drive away evil spirits.

The *Polterabend* party in Finland is organized by the bride-to-be's friends on the night before the wedding. The bride is dressed up in a special costume and paraded from place to place, often collecting money on the way. (This is reminiscent of the Scottish premarriage factory of bosseller or scrammel and the English ribbon girl custom.) As with many events of this type, the participants subvert and parody other ceremonies and rites. A *Polterabend* party in the town of Loviisa, Finland, in 1989, took the form of a mock "Lucia" party. (The Lucia ceremony is a Swedish festival of light, with associations of purity and innocence, held around 13 December. A young woman is chosen to represent St. Lucia and is dressed in a white gown with a garland crown with lighted candles on her head.) For this *Polter-Lucia,* the bride-to-be was dressed as a Lucia who looked the worse for wear, with the candles in the headdress broken and her teeth blackened. The bride made a speech from a balcony—opposite the town hall balcony where the Lucia usually makes her speech—and then was driven around the town sitting in a pedal boat with "love boat" painted on the side, carried on the back of an open truck (Lucia is driven around the town in an open truck). The "love boat" was finally launched onto the town pond.

See also Bosseller; Germany; Ribbon Girl; Rough Music/Rough Band; Scandinavia

References

Murphy, Brian M.1978. *The World of Weddings: An Illustrated Celebration.* London: Paddington.

Scott, George Ryley. 1953. *Curious Customs of Sex and Marriage.* London: Torchstream.

Virtanen, Timo J. 1994. "Public Customs and Family Traditions." In *Everyday Life and Ethnicity: Urban Families in Loviisa and Võru, 1988–1991.* Edited by Anna Kirveennummi, Matti Räsänen, and Timo J. Virtanen. Helsinki: Studia Fennica Ethnologica 2.

Polyandry

Polyandry, the practice of a woman having multiple husbands at the same time, is less common than polygyny, the practice of a man having multiple wives at the same time. Polyandry is found in both matriarchal and patriarchal societies. (Polygamy is the practice of having more than one mate at the same time. This term is often wrongly used to refer to the practice of one man having several wives, but the proper term for that is polygyny.)

Sometimes the practice of polyandry seems to be a socioeconomic necessity, such as in the Himachal Pradesh area of India, where the work of two men is required to cultivate enough food for one family. In the practice of polygyny, we can discern issues such as those of male power and wealth and female subordination. But polyandry appears to have little association with the outward manifestation of power and is not particularly associated with matriarchy or any form of female power. Indeed, in many examples of societies that practice polyandry, the woman is still subservient to the man, and in some forms of polyandry, notably the system observed among the Lele peoples of the Congo, the woman was seen as little more than a prostitute by the missionaries (and the early anthropologists) who came across the practice. And it was a system that worked alongside "regular" marriage. Among the Lele peoples, girls were betrothed in infancy to older men (aged around twenty), who would then wait for their chosen brides to grow up. The young men had a long period of enforced bachelorship, which they often resented, and it was quite usual for them to seduce married women. The young men were grouped by age—all born within a period of fifteen years or so, and each of these groups could ask to be given a common wife (otherwise known as a "wife of the village").

The woman allotted would often have been the granddaughter of a village wife. If they were not allotted a village wife, the group could find their own by abducting one from a neighboring village—actually the preferred method of obtaining a village wife as this raised the prestige of the capturing village. The group of young men worked together to produce the raffia cloth that formed the marriage payment, and they would work together to provide the appropriate services to her parents and to build the hut for the wife. She would sleep with each member of the group in order of age. Eventually she chose five or six of the men to live in her house. For these, she would cook, hoe, and fetch water as an ordinary wife. However, away from her home she was a village wife and any man could have intercourse with her with nobody's rights infringed. Eventually her house husbands would find their own wives and move out. The children of a village wife were the children of the village and belonged to no particular matrilineal line. The men living with the mother of such a child would, however, have a special responsibility for them. Sons of such a relationship could later appeal to the whole village to help provide any marriage or other payments he might incur. In the Marquesas Islands, in the Pacific Ocean, polyandry occurred because there were more men than women. But even so, the practice was largely restricted to the families of chiefs. The woman had very little authority or power; one of the husbands was usually in charge as head of the household, and the other husbands were secondary (she was properly married to the senior husband and "tied" to the other men).

Often polyandrous practice involves the woman marrying all the brothers of the family, as among the Tibetans, a patriarchal society. Here, it is the eldest brother who marries the woman when he achieves a marriageable age, with all the other brothers present at the marriage ceremony (unless they are considered too young to behave properly at a ceremony). All the brothers have the status of husband and they all live in the same house as the wife. This does not prevent one of the younger brothers from seeking a wife elsewhere—most beneficially an heiress with no brothers.

Many of the cases of polyandry cited by Westermarck (1894) were of the woman being married to a group of brothers. In many of these cases the woman does not seem to be able to choose husbands in the same way as a man chooses wives in polygynous societies. However, in both systems the first married, or the elder, of the spouses is often assigned the role of chief husband or wife. In polyandry, there seemed to be a leaning toward monogamy, so that secondary husbands or members of the group of husbands might acquire their own wives at some stage during the polyandrous agreement.

The practice of polyandry is sometimes accepted and used, but not universally, and in a telling note from one of Westermarck's correspondents, from New Caledonia in the Pacific Ocean, where polyandry was known, it was stated that "the husbands were despised by the rest of the natives."

See also Polygyny
References
Mair, Lucy. 1971. *Marriage*. Harmondsworth, Middlesex: Penguin.
Scott, George Ryley. 1953. *Curious Customs of Sex and Marriage*. London: Torchstream.
Westermarck, Edward. 1894. *The History of Human Marriage*. 2d ed. London: Macmillan.

Polygamy
See Polyandry; Polygyny

Polygyny

Polygyny is the term used for a system that allows a man to have more than one wife, often wrongly called polygamy, which can equally refer to a rarer marriage system, polyandry, where a woman may have several husbands. Polygyny often involves many rules and restrictions, and there are often social and economic reasons for the practice, which, in some cases, have also become bound up with religious observance.

The Plains Indians of North America practiced polygyny. The men did little else but hunt and fight in battles and they were exposed to grave dangers daily. Consequently, there were often more women than men in a tribe. The women carried out work within the village, preparing food, making bead and quill work items, tanning, and other chores. As a warrior increased in status he was expected to care and provide for more and more people, giving feasts and presents. It would therefore be the overworked wife who might suggest that he take an additional wife, usually his wife's younger sister.

The Christian missionaries who objected to this practice were reminded that in the Bible, Abraham, Isaac, and Jacob each had more than one wife. But polygyny (and polygamy) were not part of Christian teaching, and the early Christians viewed any form of marriage as second best to celibacy. However, Martin Luther did allow Philip the Magnanimous of Hessen to take two wives. He argued that, since Christ was silent about polygyny, and according to the Bible it was practiced among the Jews, he could not presume to forbid the taking of more than one wife.

Polygyny was part of Talmudic teaching, and North American Indians have pointed out that a number of the prominent Jewish leaders in the Old Testament had several wives. Solomon was reputed, according to the Old Testament, to have had seven hundred wives and princesses, as well as three hundred concubines (Kings 10.3), and Rehoboam had eighteen wives and three-score concubines. Talmudic teaching permitted up to four wives, and European Jews still practiced polygyny in the Middle Ages.

Muhammad followed rabbinical teaching, and the Koran follows the Jewish practice of allowing a man to have up to four wives. However, if a man engaged in polygyny, he would be expected to treat each of his wives equitably: "You may marry other women who seem good to you: two, three or four of them. [B]ut if you fear that you cannot maintain equality among them, marry one only or any slave girls you may own—this will make it easier for you to avoid injustice" (Koran 4.3). The Islamic man is allowed to take concubines. A difference between a wife and a concubine is that the wife has the protection of her father while the concubine has no protection against her husband should she need it.

The Mormon church tried to emulate the polygyny practices of the Old Testament. These practices have been controversial in the United States, and members of the Mormon church were not welcome in many places. Congress outlawed polygyny in 1862, but Mormons employed various subterfuges to circumvent the prohibition. Congress persisted in passing anti-polygyny bills, and the Mormon church finally declared the practice discontinued in 1890. There are still today a few Mormons who defy the law and have polygynous relationships.

There is no particular pattern to the practice of polygyny. The ancient Egyptians were polygynous, whereas the ancient Romans were not. The Justinian Code proclaimed it an offense, although this was changed by Mark Antony, who took two wives. In China and Japan, polygyny was allowed, as was concubinage. (The description of polygyny in China suggests that this was not true polygyny, because the law did not allow a man to take a second wife while his first wife was still alive. But he was allowed to take concubines over whom the legal wife had power and authority. The children of concubines had the same legal rights as the children of wives.) The Hindu law books do not prohibit plural marriages nor do they restrict the number of wives a man could marry. The North American Plains Indians allowed polygyny, but the Iroquois did not. Many of the Moorish tribes of North Africa did not observe polygyny, nor did the Tuaregs of Niger, the Veddah of Ceylon, and many of the tribes in South America. In societies where polygyny is permitted, the observance was, and is, not universal because not every man had the resources to support more than one wife. Often plural marriage was only indulged in by the powerful and well-off. Among some of the North American Indian tribes, only the chiefs would have more than one wife, usually, as noted above, to help him meet obligations within his tribe. Fijian chiefs had from twenty to a hundred wives, obviously an outward sign of power and wealth. Probably Solomon had his seven hundred wives (perhaps an exaggeration to further enhance his status) to show how much power and wealth he had.

Schapera (1940) studied the Kgatla people of the Bechuanaland Protectorate, South Africa, in the early 1930s. Theoretically, the Kgatla practiced polygyny, but Schapera found that it was only practiced by a minority of the population. Of seventy-four men in the age group he studied, forty-six were monogamous, twenty had two wives, seven had three wives, and only one had four wives. Thus, of this group, 38 percent were in a polygynous relationship. Dr. Livingstone, in about 1850, found that among the BaKaa people, of two hundred seventy-eight married men, one hundred fifty-seven were monogamous, ninety-four had two wives, twenty-five had three wives, and two had four wives, so that 43 percent of men were in a polygynous relationship (Freeman 1851, 280).

Schapera further adds that households of four or more wives were only found among the royal family and other prominent or wealthy people. Among the Kgatla each wife had her own household compound for herself and her children and hangers-on, along with the fields necessary to support the household. These compounds had to be supplied by the husband, and the property held there would be passed on to her children. If a widower remarried, he would have to provide his new wife with a new compound. He could not give his new wife the deceased wife's compound and fields because they were passed to her children.

Within the culture of polygyny, there may also be a hierarchy of the wives. Although the Koran instructs a husband to treat all the wives equally (if he cannot do so he should take only one wife), in other societies the first wife is usually the senior wife, with subsequent wives subservient and secondary to her. In Samoa, where a man has several wives, they each take turns at being the dominant wife for three days in rotation. A Muhammadan with four wives has to visit each in turn. Another form of polygyny was for a man to marry all the sisters within a family, known as *sororate*. Since all would be married at the same time, it could have been difficult to discern who took the role of chief wife.

Polygyny is, in many respects, tightly controlled, and anthropologists have not been very often able to find the opinions of the women in the arrangement. In many of these societies, the status of a woman is very low and she has little say about her marriage partner, with the arrangements made by her parents and the husband or his family. But evidence suggests that some of the Mormon women involved in polygynic relationships were not happy, and Scott (1953) recounts a story of eight girls who, in July 1873, in China, found themselves promised in a polygynous marriage. They tied themselves together and drowned together rather than live within that marriage.

See also Bigamy; China; India; Islamic Marriage; Mormon Church; Native American Marriage; Polyandry

References
Erdoes, Richard. 1972. *The Sun Dance People: The Plains Indians, Their Past and Present*. New York: Alfred A. Knopf.
Freeman, J. J. 1851. *A Tour in South Africa*. London: N.p.
Mair, Lucy. 1971. *Marriage*. Harmondworth, Middlesex: Pelican.
Schapera, Isaac. 1940. *Married Life in an African Tribe*. London: Faber and Faber.
Scott, George Ryley. 1953. *Curious Customs of Sex and Marriage*. London: Torchstream.
Westermarck, Edward. 1894. *History of Human Marriage*. 2d ed. London: Macmillan.

Posset

Posset, or sack posset, a bedtime drink, had a special association with marriage, including a divination game where a wedding ring would be dropped into the posset. The posset was then distributed among the unmarried people, and the person who received the ring would be the next to marry. The posset of the seventeenth century was a mixture of milk, wine, egg yolk, sugar, cinnamon, nutmeg, and other spices.

Brand (1777) suggested that the word is derived from the French word "poser," meaning to settle, as "when the milk breaks, the cheesy parts, being heavier, subside." He also gives an example of its use in a wedding: "In the evening of the wedding day, immediately before retirement of the company, Sack Posset was eaten, the bride and groom invariably tasting it first; and this was given the name of Benediction Posset." The posset was well enough known in the eighteenth century for it to warrant only the smallest passing reference in an account of a wedding in Derbyshire, England, in 1753: "The newly married couple . . . were at length put to bed . . . the stocking was thrown, the Posset drunk, and the whole concluded with all Decorum, Decency and order imaginable." Jeaffreson (1872, 1: 194) gave an account of the posset at a wedding, with a possible explanation for its use: "Beer and plum buns,— cakes swimming in a bowl of spiced ale,— were forced upon the bride as soon as she had entered the bridal chamber . . . [i]n the belief that no other combination of food and drink was so calculated to restore the exhausted energies of a delicate young lady."

A similar custom took place in France, as described in a privately printed seventeenth-century book: "In some parts of France, the bride and bridegroom are put to bed. . . . After they have been in bed about two hours, the company re-enters with a sack posset or hypocras, and all sitting round the bed, drink and laugh, and joke with the new married couple" (Gaya 1685, 22). Catholic couples in England at one time participated in a similar practice where the priest would bless the couple as they sat in bed—wearing their best dressing gowns and surrounded by their closest friends. The priest blessed the couple, their bed, and a cup of sweetened and spiced liquor known as the benediction posset (since it had been blessed). When the posset had been drunk, the bed curtains were drawn and the friends dispersed. It is clear that this could only happen in rich households.

The posset tradition, still observed in France, although much changed and much less serious, involves the bride and groom having to drink a concoction prepared by their friends from a chamber pot on the wedding night. This is variously named *rôtie, rutia, panee, panya, saucée, saucya, potee, salade, chichole,* and *la soupe.* The concoction usually consists of a mixture of white wine or champagne, chocolate, balls of chocolate cream, and biscuits. Sometimes pieces of crumpled and twisted cigarette paper are also added and sometimes leftovers from the reception meal are dumped in. When the bridal couple are thought to be asleep, one of the groomsmen takes the chamber pot filled with this brew, often decorated with ribbons, to the couple's bedroom. The bride has to taste the brew first, then her husband, and then it is passed around to the guests. In some places if the bride refuses to drink the mixture the guests punish her by making her get out of bed and walk around the room several times in only her nightdress.

See also Hot Pot; *Soupe, la*

References

Brand, John. [1777] 1900. *Observations on the Popular Antiquities of Great Britain.* Revised and enlarged by Sir Henry Ellis in 1841 and 1848. 3 vols. London: G. Bill and Sons.

Gaya, Louis de. 1685. *Matrimonial Ceremonies Displayed.* Translated into English, 1704. London: Privately printed.

Jeaffreson, John Cordy. 1872. *Brides and Bridals.* 2 vols. London: Hurst and Blackett.

Premarriage Customs

Ceremonies and events that lead up to the wedding are sometimes as important as the ceremony itself. Some have a serious purpose—legal, religious, or spiritual—such as the reading of the banns or the formal betrothal, henna nights or the ritual bathing. Courtship, proposal, and arrangement practices are important premarriage customs. And there are informal premarriage events that are organized and shared by the couple's friends, peer groups, and working colleagues. These can be embarrassing and even dangerous and usually involve alcohol consumption.

These events fall into three categories. First are the stag or hen night parties, where each of the couple, separately with their friends, indulges in a last mad fling as a single person before having to settle down into married life. The excesses of these events are legendary and often involve the participants acting completely out of character. Second are workplace ceremonies, usually for the bride, the "ribbon girl" traditions. Third are customs to help the couple set up the home, such as the Welsh bidding custom, the shower (mainly in the United States and Canada), and other localized events.

> **See also** Betrothal; Bidding; Courtship; Creeling; Engagement; Factory Customs; Hen Night; Henna; *Polterabend* Party; Ribbon Girl; Shower; Stag Night

Presents

Presents given by, between, and to the couple intending to marry have a number of different symbolic and practical purposes. They are used in the context of marriage as a way of expressing interest in a particular person, as a way to seal an engagement, and as a method for the community to help a couple set up an independent home.

During periods of courtship, the exchange and receiving of gifts was often very significant in establishing and cementing a relationship. Welsh love spoons, carved and inscribed knitting sheaths in the Yorkshire Dales, England, inscribed lace-making bobbins in other parts of England, and carved and inscribed distaffs, lace reels, and washing-beetles in Hungary, for instance, were usually a symbol of affection and the first step in courtship. The acceptance of such gifts was a sign that the interest and affection was reciprocated. The giving of gifts to elicit interest or show affection is found among many societies worldwide. For example, among the Kgatla people of South Africa, a young man would try to win the affection of a girl with small gifts such as decorated spoons or porridge-stirrers. Among the South African Zulu people, once a girl has been allowed to show her feelings for a young man, she presents him with a necklace of white beads. This represents a form of engagement, and they can then exchange presents of jewelry and are allowed to spend the nights together.

In Iceland, if a young man gave a young woman a carved mangle or a carved reel for sewing thread, this was a proposal to marry. If the girl accepted the gift, she accepted the proposal. In the Friesland area of the Netherlands, a young man sealed the engagement to marry by giving the girl a coin in a knotted shawl. Today, in many countries, the engagement is sealed by the giving of a ring—often a diamond ring. The giving of presents between a couple has traditionally been a sign of an agreement between them, and there were breach of promise cases in England where the giving (and receiving) of presents is offered as evidence to constitute proof of the agreement between the couple.

In continental Europe, it was common for a young man to give a young woman he was courting presents of decorated domestic items—distaffs, spinning wheels, chairs, bobbins, dressers. These not only showed his affection for her but also demonstrated his skills. She may give him embroidered or other decorated clothing—again to demonstrate her skills. Engagement gifts are often exchanged, again usually governed by tradition and convention. In Hungary, in the eleventh and twelfth centuries, the exchange of engagement gifts was obligatory by royal decree—usually a wedding handkerchief, shirt, and trousers from the woman to the man, and a handkerchief, neckerchief, knife, money (often hidden in an apple), shoes, and a ring from the man to the woman. In Germany, it was the custom for an engaged couple to exchange gifts on the day before the reading of the banns, usually wedding shirts and an embroidered handkerchief from the woman to the man. He gave her a pair of decorated slippers. In Yugoslavia, a young woman was given presents of clothes and jewelry by her husband-to-be as part of the formal arrangements. She offered him a present in return—by custom, of equivalent value (generally tradition dictated that all presents required one in return of similar value).

Presents given by the groom to the bride's family are a formal way of paying homage and showing respect for the family. In Muslim countries where the parents of the couple arrange the marriage, the young man buys presents for his bride-to-be, and for her mother, as a sign of respect and love. In some societies a young man was expected to supply labor to the bride's family rather than give gifts to the family. In biblical Jewish tradition, work services were required from a suitor. Gifts given to the woman's family have sometimes been seen as a form of purchase. But there is often reciprocal gift giving. Sometimes the gift of cattle, for instance, may also provide an insurance for the bride in the event of her being widowed or divorced.

Among the Zulu, the bride-price, usually cattle, given by the bridegroom to the bride's family is not strictly a purchase payment, a dowry, or a gift. It is a guarantee that he will take care of the daughter. If she is ill treated, neglected, or abused, she has the right to return to her father. The bride-price would then provide for her and her children.

By tradition, the community often helps the couple to set up the home by giving engagement and wedding presents. Guests bring presents for the home to the shower, an engagement party. Many bridal couples in Europe and the United States provide lists for their guests to choose from, sometimes registering the lists with certain stores.

See also Bride-Price; Purchase, Marriage by; Shoes; Shower; Spousal; Tokens
References
Owen, Trefor. 1968. *Welsh Folk Customs.* 2d ed. Cardiff: National Museum of Wales.
Schapera, Isaac. 1940. *Married Life in an African Tribe.* London: Faber and Faber.
Van Nespen, W. 1975. *Love and Marriage: Aspects of Popular Culture in Europe [exhibition], Antwerpen.* Brussels: Ministerie van Nederlanse Cultuur en Nationale Opvoeding.

Proxy, Marriage by

Although it is usually considered essential for both of the couple to be present to exchange vows and rings, it is not unknown for a marriage to take place with one of the couple not present. Marriage by proxy has sometimes occurred among European royal families, for purposes of a political alliance. A well-known example was the marriage of Charles I of England to the French princess Henrietta Maria in 1625, which took place by proxy at the door of Notre Dame Cathedral, after which the bride traveled to England and the couple married again at Canterbury Cathedral.

In 2003, a Russian cosmonaut and his fiancée were married while he was in space. The ceremony was conducted by a judge at the Houston Space Center using satellite video and voice links. This was a legal marriage under American law (where only one witness is required).

Marriage ceremonies have been performed with someone or something else substituting for one or both of the couple. Crawley gives an example from South Celebes (Indonesia). The bride and groom each have a representative—if the bride's representative is a man, the groom's would be a woman. The bride would not appear at the wedding but would instead be confined in a room while her deputy took her place. After the ceremony the groom was not able to see his bride but returned to his home, leaving his sword behind as his representative. Three days later he returned to his bride and reclaimed his sword in exchange for a present. The practice of people marrying trees, found in parts of India, may have been a marriage by proxy to avert the dangers of evil influences on the wedding.

See also Church Porch, Weddings in; Russian Weddings; Tree, Marriage to a
References
Crawley, Ernest. [1902] 1932. *The Mystic Rose: A Study of Primitive Marriage and of Primitive Thought in Its Bearing on Marriage.* Revised and enlarged by Theodore Besterman. London: C. A. Watts.
Monsarrat, Ann. 1973. *And the Bride Wore . . . : The Story of the White Wedding.* London: Gentry.

Purchase, Marriage by

The concept of "marriage by purchase" has been devised by anthropologists from their observations of native societies where there were gifts given, such as cattle or goats, by the man to the woman's family. Jeaffreson (1872) concluded from Anglo-Saxon laws that assigned a monetary value to a woman's virtue that a suitor bought his spouse from her father. However, Jeaffreson has misinterpreted these laws. They instead provided for retribution for rape and seduction or sexual assault as part of a payment for marriage. (He interpreted this as a step forward from "marriage by capture.") Within Anglo-Saxon society there were many distinctions of rank and class, and free women had a great deal of individual freedom.

The theory of marriage by purchase is based upon a Judaeo-Christian-Islamic view of the position of women within society in relation to men and their male relatives and from a Western view of exchange and buying and selling. Westermarck (1894) gives many examples in which apparently cattle, goats, or some other commodity is given to the family (usually father or male relatives) of the bride by the bridegroom. Or a young man wishing to marry a young woman may work for her family for a set period, as did Jacob in the Old Testament, who worked for Laban for seven years in order to marry Rachel. The theory holds that the woman has a value for the community in her childbearing potential and her work to help support the community, and this value has to be met by the man who will be taking her away from the family and community. Thus, these gifts from the bridegroom, or his family, to the bride's family, were interpreted as a purchase transaction. But the anthropologists were viewing from the outside and did not know or understand the social nuances involved in the agreement. Crawley (1902) suggested that the whole concept of marriage by purchase was based on a misunderstanding of the role of gift giving and other traditions of sealing agreements among the

people being studied. In many of these transactions there is a complicated system of gift giving and receiving, some of which are more symbolic than of any great value, between the two families or kin groups involved. In 1938, R. P. G. Hulstaert described the marriage ceremonies of the Nkundo people of the Belgian Congo (today the Republic of Zaire). The process started with the young man presenting an *inkula,* a present of two copper rings (at one time this would have been an arrow) to the woman and her kin. If accepted, the couple became betrothed. At the marriage, the groom's parents, his relatives, and the groom himself gave presents to the bride. There followed a presentation of the *ndanga,* usually a knife, to the bride's father that signified that the husband took responsibility for accidents that could befall the bride. In return, there was a presentation from the bride's family to the groom and his family that formed part of the *nkomi,* a payment from the bride's family to the groom. The marriage was fully completed, but she became his wife only after the groom had paid the *walo* to his father-in-law, a substantial payment, which consisted mainly of metal objects. When he made this last payment, the bride's family made a return payment of a present of food to the husband's family. The new husband gave presents to the wife's mother, father, brothers, and other relatives, whereupon the husband's family demanded, and received, presents from the wife's family. The husband made the final payment (the *bosongo*) of a quantity of copper rings to his wife's family.

Among the Nyakysus people, who live at the north end of Lake Nyasa (in Malawi), the marriage only becomes legal after the handing over of cattle by the bridegroom's representative to the bride's. This cements the marriage and allows her to bear legitimate children. The giving and receiving of the cattle is a bond that unites the families. However, even after giving the cattle, the son-in-law is expected to do a certain amount of work on her father's land. The marriage may be dissolved with the return of those cattle.

In the traditional Chinese wedding, the groom's family sends gifts to the bride's family, which include cash, food, and sacrifices for the ancestors, and, since the young woman leaves her birth family and becomes part of the groom's family on marriage, the bride herself takes gifts for the groom, either just before the wedding day or, if she lives far away, on the wedding day. These gifts include jewelry, kitchen utensils, bridal linens, such as sheets and pillow covers, and clothes. Consequently, there is an exchange of gifts between the two families rather than what could be viewed as a buyer/seller exchange.

Among the Zulu people in South Africa, a bridegroom had to give cattle to the woman's father or family—a form of insurance for the woman so that, should he die, reject her, divorce her with no good reason, or be violent, she could return to her family and the cattle would provide her support. This is much the same situation as with the groom giving a dowry, or settlement to the bride, or as in Saxon England, with the *morgengifu,* the "morning-gift," given to the bride on the morning after her wedding—property or wealth to support the wife should she lose her husband.

But perhaps the ancient Assyrians did have a true system of marriage by purchase, according to the Greek historian Herodotus (484–424 B.C.), with a system of public auction of young women for brides. The women in the auction were considered property of the state, and someone bidding and winning in the auction had to marry the woman he won. In this Assyrian marriage market, the women considered the most beautiful were sold first, and the money raised on their sale went toward a dowry for the less good-looking, as an inducement to buyers. The Thracians, too, had marriage markets where women were sold to the highest bidder. The purchase money went to the parents of the young woman.

In Britain an unofficial form of divorce and remarriage was the "wife sale," a practice made famous by Thomas Hardy in his novel *The Mayor of Casterbridge,* set in the early nineteenth century. This practice occurred occasionally into the twentieth century. In this practice, generally, the husband would lead his wife to the market with a halter around her neck and put her up for auction. The highest bidder took the wife and the married couple would part. On the face of it, this seems brutal and degrading for the woman, but this was a form of divorce at a time when divorce was very difficult and expensive to obtain. The outcome of the auction was rarely in doubt, with the highest bidder usually being the woman's lover.

See also Bride-Price; Dowry; Wife-Selling; Zulu Weddings

References
Crawley, Ernest. [1902] 1932. *The Mystic Rose: A Study of Primitive Marriage and of Primitive Thought in Its Bearing on Marriage.* 4th ed. Revised and enlarged by Theodore Besterman. London: C. A. Watts.
Evans-Pritchard, E. E. 1940. *The Nuer.* Oxford: Oxford University Press.
Fell, Christine. 1984. *Women in Anglo Saxon England and the Impact of 1066.* London: Colonnade Books, British Museum Publications.
Hulstaert, R. P. G. 1938. *Le mariage des Nkundó.* Bruxelles: Institute Royal Colonial Belge.
Menefee, Samuel Pyeatt. 1981. *Wives for Sale.* Oxford: Basil Blackwell.
Scott, George Ryley. 1953. *Curious Customs of Sex and Marriage.* London: Torchstream.
Westermarck, Edward. 1894. *The History of Human Marriage.* 2d ed. London: Macmillan.
Wilson, Monica. 1950. "Nyakyusa Kinship." In *African Systems of Kinship and Marriage,* edited by A. R. Radcliffe-Brown and Cyril Daryll Forde. London: Oxford University Press.

Quaker Weddings

Quakers do not believe that there is a need for clergy to act as a conduit between people and God, so worship is a silent contemplative event where Friends (as they refer to each other) contribute and share thoughts, readings, or events with the other members of the congregation. A Quaker wedding is much the same as Quaker worship. There is not a formal procession or a division between the families as is often the case in church weddings. The meeting is a silent worship, and those present are invited to contribute thoughts, wishes, poems, and readings. When the couple judge the time right they exchange vows before the congregation and a registrar. The vows usually take this form: "Friends, I take this my friend [name] to be my husband/wife, promising through divine assistance [or with God's help], to be unto him/her a loving and faithful wife/husband, so long as we both on earth shall live." After the exchange of vows, the couple again take their seats, after exchanging rings. Originally, Friends would not have worn rings. Toward the end of the meeting, the couple and the chief witnesses sign a Quaker certificate. The certificate is read out to the meeting, and after the meeting has ended all the members sign the certificate as witnesses.

In keeping with the traditions of simplicity implicit in Quaker worship, the wedding outfits of the bride and groom are not likely to be elaborate. A description of a Quaker wedding in 1838 described the bride as wearing "a pale gray gown, a cap and a white shawl, with a large veil thrown over her head and face" (from the Diary of Lady Charlotte Bury, 1838, quoted in Heseltine 1951, 173). Similarly, distractions such as photography or videos are avoided (unless there are special circumstances). No registrar or elder pronounces the couple as man and wife, and it is not necessary, legally, for any such pronouncement to be made. In a court case in England, in 1953, *Quick v. Quick,* the couple had exchanged vows, but as the bridegroom was putting the ring on the bride's finger, she threw the ring down and declared that she would not marry him, and left the church. But the court declared that legally the marriage had been completed. However, it is implicit in law that a third party should make a declaration as confirmation of the marriage, which is why the Quaker certificate of marriage is read aloud to the meeting.

Quakerism arose in seventeenth-century England, and during this period, in 1653, the Puritan government declared marriage to be a civil ceremony to be performed before a registrar or justice of the peace. George Fox, the founder of Quakerism, wrote: "For the right joyning in marriage is the work of the Lord only, and not the priests or magistrates; for it is God's ordinance and not man's: and therefore Friends cannot consent that they should joyn them together; for we marry none, it's the Lord's work, and we are but witnessess." A 1656 epistle from Margaret Fell stressed three principles as the basis for Quaker procedure—adequate preliminaries (preparation), open ceremony (exchange of declarations and the signing of the certificate), and efficient registration.

A thorough and open procedure was especially important after the Restoration in 1660. When the *Book of Common Prayer* was introduced in 1662, and with the Act of Uniformity and the restoration of church courts (with responsibility for proving wills), the legality of Quaker marriages was brought into question. The Bishop of Salisbury reported upon Quaker meetings in 1669. He referred to a Quaker's wife as "his Company keeper, or pretended wife." In another account the Bishop noted that "he keeps a woman as his wife to whom he was never married." The marriages of those mentioned were well documented in the Quaker register books. From 1661, Friends had success in gaining judgments from the courts that their marriages were valid in civil law.

The preliminaries for a marriage called for the couple to appear at the monthly meeting where the woman was a member to declare their intention to marry. The meeting appointed members to investigate and report on whether there were any impediments to the marriage taking place. The following month the couple would declare their intention a second time, and, if the reports were satisfactory, they would be told that they could go ahead with the marriage.

The formal enquiry procedure was discontinued in Britain and Ireland in 1872 because the couple was now required to put a notice in the office of the superintendent registrar, which provided enough of a safeguard against clandestine or irregular marriages.

Neither do the couple now have to make a public declaration to the meeting in person but may declare their intentions in writing. Although these changes appear to diminish the "corporate" involvement in the marriage, the meeting at which the marriage occurs has a very inclusive feel, so that all those attending are personally involved.

See also Civil Ceremonies; Commonwealth Period
References
Heseltine, G. C. 1951. *A Bouquet for a Bride.* London: Hollis and Carter.
Milligan, Edward H. 1994. *Quaker Marriage.* Kendal: Quaker Tapestry Scheme.

Quintain

Quintain, an old jousting sport, involves an upright post with a swiveling crossbar, with a flattened target on one end and a weight, generally a sandbag, on the other. When the flat surface is struck, the crossbar turns and the striker has to be quick to avoid being hit by the sandbag. The quintain was a popular pastime at weddings and continued in use at Welsh weddings into the nineteenth century. As the groom's party proceeded to the bride's home to collect her to take her to the church, they would come upon barriers that the bride's party had placed across the road. One of these might be the quintain (in Welsh, *cwinten* or *gwyntyn*). In some parts of Wales, *cwiten* became the word used for the straw rope barriers held across the roadway to bar the way of the groom's party.

Peter Roberts in *The Cambrian Popular Antiquities* (1815) described the procession of the groom's party:

> And the cavalcade being all mounted, set off at full speed, . . . for the house of the bride. The friends of the bride in the mean time having raised various obstructions to prevent their access to the house of the bride, such as ropes of straw across the road, blocking up the regular one, &c., and the *quintain;* the rider in passing struck the flat side, and if not dextrous was overtaken, and perhaps

dismounted, by the sand-bag, and became a fair object for laughter. The *gwyntyn* was also guarded by champions of the opposite party; who, if it was passed successfully, challenged the adventurers to a trial of skill at one of the four and twenty games—a challenge which could not be declined; and hence to guard the *gwyntyn* was a service of high adventure.

Quintains at weddings were not confined to Wales. Dr. Plott, in *History of Oxfordshire* (1677), after describing a quintain set up in the village of Deddington, Oxfordshire, England, continued: "It is now only in request at marriages, and set up in the way for young men to ride at as they carry home the bride; he that breaks the board being counted the best man" (quoted in Strutt 1801).

In a nineteenth-century history of Northamptonshire, England, by the Reverend R. S. Baker, *The History of Northamptonshire,* an account is given of the quintain used in the village of Brington:

> The last and indeed the only instance of this sport which I have met with in this county was in 1722, on the marriage of two servants at Brington, when it was announced in the *Northampton Mercury* that a quintain was to be erected on the green at Kingsthorp, "and the reward of the horseman that splinters the board is to be a fine garland as a crown of victory, which is to be borne before him to the wedding house, and another is to be put round the neck of his steed; the victor is to have the honour of dancing with the bride, and to sit on her right hand at supper."

Although there seem to be few references to this practice in England, it was obviously widespread. It provided part of the amusement for Queen Elizabeth I when she stayed at Kenilworth Castle, Warwickshire, in 1575. There was "a solemn country bridal" where a quintain was set up, and the "bridegroom had the first course at the quintane, and broke his spear" (Strutt 1903, 110).

See also Barring the Way; Wales
References
Baker, Reverend R. S. *The History of Northamptonshire.*
Hone, William. 1841. *The Table Book.* London: Thomas Tegg.
———.1827. *The Every-Day Book.* London: Thomas Tegg.
Owen, Trefor. 1968. *Welsh Folk Customs.* 2d ed. Cardiff: National Museum of Wales.
Roberts, Peter. 1815. *The Cambrian Popular Antiquities.* N.p.: n.p.
Strutt, Joseph. [1801] 1903. *The Sports and Pastimes of the People of England.* Enlarged and corrected by J. Charles Cox. London: Methuen.

Racing

Atkinson (1841) described a custom that he observed at Danby-in-Cleveland, Yorkshire, where the members of the congregation raced for ribbons donated by the bride. After the wedding, all the guests went into the field adjoining the church, and there they ran footraces for the ribbons. He also noted that before his incumbency the race would have been on horseback, cross-country, to the bride's house, where, again the winner received a ribbon from the bride. This was not an isolated custom. There is a record of a similar race being run at Hornsea in East Riding of Yorkshire, England, in 1848, where the races were run after the bridal party had returned from the church. The winner received a ribbon that he wore in his hat. In later years the prize was increased to a scarf or a handkerchief.

Similarly, in North Yorkshire, the race to the bride's house began as soon as the ring was put on her finger. The winner had the right to remove the bride's garter from her leg. Sometimes the racers waited until the wedding ceremony had finished, and, as usual, the prize was a ribbon, which the winner wore in his hat. If the distance from the church to the house was two or three miles or more, the race would be on horseback. This practice is similar to those linked with the wedding favors and the bride's garter— guests would scramble to remove the bride's garter before she left for the bedroom. To facilitate the removal of the garter and to "prevent a curious hand from coming too near her knee" (and make it less embarrassing) she would attach ribbons to it. There are accounts from the north of England where the members of the congregation would race to pluck the bride's garter immediately after the wedding ceremony with the winner parading it around the church in triumph. To avoid being injured in the scramble, the bride would often give out a garter that she had in her bosom.

Henderson (1866) noted that at Melsonby, near Darlington, County Durham, the bride acted as the winning post for the race by holding the ribbon in her hand—the winner also claimed a kiss on receiving the ribbon. He also commented that on one occasion the bride, a Methodist, refused to give a ribbon for the races, and she was ostracized by the youths "firing the anvil" at her. In a slight twist to the practice, Henderson also mentioned racing in Cleveland, North Yorkshire, where the bridegroom gave the ribbon prize. All who wished to take part in the race began as soon as they were in sight of the house where the wedding feast was to be held, and all the competitors in the race were entitled to a glass of spirit, which they were not slow to claim.

A similar practice, known as "racing for kail," was found in the northeast of Scotland. When the wedding party, processing back to the house for the reception, got near the house, the unmarried began a race to "win the kail." It is not clear if they received any form of prize, but it was thought that the winner would be the first in the party to be married. Another variant of the race, from Ireland, was a race for the bottle. Again it was a race to the bride's house, but this time the winner received a bottle of whiskey. The winner would hand the bottle to the bridegroom to take a drink; he would then pass it to his bride, who would take a drink. The bottle was then passed around the company. A little whiskey was to be left in the bottom of the bottle, which would be thrown away by the bridegroom. This is reminiscent of the "loving cup" custom, in which the whole company drank from the same cup passed around. The practice of leaving a little whiskey in the bottom and then throwing it away is similar to a practice from North Yorkshire, England, where the bride would eat a piece of the wedding cake and then throw the rest of the slice over her shoulder; this was said to signify that the couple would always have enough and some to spare.

Racing, with prizes, appears as part of the amusements at weddings in Cumberland, England. A correspondent to Hone's *Table Book* (1841, 374) notes that in Cumberland, England, it was the practice to hold a "bidden wedding" on the eve of the wedding. "A couple of respectability and slender means" would publicize their wedding through the local newspaper, the *Cumberland Pacquet,* with an advertisement in which the editor "set off the invitation in a novel and amusing manner, which never failed to ensure a large meeting, and frequently the contributions made on the occasion, by the visitors, were of so much importance to the new married couple." Hone also prints an advertisement that appeared in the *Cumberland Pacquet* (June

1803) that announced a "Public Bridal," which seems to have taken place after the marriage. But the term "public bridal" that headed the advertisement suggests that it was a similar event to the bidden wedding or the bridewain:

> JONATHAN and GRACE MUSGERAVE purpose having a PUBLIC BRIDAL, at Low Lorton Bridge End, near Cockermouth, on THURSDAY, the 16th June, 1803; when they will be glad to see their Friends, and all who may please to favour them with their Company;—for whose Amusement there will be various RACES, for Prizes of different Kinds; and amongst others, a Saddle, and Bridle; and a Silver-tipt Hunting Horn, for Hounds to run for.—There will also be Leaping, Wrestling, &c. &c. (Hone 1841, 374)

It is not clear if any collection for the couple was made at this event.

See also Anvil, Firing of; Favors; Garter
References
Atkinson, J. Canon. 1841. *Forty Years in a Moorland Parish.* London: Macmillan.
Gregor, Rev. Walter. 1881. *Notes on Folklore of the North East of Scotland.* London: Folklore Society.
Henderson, William. 1866. *Notes on the Folklore of the Northern Counties of England and the Borders.* London: Longmans, Green.
Hone, William. 1841. *The Table Book.* London: Thomas Tegg.

Ribbon Girl

"Ribbon girl" is the name given by folklorists to a prewedding event that occurs on a woman's last day at work before her wedding, mainly in factories in England and Ireland and sometimes in offices and markets. A similar custom found in Scotland is known as "creeling the bride" or "bosseller." The woman is decorated with ribbons, streamers, risqué rhymes and slogans, heart shapes, and sometimes presents, such as kitchen utensils. The girl, so decorated, is led in procession around the workplace and then accompanied

"Ribbon Girl," Romford, Essex, England, 1972. (Author's collection)

home, showered with confetti as she leaves work. The ribbons and streamers were often made from wrapping paper used by the factory or parts of items made at the factory. For example, at a factory that produced spark plugs, these are hung on her coat. A photograph in the *Yorkshire Evening Press* in March 1968 of a girl who worked in a tailors' workshop in Selby, Yorkshire, showed her leaving work with spools of thread tied to her coat. A woman's colleagues would also make paper rosettes and streamers.

In offices, the woman's desk might be decorated with paper rosettes on her chair, over her computer, and on the desk, and with streamers going from a central point above the desk to the four corners of the desk. Sometimes a veil is made from paper and net for her to wear. In some instances she will wear the veil all day, and sometimes only at the end of the day when she is paraded home. Sometimes the headdress may be a dunce's cap or made from toilet paper. In markets, she may be wheeled around in a decorated wheelbarrow and then paraded home. Sometimes the woman is tied to a lamppost as part of the celebrations. If the girl uses a car or bicycle to get to work this may be decorated by her workmates.

And there are examples of such events happening to young men. The man may be dressed up as a mock bridegroom and paraded out of the workplace at the end of the day. Sometimes the event resembles the traditional ceremonies that used to be carried out to celebrate an apprentice finishing his studies. Indeed, in some workplaces, these premarriage events are only performed on apprentices. A description of the event, from a diesel engine plant in Stockport, England, in 1972, involved the man being cheered as he went to his bench, where he found a mock wedding cake composed of fireclay and engine parts. His friends had decorated a chamber pot with the bride and groom's names, good luck messages, and an eye in the bottom with the words "I can see you." During the morning the chamber pot was suspended from an overhead crane that he had to climb to retrieve it as the onlookers banged hammers and spanners on benches and metal to make as much noise as possible.

The man's jacket was taken, and the lining and pockets were filled with confetti and heavy pieces of iron. The pockets were often sewn up as well. After work the bridegroom and his friends went to a public house where they all drank from the chamber pot. Men's celebrations often seemed to be more boisterous and to go to more extremes than the women's. In 1994, at Biggar on the English-Scottish border, a bridegroom-to-be was seen blackened and naked and chained to a lamppost with women and men jeering him. He was eventually unchained and dragged through the streets and thrown off the bridge into the river. His fiancée did not see any of this. She was being taken around by her "friends" and getting very drunk (Monger 1996). There seems to be an element of role reversal in these celebrations. Another example, again from an engineering establishment, involved the man's colleagues stripping his clothes from him, covering him with sawdust and syrup, and dressing him up in stockings and pants—his shirt taken and decorated with pictures and slogans written in lipstick. He and his workmates then went to the local tavern where he had to buy the drinks. He was delivered home very drunk. This is very similar to "stag night."

At one time a woman would no longer work outside of the home after marriage, as remembered by a Mrs. Helen Stewart, a Glaswegian woman, talking about her own marriage in the 1930s: "The day before . . . I left work at the mill (you didnae go back once you were married)" (Blair 1985, 103). In some professions and jobs (such as teaching) a married woman lost the right to work in that job or profession. Consequently, to a great extent there was very much an element of "sending-off" and recognition and celebration of the change in the woman's societal status. This is also exemplified in the men's celebrations, which are analogous to apprentice-finishing events. There is also an element of the workmates taking part in the wedding celebrations themselves, and of marking the event. From the point of view of the bride-to-be, the fact that she was subjected to the sometimes embarrassing public celebrations was a tangible demonstration that she was part of the community. One woman described it this way (Monger 1996): "Even though it was a little embarrassing we would have hated to have missed it."

There are few accounts of these types of customs before the twentieth century, although this may be because no folklorist or social commentator had seen or recorded them. There is one nineteenth-century account (possibly from about 1836) of a similar custom from a printing works in London, England, from a book by Charles Manby Smith (1857), which happened among the men after the wedding. The ceremony involved parading the newly married man through the workplace, accompanied by a mock bride and groom, while the work colleagues banged the benches to make a form of rough music to mark and celebrate the fact of the marriage.

For many people in industrial societies, the work community and the social community do not necessarily overlap. And the work community is usually not invited to attend the wedding, so it makes its mark, or takes part in the wedding, through customs such as the ribbon girl custom. Where the work and social communities are mostly the same, it is rare to see a premarriage celebration of this nature.

See also Cars; Chamber Pot; Creeling; Factory Customs; Hen Night; Rough Music/Rough Band; Stag Night

References
Blair, Anna. 1985. *Tea at Miss Cranston's*. London: Shepheard-Walwyn.
Monger, George. 1996. "Pre-Marriage Ceremonies: A Study of Custom and Function." *Lore and Language* 14: 143–155.
———. 1975. "Further Notes on Wedding Customs in Industry." *Folklore* 86, no. 1 (spring): 50–61.
———. 1971. "A Note on Wedding Customs in Industry Today." *Folklore* 82, no. 4: 314–316.
Smith, Charles Manby. [1857] 1967. *The Working Man's Way in the World*. London: Printing Historical Society.

Rice

Jeffreason (1872) wrote: "My friend Mr. Moncure Conway, tells me that not long since he was present at a wedding in London, where rice was poured over the head of the bride. The groom and bride of this wedding were English people, moving in the middle rank of prosperous London." These comments suggest that rice did not appear in weddings in Europe until the nineteenth century. Rice soon became established as part of the marriage celebrations. By 1880 the folklorist T. F. Thiselton Dyer wrote that rice was showered onto the couple as they departed from the bride's home to promote success and happiness in their new life together. Despite the objections of some nineteenth-century clergymen, the scattering of rice on the newlywed couple has become a well-known part of the celebrations. Today rice has been replaced with paper confetti.

It was once more common, in England, to scatter wheat over the heads of the couple. Thomas Moffet in his *Health Improvements* (1665) wrote: "The English, when the bride comes from church, are wont to cast wheat on her head: and when the bride and bridegroom return home, one presents them with a pot of butter, as presaging plenty, and abundance of all good things." In countries where rice is a staple food it has associations with wealth and fertility. In India, rice is used at all auspicious occasions and is thought to give strength and virility to men. Rice tinged with turmeric powder or, among the more affluent, saffron, is presented to guests as an invitation to the wedding feast. In the Kerala district of southwest India, a *para* (measure) containing rice with a coconut sprout in the center is a central element at the marriage ceremony. Agriculture in this area is based around rice and coconut cultivation, which are consequently used as fertility symbols at weddings. In some parts of India, the bridal couple stands on a pile of rice, and guests throw a little rice onto the pile at the finish of the recitation of each text. The bride and groom also pour a little rice onto the sacrificial fire or offer rice to the household deity. Sometimes rice is sprinkled onto the bridal couple. It is also thought that rice is effective in scaring away demons.

A Chinese legend is said to explain how rice can be effective against demons. A sorcerer named Chao, in the province of Shansi, was consulted by a man about to be married; Chao told the man that he would die in six days. Unhappy with this prediction, the man consulted a sorceress, named Peach Blossom, who gave him the same prophecy but promised to prevent the catastrophe with charms. Chao was astonished to see the man walking about on the seventh day and, realizing that Peach Blossom's power was greater than his,

determined to destroy her. He went to her parents, pretending to seek her in marriage for his son. Her parents consented, and marriage cards were exchanged. However, an unlucky day was chosen for the wedding when the Golden Pheasant was in the ascendant, so that when she sat on the red nuptial chair, the spirit bird would destroy her with its powerful beak. Peach Blossom knew what was happening and ordered rice to be thrown out of the doors, which the spirit bird went to eat. While the spirit bird was thus preoccupied, she stepped into the bridal chair, and the marriage continued with her unscathed. Sometimes today, and more often in the past, rice is thrown into the air as the bride is carried out of her parents' house to be taken by sedan chair (or now sometimes in a decorated car) to the groom's house. It is said that the rice is thrown to distract the chickens so that they do not peck the bride as she leaves. However, it may well have originated to appease bad or malevolent spirits.

See also Almonds; Bride-Cake; China; Confetti; India

References

Coapta, Shakti M. 1971. *Plant Myths and Traditions in India.* Leiden: Brill.

Dyer, T. F. Thiselton. 1880. *English Folk-Lore.* 2d ed., revised. London: D. Bogue.

Jeaffreson, John Cordy. 1872. *Brides and Bridals.* 2 vols. London: Hurst and Blackett.

Moffet, Thomas. 1665. *Health Improvements.*

Rings, Wedding and Betrothal

The giving and receiving of rings at the engagement, or in earlier times, at the betrothal, and at the wedding are an important part of the Western wedding tradition. The exchange of rings upon betrothal was a well-established practice in the Middle Ages and in Shakespeare's time. These were often posy rings, which had a motto inscribed on the inside of the ring—for example, "Our contract was Heaven's act" (posy is probably a corruption of "poetry") and a reference to the motto inscribed within the ring). Similarly, the rings of the ancient Greeks and Romans were

Marriage rings. Left: Italy, seventeenth century, gold, gift of Rose and Benjamin Minsk Collection, M45. Right: Probably Venice, eighteenth century, gold (hammered, engraved, and filigree), gift of Mrs. Arthur Miller, JM9-47. Photographed by Coxe-Goldberg Photography. (The Jewish Museum, New York/Art Resource, New York City)

often inscribed with a motto to suggest the mystic power of the ring.

A popular form of betrothal ring was the gimmal ring, two or three interlocking rings that joined together to form one complete ring. Many of these had a central motif of two hands clasped over a heart. The ring would be solemnly broken over the Bible, before witnesses, at the betrothal, each of the couple receiving a part of the ring. If the ring consisted of three pieces, one of the witnesses took the third part. At the wedding the pieces of the ring would be reunited.

The engagement ring is now usually a gold band with precious stones and is a sign of being promised in the same way that a Kalderash Gypsy girl would wear a gold coin around her neck to indicate that she is promised in marriage. At a formal betrothal in twelfth-century England, a promise of the dowry—an endowment from the groom to the bride—was made public. The modern-day engagement ring appears to be viewed in a similar way, as a sign of the promise to marry, but also seems to be seen as indicating the husband-to-be's generosity and the depth of his affection.

It is unclear when the giving or exchanging of rings upon marriage came into being, but the Roman bridegroom would send an iron ring to the bride before the wedding as a symbol of how lasting their union should be and of the frugality that they were to observe together. Nor is it clear why the wedding ring is usually worn on the third finger of the left hand. The left hand has often been considered as unlucky or bad. Well into the twentieth century in Great Britain and the United States, left-handed children were forced to write with their right hand at school. Perhaps the reason for putting the ring on the third finger of the left hand was the belief that a vein or nerve went from this finger to the heart. This finger was known as the *medicus finger* because of this supposed vein. A seventeenth-century writer, Levinum

Lemnius (writing in 1658), claimed to have revived women who had fainted by pinching the wedding ring finger and rubbing the gold ring with a little saffron. He claimed that this restored forces passing to the heart "and refresheth the fountain of life unto which this finger is joined." Another reason put forward for the use of this finger is that the left hand is, as a rule, not used as much as the right and that the third finger (it is said) cannot be extended on its own—thus the ring is less likely to be worn out or damaged.

It would appear that before the Reformation in Europe the wedding ring was worn on the right hand (as would seem logical if the couple are forming a new partnership with mutual support, with the right being considered the good side—being a right-hand man or woman indicates an essential role in a working relationship). In *The History of the Reformation,* published in 1661, Peter Heylyn wrote "that the man should put the wedding ring on the fourth finger in the left hand of the woman, and not in the right as hath been many hundreds of years continued." The Greek Orthodox church directs that the ring be put on the right hand. The Anglican (Church of England) *Book of Common Prayer* directs that the ring should be put on the third finger of the left hand. And, further, the wedding ring has not always been worn on the third finger and sometimes not worn at all. Eighteenth-century portraits of married women showing the left hand do not always show a wedding ring. During the late sixteenth and the seventeenth centuries, it was the fashion for women to wear the ring on the thumb. Most likely it was not until the nineteenth century that the ring was worn continuously.

Early Quakers preached against the wedding ring. But today Quakers exchange rings at weddings. Even the early Quakers rejected this teaching to not wear a wedding ring and asserted their right to the ring.

During the Commonwealth Period in Britain (1649–1660) when the monarchy was abolished and a Puritan Parliament ruled the country, the use of the wedding ring was forbidden because of its "heathenish origin." Samuel Butler, in his long, three-part burlesque poem, "Hudibras" (1663), which attacked the Puritans, referred to this:

Others were for abolishing
That tool of matrimony, a Ring
With which th' unsanctified Bridegroom
Is married only to a thumb
(As wise as ringing a pig
That used to break up ground and dig)
The bride has nothing but her will,
That nulls the after marriage still.

Although the wedding ring and marriage in church using the *Book of Common Prayer* service were forbidden during this period, the Presbyterian minister of Finchingfield, Essex, performed the marriage service of one of his daughters using the *Book of Common Prayer* and a ring to ensure that she would not be returned to him for want of a legal marriage.

Many today consider it unlucky to remove the wedding ring after it has been placed on the finger in church, a belief that probably dates back to the nineteenth century when it became common to wear the ring continuously. Previously, although the ring was considered essential for a marriage, keeping the ring was not, and there were references to such items as the church keys being used in place of a ring. In southwest Ireland it was thought that a marriage would not be valid unless a gold ring was used. Tradesmen who supplemented their income by hiring out gold wedding rings probably were the source of this idea. There were also cases of rings being borrowed for the ceremony, and in Yorkshire, England, it was considered lucky to be married with a borrowed ring. It is a North American belief that it is best to buy the wedding ring from a mail-order firm because rings in shops may have absorbed bad luck from people who have tried them on. In some parts of England it was considered acceptable for the wedding ring to be tried on before the wedding, but not worn. Some said that the ring should not even be tried on before the wedding; to do so was probably seen as tempting fate.

Efforts were undertaken to prevent mock weddings (for purposes of seduction) using rings made from rushes. In 1217 the Bishop of Salisbury announced: "Let no man put a ring of rush, or any other material upon the hands of young girls, by way of mock celebration, for the purpose of seducing them, that while believing he is only perpetrating a jest, he may not in reality find himself bound irrevocably to the connubial state." There are records of curtain rings and even a ring made from a piece of kid glove (at a clandestine wedding) being used. The residents of the island of St. Kilda, off the coast of Scotland, used a piece of woolen thread as a ring at the wedding ceremony. The wedding ring was not worn, but married women wore a white frill at the front of the head shawl that distinguished them.

The use of a precious metal, and especially such a durable one as gold, perhaps confers a permanence on the union that these makeshift rings do not. It is thought to be unlucky to drop the ring before or during the ceremony. If either the bride or groom drops it, the early death of the culprit is foretold. If it rolls away from the altar steps, this is a bad sign. If it stops on a gravestone, the early death of one of the couple is expected. If the grave is that of a woman, the bride will die first, and vice versa. The ring is said to signify that the affections of the couple will never end, and it is made from gold to signify the durability of the marriage. Superstitions and beliefs have built up about the ring after the wedding. In most European countries, breakage or loss of the ring foretells that the marriage will be broken, either by the death of the husband or the loss of his affections.

There was a saying, "As your wedding ring wears, your cares will wear away." Some see the wearing away of the wedding ring as a sign that the marriage is wearing away, and if the woman's ring falls apart from wear, she will soon lose her husband. It has become (probably from the nineteenth century) unlucky to remove the ring after it has been placed on the finger in church, although in some places it is thought safe to remove the ring after the birth of the first child. If the ring falls off by accident, bad luck can be avoided if the husband replaces it. Possibly related to the idea of a vein running between the ring finger of the left hand and the heart, in some parts of Britain it was considered to have some healing properties, so that stroking the ring finger along any sore or wound would help heal it; similarly, a cure for sore eyes was to rub them with a wedding ring. The same treatment could also be applied for a sty in the eye. Finally, if a single person passed a sliver of wedding cake three times through a wedding ring and then put it under her (or his) pillow, he or she would dream of the future spouse.

See also Divinations

References

Cunnington, Phillis, and Catherine Lucas. 1972. *Costume for Birth, Marriage, and Death.* London: Adam and Charles Black.

Dyer, T. F. Thiselton. 1880. *English Folk-Lore.* 2d ed., rev. London: D. Bogue.

Heylyn, Peter. 1661. *The History of the Reformation.* N.p.: n.p.

Hone, William. 1841. *The Table Book.* London: Thomas Tegg.

Jones, W. 1877. *Finger-Ring Lore: Historical, Legendary, and Anecdotal.* London: Chatto and Windus.

Tegg, William. 1877. *The Knot Tied: Marriage Customs of All Nations.* London: William Tegg.

Wright, A. R. 1928. *English Folklore.* London: E. Benn.

Rosemary

Gilded rosemary accompanied the bride at an "old English Wedding," according to Tegg (1877): "A gay procession formed part of the humbler marriages; the bride was led to church between two boys wearing bridelaces and rosemary tied about their silken sleeves, and before her was carried a silver cup filled with wine, in which was a large bunch of gilded rosemary, hung about with silk ribbons of all colours." This seems to be paraphrased from Deloney (1597), whose story was set in the reign of Henry VIII.

Rosemary was carried or worn extensively at weddings in the seventeenth century, and probably before, and was believed to help the memory of the wearer; in Shakespeare's *Hamlet,* Ophelia gives a sprig of rosemary to her brother with the words, "There's rosemary, that's for remembrance; pray you, love, remember." Guests carrying it at a wedding was symbolic of the steadiness with which the couple should remember their mutual vows of affection. (Mourners at a funeral, to show that they would bear the memory of the deceased with them, also carried rosemary.) Dr. Roger Hackett, in his bridal sermon entitled "A Wedding Present," in 1607 (Jeaffreson 1872, 1: 190), suggested that rosemary not only aided memory but was indicative of the man's rule and that it also gave the heart wisdom, love, and loyalty:

> The rosemary is for married men, the which, by name, and nature, and continued use, man challengeth as properly belonging to himself. It overtoppeth all the flowers in the garden, boasting man's rule; it helpeth the brain, strengtheneth the memory, and is very medicinal for the head. Another property is, it affects the heart. Let this *ros marinus,* this flower of man, ensign of your wisdom, love, and loyalty, be carried not only in your hands but in your hearts.

In many parts of Britain, rosemary was, and is, known as the plant of friendship, and it was thought that households with a rosemary bush in the garden would never be short of friends. Hackett, however, would not have approved of the practice of gilding the rosemary, or of gilded ginger, which was sometimes included with knives and other wifely paraphernalia attached to the new bride's girdle, because in the same sermon he urged brides to wear not gilded flowers, but natural ones, with their "native fragrance." According to custom and etiquette, guests each carried a sprig of rosemary and dipped it into the loving cup tankard before drinking a pledge to the bride and groom. The newly-weds would, themselves, dip a sprig of rosemary into the wine cup before they drank to ensure their own happiness and the continuance of love between them. Apart from wearing and carrying sprigs of rosemary, there were also frequent references to the pathways to and from the church being strewn with rushes and flowers, and rosemary was often specifically mentioned.

The plant was associated with the Virgin Mary and was considered to give protection against evil spirits, injury, and lightning and believed to bring success to any enterprise. A story says that the flowers were originally white but became blue when, in the flight to Egypt, the holy family stopped to do some washing and Mary hung her robe on a rosemary bush to dry. (Blue is also associated with the Virgin Mary.)

If a girl wanted to see her future husband she should sleep with a sprig of rosemary and a crooked sixpence under her pillow and he would appear in her dreams. Another common belief associated with rosemary is that it only thrives where the woman is the dominant partner in the marriage.

See also Divinations; Flowers

References

Deloney, Thomas. 1597. *History of John Newchombe, the Wealthy Clothier of Newbury.*

Jeaffreson, John Cordy. 1872. *Brides and Bridals.* 2 vols. London: Hurst and Blackett.

Monsarrat, Ann. 1973. *And the Bride Wore . . . : The Story of the White Wedding.* London: Gentry.

Tegg, William. 1877. *The Knot Tied: Marriage Customs of All Nations.* London: William Tegg.

Vickery, Roy. 1995. *A Dictionary of Plant Lore.* Oxford: Oxford University Press.

Rough Music/Rough Band

This was a form of communal punishment meted out for matrimonial offenses, such as wife-beating, suspected immorality, a wedding under dubious circumstances, or any offense of a sexual nature. A group of men or boys beat on kettles, frying pans, or iron pots and blew whistles and horns outside the house of the wrongdoer. Sometimes an effigy would also be burned and rhymes about the person recited. Another form of punishment was to beat a bundle of straw outside the house of a known wife-beater.

The rough band and beating of the straw displayed to the wrongdoer that the community was aware of the crime and that the community was bringing the problem out into the open. The punishment acted as a way of shaming the wrongdoer before the entire neighborhood. In East Anglia, the rough band lost its role as a punishment and became part of the celebration of a wedding well into the twentieth century. Friends and neighbors of the couple would make rough music outside the reception (which was often held at the family home of either the bride or groom) by beating kettles, tin baths, old iron pans, and anything else that could be used to make a noise. The band would be rewarded with a drink and sometimes food as well.

In the state of Georgia, in the United States, a similar custom known as serenading, or sometimes shivaree or charivari, was popular during the nineteenth century (and into the twentieth century). After the ceremony, the friends of the bride and groom followed them to his house. The bride and groom would go up to the bedroom, whereupon the serenading would start. The serenaders would have a wide variety of instruments and noise-making implements—banjos, fiddles, pots, and pans—and they would make as loud a noise as possible, even running sticks along iron fence railings. The din would be maintained for several minutes, until the bride and groom would go to the bedroom window and invite the serenaders in for food and drink. If they were not invited in, the row was maintained for much longer. This tradition continues in some parts of the United States, notably in rural areas of Iowa, but often sometime after the wedding. The serenaders arrive during the evening and expect to be invited in and be rewarded with refreshments.

In Galicia, Spain, weddings were often a very private affair, taking place in secrecy at night, and for older children and youths, finding out the time and date of the wedding was a kind of sport. If the friends and neighbors of the couple found out the details of the wedding they would wait outside the church for the newlyweds and serenade them as they emerged, with the noise of bells, tambourines, and scallop shells (rubbing the rough surfaces of the shells together) and screaming and shouting. If those who had been appointed to give away the bride and groom did not throw money for the serenaders to scramble for, the couple and their relatives would be followed home by the band. If enough money was thrown to the crowd, they would adjourn to an inn to hold a party for the newlyweds.

This is reminiscent of an "old institution of the London vulgar—one just about to expire," described by Chambers (1863, 360):

> The performers were the butchers' men,—
> "the bonny boys that wear the sleeves of
> blue." A set of these lads, having duly
> accomplished themselves for the purpose,
> made a point of attending in front of a house
> containing a marriage party, with their
> cleavers, and each provided with a
> marrowbone, where with to perform a sort
> of rude serenade, of course with the
> expectation of a fee in requital of their
> music. Sometimes, the group would consist
> of four, the cleaver of each ground to the
> production of a certain note; but a full
> band—one entitled to the highest grade of
> reward—would be not less than eight,
> producing a complete octave; and, where
> there was a fair skill, this series of notes
> would have all the fine effect of a peal of
> bells. When this serenade happened in the
> evening, the men would be dressed neatly in
> clean blue aprons, each with a portentous
> wedding favour of white paper in his breast
> or hat. It was wonderful with what quickness
> and certainty, under the enticing
> presentiment of beer, the serenaders got
> wind of a coming marriage, and with what
> tenacity of purpose they would go on with

their performance until the expected crown or half-crown was forthcoming.

See also Cars

References

Chambers, Robert. 1863–1864. *The Book of Days.* Vol. 1. Edinburgh: W. and R. Chambers. Philadelphia: J. B. Lippincott.

Ewart Evans, George. 1966. *The Pattern under the Plough.* London: Faber and Faber.

Rey-Henningsen, Marisa. 1994. *The World of the Ploughwoman: Folklore and Reality in Matriarchal Northwest Spain.* Helsinki: Academia Scientiarum Fennica.

Russian Weddings

Weddings in Russia illustrate the human propensity for ceremony. After the Russian Revolution in the early twentieth century, the Communist Party attempted to make marriage a quick event with a simple registration before a party official. It became evident to party officials, however, that people would insist on more than a signing of a certificate in a dreary office. Russian weddings had traditionally taken place over several days, and the Soviet government considered that this wasted productive time. But Russians like to celebrate, especially weddings, and today one of the biggest concerns for the organizers of a wedding is whether or not enough alcohol has been provided.

Russians generally marry young, soon after leaving school or university, and a law that passed through the Duma (the Russian Parliament) in 2002 even allowed marriage between the ages of fourteen and sixteen, in special circumstances with permission of the authorities. Sixteen is the age of consent (among Muslim populations the age of consent is fourteen). Russians have freedom in the choice of marriage partner, and the engagement is low key. There is no engagement ring—the plain gold bands that the couple exchange during the wedding ceremony are referred to as the "engagement rings"—the man simply asks the woman to marry him, and he may give her flowers. There is no public announcement, but close friends and family are, of course, told of the plans to marry.

The date of the wedding is dependent upon a date being available at the Department of Registration of Civil Statuses (ZAGS) but usually takes place between one to three months after registration. The couple have to apply in writing to ZAGS to register their marriage and pay a fee, but by law there has to be at least a month-long waiting period (to allow the couple time to reconsider); during Soviet times this period was three months. ZAGS gives the couple a date for the registration. Russians at this stage do not say that they are "engaged" but instead that they "handed in the application." After applying to ZAGS there is a great deal of preparation to be done. Today, most commonly, both families share reception expenses—before perestroika, the bride's family would have provided the reception. The bride's dress is usually made for the occasion. Rarely she rents a dress or wears one passed down to her from a member of her family. Often she will make it herself; most brides wear a white dress, although some wear a suit of white or a pale color. Cars have to be organized for the wedding party. The black limousine is still a great luxury in Russia, and one is hired for the bride if the family can afford it. (Generally, friends and family with cars will take part in the procession of cars to the ceremony.) Each of the couple appoints a "witness," usually the best friends of the bride and the groom. The witnesses will preside over the celebrations at the reception. They prepare a script of speeches and competitions that they will perform during the celebrations; they meet several times before the wedding to make these preparations, rehearsing and preparing posters and jokes to be pinned up when the groom arrives for his bride on the wedding day.

The wedding celebration usually lasts at least two days but can last up to a week, depending on the stamina of their friends and the amount of food and drink provided. On the wedding day the groom's family and friends meet at his home, and the bride and her family and friends meet at the bride's home. The groom goes to the bride's home to collect his bride. He must allow plenty of time for this—most Russians live in apartment blocks, and he must "fight" his way up to the bride's home. The higher up she lives, the more effort he has to put into collecting his bride. The stairway is filled with posters and jokes about married and family life. At each flight of stairs there is a challenge for the groom and his followers. The bride's friends bar his way with questions and challenges that he, with the help of his friends, has to overcome in the effort to achieve his goal. Questions put to the groom may include a group of baby photographs from which the groom has to choose the photograph of his bride. If he answers incorrectly, he has to pay to pass to the next flight of steps. He may have to sing or dance to get past the friends. If the building has an elevator, the bride's friends will have blocked it. He may even climb the outside wall or enter from the roof.

The bride and groom go to ZAGS for the ceremony accompanied by their closest friends and family (the number going depending on the number of cars available). The rest of the guests will join the party at the reception. The bride and groom each go to ZAGS in different cars; the bride's car is usually decorated with a doll on the hood or two stylized golden rings on top—the crossed rings are a Russian symbol of marriage and are often seen on wedding invitations. On the way, the cars may encounter barriers across the road—the groom has bottles of wine in his car to pay for passage through the barriers. The ZAGS ceremony, the *brakosochetanie,* is simple: the bride and groom are asked if they want to marry each other. They answer and exchange rings. Rings are worn on the ring finger of the right hand (wearing a ring on the ring finger of the left hand means that the person is either divorced or widowed). The registrar says a few words of greeting and the official

music of the marriage ceremony (the Mendelssohn wedding march) is played. The guests present flowers to the bride, and all drink champagne.

Many couples opt for a church marriage, but the church marriage ceremony has no official status in Russia. Before a church marriage can take place, the couple must undergo the civil ceremony at ZAGS a few days beforehand. The full church ceremony is very long, and all stand during the ceremony (there are no pews in Russian churches). Most couples usually have a shortened version of the service.

After the ceremony, the couple leave the guests, accompanied by the witnesses and perhaps a couple of cars of close friends, for a tour of city sites, visiting memorials to those who died in World War II or the Russian Civil War (1918 to 1922) or graves or memorials of famous people and lay flowers at these sites. The BBC reported in 1998 that the site of the killing of Tsar Nicholas II and his family has become a focus for such pilgrimages by newlyweds. This tour of the city lasts for two to three hours before the couple join their guests for the reception.

It is rare for there to be more than about a hundred guests. If there are more than fifty, a restaurant may be hired. But most often the reception is held in the home. The guests are usually family and close friends (family members living in other cities, towns, or villages are not likely to attend because of the difficulties and costs of travel in Russia). The couple, close family, and the witnesses sit at the head table. There is not usually any particular seating plan for the other guests. One of the witnesses now gives the first toast—*Za Molodykh,* "for the newlyweds." Before the toast is drunk, the parents of the couple give speeches and one of the witnesses may read a poem of welcome to the guests. The first toast is champagne, and after the first sip one of the guests announces that the champagne is bitter *(Gor'ko),* and all the guests chant *Gor'ko, Gor'ko.* The way for it to be sweetened is for the couple to kiss. The two stand and kiss for as long as possible—the guests count as they kiss. If the guests do not think that the kiss was long enough, they demand another kiss. This happens after every toast, and there are many toasts drunk at the reception. The second toast is to the parents of the couple, with the couple making speeches of thanks to their parents. Again at the toast the shout of *Gor'ko* will go up, with the consequent kissing. The toasts continue, with the witnesses calling on the guests around the table to lead toasts. Each guest gives a present to the couple (usually an envelope containing money). Between toasts, guests eat and talk and the witnesses entertain the guests with poems and jokes and make fun of the couple by asking them questions. After a time, it happens that the guests begin to get too drunk to give toasts, and the witnesses collect the rest of the presents on a tray.

After this there is dancing before the main course is served, with the bride and groom leading off the dancing. During the dancing and mingling, the bride may be "stolen" by the groom's friends. He has to pay a ransom, with haggling to agree to the amount to be paid. This may happen several times during the evening. During the evening, the bride's friends steal the bride's shoe, and again the groom has to pay a ransom for the return of the shoe, the sum being the subject of negotiation. Eventually the main course is served, and dancing and drinking resume. There is no custom of cutting a wedding cake in Russia, but at the end of the reception guests are served cake, and this is the end of the first day of celebration.

The second day of celebration is slightly less raucous, as would be expected for a group of people suffering from hangovers from the first day. The party is held at the couple's new home, which may be the home of the bride's or groom's parents, and begins in the late morning or early afternoon. Although all from the previous day are invited, the second day of celebration is usually attended by family and close friends only. During this celebration the most popular drink is

beer, and the guests have to "hire" knives, forks, and spoons from the family. The money raised goes to the newlyweds. There is less food prepared for the second day—usually borscht (beet soup with vegetables and meat) or a freshwater fish soup (with potatoes and onions). This is followed by a main course of pelmeni (a noodle dough encasing a filling, somewhat like ravioli). This is accompanied by many toasts and the inevitable *Gor'ko*. After the meal the bride goes through a ritual of cleaning the floor. The guests make a mess on the floor that she has to clean up. The mess is made with coins and banknotes—the more coins scattered around, the harder the bride has to work. All the money she clears up belongs to the couple. The witnesses also arrange competitions and raffles to raise more money for the couple.

The celebrations usually last two days and begin on a Friday so that the guests have Sunday to recover. It is considered impolite to stay sober, and the food is usually so abundant that it is said that if you are going to a wedding it is advisable to not eat for three days before and that you will not need to eat for three days after. There are some new traditions following the attempted suppression of such things by the authorities, but there are elements that remain from before the Revolution and that are found in other parts of the world.

Before the Russian Revolution, marriages were arranged through a matchmaker, usually a member of the groom's family, who would visit the prospective bride's home at night. If the family agreed to the marriage, discussions would continue and a present would be sent to the bridegroom as a token of acceptance of the proposal. The groom's family paid some money to the bride's family for the cost of the wedding and the bride's clothes. The discussion also included what the bride was expected to bring to the new home—clothes, bedding, and household goods. Once the negotiations were satisfactorily completed, a formal betrothal party was held, and in some places the groom-to-be ceremonially burned the girl's spindle to symbolize her change of status from spinster to betrothed/married woman. During her betrothal, she was released from household duties while she prepared for her wedding and the accompanying celebration, which could last for a whole week.

The night before the wedding, a decorated tree, which symbolized her free virgin days, was dismantled, and the bride and groom exchanged small bunches of twigs. These were used by the bride at her ceremonial bath the next morning. This took place in a neighbor's house using water brought by her friends from a variety of wells. Her friends helped her dress, and after a blessing from her family, she would sit at the table with her bridesmaids and await the arrival of the groom and his party. The groom's party would process to the bride's house led by a man carrying a cask of beer, and along the way the bride's friends would have erected barriers that the groom's supporters would bribe their way past with wine and sweets. At the house the bridesmaids might have barred the way, demanding a ransom for the bride. Eventually the groom's party was allowed into the house, and everyone would sit down to a large meal—except the bride and groom, who were not allowed to eat before the ceremony. After the meal the bridal party formed a procession to the church. As it left the house, guns were fired into the air, whips were cracked, and everyone made a huge noise as an icon was carried three times around the party to ward off evil spirits. The church ceremony, as noted above, could last several hours, and the wedding party was not allowed to sit down at any stage. Everyone observed proper decorum in the church.

After the church ceremony, the bride's hair was plaited in the style traditionally worn by married women, and the party returned to whichever house was to be the venue of the celebrations. Here the bridegroom was allowed to take part in the subsequent feasting, but his bride wrapped herself in a shawl and, although sitting next to him at the top of the table, had to remain quiet and only participate in the celebrations by giving sweets to members of her new family. They gave her money in return. At the end of the feasting the couple were ceremoniously bedded. The next morning, the groom's "best man" and the matchmaker's wife roused the couple (accompanied by a rough band beating pots and pans) so that the bride's bloodstained nightdress could be displayed to prove her virginity. The party then went to the bride's parents' house. Here the groom put money into a glass of drink to offer to his mother-in-law in recognition of the care she had taken of her daughter. The party then moved to the groom's house. It was not until the following day that the bride was able to remove her shawl and join the party, at which time she would be tested and asked questions to see if she would make a good wife. The celebrations for the relatives would continue for several days.

Post-Revolution Russian family codes (1918, 1926, and 1936) were intended to free people from religious authority and from the grip of custom—and also to stop the loss of work time to marriage celebrations. Couples were allowed to either register as a couple or simply set up home together and be regarded as married. This did not work, and in 1944 the new Code of Family Law declared that only a registered marriage gave the rights and obligations of a married couple.

The 1926 code laid down the procedure for registering a marriage at ZAGS. This involved the couple declaring that there was no impediment to the marriage and guaranteeing that they had declared any former marriages and children and had given honest details of their health. The registrar warned that they would be committing a civil offense if they had not been honest. They would then register the marriage and the details would be entered into their passports. In 1959, in Leningrad, in response to the demand for more wedding ceremony, the first "wedding palace" was opened. There was piped music and shops to buy gifts and flowers. After the ceremony photographs could be taken and wine drunk. After perestroika, as in many countries around the world, marriage remains a civil ceremony, but the old Russian ways of celebration have come back.

See also Barring the Way; Cars; Civil Ceremonies; Rings, Wedding and Betrothal; Rough Music/Rough Band

References

Murphy, Brian M. 1978. *The World of Weddings: An Illustrated Celebration.* London: Paddington.

"Russian Wedding Protocol: Parts 1, 2, and 3." Available at *http://www.womenrussia.com/ wedding.htm* (accessed April 2003).

"Uncovering Russia's Past." 3 February 1998. *BBC News Online.*

S

Sameh People

The Sameh people (the Lapps) inhabit an area in the far north of Norway, Sweden, Finland, and Russia where the sun shines at night during the summer and there is almost perpetual darkness during the winter. These nomadic people exist by herding their reindeer and bartering for products. Within this culture, there are few chances to meet a person of the opposite sex, so when a trading meeting takes place, the unmarried are on the lookout for a future spouse. After approaching a girl and finding that the two are of like mind, the young man goes to her parents' abode, makes a steaming hot jug of coffee, and places it in front of them. If they ignore the coffee, he knows that he has been rejected. If, on the other hand, they pour the coffee until it overflows the cup, he knows that he has been accepted. This is a binding engagement and may be marked by the young man giving the girl a ring. The man gives her another ring when the marriage is solemnized, and he may also give her a third ring at the birth of the first male child.

Although most Sameh are strict Lutherans, the wedding may not be blessed by the church for a time (sometimes only after the birth of a couple of children). For the Sameh, the best time for a wedding is Eastertide when their churches are decorated in dazzling colors. The marriage feast itself can last up to about three days, with drinking and the chanting of improvised lyrical poems called *joiks*. The *joiks* at weddings usually tell of the bride and groom, describing their virtues but also unsparingly pointing out their faults and telling of episodes from their life. During the feast, a male relative goes among the guests with a bowl into which they drop money. Some make promises of gifts of reindeer or of a calf. These promises are duly noted and followed up so that the couple may begin their married life with a herd of reindeer. The couple set up their new home either with the bride's mother or in their own tent alongside her mother. The Sameh see the mother as the stabilizing influence and the essence of the family unit.

The costume of both the bride and groom is the traditional Sameh costume, which is influenced by both Scandinavian and Russian designs. But it also subtly shows off their wealth. Gold and silver clasps fasten woolen shawls, and the bride's bodice is adorned with jewelry. The width of the groom's belt, decorated with silver and gold coins, indicates his wealth and status.

Johan Turi, a nineteenth-century traveler, reported that Lapp weddings were arranged through a form of barter and included a payment of a bride-price (Baldizzone 2001). The young man would approach the woman's parents accompanied by a guarantor, who acted for the young man. If the girl came out and unharnessed her suitor's reindeer, that was a sign that she accepted his proposal. There followed negotiations. The young man's guarantor extolled his virtues, and her parents praised her to try to keep the bride-price high. Eventually they would agree to a price.

See also Bride-Price

References

Baldizzone, Tiziana, and Gianni Baldizzone. 2001. *Wedding Ceremonies: Ethnic Symbols, Costume, and Rituals.* Paris: Flammarion.

Murphy, Brian M. 1978. *The World of Weddings: An Illustrated Celebration.* London: Paddington.

Same-Sex Marriage

Authorities in many countries do not recognize gay, or same-sex, marriages, but many same-sex couples are going through ceremonies in which they pledge themselves to each other in a form of marriage. Same-sex marriages are recognized in some European countries and Canada. In Great Britain in 2002, proposals were made for same-sex couples to be able to register their relationships after living together for a minimum period, which would give some of the rights of kinship, inheritance, and other benefits that married couples have. But there is today no recognition of same-sex marriage in Great Britain.

In the United States, there are laws that essentially forbid same-sex marriages. Thirty-seven states have defense of marriage acts, which define marriage as being between a man and a woman. Although there is considerable tolerance of same-sex partnerships and lifestyles, public opinion against same-sex marriage is about 60 percent. But many Americans support a form of civil union for such couples. Couples have, over the years, applied for licenses to marry, and the applications have been turned down on the grounds of "tradition," or because, as in Kentucky, there are laws on the books against sodomy. However, in June 2003, the U.S. Supreme Court struck down the Texas anti-sodomy laws, and this has given gay couples confidence to launch further legal challenges. The state of Massachusetts became the first to legally allow same-sex marriage in May 2004. Earlier in the same year thousands of same-sex couples went through a marriage ceremony in San Francisco, but the marriages were not recognized by the state of California, and a mayor in New York was being prosecuted for conducting a same-sex marriage. The issue is obviously contentious in the United States. The president, George W. Bush, supports an amendment to the Constitution to define marriage exclusively as between one man and one woman. This debate and controversy in the United States had been raging at least since the second half of the twentieth century. In 1968, a Pentecostal minister in Florida, Troy Perry, established the Metropolitan Community Church after being expelled from the Pentecostal church for divorcing his wife and admitting his homosexuality. His church was established for, and run by, gay men and women. Perry and his associates have presided at a number of same-sex weddings. Seligson (1973) gave an account of one of these, a lesbian wedding, which mirrored the usual wedding in most ways, except that all the participants were women (the "father" of the bride, who appeared to be an "elderly, husky man in a tuxedo," for example, was a woman dressed as a man).

In June 2003, the provinces of Ontario and British Columbia, in Canada, legalized same-sex marriages at the same time as the federal government was drafting legislation to allow these marriages throughout the country. Thus, many American gay couples travel to Canada, usually to the Canadian side of Niagara Falls, to get married. They then find themselves in the position of being a legally married couple in Canada but not in their own country. By marrying, same-sex couples wish to make a pledge to each other

Phyllis Lyon, on the left, and Del Martin, who have been together for fifty-one years, embraced after their marriage at City Hall. They were the first legally married same-sex couple in San Francisco. Witnessing the ceremony were, left to right: Kate Kendell, executive director of the National Center for Lesbian Rights; Roberta Achtenberg, senior vice president of the San Francisco Chamber of Commerce; and members of mayor Gavin Newsom's staff, including Steve Kawa, chief of staff, and Joyce Newstat, director of policy. (Liz Mangelsdorf / San Francisco Chronicle / CORBIS)

and in a very symbolic way to normalize their relationship, although this still does not give them the rights of heterosexual married couples in the United States. It is ironic that a high percentage of heterosexual couples during the latter half of the twentieth century are opting to live together without getting married. The gay community seeks to be married and have the marriage and the commitment overseen, sanctioned, and recognized by the government.

Same-sex couples living together as husband and wife is not only a modern phenomenon, although in the past, when homosexuality was illegal in Britain, couples had to resort to subterfuge. In 1776 the *Gentleman's Magazine* wrote about two women who lived together as husband and wife by mutual consent for thirty-six years. They kept a public house in Poplar, London, and it was only on

her deathbed that the wife told her family the secret of her marriage. The article stated that "both had been crossed in love when young, and had chosen this method to avoid further importunities."

See also Civil Ceremonies

References

Chambers, Robert. 1863–1864. *The Book of Days.* Vol. 1. London: Edinburgh: W. and R. Chambers. Philadelphia: J. B. Lippincott.

Dyer, Clare. 2002. "New Legal Rights for Gay Couples." *Guardian,* 7 December, 11.

Seligson, Marcia. 1974. *The Eternal Bliss Machine: The American Way of Wedding.* London: Hutchinson.

Young, Gary. 2004. "Massachusetts Performs First Gay Marriages." *Guardian,* 17 May, 13.

Saucée, la

See France; *Soupe, la*

Scandinavia

Traditional weddings in Finland until the mid-twentieth century showed differences between east and west Finland, although there were many similarities. Like other Scandinavian countries, the Finnish are mainly adherents of the Lutheran church, founded by Martin Luther (1483–1546), an Augustinian friar who led the German Reformation. Much time was spent preparing for weddings and making household things to show off abilities. Ornamented spinning wheels or distaffs, for example, would be made by a prospective bridegroom to give to his bride-to-be. A girl would collect and make the necessary clothing and household items required to set up home, and she was also expected to make many gifts to be distributed at the wedding—socks, belts, ribbons, and gloves. These she kept on display in her bedroom so that prospective bridegrooms could see her handiwork during courtship. In Finland, a courting couple was allowed to spend the night together in her bedchamber, a practice known elsewhere as bundling, usually strictly controlled to deter sexual activity.

Western Finland had influences from Russia, and the wedding was a big social occasion for all in the community that could last for several days, even up to a week. In eastern Finland, the celebrations were confined to members of the family, and guests outside the family group were not invited. The friends of the bride usually organized a *Polterabend* party. They dressed the bride in a special costume and paraded her through the town or village, making a great deal of noise and often collecting money on the way, her last fling before taking on the mantle of a respectable married woman. Sometimes there is an element of subversion about the party. For example, the bride may be dressed as St. Lucia, looking the worse for wear and parading around the town in a parody of the winter procession for the St. Lucia Festival of Light.

A characteristic of Scandinavian weddings is the dressing of the bride with a crown, usual until the late nineteenth century, when the crown began to go out of favor. On her wedding day, the bride would be prepared by a "bride-dresser," who would own and hire out the crown and other jewelry to decorate the bride. The crown was a large, cone-shaped headdress decorated with silver or gilded trinkets (in the south of the country the crown may be crescent-shaped). The woman would wear her best clothes and all her betrothal jewelry; if this did not suffice, she might borrow pieces from her friends or rent pieces from the bride-dresser.

An important part of the preparations was the combing of the bride's hair and the securing of the crown to her head. The crown had to be well secured, because in some places she would have to wear the crown continuously for the several days of the celebrations, even sleeping sitting upright and wearing the crown. In western Finland, the wedding ceremony was often performed underneath a bridal canopy or *pallium,* sometimes referred to as the "bridal heaven," a silk cloth fixed to the ceiling of the room or a cloth supported by the bridesmaids and groomsmen. At the celebrations it was often the custom to "dance" the crown off the bride's head, i.e., when the crown was removed, the bride's head was covered with a linen or silk cap or a scarf. All married women in Finland covered their heads—only unmarried women were allowed to go out with their heads uncovered.

Marriage in Norway begins with the betrothal, which may take place months, or even years, before the marriage ceremony. At this formal event, the two stand before the clergyman in front of the congregation and are asked whether, in the presence of God and the witnesses, they desire to be betrothed to one another. After answering, they exchange rings—plain gold bands that are worn on the ring finger of the left hand. The two then exchange presents. The man presents a psalmbook, jewelry, or clothes; the woman gives her future husband clothes that he will wear on the wedding day.

A Norwegian wedding procession from the late nineteenth century. (Illustration from Richard Lovett's Norwegian Pictures, *published by the Religious Tract Society, London, 1885.)*

The wedding usually takes place on a Sunday. On the wedding day, the bride and bridegroom lead a procession of their friends to the church, either on foot or on horseback. In some cases the journey to the church could be by boat, which is decorated for the occasion, and on some occasions, guns are fired from the boats to celebrate the event. The procession is usually led by a fiddle player, who may be accompanied by other musicians. In the church the priest addresses the couple and asks each in turn if he or she will take the other as husband or wife, to which they reply in the affirmative, with a bow of the head. The two then kneel with joined hands, and the priest announces that they are married; the service finishes with the priest pronouncing a benediction and giving the sign of the cross. They move their rings from the left hand to the right. The festivities, which may take place at the best restaurant in the town, usually last at least three days, with eating, drinking, and dancing. Guests, and even the bridal couple, may have traveled a long distance for the wedding. The party might have been brought over a fjord to the church (with the bride wearing her crown and a fiddler playing in the bows of the boat).

In some districts, during the dancing, the bride takes part in "dancing off her crown." For this she is blindfolded and stands in the middle of a ring formed by the unmarried girls. She takes off her crown and places it on the head of the nearest girl she can reach. This girl is thus the next to be betrothed. She then takes the bride's place in the ring, and the dance continues, with her placing the crown on another's head, until the crown has been passed around the party. The bride then toasts all the unmarried girls, wishing them a speedy betrothal, and joins the married women. The bridegroom, meanwhile, has danced with all the unmarried men, bidding them farewell. He is then hoisted onto their shoulders. There follows a mock fight staged for him, between the bachelors and the married men. Eventually the Lutheran priest leads the wife, and then the husband, to the bridal chamber, where he delivers a sermon suitable for the occasion. The guests at the door give the couple good wishes, the groom gives each man a glass of brandy, and the bride gives each woman a glass of wine.

The bride usually wears the traditional dress, the *bunad,* an outfit usually presented to her upon her confirmation at around age fifteen. Each region has its own distinctive style, but generally the outfit comprises a long woolen skirt, an apron, a linen shirt, a cap, a waistcoat, and sometimes a shawl. A matching purse may also be included. The outfit is heavily embroidered with traditional regional designs and is embellished with silver brooches or silver squares on a leather belt. The bride often wears a bridal crown made from beaten silver, which may be brassed to imitate gold, approximately four to eight inches high. Her hair is worn loose, and sometimes long ribbons hang down her back, under the crown but over the hair. Crowns are sometimes family heirlooms. In some districts it was common to have communal crowns that would be lent to the brides. The groom may also wear richly embroidered national dress.

In Sweden, a marriage is first and foremost a civil event, so that a couple wishing to marry have to apply to the parish authorities, who will issue a certificate showing that there is nothing to prevent the marriage (the *hindersprövning*), after which they may opt for a Church of Sweden wedding or may apply to the district court where a registrar will follow a form of service, with vows exchanged and a marriage license issued.

> **See also** Betrothal; Bundling; Crowns; Dress, Wedding; *Polterabend* Party; Sameh People; Tokens
> **References**
> Braddock, Joseph. 1961. *The Bridal Bed.* New York: John Day.
> Lovett, Richard. 1885. *Norwegian Pictures.* London: Religious Tract Society.
> Sihvo, Pirkko. 1975. "Finland." In *Love and Marriage: Aspects of Popular Culture in Europe [exhibition], Antwerpen,* edited by W. Van Nespen. Brussels: Ministerie van Nederlanse Cultuur en Nationale Opvoeding.
> Virtanen, Timo J. 1994. "Public Customs and Family Traditions." In *Everyday Life and Ethnicity: Urban Families in Loviisa and Võru, 1988–1991,* edited by Anna Kirveennummi, Matti Räsänen, and Timo J. Virtanen. Helsinki: Studia Fennica Ethnologica 2.

Shift, Marrying in a

It was once commonly believed in England that if the woman went to the altar partly, or "entirely, divested of clothing," or wearing only a shift, or *en chemisette,* her husband would not be liable for her debts. When a man married a woman he acquired an interest in her estate and also her debts. If she, therefore, went to him without any estate or possessions he would not have any responsibility for her debts. An account from the parish register of Much Wenlock, Shrop-

shire, England, for 1547 notes: "Here was wedded Thomas M. Smith and Alice Nycols, which wedded to him in her Smock and bareheaded." Another account, from Saddleworth, Derbyshire, England, from 1774, recounts how the bridegroom, a widower, aged about thirty, married a widow, aged nearly seventy, who was slightly in debt. He made her get married wearing only her shift. As this was in February the weather was very cold. The bride began to shake and shiver uncontrollably, and the minister covered her with his coat.

> **See also** Dress, Wedding
> **References**
> Chambers, Robert. 1863–1864. *The Book of Days.* Vol. 1. Edinburgh: W. and R. Chambers. Philadelphia: J. B. Lippincott.
> Cox, Charles J. 1910. *The Parish Registers of England.* London: Methuen.

Shoes

Brides in the West are often given lucky charms to carry with their bouquets. These may include foil-covered cardboard horseshoes, black cat toys, and foil-covered shoe shapes. (Horseshoe and shoe shapes are also found in "lucky charm" confetti.) Shoes and old boots are often attached to the bumper of the newlyweds' car when they depart for their honeymoon, and in earlier times the couple would depart for their "wedding tour" with a shower of old shoes or satin slippers thrown after them. By the late-nineteenth century, this practice was well established in the United States, and there was a belief that if a shoe or slipper landed on top of the wedding carriage the couple would be sure to have good luck. At the wedding of Alice Lee Roosevelt in 1906 a slipper was put on top of the departing car for good luck.

The inclusion of the shoe in weddings is often said to derive from Anglo-Saxon times when, it is said, the bride's father would pass one of the bride's shoes to the groom who would then tap her on the head with it. This is sometimes interpreted as a transfer of authority over the woman from the father to her new husband. However, there was probably more equality between the sexes in Anglo-Saxon society (with, for example, women being able to own land in their own right). But many writers suggest that the shoe was a symbol of authority, citing passages from the Bible, such as Ruth 4.7: "Now this was the custom in former times in Israel concerning redeeming and exchanging: to confirm a transaction, the one drew off his sandal and gave it to the other, and this was the manner of attesting in Israel." But in Deuteronomy 25.9, in the ceremony whereby a widow is rejected by her husband's brother in marriage, she publicly loosens his shoe from his foot and spits in his face. In the Middle East, to hit a person, or his or her image, with a shoe is considered a high insult and implies that the person is less than the dust beneath the hitter's feet.

Ditchfield (1896), after stating that the throwing of old shoes after the couple was symbolic of the transference of authority, noted a custom from Kent where the shoe was thrown by the principal bridesmaid, and others ran after it. The girl who got the shoe would be married first. Her shoe was then thrown at the men—the one hit by the shoe would be the first among them to be wed. Similarly, in Germany after the couple had retired to the bridal chamber, the tradition was to throw one of the bride's shoes among the guests for them to scramble for it. If it was caught by a single person, he or she would soon be married. A Greek tradition is to write the names of the unmarried women on the soles of the bride's shoes; those whose names were erased from the shoe by the end of the day, after all the dancing, would be married soon. It was expected in a household with several daughters that they would be married in order. If a younger daughter married before her elder sister, the latter might try to change her luck by serving at her sister's wedding without shoes. Crombie (1895), writing about shoe-throwing at weddings, noted that in many traditions the generally accepted gift of the bridegroom to the bride or to her relatives was a pair of shoes.

We find traditions of shoe-throwing to bring good luck in many places in the British Isles. In *Great Expectations,* by Charles Dickens (published in 1861), when the hero, Pip, leaves his home to go to London he says: "The last I saw of them was, when I presently heard a scuffle behind me, and looking back, saw Joe throwing an old shoe after me, and Biddy throwing another old shoe." In Ireland, an old shoe would be thrown after someone going to a fair to bring luck. In the Isles of Man, an old shoe would be thrown after the bride as she left home, and one would be thrown after the groom as he left home to go to the church. If, on the way back from the church, one of the spectators or guests removed one of the bride's shoes, the bridegroom would have to pay a ransom. Tegg (1877) described how a newlywed pair would have to pass through a double file of friends and domestics, each of whom carried a slipper. As they departed, the slippers were flung after the carriage for good luck.

Hone (1841) gave an account of a custom known as "trashing." This involved old shoes being thrown at a bridal couple who had not contributed to the local scholars' convivialities. Hone noted that this was later carried out indiscriminately as a piece of fun, sometimes with turf or clumps of mud substituted for shoes. Similarly, in the Orkney Islands, where the custom was for the bridegroom to donate a football (or the money for a football) to the children of the bride's parish, if the ball or the money was not forthcoming, the children would demand their "ba' money." If it was not paid, the people of the bride's parish would take the bride's shoe.

The question of why shoes are used as a symbol of good luck is unclear. The transference of authority theory is tenuous and is usually based on an interpretation of the biblical passages. However, these, notably the passage from Ruth 4.7, suggest that the shoe may be symbolic of a confirmation of a transaction or event, and, indeed, an essential part of the Anglo-Saxon wedding, especially among the landed classes, was the transaction of the dowry. It may, therefore, simply be that the spectators at a wedding threw old shoes after the wedding couple (or today tie old boots and shoes to the car bumper in a continuation of the tradition) as an unconscious confirmation of the wedding with the conscious act of wishing the couple good luck.

But it is not just in Christian tradition that shoes play a role in the event. At a Punjabi wedding, when the groom begins the ceremony by chanting some mantras, the bride's female friends will try to take his shoes for him to buy back after the ceremony. During the evening at a Bangladeshi wedding, a group of the bride's friends try to steal the bridegroom's shoes while a similar number of the groom's friends try to stop them. Once taken, the shoes are sold back to him, with a certain amount of ritual haggling. (A spare pair of shoes may have been taken along for the bridegroom to give him and his party a bargaining tool.) Similarly, at an Indian Muslim wedding, at specified times during the celebratory meal, the groom has to haggle with the bride's sisters for a glass of milk and for his shoes, which they had earlier stolen from him. At a Russian wedding celebration, the friends of the bride and groom will "capture" the bride's shoes, for which the groom has to pay a ransom.

There are also beliefs that the spirit or life essence of a person can linger within their shoes. A Chinese tradition was that if a betrothed girl died before her wedding her betrothed would go to her parents' house and ask for her shoes. These he would take to his home, stopping at street corners to call upon her to follow. On arriving at his home, her spirit was informed of the fact, and the shoes were placed either on or under a chair at a table. Incense was burned on the table, and a tablet placed in her memory among the family ancestral tablets. Everything was done as if she were present and wearing the shoes. It is considered by some that the idea that a life essence can be contained within an old shoe may contribute to the belief that an old shoe will bring luck.

See also Ba'siller; Cars; Dancing in a Hog (Pig) Trough; Dowry; Russian Weddings; Stockings, Throwing of

References
Crombie, James E. 1895. "Shoe Throwing at Weddings." *Folklore* 6, no. 3: 258–281.
Ditchfield, P. H. 1896. *Old English Customs.* London: Methuen.
Hone, William. 1841. *The Table Book.* London: Thomas Tegg.
Jeaffreson, John Cordy. 1872. *Brides and Bridals.* 2 vols. London: Hurst and Blackett.
Monsarrat, Ann. 1973. *And the Bride Wore . . . : The Story of the White Wedding.* London: Gentry.
Tegg, William. 1877. *The Knot Tied: Marriage Customs of All Nations.* London: William Tegg.

Shower

The wedding shower, a tradition in North America, is a party for the bride's female friends and female relatives to which the guests bring gifts for the bride, usually ones for the home or items of lingerie. The shower gift is often considered secondary to the wedding present. The shower is known in Britain mainly as a custom from the United States. These events are reminiscent of the Welsh tradition of bidding and other, sometimes localized, events at which the community contributes household goods to the couple to help them in setting up their home, found in many parts of Britain.

Sometimes the shower includes a "money tree," a gilded branch upon which the guests hang bags of money or clip dollar bills. In New Zealand, five showers were held for a vicar by his five parishes in the 1980s, so that each could help the couple set up home (Monger 1996). (In New Zealand, parishes individually pay for their clergy.) In Trinidad, the shower is thought to have originated in the mid-1940s and is an event organized by the bride's girl-friends a few days before the wedding. The bride-to-be is invited for a final drink as a single woman. An umbrella or garden shade is decorated with gifts, which may include money, for the new household. After some speeches and teasing, there is calypso dancing and traditional foods—rice, peas, fried chicken—and alcohol. Trinidadian women drink very moderately, but at this party the bride-to-be can become quite intoxicated.

A Canadian version is the community shower, a late twentieth-century innovation that is usually arranged by a family member or friend and is open to both men and women. The community is invited via an advertisement in the local newspaper, and a collection is made before the event for presentations during the evening. On the evening, a further collection is made, and guests are asked to put money or a favorite recipe into an envelope, which is then pinned to a tree branch or hung by a ribbon from a light fixture. Tickets are also sold for the drinks, the proceeds of which go to the couple. During the event there may be a mock marriage, speeches, and "folk-poetry," referring to the couple.

Eichler (1924, 195) suggested that the shower originated in Holland where, so the story goes, a pretty young girl wanted to marry an impoverished miller. Her father forbade the marriage and told her that if she insisted on marrying the young man she would not be given the dowry he had set aside for her. However, the miller's neighbors, to whom he had given good service, heard about this and were sorry about it. They did not have money to provide her with a replacement dowry so they decided to contribute gifts to help furnish their home, coming to the young woman in procession to give her their gifts. Some years later an Englishwoman wished to give a marriage gift to a good friend about to be married but thought that what she could give was too slight to express her feelings for her friend. She remembered the story of the Dutch girl. She therefore found a number of friends in a similar predicament and suggested that they all come together and present their gifts at the same time. The "shower" was successful and caused a great deal of favorable comment in fashionable cir-

cles, and "it became definitely established as a social custom, and has remained ever since."

See also Bidding; Presents

References
Eichler, Lillian. 1924. *The Customs of Mankind.* London: William Heinemann.
Greenhill, Pauline. 1985. "Contemporary Folk Poetry in Southern Ontario." Ph.D. thesis, University of Texas, Austin, 112–122.
Monger, George. 1996. "Pre-Marriage Ceremonies: A Study of Custom and Function." *Lore and Language* 14: 143–155.
Monsarrat, Ann. 1973. *And the Bride Wore . . . : The Story of the White Wedding.* London: Gentry.

Sigheh
See Temporary Marriage

Sikh Weddings

In Sikhism, the major religion of northern India, marriage is seen as not only the joining of two families but also as a merging of two souls. In Sikh philosophy the goal is to be able to merge one's soul *(atma)* with God *(Parmatma),* and in marriage, in the merging of the souls, the couple should assist each other to achieve that goal. The wedding ceremonies can be officiated by any Amritdhari Sikh, that is a man or woman who has been initiated into the Amrit tradition and who follows the Sikh code in daily life. The essential premarriage ceremony begins with the formal betrothal, the *shagan,* which may be held at either the groom's family home or at the Sikh temple, *gurdwara.* At this ceremony the families exchange gifts and make the formal agreement to the marriage—no dowry agreement is made, unlike marriages in many Hindu or Islamic cultures, because Sikh tradition condemns dowry payments and teaches that the bride's father should only offer his daughter in the wedding agreement. The bride and groom may exchange rings. The ceremonies begin three days before the wedding day with the *akhand paath,* a three-day reading of the *Sri Guru Granth Sahib* (the holy book). During this period, the bride and

The ritual of mania *at a Sikh wedding, in which the bride is fed sweets on the night before her wedding. Also, the ritual of* mehndi *on the night before a Sikh wedding, in which a bowl of haldi and turmeric is used to purify the skin. (Sheldan Collins/CORBIS)*

groom undergo the *myah* ritual—they are cleansed every morning and evening by their respective families by having their hands, feet, and faces massaged with flour, tamarind powder, and oil to purify them in preparation for their new lives.

The night before the wedding both the bride and groom have their hands and feet decorated with *mehndi,* a paste of henna, lemon juice, oil, and water in which tea leaves had been steeped. The paste is said to indicate the strength of the love between the couple—the darker the *mehndi,* the stronger the bond of love. After the bride has had the *mehndi* applied to her hands and feet, she is adorned with twenty-one red and cream ivory bracelets at the *chooda* ceremony; ornaments, called *kalira,* are attached to the bracelets by her maternal aunt and uncle. These ornaments make it impossible for her to carry out any housework. The woman wears these bracelets throughout the wed-

ding ceremony and for forty days after. This allows her time to settle into her new household after the marriage.

The wedding itself usually takes place in the morning. The couple are finally prepared, and in the *nath* ritual, the bride's uncle will fit a traditional nose ring to her. The groom's costume must conform to five elements of Sikh traditional dress—the *kangha* (comb), *kesh* (uncut hair), *kaccha* (shorts), *kara* (bracelet), and *kirpan* (saber). On the wedding day hymns are sung at the *gurdwara* (temple) before the wedding parties arrive, and, as the groom and both families arrive, hymns specifically for them are sung. When both the wedding parties have arrived (but not the bride), the families exchange gifts. In doing so, they are accepting each other as being joined by the marriage. This ceremony, called the *milnee* (or *milni*), is accompanied by hymns from the holy book. After this preliminary, the wedding ceremony, *anand karaj* (ceremony of bliss), begins with the *kirtan,* which involves the musicians, the *ragis,* singing hymns. Then either both the bride and groom, who have been sitting with the congregation, are invited to sit before the *Gru Ganth Sahib,* the holy book, or the groom first sits in front of the book and the bride is led up to him, escorted by her mother and best friend. In either case, the bride finishes by sitting at her groom's left before the holy book. The officiant usually then presents a homily to explain the Sikh view of marriage, the spiritual importance of the union, and the obligations as husband and wife.

The couple and their parents now stand for prayers asking for God's blessing on the marriage before the most significant event of the ceremony begins—the *palaa* ceremony. A pink- or saffron-colored shawl is folded lengthwise, and one end is placed over the groom's shoulder and into his hands. The other end is given to the bride as the *ragis* sing a prayer called the *shabad palai.* The shawl represents a physical bond that is symbolic of the spiritual link between the couple. The couple then stand and a series of four prayers is read by the officiating priest and sung by the *ragis.* These prayers are called the *laavan* ("breakaway"—at the marriage, the bride is breaking away from her family). The first prayer is spoken (and translated if necessary) and then sung by the *ragis* as the couple walk clockwise around the *Gru Ganth Sahib,* joined by the *palaa,* the groom leading the bride. They finish the circuit as the *ragis* finish singing the prayer. They bow to the holy book, and then sit waiting for the next prayer. Each time the couple walk a circuit of the holy book. After the *laavan,* the couple are showered with flower petals by the congregation, and the priest closes the ceremony with a few words and pronounces the couple man and wife. Their first act of marriage is to feed each other with fruit. A song of bliss is sung and "blessed food" *(gurupahad)* is distributed to the congregation.

See also Confetti; India
References
Gurmukh, Singh. "Sikh Marriage." Available at *http://www.bbc.co.uk/religion/religions/sikhism/features/rites/weddings2.shtml* (accessed 1 June 2004).
"The Sikh Wedding Ceremony." Available at *http://www.clickwalla.com/listing.asp?sectionId= 322* (accessed 1 June 2004).

Slave Weddings

Slaves on the plantations of the South in the United States and in the West Indies were discouraged from forming any stable family groupings and from getting married. But plantation owners and militia took female slaves as mistresses (the offspring became the property of the slave master) and some married slave women. Captain John Stedman, who served in the Scots' Brigade in Dutch Guiana (now Suriname), in South America, in 1772, married a young woman who was the daughter of a slave woman and a "respectable gentleman." When he returned to Holland, he had to leave her behind as she was still a slave and he could not afford to buy her freedom. Their son, however, went to Holland with Stedman.

In the American South, slaves were encouraged to have children, who became slaves for the owners. If they were sold, their fecundity was a selling point. The marriage of slaves was allowed, but these marriages had no legal status and the events were viewed as a pleasant diversion by the white slave owners. There were descriptions of the weddings in the diaries of white women, sometimes described as humorous. But for the participants these were solemn affairs. Scriptures were read and pledges were made. Slaves were discouraged from following their tribal religions and many embraced Christianity and sought the sanction of their adopted religion. There were stories of devoted slave couples working extra hours to be able to buy themselves out of slavery so that they could work to free their loved ones. The white family was often deeply involved in the wedding arrangements and often officiated at the wedding, especially if the slaves were house servants. The wedding of house servants was sometimes performed in the owner's house and officiated at by a white minister. The owner's wife might lend clothes or materials to make the wedding dress. Sometimes the owner would provide the wedding reception feast and a wedding cake. Or a black spiritual leader might be asked to officiate. It was not unknown for the plantation owner to marry the couple, usually after supper, at his house, with very little ceremony, asking them simply to hold hands as he read passages from the Bible and then declaring them married (and to be ready for work in the morning). The identity and profession of the officiating officer was actually of little importance since the marriage had no standing in law.

The marriage of slaves from different plantations was discouraged but not unknown. Some plantation owners did try to buy the intended spouse from the other plantation or tried to sell his slave to the other plantation. If this could not be arranged, some owners gave time for conjugal visits. However, there was no guarantee that the couple would remain on adjoining plantations. There is the case of a couple from different plantations getting married; the man was allowed to visit his wife on Wednesdays and Saturdays. When he visited on a Saturday, she had been sold, and he never learned where she had gone.

Slave owners did not allow the slaves to practice their tribal religions and many embraced Christianity, but the solemnity of their beliefs and wish for proper Christian marriage was not treated seriously. Marriages that did take place had no legal basis and the couple could be separated at the whim of the plantation owner. In both Jamaica and the United States, this established a social ethos that was seen as immoral, promiscuous, and irresponsible by the white population, but it is a social milieu that the system of slavery promoted and established.

Attempts by the slaves to form family units within the Christian accepted norm were not treated seriously by the authorities.

See also Jamaica

References
Oliver, Paul. 1990. *Blues Fell This Morning.* 2d ed. Cambridge: Cambridge University Press.
Sides, Sudie Duncan. 1974. "Slave Weddings and Religion." *History Today* 24, no. 2: 77–87.
Thompson, Stanbury, ed. 1962. *The Journal of John Gabriel Stedman, 1744–1797.* London: Mitre.

Soupe, la

La soupe (la saucée, saucya, or *la rôtie)* is a French marriage custom that begins after the main reception, during which much wine has been drunk, as the newlywed couple try to leave. The young people at the reception try to keep the couple as long as possible. After the couple manage to escape from the group, the guests prepare a mixture in a chamber pot known as *la soupe.* The mixture includes leftovers from the meal—champagne, cake, biscuits, wine, cheese, and vegetables. The group then searches for the couple and makes them eat some of the mixture.

A description of this practice from Orleans in France says that the guests mixed wine, cake, chocolate, and other things in a large bowl; the guests then went to the bride and groom's room at about four in the morning and presented them with this concoction, which the couple was supposed to consume with some show of enjoyment. In the case described, the couple declined.

This raucous event seems similar to a much earlier practice found in England, especially during the Catholic periods, and in many parts of Europe, especially among the gentry class. The bridal bed was blessed by the priest and the guests accompanied the bridal couple to bed. Once the couple was in bed, the priest blessed a cup of sweetened and spiced wine, known as the benediction posset, which in the seventeenth century was described as made from milk, wine, egg yolk, sugar, cinnamon, and nutmeg, which all the company drank. When this was finished, the company left the couple. But the guests often continued to play tricks on the couple or sing bawdy songs outside the bedchamber door.

See also Bed, Marriage; Chamber Pot; Posset

References
Buisson, Giles. 1984. "Une veille coutume nuptiale: La rôtie." In *Du berceau à la tombe: les rites de passage,* edited by Françoise Lamotte. Paris: Revue du Département de la Manche, Tome 26.
Furnborough, Peter, and Elizabeth Atkins. 1973. "Traditions and Language in Orleans and the Vale de Loire." *Lore and Language* 1, no. 9: 16–19.
Van Gennep, Arnold. 1932. *Folklore du Dauphiné.* Vol. 1. Paris: Librairie orientale et américaine.

South America

The Spanish settlers and governors imposed their culture and religion onto the South American populations. Thus, the countries of South America are mostly Roman Catholic and follow church practices in marriage. Many of these practices are similar to those found in contemporary Europe. In some countries, such as Peru, marriage is a civil ceremony that may be followed by a Roman Catholic service.

Argentinean weddings, too, follow the European model. Until around the early twentieth century, in Argentina, there was little, if any, free association of the sexes; a girl saw little of life outside the walls of the home or of the convent schools. Even after marriage most women remained in some degree of seclusion. In Argentina, the bride will usually wear a white wedding dress with a blue petticoat beneath, the latter representing the "something blue" that a bride should wear. But it is not usual for the couple to have a best man and bridesmaids; their parents fulfill this role at the ceremony. It is common for the grandmother of a girl about to be married to give her a ring for the wedding; this ring would have been given to her by her grandmother on the day of her wedding. The ring is handed down in the family from generation to generation and is supposed to

bring love and happiness. If she loses the wedding ring, superstition says that this presages the end of her marriage—she must ensure that she never loses this ring.

In Brazil, European and U.S. traditions are observed, such as the superstition that the groom should not see his bride in her wedding dress before the wedding and that the bride should wear "something old, something new, something borrowed, something blue." The rings are usually engraved with the couple's names—the bride's ring has the groom's name and the groom's ring, the bride's.

In Colombia, the bride's dress usually has touches of gold in the white and the dress is the focus for a divination—each bachelor puts a shoe under the bride's dress; the groom picks one of the shoes and the owner will be the next to be married. The wedding cake is placed in the middle of the dance floor and is usually the first thing to be eaten at the reception. In Chile, it is usual for the couple to wear their wedding rings before the ceremony, but on their right hands. The rings are changed to the left hands during the ceremony.

The governor of an area in ancient Peru would, every year or every two years, arrange for the marriage of all the young men, aged twenty-four and older, and all the young women from eighteen to twenty years of age. Apparently, the young men and women formed a circle around the governor, who called them by name, in turn, presenting them to each other and obtaining a promise from them of mutual fidelity, whereupon they would be expected to marry. However, Westermarck (1894) wrote that this practice was performed by the king for the marriageable men and women from among his own family, and that the governors of the provinces had to follow suit. He cited this practice as being an example of an old non-European form of civil marriage.

Among the Inca, by law, a son should obey and serve his father until the age of twenty-five and not marry without his parents' consent.

The consent of the girl's parents was also essential—without this consent the marriage would be declared invalid and any children considered illegitimate (it would be the rare and brave parent who would object to the choice made by the king or his representative).

Today in Peru, couples choose marriage partners and meet through social events. Before the wedding the bride and groom have a bachelor party, separately or together. Although Peru is a Catholic country, the wedding is a civil ceremony. As in many countries where the officially recognized wedding event takes place before a registrar, many couples follow the civil ceremony with a religious service. The woman wears a white dress, and the man a tuxedo or suit. The marriage is followed by a wedding reception attended by the family and friends, usually paid for by the bride's parents, although it is becoming more common for the couple to pay for the reception themselves. After the reception the couple go away for their wedding night and a honeymoon.

See also Christian Weddings; Civil Ceremonies; Dress, Wedding; Honeymoon; Mexico; Rings, Wedding and Betrothal; Spain

References

Murphy, Brian M. 1978. *The World of Weddings: An Illustrated Celebration*. London: Paddington.

Westermarck, Edward. 1894. *The History of Human Marriage*. 2d ed. London: Macmillan.

Information available at *http://www.world-weddings.net/south_america* (accessed 1 June 2004).

Personal communication, Giovanna Salni. Peruvian Embassy, London, 22 April 2003.

Spain

Courtship and marriage traditions in Spain have changed markedly over the years. During the twentieth century, the formality of and the regional differences in courtship, engagement, and wedding ritual began to disappear, although in some places there are still remnants of the old ways. Contemporary courtship has little of the formality of the past. A couple today may meet as work col-

leagues or socially, spend time getting acquainted, and then inform their parents that they are going to be married. Although most couples get married in a church, the actual marriage is a civil event, and it is not unusual for the registrar to attend the church wedding to ensure that the couple sign the civil marriage contract. (Some couples opt for just a civil ceremony.)

Some of the "old ways" presented some danger. In Ibiza, for example, a man would shoot at a spot near his favored girl's feet with a gun, and in Valencia he would put a bullet into the ceiling, firing through a window. Slightly less dangerous methods of a man expressing his interest in a girl were to let off fireworks or, in Levant, painting a wall of the house. In Extremadura, a stick would be thrown onto the house porch or the girl would be given a neckerchief. Somewhat more subtly, a young man might follow the young woman who interested him or loiter near her home. To indicate that she reciprocated that interest she would make an appearance on the balcony of the house. Courting couples had to sneak time alone to get to know each other—talking at night through the lattice work of the window in the Andalusian region, meeting in the orchards in Levant, meeting under the porch in northern Spain or as the man stood on a small portable ladder at the window. The couple wrapped themselves in a blanket to keep warm in La Mancha. In Andalusia, the couple talked through the "cat-flap" in the gate, an opening to allow the household pets to get in and out. The couple would lie on the ground (on mats) and talk to each other through the hole.

Traditionally, once a couple became engaged—the young man's parents approached the young woman's parents to officially propose—there would be an exchange of presents, such as a decorated, carved wooden distaff given by the young man to the woman or a decorated wooden spoon or an ornamented chest for baby clothes. She would give him a present of an embroidered shirt or other items of clothing that she had made and embroidered. Meanwhile there would also have been negotiations between the parents regarding each family's contribution to the new household. These agreements would generally have been verbal, though in Catalonia and Aragon there would be a written agreement. The written and the verbal agreements had the same standing.

Some people still have a party on the eve of the wedding at which the couple, with their parents, receive presents and money for the new household. In the past, the marriage gifts would have been made and embroidered by the givers. Today it is common, even in the smallest villages, to place a "marriage-list" in one of the shops for people to choose from. The bride's party and the groom's party might go in procession to the church, sometimes processing separately and sometimes meeting at the bride's home. In Catalonia, the road may be barred with ribbons stretched across the way to block the path of the bridal procession. Once the bridegroom has paid for the party to pass the blockade, the ribbon is cut and the bride pins the ribbon to her wedding dress. There are several Spanish traditions that force the bridegroom to pay money to the community; in Santander, the unmarried young men would abduct the bride before the wedding so that the groom had to pay a ransom to get her back.

The solemnization of the wedding was, and is, followed by a wedding feast. In La Mancha, it was usual for the men of the family to wear aprons and serve the meat to the company. On the Canary Islands, the "pot with seven meats" was usual—chicken, rabbit, pork, pigeon, lamb, beef, and partridge. During the feast there were traditional dances and tricks played on the couple. In Catalonia, the bride's shoe is stolen and the groom has to negotiate a price for its return. Many of the pranks are focused on the wedding night. Little bells are hung on the mattress or the bed is unscrewed so that it may collapse. The couple may be serenaded under the bedroom window. In some areas a couple may depart for their wedding night as soon as they had been married (in Levant it was not unusual for the couple to elope). In the matriarchal areas of Galicia, couples would keep the wedding day secret, perhaps being married at night with little fanfare and no wedding feast. However, the young people of the area would go to great lengths to find out the date and would serenade the couple with "rough music" until they threw money to the serenaders so that they could go and drink the health of the bride and groom. The Galician marriage system is known as a "visiting marriage"—the couple do not live together after marriage but come together clandestinely. During the latter part of the twentieth century, the white wedding and extensive wedding feasts became increasingly popular.

See also Barring the Way; Bed, Marriage; Courtship; Rough Music/Rough Band; Shoes

References

Escudero, Maria Luisa Herrera. 1975. "Spain." In *Love and Marriage: Aspects of Popular Culture in Europe [exhibition], Antwerpen,* edited by W. Van Nespen. Brussels: Ministerie van Nederlanse Cultuur en Nationale Opvoeding.

Rey-Henningsen, Marisa. 1994. *The World of the Ploughwoman: Folklore and Reality in Matriarchal Northwest Spain.* Helsinki: Academia Scientiarum Fennica.

Spousal

The word "spousal" has lost its original meaning and significance over the years and has come to mean the marriage. "Spouse" now signifies a marriage partner. But originally "to espouse" meant to make a contract for an immediate or future marriage, and the term "spouse" signified a person promised in marriage, not one's marriage partner as in contemporary usage. Properly, the term *sponsus* should be used for the male partner and *sponsa* for the female partner. The spousal or espousal constituted the main part of the marriage contract, to be ratified on the wedding day, and by the sixteenth century it came to have several meanings, depending on the context. The definitive treatise on spousals, written in the seventeenth century by Henry Swinburne, was the *Treatise of Spousals or Matrimonial Contracts.* Swinburne explained that the church distinguished between two types of espousal, differentiated by the form of words used in the espousal agreement. If the vow was of the form "I *do* take thee for my husband," then the espousal was considered *de præsenti* and was an indissoluble contract and tantamount to being married—and in the strictest sense could only be broken by death. One of the church reforms introduced by King Henry VIII was the ending of the *de præsenti* espousals. The other form of espousal, *de futuro,* depended on the couple using the words "I *will* take thee," indicating a promise for the future. Although binding, it was possible to break this contract, by mutual agreement or if one of the party did not fulfill the promises or conditions contained in the original promise, such as the failure to wed or perform the marriage ceremony at a particular time or within a specified time frame. Similarly, if one of the couple was found guilty of heresy, apostasy, or infidelity, the contract could be null and void. Disfigurement of one of the couple was also a cause for nullification, as was prolonged absence or another "just and reasonable cause," which could allow the ending of the espousal by one of the couple, without the consent of the other, or by judicial decree of an ecclesiastical judge.

Entering into a *de futuro* contract placed the couple into a marital no-man's-land—neither married nor single. If the couple then consummated the relationship, which implied consent in the present, they would be considered married, the contract could not be broken, and was legally binding for life. Children conceived or born during the period between espousal and the wedding were considered legitimate. A woman was unable to enter into betrothal or marriage with another while espoused *de futuro.* But she and her partner could be liberated from the contract by mutual consent, which would free them to enter

into another contract. If the couple broke the spousal contract, the man was liable to return all the gifts given to him by his *sponsa;* if the agreement had been sealed with a kiss, the woman was allowed to keep half the presents he had given her; otherwise, she would have to return all the presents. One of the usual presents to the *sponsa* was a ring that she wore on her right hand, which would be transferred to her left (or another ring given) at the subsequent marriage. The wearing of the "engagement" ring on the right hand continued into the nineteenth century.

It was not uncommon for young children to be espoused—the final wedding could not take place until the boy was fourteen and the girl twelve. These arrangements could be undone since, by definition, they were *espousals de futuro,* but one of the basic tenets of wedding agreements has been that of consent of both parties, and young children could not be considered to have given their informed consent, which sometimes caused a great deal of controversy.

As spousals could take place either in public or in private, the exchange of gifts and sometimes the wearing of a ring or other token, such as a coin, was the outward manifestation of the agreement, as was the giving of gifts and love tokens. Carved, engraved, or otherwise decorated knitting sticks, lacemaking bobbins, fair prizes, handkerchiefs, and other small gifts were given to seal the agreement. The fact that espousals could be made in private and the complex laws concerning espousals led to a great deal of litigation. Macfarlane (1986) gives some examples from ecclesiastical depositions, such as a case in 1576 in which an Essex woman swore that the "gifts" of a silver ring and a silver whistle that it was said she gave the man were actually taken from her by force and trickery. Consequently there was no agreement to marry.

See also Betrothal; Engagement; Handfasting
References
Jeaffreson, John Cordy. 1872. *Brides and Bridals.* 2 vols. London: Hurst and Blackett.

Macfarlane, Alan. 1986. *Marriage and Love in England, 1300–1840.* Oxford: Basil Blackwell.

Stone, Lawrence. 1990. *The Family, Sex, and Marriage in England, 1500–1800.* Abridged and revised ed. London: Penguin.

Swinburne, Henry. 1686. *Treatise of Spousals or Matrimonial Contracts.* London: N.p.

Stafell

Stafell was a custom in Wales, found in Carmarthenshire and Breckonshire, for the taking of the bride's goods to the new home and came to be associated with the giving of gifts for the home and referred to the bride's "bottom drawer." The word *stafell* means "room" but came to mean the goods and chattels that the bride took with her to set up the home. This custom was sometimes called "bringing home the *stafell*" or, in Cardiganshire, Wales, "setting forth the marriage chamber," which happened a day or two before the wedding. The *stafell* seems to have combined two events into one. The first was the preparation of cakes, bread, and cheese for the marriage feast, and the second was the furnishing of the marital home, which involved moving the bride or sometimes the bridegroom's furniture. Hone (1827, 792) gives a description of the *stafell* (which he called *starald*) from the eighteenth century:

> When a farmers daughter, or some young woman, with a fortune of from one hundred to two hundred pounds, marries, it is generally very privately, and she returns to her father's house for a few weeks, where her friends and neighbours go to see her, but none go empty-handed. When the appointed time arrives for the young man to take home his wife, the elderly women are invited to attend the *starald,* that is, the furniture which the young woman provides; in general it is rather considerable. It is conveyed in great order, there being fixed rules as to the articles to be moved off first, and those which are to follow. I have thought this a pleasing sight, the company being all on horseback, and each matron in her appointed station, the nearest relatives going first; all

have their allotted basket or piece of small furniture, a horse and car [a form of horse-drawn vehicle] following afterwards with the heavier articles.

Similarly, Gregor (1881) described the taking of the bride's *providan* to her new home where an almost set and ritualistic order of packing and processing was observed. Owen (1961) wrote that in Carmarthenshire only respected married women were invited to take part in and accompany the *stafell;* this was considered an honor for the women invited. The mothers of the bride and groom would oversee all the arrangements "like two ladies," and apparently this may have been the first time that the two women had met. Once the procession was over and the furniture and household goods were safely delivered and in their place, the women relaxed with tea and wine drinking. Owen (1961) mused that it may be stretching matters too far to suggest that this ceremony in some way represented the older married women accepting the younger woman into their ranks, but it does have the appearance of the reverse of the hen night (or stag night) where the bride-to-be celebrates, often to excess, with her friends before officially entering coupledom. It was generally the rule that the couple set up the home, ready to move into, before the wedding. But it was sometimes the case that the *stafell* took place after the wedding—that is, it occurred when the couple moved into their new home, even if this was after the wedding. Whenever it took place, the practice remained a women-only custom.

Some evidence provided by Owen (1968) suggests that from the late eighteenth century to the early nineteenth century, the *stafell* in Breckonshire had become an extension of the bidding custom (a party for all the women or all the men of the community where financial contributions were made to the couple with accounts kept of each donation), but in this case gifts in kind were given rather than money.

See also Bidding; Bottom Drawer; Home,
    Setting Up; Presents; Shower
References
Gregor, Rev. Walter. 1881. *Notes on Folklore of the
    North East of Scotland.* London: Folklore
    Society.
Hone, William. 1827. *The Every-Day Book.*
    London: Thomas Tegg.
Owen, Trefor M.1968. *Welsh Folk Customs.* 2d ed.
    Cardiff: National Museum of Wales.
————. 1961. "A Breconshire Marriage
    Custom." *Folklore* 72: 372–384.

Stag Night

The stag night is a twentieth-century invention, an all-male affair usually organized by
the best man or close friends at which the
groom-to-be bids farewell to his single status
and his unmarried friends, with a celebration
usually involving copious alcohol. The intention of the friends is often to get the groom-
to-be as drunk as possible. Often jokes are
played on him—sometimes with some level
of underlying malice. For obvious practical
reasons, the stag night has come to be held a
few days before the wedding. Toward the end
of the twentieth century, women began to
have similar celebrations known as hen nights,
and nightclubs began to see these as business
opportunities with special promotions. A similar type of event is found in Finland with the
Polterabend party at which the bride-to-be and
her friends parade around the streets and have
a loud, raucous celebration to mark the end of
the bride-to-be's single life.

See also Bosseller; Hen Night; *Polterabend* Party;
    Premarriage Customs; Ribbon Girl
References
Ballard, Linda May. 1998. *Forgetting Frolic: Marriage
    Traditions in Ireland.* Belfast and London:
    Institute of Irish Studies, Queens University,
    Belfast, and Folklore Society, London.
Gillis, John R. 1985. *For Better, For Worse: British
    Marriages, 1600 to the Present.* Oxford: Oxford
    University Press.

Stockings, Throwing of

The bedding of the bridal couple was once
carried out as a public ceremony. Today the
couple retiring to bed is left as a private matter, but there still remains an element of public announcement with the decoration of the
going-away car and tricks played on the couple, such as sprinkling them with confetti to
ensure that the couple are marked as newlyweds. The French *la soupe* custom has similarities to sixteenth- and seventeenth-century bedding customs. An element of those
bedding customs, often remarked upon by
travelers and diarists, was the throwing of the
stockings. Scott (1953, 229) quoted some
lines from *The Gentleman's Magazine* (published between 1731 and 1914, Scott gives
no attribution as to date or author):

> Bid the lasses and lads to the merry brown
>   bowl,
> While rashers of bacon shall smoke on the
>   coal:
> Then Roger and Bridget, and Robin and
>   Nan,
> Hit 'em on the nose with the hose [stocking]
>   if you can.

This refers to the throwing of the stocking, a practice recorded by Samuel Pepys and
described by Francis Maximilian Misson
(1698):

> The Bridesmen take the Bride's stockings,
> and the Bridesmaids and Bridegroom's; Both
> sit down at the Bed's Feet, and fling the
> Stockings over their Heads, endeavouring to
> direct them so as that they fall upon the
> marry'd couple. If the Man's Stocking,
> thrown by the Maid, fall upon the
> Bridegroom's Head, it is a Sign she will
> quickly be marry'd herself; and the same
> Prognostick holds good of the Woman's
> Stockings, thrown by the Man. Oftentimes
> these young People engage with one another
> upon the Success of the Stockings, tho' they
> themselves look upon it to be nothing but
> sport.

This custom took place at weddings of all
levels of society, from royalty to peasantry.
Although bedrooms of couples at the bottom
end of the social scale may have been simple,

a bridal chamber was often part of the wedding house provided by the church authorities and used by wedding parties for the marriage feast. Traditions of throwing the bride's or groom's stocking continued among some groups of people into the nineteenth century. Gregor (1881) noted that among the fishing community at Gardenstone the bridal bed was made up by a woman who was currently breast-feeding a baby, in the belief that if any other woman did so there would be no family. At the *beddan,* the unmarried filled the room, and the bride went to bed first. The bridegroom took off his stocking and threw it among the crowd. The one who caught it would be the next to marry. Similarly, in other places, Gregor noted that when the bride was in bed, one of her stockings was handed to her, which she threw over her left shoulder to the onlookers. The guests scrambled for the stocking, and the winner of the stocking would be the next to marry. This is reminiscent of the contemporary practice of flinging the bride's bouquet to the unmarried guests. To foretell her fortune in married life, a bride, as she prepares for bed on her wedding night, could throw a stocking over her left shoulder. If it lies in a straight line on the floor, her luck would be continuous; if not, her luck would be changeable.

See also Bed, Marriage; Bouquet; Divinations; France
References
Gregor, Rev. Walter. 1881. *Notes on Folklore of the North East of Scotland.* London: Folklore Society.
Jeaffreson, John Cordy. 1872. *Brides and Bridals.* 2 vols. London: Hurst and Blackett.
Misson, Francis. [1698] 1719. *Memoirs and Observations in His Travels over England.* Translated by J. Ozell. London: Printed for D. Browne.
Scott, George Ryley. 1953. *Curious Customs of Sex and Marriage.* London: Torchstream.

Strawboys

A tradition, found in many parts of Ireland, was for the wedding party, after the solemnization of the marriage, to be visited by a group of mummers (actors) known as strawboys. The mummers wore a straw conical mask, sometimes wore a straw skirt, or were completely covered with a straw costume. The group were usually men, and some (Hilliard 1962) have suggested that in County Kerry it would have been seen as sacrilegious for a woman to be in the strawboy party. The strawboys would visit the wedding house and dance with the women. The leader of the group, who would have a slightly more elaborate mask with some ornamentation on the apex, would claim the right to dance with the bride. In County Kerry, the strawboys would usually visit the bride's house on the eve of the wedding. The whole ceremony was carried out in silence and was associated with bringing luck and good fortune to the bride and groom. The strawboys themselves did not only appear at weddings. In some areas they would perform a folk play at other traditional festivals or be part of other customs.

See also Chimney Sweep
References
Gailey, Alan. 1968. "Straw Costume in Irish Folk Customs." *Folk Life* 6: 83–93.
Hilliard, Richard. 1962. "Biddies and Straw Boys." *Ulster Folklife* 8: 102.

Suttee

Suttee was the practice whereby a widow committed suicide by throwing herself onto the funeral pyre of her deceased husband. On the Indian subcontinent, the practice of *suttee* was outlawed by the British government, the colonial power, in 1829. However, the practice continued surreptitiously and is still occasionally practiced. In August 2002 a judicial enquiry was undertaken after a widow committed *suttee* in the village of Tamoli in the Madhya Pradesh district of India (Harding 2002, 8–9). Within Hindu tradition, even today, the ideal wife is *pativratā,* meaning she whose vows *(vrata)* are to her husband *(pati).* She is expected to devote her life to her husband whom she should regard as her god; ideally she should die before he does, but if

Several pairs of dye-stained red palm prints border a village archway in Rajasthan, India, left as testaments by women on their way to perform suttee, *the outlawed but ancient practice of suicide on a husband's funeral pyre. (Sheldan Collins/ CORBIS)*

by some mistake he dies first, she should kill herself on his funeral pyre. *Suttee* dates back to at least the tenth century and has its origins in the Hindu belief that a woman who sacrifices herself on her husband's funeral pyre will achieve divine status and become a manifestation of the god Shiva's consort. However, the practice is also said to have its origins in preventing or deterring wives from poisoning their husbands (apparently a very common occurrence in India at one time). In the *Padmapurana,* a series of ancient religious poems, which are a form of Hindu equivalent of the Bible, the duties of the wife are outlined—that whatever his faults, she should obey him, give him obeisance, see to his every whim, and treat him as her god, and "she must, on the death of her husband, allow herself to be burnt alive on the same funeral pyre; then everybody will praise her virtue" (Braddock 1961, 187). With these instructions it is not surprising that a woman would

be moved to poison an abusive and selfish husband.

It was only later that the religious idea of the widow receiving her reward in heaven was instituted so that the widow would be induced to voluntarily go to her death rather than be dragged screaming to the pyre. Her failure to commit *suttee* would subject her to perpetual infamy, she and her family would be degraded, and she would be treated as a social pariah. Today in Hindu society, a widow continues to have very low status— she may not remarry, she is not allowed to take part in ritual, and she is generally ostracized. And although there is a law that imposes life imprisonment or death on those aiding and abetting *suttee,* the treatment of widows could be said to be worse than death.

The act of *suttee* was usually carried out with great solemnity and dignity. The funeral pyre was prepared with a form of arbor constructed at one end. The body was placed in the pyre with the head opposite the opening and the feet toward the west. The widow would be accompanied to the site by Brahmins with whom she would pray and converse. She would bid farewell to her relatives and distribute her bracelets and other jewelry and ornaments among them, sometimes retaining the *tali,* the amulet placed around her neck by her husband on their wedding day. She would be led around the pyre three times before climbing the steps up to the mound, pressing her hands on his feet and then taking her place next to his head. The pyre was then set alight either by the widow herself or by a relative.

There were some regional differences in the actual performance. In Bengal, the widow was tied to the corpse and both bodies were covered with bamboo; in Orissa, the body was burned in a pit and the widow threw herself into the fire; in some provinces she would be drugged with opium. In Bali, widows were usually killed with a dagger thrust before being burned; however, in most cases the woman would be asphyxiated by the smoke before being burned. There were cases of widows running in agony out of the pyre only to be pushed back by the spectators. In the sacred books of the Hindu it is written:

> The woman who mounts the funeral pile of her deceased husband equals herself to Arundhoti, the wife of Vishista, and enjoys bliss in heaven with her husband. She dwells with him in heaven for thirty-five millions of years, which is equal to the number of hairs upon the human body, . . . She who thus

goes with her husband to the other world purifies three generations, that is the generation of her mother's side, father's side and husband's side; and so she being reckoned the purest and the best in fame among women, becomes too dear to her husband and continues to delight him during fourteen Indras, and although her husband be guilty of slaying a Brahmin or friend, or be ungrateful of past deeds, yet his wife capable of purifying him from all these sins. (Scott 1953, 293)

Even today Indian women go to visit and worship at shrines erected to those who have committed *suttee* to ask for help with various problems. India is not the only place, though it is the best-known example, of the practice of *suttee* occurring. Such acts have been reported among the Native American Indians and in the Fiji Islands, Ghana, and Zaire.

See also Hindu Weddings; India
References
Braddock, Joseph. 1961. *The Bridal Bed.* New York: John Day.
Harding, Luke. 2002. "The Ultimate Sacrifice." *Manchester Guardian,* 23 August, G2, 8–9.
Leslie, Julia. 1994. "Recycling Ancient Material: An Orthodox View of Hindu Women." In *Women in Ancient Societies,* edited by Léonie J. Archer, Susan Fischler, and Maria Wake. London: Macmillan.
Scott, George Ryley. 1953. *Curious Customs of Sex and Marriage.* London: Torchstream.
Westermarck, Edward. 1894. *The History of Human Marriage.* 2d ed. London: Macmillan.

Sweden

See Scandinavia

T

Temporary Marriage

Temporary marriages are found in some Muslim communities, particularly among Shiite Muslims, and are known as *sigheh* in Iran and *muta'a* in Iraq. These are formal arrangements that can last from a few hours to many years. Temporary marriage is considered legal by the religious establishment and appears to allow for a degree of sexual freedom for the man (who is allowed up to four wives), getting around the problem of adultery and sex outside the marriage, which is punishable by stoning, or, at the least, lashes and fines. The *sigheh* is entered into in much the same way as a regular marriage contract. The man has to pay the woman an amount of money called a *mehriyeh* (for a year's contract, the average payment is around 14 gold coins, or approximately $1,120). Any children from this arrangement are considered legitimate, and there is no stigma attached to them. The contract is drawn up by a cleric, and this contract may last for as little as one hour up to a year. The cleric sits with his copy of the Koran and a ledger of the names of the couple with the dates. The cleric blesses the "marriage," which is recognized as a marriage by Shia Muslims but has no validity in the secular courts.

A man may have as many *sigheh* relationships as he likes, even if he is married conventionally. A married woman is not allowed to enter into a *sigheh* arrangement, and an unmarried woman should have the permission of her father, which would not be given, since virginity is considered highly important for a bride. The women who enter into *sigheh* relationships are therefore usually divorced or widowed, and they are viewed as something between a mistress and a prostitute. The practice of *sigheh* is officially sanctioned by the Iranian authorities, although it is not often openly talked about. During the Iran-Iraq War in the 1980s, the authorities encouraged *sigheh* for war widows so that they could receive some money to help them, and there have been suggestions that this could be available for young people to get to know each other before marriage. (It is said that Muslim college students in America have used this practice to circumvent the Muslim prohibition of premarital sex.) However, due to the traditional view of virginity in brides and the concept of an unmarried woman having sex as bringing dishonor upon the family, this is unlikely to become socially acceptable.

Many educated young feminists in Iran, still subject to Islamic laws that they see as repressive for women, strongly object to this practice and see it as legalized prostitution that men are able to make use of when they are traveling or their wife is indisposed. In Iraq, *sigheh* or *muta'a* relationships were banned and rare during the reign of Saddam Hussein, a Sunni Muslim. The arrangement is not accepted and is condemned by Sunni Muslims as outdated and open to abuse. Shiite Muslims consider this view to be blasphemous, since the practice was sanctioned by the Prophet Muhammad as a way to secure some financial security for widows. After the 2003 Iraqi war that deposed Saddam Hussein, the practice of *muta'a* became common, with war widows desperate for money to feed and clothe their families. However, a woman who enters a *muta'a* relationship often does so with a sense of shame, and she is often considered little more than a prostitute.

See also Islamic Marriage

References

Allam, Hannah. 2003. "Temporary Marriage Returns to Iraq." Available at *http://www.TwinCities.com* (accessed 31 August 2003).

Judah, Tim. 2002. "A Revolution Crumbles." *Manchester Guardian Weekend,* 5 October, 90.

Steavenson, Wendell. 2002. "Marriage for a Night." *Prospect* (October): 60–63.

Thailand

In Thailand, a Buddhist country, there is no overt religious or civil ceremony for weddings. To Buddhists the wedding is a civil contract, although one that can be blessed by monks. The couples are married by their mothers, with the ceremony overseen, witnessed, and blessed by three Buddhist monks. Both the man and the woman usually wear mainly white. The woman wears a plain white dress and the man a white tunic, which may have some decoration. On the allotted day the bride will go to the place for the marriage, with no pomp or ceremony, and await the bridegroom there. He is escorted to the marriage location by a group of young men, who parade before him, beating drums and chanting. When he is near his destination, the party's progress is blocked by a flimsy barrier,

The mothers of the bride and groom put rope around the couple's heads simultaneously. Each monk takes a bunch of green twigs, which he dips into a golden bowl of perfumed water and sprinkles over the couple. (Courtesy of Mollie Grainger)

Buddhist monks at a Thai wedding. (ML Sinibaldi / CORBIS)

consisting of a gold chain, which is held across the path by the bride's friends and relatives. The groom has to pay a toll to pass this barrier. Further along, his party encounters another barrier, much stronger and held by the bride's parents. Here he has to bargain for his bride. He may make a token gesture of attempting to break through the barrier without paying, but in the end a bargain is struck, and he and his party are allowed through.

These preliminaries over, the monks begin by chanting and praying while holding a rope between them. The mothers of the couple make two loops on the rope, and each places one of these around the head of her new son- or daughter-in-law; this has to be done simultaneously and is symbolic of the two women accepting each other's child as part of the family. The monks, still holding the end of the rope, continue their chanting, and each takes a bunch of green sticks and dips them into a gold bowl containing water infused with herbs and sprin-

kles the couple with the water. The mothers next remove the rope from the heads of the couple, again simultaneously, and the bride and groom move to the prayer seats. Here the rope, now loosed from the monks, is once again put around the couple's heads by the mothers. Each of the two women then makes three paste dots, in the shape of a triangle, on the forehead of her new son- or daughter-in-law. Once this is done, all the witnesses to the marriage, who are older than the couple, pour the remainder of the water through the hands of the bridal couple. Finally the rope is removed from the heads of the bride and groom and the ceremony is complete. Before the wedding, the monks are given gifts; after the ceremony the couple serve the monks a meal and then present them with more gifts.

See also Barring the Way
Reference
Personal communication, Mrs. M. Grainger, 3 March 1989.

Threshold, Carrying over

The husband carrying his new wife across the threshold is often said to date or be derived from the Rape of the Sabine Women, who were carried off against their will, as described by the Roman historian Livy, among others. This was also said to have been the origin of other Roman wedding practices, such as the bride running to her mother and being carried away by force by the bridegroom and his friends. But in Rome, the bride was carried into the house by a group of people rather than just by the bridegroom, and the rite of entering the house was a public event rather than the more private rite as now practiced in Europe and America. Although it seems reasonable to interpret the carrying over the threshold as being a form of benign capture derived from an older rite of marriage by capture, it may be more related to wedding traditions in which the bride makes a show of reluctance and modesty with no unseemly haste to break away from her family and start a new unit.

Transitional times in life are often seen as vulnerable times—the changing of the year or seasons, the embarking on an adventure—and crossing the threshold can be seen as being the true beginning of the married couple's life together. For example, it is considered bad luck for the bride to stumble over the threshold, seen as an omen of an unhappy marriage. But there also appears to be a fear of malevolent sources destroying the marriage with sorcery placed at the threshold. In Ben Jonson's "Masque of Hymen," the bride is warned to ensure that she steps boldly over the threshold:

> Haste, tender lady, and adventure;
> The covetous house would have you enter,
> That it might wealthy be,
> And you, her mistress, see:
> Haste your own good to meet;
> And lift your golden feet
> About the threshold high,
> With prosperous augury.
> (Jonson 1606, 75)

Henry Morley, the editor of an 1890 edition of this work, noted that at the entrance of the bride it was customary to give her the keys to signify that she was the mistress of the house; he also noted that she must not touch the threshold as she entered the house, but be carried over it. This was to avoid any "sorcerous drugs, used by witches to be buried under that place, to the destroying of the marriage, or the power of generation" (Jonson 1606, 75). A means of protecting a bride's new house against witches and sorcerers was for the bride to place a bowl of salt and a broom at the door; a witch would have to count the grains of salt and the straws in the broom before entering the house, a task considered impossible between the hours of midnight and dawn, thus effectively protecting the inhabitants of the house. In Vosges, France, a bride was carried from her home to church by two men in an effort to evade incantations that could damage the marriage. The Berber people of Morocco are still today concerned that witchcraft could disrupt the couple's married life, and the date and venue of the wedding are kept secret until the last moment; the bride's feet must not touch the ground on her wedding day. These are related to beliefs that the life force resides in the feet and with attempts to prevent malevolent spirits from affecting the bride and the marriage by entering through the feet.

In the Zoroastrian wedding, the bridegroom processes to the bride's house, where the doorjambs are smeared with turmeric, the yellow color of which is symbolic of the life-giving properties of the sun. The groom has to pass through this gateway, with his right foot first and without touching the threshold. He is met by his future mother-in-law, who marks his forehead with a red pigment, into which she presses rice. More rice is thrown over him.

The act of lifting may have some symbolic relation to the passing from one phase of life to another, as in the petting stone tradition, in which the bride is lifted over the petting stone, or an improvised barrier outside the church, by two young men on either side of the bride. The groom leaps over the stone after her and then drops a coin into the hands of the "bride-lifters." Etiquette demanded that the bride should show some reluctance to jumping over the stone to show an appropriate degree of modesty. If she was too keen to jump the stone, it was thought that she displayed too much independence.

Lifting the bride over the threshold was not the only threshold custom observed. As noted above, in seventeenth-century England she may be presented with the house keys to symbolize her becoming the mistress of the house. Gregor (1881) wrote that a bride entering her new home was met at the door by two of her female friends, one with a towel and the other with a basket full of bread of various types. The towel was put over her head and the bread was poured over her, to be gathered by children who had collected around the doorway: "In former times the bride was then led to the hearth, and after the fire had been scattered, the tongs was put into her hand, and she made it up." So not only was she met at the threshold and doused in bread—symbolic of plenty—but she was also led to the heart of the home (the hearth) to make up the fire, making her mistress of the home.

It was a common practice in the northeast of England and in Scotland for a piece of cake, shortbread, or buns to be thrown or broken over the bride's head at the threshold of her parents' house when she and her new husband arrived back from church. In parts of Scotland a currant bun was broken over the bride's head by the bridegroom's mother or nearest female relative before the just-wed bride entered the house. It was considered unlucky if the bun was broken over the head of anyone else. In Yorkshire, England, to ensure future weddings, hot water was poured over the doorstep as the bride and groom left the reception in the belief that before the water dried another marriage would be agreed upon. This practice, sometimes re-ferred to as "keeping the threshold warm for another bride," was mentioned by a correspondent to the journal *The Athenæum* (16 November 1867):

> At a wedding in Holderness, the other day, at which my granddaughter assisted, a ceremony was performed there I had not observed before. As soon as the bride and bridegroom had left the house, and had the usual number of old shoes thrown after them, the young folks rushed forward, each bearing a tea-kettle of boiling water, which they poured down the front door-steps, that other marriages might soon flow, or as one said, "flow on."

Among the Bulgarian Gypsy (Roma) community, the bride may carry a small child in her arms as she crosses the threshold of her new home as a wish for children of her own.

See also Cake, Wedding; Capture, Marriage by; Feet; Petting Stone; Shoes; Zoroastrian Weddings

References

Charles, Henry. 1939. *Materials toward a History of Witchcraft.* Vol. 2. Philadelphia: University of Pennsylvania Press.

Gregor, Rev. Walter. 1881. *Notes on Folklore of the North East of Scotland.* London: Folklore Society.

Jonson, Ben. [1606] 1890. *Masques and Entertainments.* Edited by Henry Morley. London: RKP.

Monsarrat, Ann. 1973. *And the Bride Wore . . . : The Story of the White Wedding.* London: Gentry.

Tibet

As followers of Buddha, there is no overt religious ceremony in a Tibetan marriage. Much of the ceremonial is centered around the woman leaving her parents' home. All is accomplished with the blessing of a lama, who, after careful study of signs, almanacs, and the gods, selects the most auspicious day for the wedding. Tibet is a large and mountainous country where customs and practices for weddings can vary from valley to valley. Although Tibetans are nearly always monogamous, they do have a reputation for polygyny and, in some places, polyandry. Polygyny was practiced only by the wealthy and the Tibetan nobility; polyandry usually involved a woman marrying all the brothers of a family—the eldest brother chose and married her, after which the younger brothers automatically became husbands. The elder brother was the master of the household, and the younger brothers had rights only when he was away. Sometimes a woman would marry a father and son. Polyandry perhaps avoided the necessity to split the family estate or solved the problem that, due to the nature of the land, more than one man's work was required to support a family. Similarly, a man sometimes marries all of the sisters in a family, and he may even take their family name, especially if there was no son and heir in the family. Again this prevented the family estates being split. In this respect the polygamous practice differed greatly from that allowed by the Muslim religion.

During the late twentieth century, it became usual for young people to choose marriage partners. The age of marrying varied among groups, ranging for women from about sixteen to twenty or twenty-five years of age. The style of marriage differs in different parts of Tibet. In some places, the couple would not have known of the wedding until just before, because the negotiations had been carried out only between the parents in secret. The girl's parents are usually not required to formally provide a dowry for their daughter, although as a matter of convention they often provide domestic items to help the couple set up their new home.

The wedding celebration begins with banquets two or three days before the actual marriage. Relatives and friends visit the family with presents, including money, food, and clothing. At the end of this period, the bridegroom's parents send representatives to escort the bride back to the groom's home. This entourage takes a payment known as "breast money" or the "milk price," to compensate the bride's mother for the loss of her daughter and be a remuneration for bringing up her daughter. Sometimes a female yak is given to the mother as the "milk price." On the wedding day the bride's parents hold a farewell banquet for her, followed by an emotional farewell as she is placed on horseback and escorted to the home of the groom (her face may be covered with a cloth so that none may glimpse her during this procession). At the groom's house, her way is barred until a man with a warlike appearance wields a charmed sword to cut apart the demons that rode with the bridal party. The groom's mother meets the bride with sour milk, baked flour, sugar, and butter and leads the party into another banquet. A priest may be present to inform the gods and spirits of the addition to the household. The groom's parents distribute pieces of silk to the couple and the guests, making the couple man and wife.

Brides of the Tibetan nomads of Amdo and Kham are elaborately dressed. Her hair may be braided with one hundred and eight braids and finished with a band of coral and turquoise beads attached to the braids (unmarried girls wear their hair in two large plaits). Coral and turquoise are both highly prized by the Tibetans, and the red coral ensures that a bride will be happy. Red is a color that augurs well and is also the color of marriage. The one hundred and eight braids demonstrate that she has loving and good-natured parents. In Kham, the bride may have an amber ball surrounded by coral on the top of her head. Elsewhere she may wear a turquoise-encrusted headband with a larger semiprecious stone at her forehead. Although there is no recognized dowry, a bride may be given a broad silk belt (a *charma*) studded with silver nails *(borchen)* or a silver medallion known as a *losar*. A nomad bride would be given a silver necklace with a hook, which was originally used for hanging a milking pail. This is an emblem of marriage and represents the pail of milk that the new mother-in-law traditionally presented to the bride.

Among nomadic peoples in Tibet, arrangements for marriage are negotiated between the families using a neutral intermediary (a member of neither family). The goods—yaks, skins, and textiles—that the groom will bring to the new home are negotiated. This is sealed with a fermented barley drink called *chang* and the exchange of gifts. These gifts are known as *nathag tak* or "nose rope." Once accepted, the parents of the bride cannot back out of the agreement. The day before the wedding, the groom and his party arrive at the bride's house (or tent) with a horse on which she will be carried away. He is welcomed with an exchange of white scarves. Much drinking of *chang* follows, and the groom and his party lodge with the bride's family for about three days before they, with the bride, return to his family. At this point a female yak may be presented to her mother as the "milk price." Dressed up and bedecked with jewels, the bride wears an engraved silver reliquary (a *gao*) around her neck that protects her from evil spirits as she makes the transition from the protection of her family gods to the protection of her husband's family god, with whom she has yet to find favor. A girl meets this returning bridal party and gives the bride a pink scarf to put over her mouth and ears before she dismounts. The bride is thus led to her new family where a red carpet, decorated with the swastika, is laid for her to dismount. As the bride crosses the threshold of her new home she is given a cup of yogurt. She flings a few drops to the sky with her right hand and prays for the protection of the Buddha and of the mountain gods—the "offering of the yogurt of the oath." With that the marriage is completed.

See also Arranged Marriage; Dowry; Polyandry; Polygyny

References

Baldizzone, Tiziana, and Gianni Baldizzone. 2001. *Wedding Ceremonies: Ethnic Symbols, Costume, and Rituals.* Paris: Flammarion.

Braddock, Joseph. 1961. *The Bridal Bed.* New York: John Day.

Murphy, Brian M. 1978. *The World of Weddings: An Illustrated Celebration.* London: Paddington.

Tokens

Tokens are given to declare affection and to seal a betrothal. In some cultures, tokens form part of the courtship ritual. Carved domestic items, such as distaffs for spinning in Finland, may be given as a token of love and also to demonstrate the lover's practical abilities. In Germany, a carved and decorated washboard or a mangle board may be given. Other gifts include combs, necklaces, and gingerbread molds (in Czechoslovakia). In Britain, love tokens reflected local industry and pastimes. The Welsh love spoon could be an anonymous declaration, like a Valentine, or an overt and outward declaration of love and intention. In bobbin lace–making areas of Great Britain, young men would make and decorate lace bobbins as a statement of love. In the north of England, specifically in the Yorkshire Dales area, where there was a very strong knitting tradition (women knitted at all times between doing other chores), all women had one or several "knitting sheaths" or "knitting sticks" usually carved from wood to hold the knitting needles. These were presented as love tokens by young men, sometimes with the couple's initials and a date or with hearts. Some of the motifs are reminiscent of the Welsh love spoon—chains or free-running balls in an enclosure. Other favorite gifts were combs and stay busks (corset stiffeners). Young women could receive gifts from a number of prospective suitors. At the courtship stage, more tokens were exchanged.

Such tokens of love were not always so elaborate—a lock of hair or a broken silver coin, each of the couple having half the coin. The couple sharing half a coin was sometimes a sign of being almost engaged; oaths and prayers might be said over the coin parts and the pieces strung on ribbon and worn around the neck. These tokens were considered lucky, and even protective, and some believed that they would protect against death and devils. This form of token was used by couples who were separated for some years as a proof of identity when they were reunited. This theme is found in a number of folk songs and ballads throughout Western Europe. In the English folk song "Gosport Beach," collected by Sabine Baring-Gould in Halwell, Devon, in 1889 (Reeves 1961), a couple had to part (he was a sailor), but he promised to marry her upon his return. She, as a token of the pledge, broke a coin in two, with each keeping half:

> So we kissed, shaked hands, did part, tears
>   from her eyes did flow,
> I left her broken-hearted, on board she might
>   not go.
> As pledge and token of our love her gold she
>   broke in two,
> One half she gave to her true love with
>   Adieu, sweetheart, adieu.
> When six long months were ever gone, from
>   Chatham down came he
> He said, my handsome fair girl, I'm come to
>   marry thee.
> Then to the church they took their way, a
>   married life to try,
> And I hope they will live happy both until the
>   day they die.

In other songs the young man returns, sometimes from war, after several years. She does not recognize him, and he tests her constancy. When she proves true to him, he reveals who he is but has to prove his identity by producing his half of the broken token. In the song "The Broken Token," collected by George B. Gardiner at St. Denys, Southampton, Hampshire, England, in 1906 (Reeves 1961), the token is a ring:

> When he found out his true love was loyal,
> It's a pity, said he, true love should be
>   crossed,
> For I am thy young and single sailor
> Safe returned for to marry you.
> If you are my young and single sailor
> Show me the token which I give you,
> For seven years makes an alteration
> Since my true love have been gone from
>   me.
> He put his hand into his pocket,
> His fingers being both long and small,

> He says, Here's the ring that we broke
>   between us.
> Soon as she saw it, down she fell.

Sometimes a coin may be cut into more than two pieces, with the additional pieces being given to one or more witnesses to the contract or promise of the couple; the pieces were brought back together to seal the final contract. The gimmal ring, said to have been developed by the French, was a circular love token, two circlets entwined to form a whole ring. Sometimes the gimmal ring was composed of several circlets so that, again, parts of the ring would be given to the witnesses. The giving of a ring is usually a symbol, and a gift, given on engagement, betrothal, or spousal. The betrothal or spousal could be as binding as the actual marriage ceremony. A public betrothal included the recitation of vows, some of which were subsumed into the Anglican church wedding service, and might be sealed with a kiss and the exchange of gifts—often a ring. Sealing the betrothal with a kiss, sometimes termed a "wet bargain," meant that if the marriage did not proceed, the man would have to return all gifts given to him. The woman only had to return half the gifts. If no kiss was exchanged, the couple both had to return all gifts to each other. The giving of marriage gifts or tokens led to disputes regarding whether or not a person was promised in marriage. The token could be almost anything, including coins, gloves, and, rarely, handkerchiefs or shoes; but disagreements occurred regarding whether the gift was given in friendship or as a marriage token. The context in which it was given determined whether a gift was considered a marriage token, and obviously the giving of a token before witnesses was preferable.

The exchange of tokens between the man and the woman did not have to be equal, and rarely did the woman initiate the giving of marriage tokens. In making the marriage contract, the man gave a token to show his good intentions, and the woman gave a verbal reply, her promise to marry. That the woman was not expected to initiate the giving of to-kens is illustrated by a few sixteenth-century cases from the ecclesiastical courts of Durham, England, where women gave to-kens, which were not reciprocated, and then maintained that a contract of marriage had been entered into. This was denied by the men. On the other hand, there are cases where men tricked women into giving them small personal items, later claiming them to be gifts and marriage tokens.

See also Betrothal; Love Spoons; Rings, Wedding and Betrothal

References

Brears, Peter C. D. 1981–1982. "The Knitting Sheath." *Folklife* 20: 16–40.

Hartley, Marie, and Joan Ingilby. 1951. *The Old Hand-Knitters of the Dales.* Clapham, via Lancaster, Yorkshire: Dalesman.

Hostettler, Agnes. 1973. "Symbolic Tokens in a Ballad of the Returned Lover." *Western Folklore* 32, no. 1 (January): 33–38.

Jeaffreson, John Cordy. 1872. *Brides and Bridals.* 2 vols. London: Hurst and Blackett.

Reeves, James. 1960. *The Everlasting Circle: English Traditional Verse from the Mss of S. Baring-Gould, H.E.D. Hammond, & George B. Gardiner.* London: William Heinemann.

Rushton, Peter. 1985–1986. "The Testament of Gifts: Marriage Tokens and Disputed Contracts in North-East England, 1560–1630." *Folklife* 24: 25–31.

Tree, Marriage to a

Although this practice could be seen as an ex-treme form of expression of love for the en-vironment, being apparently married to a tree was a practice found among several groups in India. In the Punjab, for example, to get around the prohibition against a man marrying for the third time (although in Hindu tradition a man may marry up to four times and a woman only once), he may marry a babul tree or an akh plant as a third mar-riage, so that his next marriage would be to his "fourth" wife. Among the Mundas people in India, anthropologists noted that after a fake fight for the bride, the couple were anointed with turmeric and then the bride was wedded to either a mahwa or a mango tree and the groom to a mango tree. Each touched his or her tree with *sindur* or vermil-ion powder, hugged it, and were tied to the tree. Similarly, among the Kumis people, the bridegroom was married to a mango tree—he embraced it, was tied to it with thread, and daubed it with red lead; the bride simi-larly married a mango tree, after which she was carried home in a basket while her groom was taken to the home on a platform carried by the men.

Various theories and explanations for this practice have been put forward. Sumner (1906) suggested that, because it was ex-pected that an older brother should marry before his younger sibling, older brothers would be married to trees so that younger brothers would be free to marry. But in a so-ciety where marriages were arranged, it was likely that the brothers would have been mar-ried in order. Other anthropologists have suggested that this form of ceremony was a fertility rite or that it was a rite of initiation into a totemic clan. There seems to be little evidence for such conclusions, although Frazer (1922) said that when a Hindu planted a grove of mangoes, neither the man nor the woman would eat the fruit until one of the mango trees, representing the bridegroom, was married to a nearby tamarind tree grow-ing near the mango in the grove. If no tamarind was nearby, a jasmine tree acted as the bride. The "marriage" was carried out with the due ceremony of a Hindu wedding with feasting.

The actual explanation may be more pro-saic. Tree marriage was used to overcome the contradiction caused by being allowed to have four wives but not being allowed to marry for a third time. Crawley (1902) wrote that it was the custom among the Kendara Kumbis for a girl to have the chance to marry only once in every twelve years, so that if she was unmarried on her twelfth birthday she would have to wait another twelve years, until she was twenty-four, be-fore she would be allowed to marry. To over-come this problem, she would be married to a bunch of flowers, which were then thrown down the well, making her a widow and freeing her to marry at any time. The practice may also have been used to divert evil influences from the couple. In Hinduism, if the astrologers foretold misfortune in marriage for one of the couple, that person was first married to an earthenware pot.

See also Hindu Weddings; Proxy, Marriage by

References
Crawley, Ernest. [1902] 1932. *The Mystic Rose: A Study of Primitive Marriage and of Primitive Thought in Its Bearing on Marriage.* 4th ed. Revised and enlarged by Theodore Besterman. London: C. A. Watts.
Frazer, James G. [1922] 1970. *The Golden Bough.* Abridged ed. London: Macmillan.
Sumner, William Graham. [1906] 1940. *Folkways.* New York: Mentor Books.

Trousseau

In the Netherlands, the trousseau referred to the linen that a prospective bride prepared and packed into her linen chest in preparation for her marriage, and this same form of preparation was traditional in other European cultures. In Germany, the trousseau was the collection of items for the household, and at one time the German government imposed limitations or rules for what could be in a trousseau, the contents depending on social status. There has developed a clear difference between the trousseau and what is referred to as the bride's "bottom drawer" or "hope chest." The bride-to-be begins to supply the bottom drawer in the time leading up to her marriage. The hope chest consists of household and other items that a girl may buy or collect in the expectation of getting married at some future time. In this respect the Dutch example above may be properly considered a trousseau since the bride-to-be begins to prepare the linen only after the marriage has been arranged.

The trousseau thus is generally defined as the bride's outfit of clothes for her wedding and honeymoon, which she (or her family) pays for. Some late-nineteenth- and early-twentieth-century etiquette books gave extensive lists of items for the trousseau, some very extravagant. A certain Lady Greville, writing around 1892 and quoted in "Two Ladies of England" (1932), said that the simple rule was to buy a dozen of everything. Some magazines counseled against extravagance, suggesting that only a half dozen of each type of undergarment was necessary. Some retailers advertised that they specialized in the supply of trousseaus. Some supplied trousseau packages at set prices.

In the Islamic world, the trousseau, or money for the trousseau, is provided by the groom's family; this amount is agreed upon at the time of the final negotiations for the marriage, along with the agreement on how much should be spent on household goods and what these will be. But again there is a clear distinction between the provision of clothes for the bride for the wedding and the setting up of the home.

See also Bottom Drawer; Egypt; Germany; Netherlands

References
Ballard, Linda May. 1998. *Forgetting Frolic: Marriage Traditions in Ireland.* Belfast and London: Institute of Irish Studies, Queens University, Belfast, and Folklore Society, London.
"Two Ladies of England." 1932. *The Bride's Book or Young Housewife's Compendium.* London: Gerald Howe.
Van Nespen, W., ed. 1975. *Love and Marriage: Aspects of Popular Culture in Europe [exhibition], Antwerpen.* Brussels: Ministerie van Nederlanse Cultuur en Nationale Opvoeding.

Turkey

A young man in Turkey was considered eligible for marriage at puberty (around thirteen or fourteen years old). A girl would have been preparing for marriage for much of her life, sewing and preparing household linens and clothes to form part of her dowry, and at the age of around twelve, about the time of puberty, she would begin to wear the veil and be considered a marriageable young woman. These ages were changed after Turkey became a republic in 1923. The 1926 Civil

Code decreed that the age of eighteen was when a child came of age. This age could be lowered to fifteen by the courts. The courts were overwhelmed with applications for the lowering of the age, and in 1938 the ages were lowered to seventeen for men and fifteen for women. As a Muslim country, the tradition had been that children should be married as soon as possible after puberty, a factor not taken into account by the legislation. The marriage partner may be chosen by the parents of the couple, and the choice may be made to cement alliances or to increase power and wealth, or, quite commonly, to link families of similar trades and professions. It was not uncommon for two families to betroth their children when they were infants. Today, in many parts of Turkey, it is not unusual for young couples to fall in love, with a great deal of free choice. But even so, although the couple will declare love for each other in song, it is the parents of the man who propose to the family of the woman.

Finding a bride for a young man considered ready to marry was accomplished by his mother. She called upon the women in families where she knew there was a daughter of marriageable age. At each house she, with her advisers, would announce the reason for the visit and would be entertained as the young woman, dressed in her best, served coffee to the visitors. During the coffee drinking, the prospective bride was inspected by the young man's mother. When the woman handed her coffee cup back to the prospective bride, the girl could retire. Sometimes a more thorough examination was held at the women's baths. The girl was expected to appear at a certain time so that she could be inspected by the prospective husband's mother and retinue. She had to pretend to be unaware of what was going on. Once a bride had been chosen, the young man's mother would formally propose to her family, giving details of his family, background, and prospects. Once the women had made the agreement in principle, the two fathers took over and would investigate the social and financial standing of

the other's family. If all proved satisfactory, they would then proceed with the betrothal and dowry contracts.

In both cases—free choice and arranged marriage—the pledge to marry, or the contract, is handed to the young woman in public. The family of her future husband gives the young woman clothes and veils for the wedding—skirts, belts, and ribbons for the waist, stockings, a long shirt, and everything necessary to dress her hair. In the cities, the girl is offered white robes and veil, flowers to be put in the hair, and other dresses. A copy of the contract is kept by both families, and the exchange of contracts, before two witnesses, who had to be Muslims, constituted the marriage. There is no religious ceremony—the wedding feast and the preparations for the wedding feast provided the ceremony. An auspicious day for the feast is chosen, usually a Friday or a Monday. A few days before the feast, the groom and his friends hold a celebration, with dancing and feasting, hosted by his parents. Either on the eve of the wedding or of the henna night, the bride and her guests go the baths *(haman)* to bathe and cleanse her and prepare her for the wedding. The baths are a form of beauty salon and are like clubs and meeting places. Here she is washed and massaged and body hair is removed. Her hair is washed and rinsed with the sap of various herbs. Her curls are cut off, the hair falling onto a mirror to ensure her a happy destiny. Her hair is braided with gold pieces, glass beads, and pearls attached to the braid ends to ward off the evil eye. The bride is dressed in her wedding clothes by the women, who provide her with sexual instruction and jokes. Each woman then bathes and prepares her own hair, after which all gather around the bride and proceed to her house accompanied by musicians.

The bathing is followed by henna night. The participants sit around tables with lumps of rye bread, flour, and dried fruits, with the last provided by the groom's family. The bride is surrounded by the presents given to her by the guests. Dances are performed. The bride's right hand is decorated with henna, during which silver or gold coins are pushed into the palm of her hand with the wish that it will always remain active. When the bride leaves her parents' home, a red cloth is tied to her right hand and a yellow one to her left. The next day, she kisses the hands of all the family as she leaves the house, and her father winds a belt of red and white ribbons around her waist three times with the advice, "Where you go, keep your hand, waist, and tongue shut." Talismen and amulets are tucked into the belt. At one time the father would have drawn a sword and held it close to the ground for his daughter to jump over, with the charge to bring forth children who would use the sword. After this, the family prays together and mourns the loss of the daughter and the end of her childhood.

Meanwhile, the bridegroom is being prepared to receive the bride. His hair and beard are solemnly and completely shaven, again to the accompaniment of drums, a process that can take two or three hours, during which the old people give him money and gifts. The hairdresser is paid with a napkin and an embroidered veil, and the bridegroom is dressed to await the arrival of his bride. Male and female guests from the bridegroom's group, with some riding on horses, and with one horse led by a standard bearer for the bride to ride back upon, process to collect the bride. When this group arrives, the bride covers herself with a red veil (al duvak), takes leave of her parents, and mounts the horse, and the drummers begin the wedding processional march back to the bridegroom's house. The procession may be held up several times and gifts have to be distributed. At her new home, where a flag waves, she is helped from the horse by the groom and his father. It is usual for a handful of sugar and corn to be thrown at her head. Sometimes a jug of water or a case of earth is broken on the ground in front of her. As she passes over the threshold she takes honey and butter in the palm of her

henna-decorated hand and presses it against the door; she then puts her hand into a bag of flour to ensure wealth for the household. Later she will kiss the hand of all the older people in the household. The bride is led into the house and given a higher seat than everyone else so that all can see her when her veil is removed by either her mother-in-law or her brother-in-law.

After the feast she is led to the "wedding room." In this room, decorated with greenery, flower garlands, and silk hangings, all the items of her dowry are prominently displayed. Here she receives guests who come to view the dowry and to meet her. The display of the dowry or trousseau, which includes mattresses, bedding, clothing, rugs, and donkey pack bags, displays her family's generosity and prestige in the community. This and the gifts of clothing to the bridegroom and his family are a big expense for the girl's father, despite the cash gift he received from the bridegroom's family. In the wedding room, a bed is made up for the bride, and there she awaits her new husband who is led to the room by the "aunts." His entry is an occasion for practical jokes—he may be given a sharp push in the back as he enters, a basin of water may be placed on the floor near the doorway, so that if he does not notice it or is pushed into it he will get very wet. The bride may hide behind the door. When he enters, the bride may try to stand on his feet, and he will do likewise to the bride. This provokes a great deal of laughter and joking from the "aunts" outside the room. Eventually the couple are left alone and by the next morning they are husband and wife. It is customary for the new wife to show the bed and sheets to the women of the household the next morning. The next day her head is bound and she becomes accepted into the community of married women. After the wedding feasts, the bride moves to her new husband's family home and becomes part of his family.

The 1926 Civil Code, based on the Swiss code, was enacted to modernize Turkey and its institutions, but the code violated traditional boundaries and sensibilities. Although the code outlawed polygamy and introduced some emancipation of women, it made divorce harder, although legal for women to instigate, and raised the legal age for marriage. Brides (and grooms) were also subjected to a medical examination, which outraged the Muslim sense of decency. The code decreed that marriage should take place before a registrar in a civil ceremony held in a municipal room reserved for marriages. The names of the couple are displayed in public fifteen days before the wedding and then the couple are driven to the marriage venue. The couple have to sign a register and are then given a certificate. The bride usually wears a simple dress, sometimes with a large corsage. After the civil ceremony, parents may hold a religious or traditional ceremony.

See also Arranged Marriage; Henna; Islamic Marriage

References
Braddock, Joseph. 1961. *The Bridal Bed.* New York: John Day.
Mair, Lucy. 1971. *Marriage.* Harmondsworth, Middlesex: Penguin.
Murphy, Brian M. 1978. *The World of Weddings: An Illustrated Celebration.* London: Paddington.
Tansug, Sabiha. 1975. "Turkey." In *Love and Marriage: Aspects of Popular Culture in Europe [exhibition], Antwerpen,* edited by W. Van Nespen. Brussels: Ministerie van Nederlanse Cultuur en Nationale Opvoeding.

U

United Kingdom

The United Kingdom consists of England, Scotland, Wales, and Northern Ireland. Many customs of marriage are common to these countries, with regional variations. In Wales, it was customary to hold a bidding, which raised money and goods to help the couple set up home. Similar customs with sports were found in Cumberland, and the penny wedding in other parts of England achieved the same objective. Only in Ireland do the guests driving from the church or registry office to the reception sound their car horns as on continental Europe.

Weddings take place in a church or chapel—or at a registry office usually located in a building such as a town hall or council offices—after due announcement in church (the banns of marriage) or by public notice at the registry office. The Marriage Act of 1994 allowed a wider variety of venues, for example, hotels and museum buildings, to be licensed for weddings. After a courtship, a couple intending to marry will become engaged. The engagement may be announced in the local newspapers and celebrated with a party, but will be sealed with the purchase of an engagement ring for the woman. A date is set; a venue is chosen; bridesmaids and the best man are arranged; and catering, flowers, invitations, and a honeymoon are set. It is usual for the bride and her family to make most of the arrangements and pay for the wedding; however, sometimes the bridegroom's family helps with the costs.

By law, the wedding has to be announced publicly at least three weeks before the wedding, either by banns in the church in the parish where each of the couple live or by the couple going to the registry office for the districts in which each of the couple live and giving notice to the superintendent registrar of the marriage. In this case, the couple must have lived in the registration district for at least seven days before giving notice and must wait at least twenty-one days after giving notice before the wedding can take place. In Scotland, under the Marriage Act of 1977, the banns are not now proclaimed in church before the marriage; the couple must fill out a marriage notice form not less than fifteen days before the intended wedding. The registrar, after necessary checks, issues a "marriage schedule," which the couple must collect in person a few days before the marriage. If it is to be a religious wedding, this schedule must be presented to the person officiating at the wedding and afterward be signed by that person, the bride and groom, and the two witnesses, and then returned to the registrar within three days of the wedding. An alternative to the banns is a special license; one of the couple must have lived in the registration district for at least fifteen days before giving notice at the registry office. The other member of the couple only needs to be in the country on the day of giving notice; the marriage can take place one day after giving notice.

The wedding dress is usually, but not always, white, with a veil. For a formal wedding, the groom, best man, ushers, and fathers will wear morning suits—or simply suits. Many couples observe well-known traditions—not seeing each other the night before the wedding and the bride wearing "something old, something new, something borrowed, something blue"—and may also observe local or family traditions related to a wedding. A person licensed to carry out and register weddings performs the wedding ceremony—clergy or a registrar. There must be at least two witnesses to the marriage, who sign the marriage register. The couple exchange vows according to the marriage service being performed (in a church either the service and vows laid out in the *Book of Common Prayer* or a revised service).

The main participants in the wedding are the bride and groom, the bride's father, the best man, the bridesmaids and maid of honor (usually younger female relatives of the couple or close friends of the bride), sometimes a page boy (usually a young male relative), and ushers (usually male friends or relatives of the couple). The bride's mother does not play a role in the ceremony of the wedding, but she is usually instrumental in all the arrangements for the day, helping and advising her daughter. The best man supports the groom and helps to ensure that everything on the day runs smoothly. The ushers seat the guests for the ceremony on the correct side of the church. The maid of honor or chief bridesmaid assists the bride during the day. The bridegroom and best man normally arrive first. The best man usually takes charge of the wedding rings, which he passes to the bridegroom at the proper time during the ceremony. The bride arrives accompanied by her father (or by whomever is "giving her away") and processes down the aisle (in a church) with her father. If the bride is wearing a veil it will cover her face. The bride and her father are followed to the front by the bridesmaids and are accompanied by processional music. In a church this is usually played on the organ; at other venues this may be prerecorded music or occasionally hired musicians. It is interesting to note that even late in the nineteenth century it was considered unusual (except among the wealthy) for the father or mother to attend the church ceremony. The bride and groom would be attended only by the best man and bridesmaids; it is not clear in this circumstance who would "give the bride away," as required in the marriage service. During the ceremony the bride lifts her veil from her face and leaves the church with the veil pushed back, revealing her face.

After the ceremony the bride and groom will leave the church or registry office, followed by the wedding party and the couple's immediate families. This is often when confetti is scattered over the couple, although this can happen at other times, such as when the couple leave for the honeymoon. Outside, wedding photographs are taken. The ceremony is followed by the reception, or wedding breakfast, attended by invited guests. The guests take a present for the couple, usually something for the new home. After the meal, it is usual for the bride's father, the groom, and the best man to make speeches, with the last often trying to embarrass the groom with stories of his bachelor past. Toasts to the bride and groom are drunk, and the bridesmaids are presented with small gifts. The celebration usually continues into the evening when other friends and acquaintances of the couple are invited. Often, though not always, the evening celebrations conclude with the bride and groom leaving for their honeymoon. The car may be decorated by the couple's friends with ribbons and streamers, tin cans and old shoes tied to the back, and the words "just married" put on the vehicle; confetti is usually thrown over the couple as they leave.

See also Banns; Cars; Confetti; Dress, Wedding; Veil; Wales

References

Ballard, Linda May. 1998. *Forgetting Frolic: Marriage Traditions in Ireland.* Belfast and London: Institute of Irish Studies, Queens University, Belfast, and Folklore Society, London.

Charsley, Simon R. 1991. *Rites of Marrying: The Wedding Industry in Scotland.* Manchester and New York: Manchester University Press.

Dobson, Sue. 1981. *The Wedding Day Book.* London: Arrow.

Heaton, Vernon. 1986. *Wedding Etiquette Properly Explained.* Kingswood, Surrey: Elliot Right Way.

"Two Ladies of England." 1932. *The Bride's Book or Young Housewife's Compendium.* London: Gerald Howe.

Unorthodox Marriages

Orthodoxy is imposed by custom, law, and authorities (usually ecclesiastical) wishing to control society. All marriage ceremonies conform to being a public show where the couple may, through a vow, an exchange of gifts, or other ceremonies, pronounce that they have set up a new unit within the society. This public action may then be followed by consummation of the marriage and a celebration consisting of feasting, drinking, and dancing in which the whole community marks the marriage. Custom and time establish accepted ways of doing things, and these become the official establishment norms. A ceremony outside of these norms is considered unorthodox, even when there are public vows and ceremonial events. An example of unorthodox practice was a form of wedding common in France in which the woman broke an earthenware vessel in front of the man she wished to marry. She then respected him as her husband for as many years as pieces of pot. At the end of the period the couple could separate or break another pot. Elsewhere there were broomstick weddings. The couple would each jump over a broomstick laid across the doorway, without touching the doorjambs and in front of witnesses. The "wedding" could be undone within a year and a day by the couple each jumping backward over the broom. These unorthodox ceremonies differ from irregular marriages in that the irregular marriages involve circumventing and using the orthodox ceremonies and vows in a manner not approved by the authorities.

See also Besom Weddings; Irregular Marriage

Reference

Clébert, Jean-Paul. 1963. *The Gypsies.* Translated by Charles Duff. London: Vista Books.

V

Valentine's Day

St. Valentine's Day is set aside for lovers and for declarations of love, with these declarations traditionally sent anonymously. St. Valentine was a Roman priest who, with St. Marius and his family, assisted the Christian martyrs during the persecutions at the time of Claudius II. St. Valentine was caught and sent by the emperor to the prefect of Rome, who tried to make him renounce the Christian faith. He refused to do so and was executed in A.D. 270 by being beaten with clubs and then beheaded. It is said that the execution took place on 14 February. In another telling, St. Valentine was executed in the cause of love for allowing Christian soldiers to marry in spite of a ban on soldiers marrying, imposed by Emperor Claudius. St. Valentine's association with a festival for lovers may be because his martyrdom occurred during the festival of Lupercalia—a festival of youth—on a day when boys would draw the names of girls for them to admire and accompany during the festival of Februata-Juno on the 15 February.

The practice of drawing names at St. Valentine's Day was well known in Britain long after the Romans had departed. Reference was made to this practice in *Poor Robin's Almanack* of 1676: "Now Andrew, Anthony, and William / For Valentines draw / Prue, Kate, Jilian." The London diarist, Samuel Pepys, in his diary entry for 14 February 1667, alluded to this custom of drawing names, and the consequences of being drawn, showing that it was not confined to the unmarried: "This morning came to my wife's bedside (I being up dressing myself) little Will Mercer to be her valentine, and brought her name written upon blue paper in gold letters, done by himself, very pretty; and we were both well pleased. But I am also this year my wife's valentine, and it will cost me £5; but that I must have laid out if we had not been valentines." A few days later he wrote: "I find that Mrs. Pierce's little girl is my valentine, she having drawn me: which I am not sorry for, . . . But here I do first observe the fashion of drawing mottoes as well as names, so that Pierce, who drew my wife, did draw also a motto, and this girl drew another for me. What mine was, I forget; but my wife's was 'Most courteous and most fair,' which, as it may be used, or an anagram upon each name, might be very pretty." At other times he noted the rich presents given (among the aristocracy) to a valentine, and indeed wrote in the above entry that being picked as a valentine by his wife would cost him £5 in buying a present.

Misson, an eighteenth-century traveler through Great Britain, noted a custom, according to which an equal number of unmarried

A fortune-teller "Be My Valentine," c. 1927. (Private collection)

men and women would gather, and each would write his or her name on a piece of paper. These would be put into two pots, one for the women and one for the men. The women would each, in turn, draw a name from the men's pot, and the men would draw a name from the women's. Misson noted that each would therefore have two valentines, and by custom, the valentines would be given a present. It was believed that being drawn to be valentines was a good omen for being drawn together in matrimony in later years. The cus-

tom and this belief is embodied in a children's rhyme:

> The Rose is Red, the Violets blue
> The Honey's sweet, and so are you,
> Thou art my love and I am thine;
> I draw thee to my Valentine
> The lot was cast and then I drew
> And fortune said it should be you.

Some in the church tried to suppress this custom as heathenish, lewd, and superstitious and substituted the names of saints on the paper slips, with the idea that those drawing the name of a saint would honor and emulate the saint picked. But the custom persisted. A common present for a valentine was a pair of gloves. A Devonshire, England, custom was for a girl to say to the man of her choice: "Good-morrow, Valentine, I go today / To wear for you, what you must pay, / A pair of gloves next Easter Day." The young man was expected to send the girl a pair of gloves on Easter Eve to wear to church the next day. In some instances the young man would not need the encouragement of the rhyme to send gloves to a girl he was interested in on Easter Eve. Her wearing of the gloves on Easter Day was a positive sign for their courtship.

St. Valentine's Day was not exclusively reserved for lovers but was also a time when children would go from door to door begging for small presents and often repeating a traditional rhyme. In a letter to the *East Anglian Daily Times* (a regional newspaper in the East Anglian region of England), in 1976, a correspondent recounted that at one time the children had had a day off on St. Valentine's Day, and they would walk to Barton Mere, where they were given a penny and a bun for singing a Valentine's Day song: "Good morning, Valentine / Comb your hair, / As I do mine / Two before / And two behind / Good morning Valentine / The roses red / The violets blue / The pinks are sweet / And so are you / If you'll be mine / I'll be thine / Good morning Valentine." In Norfolk, England, presents were given. Children's presents were said to have been left by Jack Valentine, Father Valentine, or Mother Valentine, sometimes with some jesting. In this area the tradition appears to have little to do with declarations of love and affection, although admirers may well have left gifts as an expression of affection. Children went to the big houses and businesses singing a song and were rewarded with small gifts or coins thrown to the children from windows. Similarly, in Northumberland, England, and in Rutland, England, groups of children went to the houses "valentining," or begging for reward for singing: "Good morrow Valentine! Plaze give me a Valentine, / I'll be yours, if ye'll be mine, Good morrow, Valentine!" Boys in parts of Worcestershire, England, would go around the village singing a valentine couplet for apples, which were fried into fritters. In Northamptonshire, England, sweet currant buns, called valentine buns, were given by godparents to their godchildren on the Sundays before and after Valentine's Day, and in Rutland, lozenge-shaped buns, called "shittles," were given to children (and old folks) on Valentine's Day. There is a tradition that on Valentine's Day the birds choose their mates, a belief that has often been referred to by poets. In the first verse of "To His Valentine," by the sixteenth-century English poet Drayton, are the lines:

> Muse, bid the morn awake,
> Sad winter now declines,
> Each bird doth choose a mate,
> This day's St. Valentine's:
> For that good bishop's sake
> Get up, and let us see,
> What beauty it shall be
> That fortune us assigns.

A custom from the west of England, described by Hone (1841), was for three single men to go out before daybreak on St. Valentine's Day to catch an old owl and two sparrows. If they managed to catch the birds and to carry them back, unharmed, to the local inn, before the females of the household had got out of bed, they would be rewarded with three pots of a mixture of warm beer and gin (known as *purl*). The men could then demand the same drink from any household in the neighborhood. The custom was supposed to remind the single girls and boys of the happiness that could be secured by an early union. The owl, because of its great wisdom, was said to influence the other birds to find mates. Divinations were performed to attempt to learn the identity of an individual's future spouse. A correspondent to a journal called the *Connoisseur,* a series of essays published from 1754 to 1756, gave an account of her Valentine's Eve:

> Last Friday was Valentine's Day, and, the night before, I got five bay-leaves, and pinned four of them to the four corners of my pillow, and the fifth to the middle; and then if I dreamt of my sweetheart, Betty said we should be married before the year was out. But to make it more sure, I boiled an egg hard, and took out the yolk, and filled it with salt; and then I went to bed, ate it shell and all, without speaking or drinking after it. We also wrote our lovers names upon bits of paper, and rolled them up in clay, and put them into water and the first that rose up was to be our valentine. Would you think it, Mr. Blossom was my man. I lay a-bed and shut my eyes all the morning, till he came to our house; for I would not have seen another man before him for all the world. (Colman and Thornton 1755)

The last sentence refers to a belief that the first member of the opposite sex you meet on St. Valentine's Day morning will be your valentine. A similar belief was that if a girl went out of the house early on Valentine's Day and the first person she met was a man, she would be married within three months (though not necessarily to that man); but if she first met a woman, she would have to wait at least a year before marriage. The first known written valentine's message was sent in 1684; however, the valentine card as we know it today did not really begin to gain popularity until around 1750. These handmade cards were gradually replaced by mass-produced cards introduced in the nineteenth century. The comic valentine came into being in 1840. Between about 1840 and 1900, the sending of valentine's cards came to be very popular, aided by the development of the penny post in Great Britain, which ensured the anonymity of the sender. Whistler (1947) gave postal figures for the number of valentines sent during the last half of the nineteenth century. In 1855 around 800,000 cards were sent through the post (presumably more were delivered by hand); after a decline in the 1860s, the figure rose to 1,634,000 in 1882. From around 1900, valentine cards began to decline in popularity, and in 1913 Elizabeth Mary Wright wrote that "the custom of writing and of sending Valentines is out of fashion and there remains little to mark the day." But today the practice is alive and well—promoted by commercial interests, from card manufacturers and sellers, to confectioners and flower merchants, to newspapers that sell space in special sections for valentine messages.

In 1938, the Shell Motor Company decided to send a valentine card to all their female clients. The first of these was designed by Claudia Freeman, and other notable designers were employed for the cards. The practice was revived after World War II and continued until 1971. The cards were sent anonymously, with no reference to the Shell Company. A collection of Shell valentine cards is held by the National Motor Museum, Beaulieu, Hampshire, England. In 1996 there were reports of one businessman in Watford, England, who, as a protest of the commercialism of Valentine's Day, developed the "anti-Valentine" card to express disinterest. He also sold bouquets of nettles, thistles, and headless flower stalks with an appropriate message (Ridgewell 1996).

Valentine's Day flourishes in cultures where there is a free choice of marriage partner. In India, where Valentine's Day began to be celebrated by middle-class Indians influenced by American and European culture around the end of the twentieth century, there has been a backlash from Hindu and Islamic conservatives, which in 2003 resulted in Hindu nationalists setting fire to valentine's cards, especially those showing couples kissing or sitting too close together, because this is seen as subverting the tradition of arranged marriages (*Independent* 2003, 14).

See also Divinations; Gloves

References

Chambers, Robert. 1863–1864. *The Book of Days.* Vol. 1. Edinburgh: W. and R. Chambers. Philadelphia: J. B. Lippincott.

Colman, G., and B. Thornton, eds. 1755. *The Connoisseur.* (Published between 31 January 1754 and 30 September 1756, and also in 1757 and 1793). London.

Hone, William. 1841. *The Every-Day Book.* London: Thomas Tegg.

Independent (London). 13 February 2003, 14.

Misson, Francis. [1698] 1719. *Memoirs and Observations on His Travels over England.* Translated by J. Ozell. London: Printed for D. Browne.

Ridgewell, Gordon. 1996. "St. Valentines Day, 1996." *FLS News* 23 (June): 16.

Whistler, Laurence. 1947. *The English Festivals.* London: W. Heinemann.

Wright, Elizabeth Mary. 1913. *Rustic Speech and Folklore.* Oxford: Oxford University Press.

Veil

Contrary to popular belief, the modern wedding veil does not derive from veils worn by brides in ancient Greece or from the "care cloth" (canopy) held over the couple during a Christian Anglo-Saxon wedding. Wardrobe accounts of Edward II of England made reference to one piece of "Lucca cloth . . . for a veil to be spread over the heads of Richard . . . and Isabella" for the wedding in 1321 of his niece Isabella to a son of the Earl of Arundel. But veils were not commonly worn by British brides until approximately the eighteenth century. In Catholic and Episcopal churches, in a practice thought to date from the synod of Milano in 1576, the veil is often used to bind the hands of the couple during the wedding ceremony (although the hands may also be bound with the priest's stole). In Spain, the bridal couple are completely covered with a cloth, called an *arrha,* and their hands are bound.

In the Jewish wedding ceremony, which takes place beneath a canopy, the *huppah,* the bride is usually also veiled. In the Old Testament, when Rebecca married Isaac (Gen. 24.50–67), she put on her veil and covered herself when she met Isaac, interpreted as a sign of her betrothal and perhaps the reason for the bridal veil in the Jewish ceremony. However, before the wedding ceremony the groom is led to the bride's room where he lifts the bride's veil to confirm that he is marrying his chosen bride. This is known as *bedeken,* from the Hebrew "to check," and recalls the biblical story where Jacob was tricked into marrying Leah, the older sister of his chosen bride, Rachel (Gen. 29.25).

Veils can be thought to be a protection from evil influences, and some societies even felt that it was dangerous to the bride for her future husband to see her. Brides also hide the face for reasons of modesty, timidity, and bashfulness. The veil can be used to confuse, to hide, to preserve a mystery, and to protect the outside world from taboo persons. There are societies where a menstruating woman and other taboo people such as mourners have to wear a veil, and in European society, a widow would have worn a veil in public. In some tribal societies, pregnant women have to wear a veil. In some Arab countries, a girl is veiled at around the age of thirteen, as a sign of her transition from childhood to womanhood. In arranged marriages it was not, and is not, unusual for the bridegroom to see his bride for the first time only when the veil has been removed after the wedding. Malicious influences are thought to be easily repelled by such items as veils and, in Chinese weddings, simple red umbrellas. The Berbers of Morocco put a great deal of effort into protecting marriage from witchcraft—by, for example, keeping the date and time of the wedding secret until the last minute. The bride wears a thick, face-covering veil throughout the three days of the marriage (even during the consummation of the marriage). The fooling role of the veil, perhaps related to the usual explanation for the presence of bridesmaids, is illustrated by a nineteenth-century account of a wedding in Lorraine, France. The bride and three companions, all of the same stature, were covered with a large white cloth, the peaks of their caps were adjusted to the same height, and the bridegroom had to touch, with a twig, the figure he thought was his future wife. The punishment for choosing the wrong woman was having to dance with her all evening and not with his bride.

The use of veils in weddings is by no means universal, and perhaps the most common form of headdress is the bridal crown. In Britain and North America the bridal veil was not common until the nineteenth century, when it became a fashionable part of the bride's costume, although bridal veils were sometimes worn in the seventeenth century, and there are some eighteenth-century references to bridal veils. An entry in *Armstrong's Norfolk Diary* for 7 February 1854, written by the Reverend Benjamin Armstrong, the vicar of East Dereham, Norfolk, England, notes the excitement in the parish because a certain Miss Dingle wore a veil at her wedding, remarking that it was supposed to be the first seen in the parish.

Many nineteenth-century veils were very long and hung down the back of the bride from her bonnet or headdress. These were always white and made from lace, specifically Brussels or Honiton lace. The fashion for wearing the veil over the face did not develop until the latter half of the nineteenth century, and the practice for the bride to enter the church with her face covered with the veil and leaving with the face uncovered was a later refinement. Despite the only-recent addition of the veil to the bridal costume in Britain and North America, it has acquired a body of folkloric beliefs. In Nottingham, England, veil embroiderers would take a long fair hair from one of the girls and work it into the veil. If it went through without breaking, a long and happy marriage was foretold; if the hair broke at the beginning, the bride would be the first of the couple to die; if at the end, the husband would be first. It is considered bad luck to show the veil to anyone outside the bride's immediate family before the wedding. It should not be put on before the wedding morning, except for fittings, and even then should not be worn with the wedding dress. If the bride does wear the veil on any other occasion before the wedding, she should not look into the mirror or the marriage will be unhappy or the bridegroom will desert her or die before the wedding. On the wedding day, the veil should be put on her head by a happily married woman, and then not until she is completely ready to go to church. She may look at herself in the mirror in her full outfit only when she is about to set off for the church. In some places, it is thought that if the bride wears her grandmother's veil, she will always have wealth. Finally, it is supposed to be lucky if the veil is torn accidentally, especially if it is torn at the altar.

See also Canopy, Bridal; Crowns

References

Armstrong, Rev. Benjamin. 1854. *Armstrong's Norfolk Diary,* 7 February.

Baldizzone, Tiziana, and Gianni Baldizzone. 2001. *Wedding Ceremonies: Ethnic Symbols, Costume, and Rituals.* Paris: Flammarion.

Crawley, Ernest. [1902] 1932. *The Mystic Rose: A Study of Primitive Marriage and of Primitive Thought in Its Bearing on Marriage.* 4th ed. Revised and enlarged by Theodore Besterman. London: C. A. Watts.

Cunnington, Phillis, and Catherine Lucas. 1972. *Costume for Birth, Marriage, and Death.* London: Adam and Charles Black.

Gutch, Mrs. 1880–1881. "A Rural Wedding in Lorraine." *Folk Lore Record* 3: 258–274.

Hostettler, Agnes. 1973. "Symbolic Tokens in a Ballad of the Returned Lover." *Western Folklore* 32, no. 1 (January): 33–38.

Monsarrat, Ann. 1973. *And the Bride Wore . . . : The Story of the White Wedding.* London: Gentry.

Murphy, Brian M. 1978. *The World of Weddings: An Illustrated Celebration.* London: Paddington.

Wales

Today, weddings in Wales are celebrated much the same as in England and Scotland, but, as in many regional areas of the British Isles, there are local customs. A correspondent to Hone (1841, 792) described a wedding in Merthyr Tydfil in Glamorganshire, where she acted as a bridesmaid "to a much valued servant." Some weeks before this wedding, a person well known in the parish went around the community inviting all to the wedding:

On the evening previous to the marriage, a considerable company assembled at the bride's father's and in a short time the sound of music proclaimed the approach of the bridegroom. The bride and her company were then shut up in a room, and the house-doors locked; great and loud was the cry for admittance from without, till I was directed, as brides-maid, by an elderly matron, to open the window, and assist the bridegroom to enter, which being done the doors were set open, and his party admitted. A room was set apart for the young people to dance in, which continued for about an hour, and having partaken of a common kind of cake and warm ale, spiced and sweetened with sugar, the company dispersed.

At eight, next morning, I repaired to the house of the bridegroom, where there had assembled in the course of an hour about one hundred and fifty persons; he was a relation of the dissenting minister, a man highly esteemed; and he was much respected on that as well as his own account. The procession set out, preceded by a celebrated harper playing "Come Haste to the Wedding"; the bridegroom and I came next, and we were followed by the large company. At the door of the bride's father we were met by the bride, led by her brother, who took their station behind the bridegroom and me; her company joining . . . the procession; we then proceeded to the church, the music playing as before. After the ceremony . . . the bride and her maid having changed their partners were met at it by the harper . . . and led the way to a part of the church-yard never used as a burial-ground; there placing himself under a large yew tree the dancers immediately formed, the bride and bridegroom leading off the two first dances. . . . By this time it was twelve o'clock, and the bride and bridegroom, followed by a certain number, went into the house where a long table was tastefully set out with bread of two kinds, one plain and the other with currants and seeds in it; plates of ornamented butter; cold and toasted cheese; with ale, some warmed and sweetened. The bride and her maid were placed at the head of the table, and the bridegroom and her brother at the bottom.

After the company had taken what they liked, a plate was set down, which went round, each person giving what they chose, from two to five shillings; this being done, the money was given to the bride, and the company resigned their places to others; and so on in succession till all had partaken and given what they pleased. Dancing was kept up till seven, and then all dispersed. At this wedding upwards of thirty pounds were collected.

In an adjoining parish it was the custom for the older people to go the evening before, and take presents of wheat, meal, cheese, tea, sugar, &c., and the young people attend next day, when the wedding was conducted much in the same way I have described, but smaller sums of money were given.

In many parts of Wales, a single-sex party, known as the bidding party, was held, where a donation was made to the couple to help them set up home. The bidding donations were carefully noted and were considered repayable at a later date. The donations made at the wedding described above were not necessarily returnable. The wedding itself could be either one where the party went on horseback (known as *priodas geffylau*) or, among the poorer people, a walking wedding *(priodas dra'd)* where the wedding party walked in procession to the church. The Hone (1841) account above stated that the bridegroom's procession—the groom accompanied by the bridesmaid—went to the bride's house to join with her and her party for the procession to the church. In some districts, especially in Cardiganshire, the bridegroom's party had to pass a number of obstacles on the way to the bride's house—straw ropes across the road, stone barricades, and sometimes a quintain (*cwinten* or *gwyntyn*)—a pole with a freely swinging spar on the top. At one end of the spar was a flat board and on the other a sandbag. The rider struck the flat board and had to be very dexterous to avoid being knocked off his horse by the sandbag. In some parts of Wales the word *cwinten* came to mean the straw rope barrier across the road.

At the bride's house, the groom would find the door barred. To gain access his group would have to take part in a question-and-answer ritual carried out in verse (called *pwnco*). Once inside, the party would have to find the bride, who had either hidden or disguised herself. Once found, she was taken toward the church with her "bodyguard" chasing behind. (Some have written that the *pwnco* took place after the wedding ceremony.) In southwest Wales, the horseback journey to the church developed into a cross-country race, the bride generally riding pillion to a person acting as her guardian. At some point during the race, this guardian would often take off in an opposite direction, chased by the bridegroom's party (with the rest following). When the bridegroom caught up with the bride and her guardian, all would proceed to the church. This practice is thought to have died out by the late nineteenth century (last reported in 1876). These races could be very dangerous, and sometimes participants were injured or even killed.

Another race sometimes found at Welsh weddings, especially in the north, was for the wedding cake, which was run from the church door to the house where the wedding reception was to be held. The race began as soon as the wedding ring was placed on the bride's finger. The races could be over a considerable distance. A young man from Llanllechid, Caernarvonshire, in the nineteenth century, ran four miles, beating thirty others, to win the race and the cake. This practice was still extant in Anglesey in 1890. After the wedding feast, which was accompanied by dancing and drinking, the company put the couple to bed; the men prepared and put the bridegroom to bed, and the women did the same for the bride. The company did not then depart, but stayed to drink the couple's health and to continue the drinking, dancing, and singing, and, as one eighteenth-century writer noted, "giving into other festivity, sometimes for two or three days together" (Pratt 1797). There was a strong sense of the whole community taking part in the wedding and helping to support the couple. These events provided social cohesion and a place for young people to meet and find future spouses.

> **See also** Bidding; Bride-Ale; Bridewain; Home, Setting Up; Penny Weddings; Racing; *Stafell*
> **References**
> Hone, William. 1841. *The Table Book*. London: Thomas Tegg.
> Owen, Trefor. 1968. *Welsh Folk Customs*. 2d ed. Cardiff: National Museum of Wales.
> Pratt, S. J. 1797. *Gleaning through Wales, Holland, and Westphalia*. Dublin: P. Wogan.

Walking on Gold

To bring luck and wealth to the couple for the future a piece of gold would be put in the bride's shoe, formerly, a sovereign (a British gold coin not now used). Often a half-crown coin would be put into her shoe instead, so that the bride was "walking on silver," because most people could not afford a sovereign. The half-crown coin was itself withdrawn when decimalization occurred in Britain. Gregor (1881) noted that in some Scottish fishing communities a bride would put a sixpence or shilling (both silver-colored coins) into her stocking or shoe for the wedding. In the United States, a new dime is sometimes put into the bride's shoe—in the heel of the left shoe—to ensure wealth and prosperity for the future.

During the Moroccan bride's preparations, a silver coin was put into the bride's slipper, and sometimes a silver coin was placed under the hand mill used to grind the corn for the flour for the wedding feast food. In Morocco, silver has associations with the moon and is considered to be protective against evil influences. (It is interesting to note that in European tradition a witch who had taken the shape of a hare could only be killed using silver bullets. And wearing a piece of silver was a charm against witchcraft and a good luck charm.) In Europe and the United States, it was not the value of the coin used that was important but the color—gold or silver. The bride being in contact with money, symbolic of prosperity, would augur well for the future.

> **See also** Tokens
> **References**
> Emrich, Duncan, ed. 1970. *The Folklore of Weddings and Marriage*. New York: American Heritage Press.
> Gregor, Rev. Walter. 1881. *Notes on Folklore of the North East of Scotland*. London: Folklore Society.
> Huddleston, Mary. 1973. "A Yorkshire Miscellany." *English Dance and Song* 35, no. 1: 24.

Wed

In Britain and the United States, the words "marriage" and "married" are used to describe the legal state of a couple setting up home together after a ceremony prescribed by authority and custom. The event, or ceremony, used to become married is called a "wedding." And this word comes from the word "wed." From a linguistic point of view, there is no common word for marriage across the European and Asian continents, but the Indo-European languages use a similar verb, *wedh*, which means "to lead" (home), expressing the act of becoming married (from the man's point of view, suggesting that in Indo-European society the woman left her house to live in her husband's, or his family's, house at marriage, and that the society was male-dominated and patrilineal). "Wed" is said to be an Anglo-Saxon word for the security that the groom gave at the espousal, or betrothal, to fulfill his part of the wedding contract. The *weds* were sureties that the suitor gave to the woman's guardians that she would be protected and maintained and were provided in the form of gifts and tokens that he gave according to his means. Wedding was, therefore, an agreement or contract between the groom and the woman's kinfolk and appears to not be a direct promise to the woman, i.e., it was not the marriage ceremony. This may explain the opprobrium, and even threat of lawsuit, which could ensue, even in recent times, should the man break off an engagement to be married.

See also Betrothal; Spousal
References
Gillis, John R. 1985. *For Better, For Worse: British Marriages, 1600 to the Present.* Oxford: Oxford University Press.
Jeaffreson, John Cordy. 1872. *Brides and Bridals.* 2 vols. London: Hurst and Blackett.
Mallory, J. P. 1989. *In Search of the Indo-Europeans: Language, Archaeology, and Myth.* London: Thames and Hudson.
Radcliffe-Brown, A. R., and Cyril Daryll Forde, eds. 1950. *African Systems of Kinship and Marriage.* London: Oxford University Press.

Wedding House

The wedding house was a building provided by the church, mainly after the Reformation, which gave wedding parties space for celebration after the solemnization of the marriage. Before this time, these celebrations had often taken place in the nave of the church. Few, if any, of these wedding houses still exist. There came to be official disapproval of the bride-ales held in the houses. These wedding houses provided space for the wedding feast, and some, such as one at Braughing, Hertfordshire, also had a bedchamber with a bridal bed, explaining how practices came to be in which guests put the couple to bed and in which the bride flings her stocking to the company. At Theyda Garnon, Essex, England, the Old Priests House that stood near the tower of the church was used for wedding feasts and was probably a wedding house. It appears to have been used for penny weddings, and tradition stated that while the bridegroom stood at one end of the table in a long white sheet and the bride at the other, a pair of white gloves would be brought in, profusely decorated with ribbons. Accounts do not make clear what happened to the gloves, but presumably they were auctioned to raise money for the couple and their celebrations. It is unclear when the church stopped providing a public space for weddings, but it is clear that the authorities dis-approved of the bride-ales and other fundraising events held to raise money for the couple.

See also Bride-Ale; Bridewain; Penny Weddings
References
Gillis, John R. 1985. *For Better, For Worse: British Marriages, 1600 to the Present.* Oxford: Oxford University Press.
King, Frank A. 1957. "Essex Wedding Customs and Superstitions." *Essex Countryside* 5, no. 19: 96–97.

Wife-Selling

In 1886, when Thomas Hardy published his novel *The Mayor of Casterbridge,* set in the first third of the nineteenth century, he caused some consternation in Victorian society. In the first chapter, a drunken husband sells his wife and baby daughter to a sailor for the sum of five guineas (five pounds, five shillings, or just over three dollars). Although this was not a totally uncommon occurrence, perhaps late-nineteenth-century literary society did not wish to have this degrading practice featured, especially since other Europeans had noted the practice in Britain and thought it was a common occurrence throughout British society and proof of Britain's low level of civilization. There are no written records of wife sales before the late seventeenth century, and some local newspaper reports from the eighteenth century suggest that it was a practice still evolving. *Jackson's Oxford Journal* (12 December 1789) referred to the practice as "the vulgar mode of *Divorce* lately adopted" (quoted in Thompson 1993).

The wife sale was quite ritualistic and in most cases was carried out with the consent of all of the parties involved, despite the public humiliation which it entailed; the financial transaction, implied in the sale, was not the major incentive for the event. Indeed, the seller usually returned part of the purchase price as luck money, or settled for a low amount that would not cover the costs of the sale. The usual method for a wife sale was for the husband to lead his wife to the market-place with a halter of rope, straw, or ribbon around her neck. The husband, or sometimes the town crier, would proclaim her good and her bad points, after which she would be sold to the highest bidder. There were some minor regional variations to this ritual; in Warwickshire the husband had to lead his wife through three turnpike (toll) gates or three villages along the road to the marketplace. As they went through the toll gates he would have to pay a toll at each gate. It was not unknown for the couple to walk out of the town some distance to return to the marketplace in the proper manner with the woman being led with a halter around her waist or neck.

This practice was sometimes a way for the woman to buy herself out of an unsatisfactory marriage—there are cases of the woman being bid for by an agent to whom she has supplied the money and of her own brothers buying her. However, it would appear that the bidder was usually someone with whom she was having an affair. There are several cases in which the bidder was someone from the couple's village who "happened" to be in the market, several miles from the village, on the right day at the right time. Often accounts suggest that the woman was only too pleased to be passed from her legal husband to the purchaser.

It was commonly believed that a wife sale constituted a legal form of divorce. Divorce in Great Britain, even well into the twentieth century, was not easy to obtain, and at one time required a bill in the House of Lords or an act from the ecclesiastical courts. It was, therefore, a recourse available to only a few people—and even then divorce carried a great deal of social scandal and stigma. Thus, the wife sale was the only form of divorce open to most of the population. Wife sale was not a legal form of divorce, but parish authorities were not averse to using it to solve a problem of a woman being a drain on the parish rates. In 1830 in Epping, Essex, England, a case came before the magistrates in which the workhouse master led a woman, dressed only in a long shift, on a halter from the George Inn to the marketplace to put her up for sale. She was sold for half a crown (two shillings and sixpence, or 12½ pence). He was issued a summons for selling goods and chattels without a license, but the case was dismissed when the magistrates did not consider a wife as goods and chattels. This practice was also used to help solve the problem caused by men going off to war. Soldiers could be away for a very long time with no news of whether they were alive or dead. After several years they would be presumed dead, and it was not unusual for a woman to remarry, causing a problem if the first husband returned.

The right of a person to sell his or her partner in marriage (husband sales were not unknown) was widely practiced, especially during the eighteenth and early nineteenth centuries. In 1837, the West Riding Sessions in Yorkshire, England, committed a man to a month in prison with hard labor for selling, or attempting to sell, his wife; this sentence shocked the people from his village and surrounding area. By the 1850s, wife-selling survived in only a few rural areas. Industrialization of the workforce and more people living in large towns and cities allowed more anonymity and ended the practice. Perhaps one of the latest records of a wife sale was in 1928 when a man told the magistrates at Blackwood, Monmouthshire, Wales, that he had sold his wife for one pound.

Even though wife-selling was seen as a form of divorce and was the only form of divorce available to the majority of the British population, it was not without stigma, as indeed legal divorce carried with it social opprobrium into the second half of the twentieth century. An account from Burford, Oxfordshire, England, tells of a wife sale in which a Burford man paid twenty-five pounds for another man's wife; the neighbors of the purchaser disapproved of the transaction and made rough music for him, to show their disapproval. He was only too pleased to pay her legal husband fifteen pounds to take her back.

See also Bigamy; Divorce; Rough Music/Rough
   Band; Shift, Marrying in a
References
Gillis, John R. 1985. *For Better, For Worse: British
   Marriages, 1600 to the Present.* Oxford: Oxford
   University Press.
Menefee, Samuel Pyeatt. 1981. *Wives for Sale.*
   Oxford: Basil Blackwell.
Thompson, E. P. 1993. *Customs in Common.*
   London: Penguin.

Wife-Swapping

In the archives of the Folklore Society in
London is an undated, but probably late-
nineteenth-century, note on black-bordered
paper, from a Mr. A. Bickley (who lived at 24
Great Ormond Street, London) to Lawrence
Gomme (president of the Folklore Society)
that refers to wife-swapping practices in
Woking, Surrey, England:

> Woking Village, Surrey. It has been a custom
> in this village for the lower stratum of the
> male inhabitants to meet at a public house
> and (informally) arrange for an exchange of
> wives. No fixed period of co-habitation was
> agreed on, but it appears normally to have
> been limited to one night. On separating the
> men proceed to the house of the allotted
> woman. As the women never objected, and
> no questions of paternity were raised, the
> habit would appear to be customary; and, ten
> years ago, the earliest instance of which I
> have knowledge, the arrangement was spoken
> of as a matter of course. I have not heard
> anything to lead to any date of origin, nor did
> the affair appear to be deemed immoral.
> There are no records of the custom but
> possibly a Research in the diocesan archives
> might reveal the raising of questions of
> discipline.

The writer does not give any indication of
the occupation of those taking part in this
practice. Temporary marriages were common among itinerant workers, such as miners and canal and railway workers. There are
accounts, from the 1760s, of itinerant miners
in South Wales taking part in mass weddings
that were not considered permanent by either party—the pair could part by mutual
consent when the miner moved on to another mine. Similarly, a practice noted in
mid-nineteenth-century Yorkshire involved
miners swapping or exchanging wives. An
agreement to part and remarry would be
made in a public house, before witnesses.
This would be followed by a feast and the
token gift made to the "bride" by the
"groom." In the Midlands, miners were also
known to have been involved in the swapping
or selling of wives. It is difficult to determine, at this distance, if the wife-swapping
mentioned in Mr. Bickley's note was part of a
form of temporary marriage. He does not
mention, and was probably unaware of, the
social milieu in which the wife-swapping
took place. However, there was, in the nineteenth century, a considerable itinerant laborer population in Woking working on the
canals at one time and on the railways at another. The practice, as described by Mr. Bickley, reads a little like the wife-swapping parties that became notorious in suburban
Britain and the United States in the 1960s
and 1970s.

Anthropologists have described instances
of wife-swapping, or wife-lending, in some
tribal societies, where it is used as a sign of
hospitality and friendship. Crawley (1902,
208) wrote that, among the Eskimo, "an exchange of wives is frequent, each party
being often happy to be released, and returning without concern," and that the
"Northern Indians" would sometimes exchange wives for the night. This exchange as
a hospitable act is reminiscent of the
episode recounted by an English traveler in
the United States in the eighteenth century,
Captain Thomas Anbury. When offered hospitality for the night in Williamstown,
Massachusetts, Anbury was surprised to find
that he was also expected to sleep with the
daughter of the house. Wife-swapping was
also used by some tribes to avert trouble;
the tribes of the Murray River, New

Guinea, would temporarily exchange wives to avoid a problem. Apparently the idea was to put a stop to the old and start again—the wife exchange provided an interval between the old and the new.

See also Besom Weddings; Bundling; Common-Law Marriage; Wife-Selling

References

Crawley, Ernest. [1902] 1932. *The Mystic Rose: A Study of Primitive Marriage and of Primitive Thought in Its Bearing on Marriage.* 4th ed. Revised and enlarged by Theodore Besterman. London: C. A. Watts.

Gillis, John R. 1985. *For Better, For Worse: British Marriages, 1600 to the Present.* Oxford: Oxford University Press.

Y

Yemen

In Yemen, an Islamic country, marriages are arranged between families. There are few prescribed formulas for weddings, and customs and practices may differ from village to village. Marriage marks the move into adulthood out of adolescence for both men and women. From about age fifteen, girls begin looking for a suitable match, although they may wait until the end of the time of education before being married. When the two families have agreed to the marriage, the financial negotiations begin. The most important item to be settled is the *mahr*—the dowry—that is paid to the bride. The size of the *mahr* is an indicator of the family's social status and the value that they place upon the bride-to-be. This may be from one thousand to six thousand dollars. The wedding festivities can be very expensive, depending upon the number of guests.

On the day of the wedding, a lunch is provided for all the guests. Such foods as *bint al sahn* (layered egg bread with a honey glaze), a stew, *salta* or *hulba* (eaten by ladling the stew with cupped bread), and lamb are served. After the meal, the men (the men and women eat separately) retire to a room to chew *qat* leaves, smoke, and talk. Often a musician is playing the traditional *oud* (a guitar-like stringed instrument) in the background. Around eight in the evening the celebrations move to the street, which is decorated with lights. The groom appears, dressed up with ceremonial sword, and there is a great deal of singing and dancing—again the men and women celebrating separately. Later the groom and his close friends and family retire to the house to relax before he is summoned upstairs to see his bride for the first time in the specially prepared marriage chamber where the marriage is consummated.

See also Islamic Marriage
Reference
Barwig, Andy. 1997. "Weddings: A Sanaani Experience." *Middle East Times.* 9 November. Available at *http://www.metimes.com/issue45/reg/09/tryemen.htm* (accessed 10 February 2004).

Yoruban Weddings

The Yoruba people inhabit vast tracts of West Africa, and today many are Muslim or Christian, having lost their own gods and their own philosophy associated with being "Yoruba." Many were taken as slaves to the New World, where they were not allowed to practice their own religions. This religion, known as Vodun (and often called Voodoo), was a "spirit" religion, which they took with them to Haiti and various parts of the United States and South America. In Brazil it is known as Candomblé and is a very misunderstood practice because of sensationalist tales and evil representations in Hollywood horror movies. The slaves were often not allowed to follow any religious practice, and even an exclamation imploring the help or grace of God could cause a whipping. The Yoruba in West Africa practice exogamy, and marriage is prohibited for any couple that can trace any form of blood relationship from any time in history. In practice this is only within living memory or knowledge and may extend back five or six generations. The rules are not strictly applied, so that in some locations a couple may marry if there are no known links at the time of the marriage. The couple would have to part if a link were to be discovered at a later date. In other places, a connection through a distant relative may only become an issue if the parents do not agree to the marriage. An additional safeguard to ensure the correct rules of consanguinity, observed in the Igbeti area, prohibits marriage between two people from unrelated kin groups resident in the same living compound. This prohibition continues even if one of the groups moves out to form a separate compound.

As with many large population groups, there are many variations of custom and tradition among settlement populations and even among compound groups. For example, there may be a spiritual quotation from a high priest, and an offering may be made to *orisha,* the spirit of love, conception, and money. The normal age for marriage for a man is between twenty-five and thirty years of age, whereas a woman will marry between the ages of seventeen and twenty-five years. In former years the first marriage would have been arranged by the couple's parents, the young man's father being the one who arranged and financed the marriage after investigating the background and family circumstances of the prospective bride. These investigations looked at the families'

reputations in regard to honesty, hereditary diseases, debt, witchcraft, and other factors. The young man's family approached the girl's family through an intermediary, and an *Ifa* oracle was consulted. If the girl's family wished to turn down the approach, her family could say that the *Ifa* oracle was not favorable. If all was well, a form of betrothal ceremony took place, the first of several. This ceremony, known as *isihun* or *ijuhon,* established the contract between the families and gave the groom exclusive sexual rights over the woman; this right was not usually exercised until she had been his wife for some time (perhaps several years). Historically, a great deal of importance was placed upon her virginity. During the period of betrothal, the young man and his friends would provide farm labor for the young woman's father as part of the "payment" obligations to her family. The final payment to her father, known as *idana,* included bitter kolanuts to symbolize long life, malaguetta peppers (atare) to symbolize fertility, and honey to signify a happy family life. Schnapps, beer, and a purse full of money were also sent; additionally, in a Christian marriage, it became usual to send a ring and a Bible. After this payment the woman was transferred to her husband's house, after which the marriage was consummated.

In contemporary Yoruba society, young men and women usually choose their own partners, although usually with their parents' consent. Virginity, although seen as an ideal, is not considered as imperative, and a couple may begin to have sex after the betrothal and before the transfer of the bride to the husband's family, so that a woman may be pregnant before the final marriage transfer. However, the exclusive sexual rights of the betrothed husband are still paramount. By tradition, a Yoruba woman would only go through a marriage ceremony once. If she remarried after divorce or the death of her husband, there would be no form of ritual; if widowed, she might marry a younger member of her husband's descent group so that she would remain in the compound with her children and retain her seniority in the group. If she opted to return to her parent's compound or remarry outside the compound, she would have to give back the marriage payment paid by her husband.

See also Consanguinity; Slave Weddings
Reference
Eades, J. S. 1980. *The Yoruba Today.* Cambridge: Cambridge University Press.

Yugoslavia

Until 1991, Yugoslavia contained many religious and national groups—Serbs, Croats, Montenegrins, Muslims, Macedonians, and Slovenes. Since 1991, Yugoslavia comprises Serbia and Montenegro. Although there were some regional differences in wedding traditions, there were many similarities across ethnic groups, so that in Muslim areas (areas with peoples of Turkish origin), where contracts were drawn up spelling out the goods the man would give to his wife, the Christians in that area followed suit. The people in the country retained many of their customs and traditions for weddings, but the socialist government did affect material culture and the way people did things. During the time Yugoslavia was part of the Soviet Republic, traditional bridal costumes and headdresses often gave way to the white wedding dress and the veil, which, instead of being handmade, could be purchased as a ready-made outfit.

Before being part of the Soviet Republic, Yugoslavian marriages were arranged between the families, sometimes through a matchmaker *(strojnik).* The matchmaker's role was to find a suitable marriage partner for the son or daughter of the house, and the wedding was a family and community event. Marriage was not a free choice of the couple. There was no segregation of the sexes, despite the expectation that a girl would be a virgin. At a limited variety of places, family parties or feasts, fairs, in church, or at some other community function, the couple could meet and exchange small gifts as tokens of affection. Elopements were not uncommon. Some parents did not object to elopement because it avoided the expense of presents, wedding parties, and banquets.

Few European societies are completely isolated from the influences of other cultures. Consequently wedding practices may change over time through political and external influences. After the agreement to marry has been made, where traditional practice is followed, members of both families or their representatives meet to discuss the practical details of the marriage—the number of guests, the presents, and the clothing to be worn by the couple. In some regions, an agreement is reached on the payments to be made by the young man's family to the bride's family to share the expenses. In the Serbian region, it is usual for both families to provide a dowry for the couple, either as goods or as money. The bride-to-be receives presents of jewelry and clothes—the amount and value depending on the affluence of the family—and she gives a present to her husband-to-be. Tradition dictates that every present should be reciprocated with one of similar value. Similarly, guests often bring food and drink to the wedding feast, and the guests must invite their hosts to a similar event. The wedding feast is usually held at the bridegroom's home. The bride and her family prepare her wedding outfit, clothing, presents for neighbors and friends, bedding, carpets, and, in some areas, furniture. The young woman and her friends work to decorate and prepare the bride's outfit and other items at a party. Her parents also contribute socks, napkins, or slippers. The outfit is packed in a decorated chest and transported to the house of her future husband where it is exhibited for the community.

Some of the decorations on the wedding goods have symbolic messages, indicating a wish for a happy and fertile marriage. Married and unmarried and young and old women wear different hoods or hats that indicate their status in the community. On her wedding day a bride wears a red wedding crown *(duvak)* decorated with ribbons, feathers, small mirrors, and collections of amulets and silver money. These were once considered protective amulets, but have become merely decorative and mark the bride as being just married. The preparation of the bride—dressing her in her bridal dress and hood (cap)—by her friends is an important step in the marriage ceremony. In contemporary marriages, the bride is likely to buy a ready-made outfit and wear a white dress with a veil. She is then escorted in a noisy procession with banners, flowers, and explosions of firecrackers. At the feast, a central place is kept for the wedding cake, which at one time had a fertility significance. The entry of the bride into her new husband's household is accompanied by rituals to ensure fertility, such as the bride holding a child. The bride's mother-in-law leads her over the threshold of the house to initiate her into the new household.

See also Arranged Marriage; Elopement; Gypsy Weddings; Islamic Marriage; Matchmaking

Reference

Kajmakovic, Radmila. 1975. "Yugoslavia." In *Love and Marriage: Aspects of Popular Culture in Europe [exhibition], Antwerpen,* edited by W. Van Nespen. Brussels: Ministerie van Nederlanse Cultuur en Nationale Opvoeding.

Zoroastrian Weddings

The followers of Zoroastrianism originally lived in Persia (modern-day Iran). The people in that area became converted to Islam, and during the seventh and eighth centuries, the followers of Zoroaster (or Zarathustra) were persecuted and fled to India, where today they are called Farsis or Parsees. According to Zoroastrian belief, marriage is considered a divine action and a righteous man's household is the second happiest place in existence. Rich Farsis can gain religious favor by leaving money to provide dowries for poor brides. Details of the wedding, which can take up to four days to complete, may vary from district to district, but there are certain actions that must be followed—the wedding should be performed before at least five specially invited witnesses; the couple must be asked by the officiating priest if they both consent to the marriage; the priest must join their hands; and at some stage in the ceremony he must tie a symbolic knot. The wedding ceremony has to be followed by the couple being blessed by the priest and with rice sprinkled over the couple.

Astrologers determine the best time for the wedding, and the beginning of the ceremony is marked by the groom, with the help of seven women, planting a mango tree that should be encrusted with nine gems. The next day the couple go through a betrothal ceremony. The women from the groom's family go to the bride's house and present her with silver coins, while the women from the bride's family visit the groom and also present him with silver coins. A priest is usually in attendance at each house, and the priests make the formal request to the parents for the couple to marry. In some districts, however, both families will be present at the request for and granting of permission to marry. After the engagement ceremony, on the third day of feast and celebrations, a lamp is lit early in the morning, and the women from each household visit each other, again exchanging gifts; the wedding dresses and rings are usually presented on this day. The next important day in the period before the marriage is when the bride's father presents the bride's dowry to the groom's family.

The second and third days of the ceremony are called *varadh patra* days and include religious ceremonies to honor and gain blessings from the ancestors. (This is reminiscent of some European practices of the couple visiting the graves of family members in the churchyard after the wedding and the contemporary Russian tradition for newlyweds to visit monuments or sites associated with dead heroes or historic events.) The wedding itself may take place at the bride's family house or in a wedding hall—just after sunset. During the wedding day and before the ceremony, both the bride *(kanya)* and groom *(var-raja* or *husband-king)* are ritually cleansed and purified by a priest (the *nahn* ceremony). The wedding procession to the bride's house is led by musicians and the officiating priests. At the house the men sit in the compound and the women in a separate part of the house. The doorjambs are smeared with turmeric, whose yellow color is symbolic of the life-giving properties of the sun. The groom has to pass through this gateway (right foot first and without touching the threshold) after being met by his future mother-in-law, who marks his forehead with a red pigment (both of the couple may be given this mark, the *kunkun,* the groom's being a vertical mark and the bride's round) and into which she presses some rice with more rice thrown over him.

The groom is dressed in white robes *(sayah),* with a garland of flowers around his neck and carrying a shawl. He sits with his male friends and relatives in the compound. The *achu michu ceremony* is performed to ward off bad spirits. This is carried out by an elderly female who brings a metal plate *(thali)* containing eggs, coconut rice, *paan* (betel nut juice wrapped in a tobacco leaf), and a small tray of water and passes this around his head three times (or seven times). An egg is cracked and put to his left. He is then allowed to enter the marriage hall. The bride, wearing a white sari, enters the hall separately from her groom after the *achu michu* ceremony has been performed on her.

The wedding itself takes place within the house or hall where two chairs face each other. Beside each chair is a little table with dishes of rice and lighted candles; the table beside the bride's chair also has jugs of clarified butter and sugar syrup, which symbolize the bride's future smooth and sweet nature. Each stand has a lighted oil light called a *diva.* While the witnesses assemble, frankincense is burned in front of the chairs. During the ceremony a servant with frankincense and a censer, with a fire lit inside, stands next to the couple. The bride and groom are seated opposite each other with a curtain held between them; the leading priest *(dastur)* joins the couple's right hands and, while encircling them with a cloth and tying the ends together, recites holy texts *(ahunwar).* Continuing to recite holy texts, the priest binds their hands together with a rawhide twine that is passed seven times around their hands, then seven times around the couple, and then seven times around the knot. As more frankincense is burned, the curtain between the couple is dropped. They scatter the rice over each other, which they had been holding in their left hands, and move their chairs so that they are sitting side-by-side with the woman on the man's left. More frankincense is burned in the censer while the couple throw rice over each other. Sometimes this is a form of competition—the one to throw the rice first is said to be the most loving and respecting of the other.

The religious part of the ceremony, the *Asirward,* follows, with the priests standing in front of the couple. The senior priest blesses the couple and gives wishes that the couple may be granted "progeny of sons and grandsons, abundant means, strong friendship, bodily strength, long life and an existence of 150 years." The priests ask the witnesses representing the groom's family and the bride's family, separately, if they consent to the marriage; the question is asked three times of each. The priest reads from the holy texts that exhort the couple to lead exemplary lives together, and blessings are made for the couple to help them achieve moral and social virtue. In some districts, the couple's robes are tied together by their friends and relatives, and they go, thus joined, to the house of the bridegroom where their feet are ritually washed (if they wear Western-style shoes, the tips of the shoes are washed). The couple take their first food together, feeding each other with curd and rice from the same dish. The guests may then sit down for the wedding feast, which usually includes a fish dish (a good omen) and sweets, and celebrations enlivened by songs.

See also Feet; India; Rice
References
Detailed descriptions of wedding ceremonial traditions in Asia can be found at *http://www.clickwalla.com* (accessed 1 June 2004).
Mallory, J. P. 1989. *In Search of the Indo-Europeans: Language, Archaeology, and Myth.* London: Thames and Hudson.
Murphy, Brian M. 1978. *The World of Weddings: An Illustrated Celebration.* London: Paddington.

Zulu Weddings

The Bantu-speaking people of the province of Natal in South Africa, the Zulus celebrate marriage over several days. Zulus have free choice of marriage partner, and there are safeguards to help marriage endure. The development of townships and the introduction of Western ways will slowly change, and probably displace, traditional tribal ways. In the Zulu wedding, there are elements of what nineteenth- and early-twentieth-century anthropologists interpreted as paying a bride-price and of marriage by capture, a doubtful theory. Soon after puberty a young woman begins to think of finding herself a husband, but she must obtain permission from the senior unmarried women in her kraal, her native village, who may make her wait for a bit. During this time she may gently flirt with young men. When she is ready, her father arranges a coming-out ceremony to introduce her to society and to make her availability for marriage formally known. He builds a wicker circle, where she remains while he and his family prepare for a party. Invitations are sent to male relatives, who offer animals for slaughter for the feast, and beer will be brewed. The day before the ceremony an animal will be killed as a sacrifice, and in the evening the young people from the kraal serenade her in her wicker cage.

On the day of the ceremony, the girls dress up and join the young woman in her cage; around midday they emerge two by two to dance for the assembled crowd, each pair try-ing to outdo the others. When the young women can dance no more, they return to the wicker circle and feast on meat and beer; the other guests also eat and drink, and after the older members of the group depart, the younger people continue their partying. From this time, the young woman always dresses up to go to the river to fetch water and attempts to draw attention to herself so that she can flirt and talk with the young men. Once she has made a choice, she is not allowed to make her feelings known until the other unmarried women give permission. Again they are likely to keep her waiting. Even when she has this permission, she will brush aside his advances. But he will know if he is accepted by signs from her sisters or other female relatives, such as setting bunches of twigs around him. When this has happened he flies a white flag outside his hut as a sign of his returned affection. It is now that the girl can let her feelings be known, and she presents him with a necklace of white beads. This represents a form of engagement; presents of jewelry are exchanged, and they are able to spend the nights together. However, they should not engage in sexual intercourse. If they do have sexual intercourse then the man has to pay a fine and the wedding is brought forward.

During this engagement period the girl is likely to stay in the man's family kraal, and the arrangements and negotiations for the bride-price take place between the families. This will usually involve a matchmaker who acts as a go-between for the two families. The bride-price, *lobola,* is not strictly a purchase payment, nor is it a dowry. It is a guarantee that the intended bridegroom gives to the young woman's father to ensure that he will take care of his daughter. If she is ill-treated, neglected, or abused she has the right to return to her father; the *lobola,* usually paid in cattle, will help provide for her and her children. If the husband sends her back to her father for bad behavior, the *lobola* has to be repaid. If the woman is unable to have children, or dies before having any children, the man

A Zulu mother puts the finishing touches on her daughter's wedding costume. (Roger De La Harpe; Gallo Images/CORBIS)

can demand another wife from her father without the necessity of paying a further *lobola.* The average *lobola* would be around three to five cattle, but this varies from district to district and with the status of the families involved.

Before the bride leaves her home kraal for the wedding the following day at the bridegroom's kraal, her father slaughters one of the *lobola* cattle and, after removing the gallbladder, pours the contents over her arms, legs, and face. While doing this, he addresses the spirits of the ancestors to inform them of her change of status. The older women of the kraal take the bride aside and instruct her in how to be a dutiful wife and daughter-in-law. She then leaves her old home in a procession accompanied by the matchmaker and the men from her kraal. She bears gifts—beads, mats, and baskets—that she will present to members of the bridegroom's kraal. The party may wash in a river that they may cross to get to the bridegroom's home, and the

girls anoint themselves with *amaka,* a concoction prepared by crushing and pounding *impepo* leaves with fat—this fragrant concoction is said to have aphrodisiac properties. When the bridal party arrives at the bridegroom's kraal, they are shown to their specially prepared hut and are presented with a goat, which will be slaughtered for their breakfast the next morning. The bride's group and the groom's group stand on either side of the kraal and shout insults at each other until they are speechless and exhausted.

The next morning the bride and her friends bathe in the river and dress themselves for dancing, decorating themselves on the arms and legs with designs in red and white ocher, and they tie bags of pebbles to their ankles to make a rhythmic rattle as they dance. The bride wears a veil of beads and twisted fig leaves and ties oxtail fringes to her elbows and knees and a goat's hair fringe around her neck. She carries a miniature assagai, a large knife, point-up, to denote her virginity. The bride's party begins the dancing, led into the kraal by the men from the bride's kraal with their shields uplifted. After the dancing the bridegroom's father welcomes the bridal party to the kraal (remarking on the bride's beauty and good character). The whole bridal party dances a wedding dance to show the groom's ancestors that the young woman is joining their family. Meat and beer are fed to the bridal party as the groom's party dresses in their finery to be ready for the next round of dancing.

The bride and groom sit on a mat with a screen between them. The screen is taken away, and she begins her dance, which is vigorous and sensual. During this dance, she appears to be fending off imaginary enemies with her assagai and small shield. When nearly exhausted, her father taps the ground and she immediately stops her dance. The groom and his supporters now begin their dance, during which he sings his own praises and congratulates himself for his choice of bride. Again, as suddenly as the dance started, it stops, and all sit opposite the bridal party, leaving a gap between the bride's group and the groom's. The bride's nearest male relative drives three cattle between the two parties; these are a gift to the bridegroom's kraal. When the cattle have passed, the bride throws herself to the ground and begs the groom to take her as part of the family. The bride's father then extols her virtues and her faults, requests that she be given a good home, and promises that she will bear children. He also calls upon his son-in-law to cherish her and be a kind and understanding husband. The couple now appear before a government official who will formally ratify the marriage. The bride returns to her hut and eats food that she brought with her. Everyone else feasts, drinks, and dances.

The next morning the groom's family provides an ox, which has to be killed with a single blow. The groom's supporters remove the gallbladder and force their way into the bride's hut, resisted by the bride's female supporters, and pour the contents of the gallbladder over her. She then goes with her companions to the river to bathe. The ox meat is eaten by the bride's party during the day, although she eats none of it, and in the evening the groom's party once again force their way into the bride's hut. This struggle and mock fight continues until one of them strikes the bride on the ankle with a stick, whereupon she begins to sing and is escorted to the groom's hut where they are left alone to consummate the marriage. When this is achieved, she cries and shows grief to indicate that she is no longer a virgin, and sometimes she indicates this transition from girlhood to womanhood by pointing the small assagai, which she carried in her first bridal dance, downward.

See also Bride-Price; Bundling; Capture, Marriage by; Dowry

References

Morris, Donald P. 1968. *The Washing of the Spears.* London: Sphere.

Murphy, Brian M. 1978. *The World of Weddings: An Illustrated Celebration.* London: Paddington.

Ritter, E. A. 1971. *Shaka Zulu.* London: Book Club Associates.

Index

About the Author

George P. Monger is a freelance museum conservator, consultant, and folklorist based in East Anglia, U.K., and has a particular interest in marriage traditions. He has published papers and reviews in folklore and ethnological journals.